English Linguistics

A Coursebook for Students of English

by
Thomas Herbst

De Gruyter Mouton

ISBN 978-3-11-020367-7
e-ISBN 978-3-11-021548-9

Library of Congress Cataloging-in-Publication Data

Herbst, Thomas.
    English linguistics : a coursebook for students of English / by
Thomas Herbst.
        p. cm.
    Includes bibliographical references and index.
    ISBN 978-3-11-020367-7 (pbk. : alk. paper)
    1. Linguistics.   2. Language and languages.   3. English lan-
guage – Textbooks for foreign speakers.   I. Title.
    P121.H56   2010
    428.2'4–dc22
                                                    2010017332

Bibliographic information published by the Deutsche Nationalbibliothek

The Deutsche Nationalbibliothek lists this publication in the Deutsche Nationalbibliografie;
detailed bibliographic data are available in the Internet at http://dnb.d-nb.de.

© 2010 Walter de Gruyter GmbH & Co. KG, Berlin/New York

Cover image: Patrick Heron, detail from *Window for Tate Gallery St Ives* – © Estate of
Patrick Heron. © Tate, London 2008. All rights reserved. DACS, UK and VG-Bild-Kunst,
Bonn, Germany.
Printing: AZ Druck und Datentechnik GmbH, Kempten
∞ Printed on acid-free paper

Printed in Germany

www.degruyter.com

Contents

Preface.. xiii

The English language and linguistics

1	Facts about English..1
1.1	English world-wide..1
1.2	Regional and social variation.................................3
1.3	Historical variation 4
1.4	The character of English..6
1.4.1	English as a Germanic language.............................6
1.4.2	Language typology 9
1.5	The linguistic analysis of English.........................10
2	Principles of modern linguistics 12
2.1	Basic concepts of linguistic structuralism 12
2.1.1	Principles of linguistics since de Saussure 12
2.1.2	The character of the linguistic sign.......................14
2.1.3	Synchronic and diachronic study of language......16
2.1.4	The importance of relations 17
2.1.4.1	The value of the linguistic sign.............................17
2.1.4.2	Syntagmatic and paradigmatic relationships 19
2.1.5	Schools of structuralism 20
2.2	Linguistics and descriptivity..................................20
2.3	The principles of structuralism and foreign language teaching...22
2.4	Areas of investigation...25
3	Language, intuition and corpora............................27
3.1	Language 27
3.1.1	Some basic distinctions..27
3.1.2	Competence and performance: the language of the individual 28
3.1.3	Language as a social phenomenon 29
3.1.4	*System* and *Norm* – language use........................29
3.2	Finding data: traditional methods 31
3.2.1	Principal options...31

3.2.2	Introspection and elicitation	32
3.2.3	Authentic language material: citations and corpora	33
3.3	Corpus linguistics	33
3.3.1	Corpora of English	33
3.3.2	What we can do with corpora	37
3.3.2.1	Corpus analysis	37
3.3.2.2	Corpora and foreign language teaching	40
3.3.3	Corpus design and corpus size	41
3.4	Introspection, corpus analysis and views of language	42

Sounds

4	The sounds of English: phonetics	43
4.1	Sounds as the starting point of linguistic analysis	43
4.2	Phones	43
4.3	Articulatory, auditive and acoustic phonetics	45
4.4	Description of sounds in articulatory terms	48
4.5	Syllables	53
4.6	Suprasegmental elements	54
5	Phonology	56
5.1	The function of speech sounds	56
5.1.1	Phonemes and allophones	56
5.1.2	Phonetics and phonology	58
5.2	The description of phonemes	58
5.2.1	Consonant phonemes	58
5.2.2	Vowel phonemes	60
5.2.3	Phonemic principle of pronunciation dictionaries	64
5.3	Phonotactics	65
6	Phonetic "reality"	67
6.1	Problems of the phoneme concept	67
6.1.1	The problem	67
6.1.2	Phonetic value of phonological features	68
6.1.3	The bi-uniqueness requirement	71
6.2	Pronunciation in connected speech	73
6.2.1	Weakening of elements	73
6.2.2	Linking phenomena	74
6.2.3	Weak forms	75
7	Contrastive aspects of phonetics and phonology	76
7.1	Levels of contrast	76
7.2	Phoneme and phone inventories of English and German	76

7.3	Rule-governed differences	79
7.4	Suprasegmental differences	80
7.5	Pedagogical implications	81

Meaning-carrying units

8	Morphology	83
8.1	The concept of the morpheme	83
8.2	Types of morpheme	85
8.3	Problems of a static morpheme concept	87
8.3.1	The problem	87
8.3.2	Portmanteau morphs	87
8.3.3	Zero-morphs	88
8.3.4	Morphological and phonological conditioning	89
8.4	Inflectional morphology: historical background	91
8.5	Further problems of morphological analysis	92
9	Word formation	95
9.1	Words	95
9.1.1	Words and lexemes	95
9.1.2	New words	98
9.2	Word formation	100
9.2.1	Introduction	100
9.2.2	Formal types of word formation: a survey	102
9.2.3	Semantic description of word formations	105
9.3	Word formation and morphology	108
9.3.1	The overlap between word formation and morphology	108
9.3.2	Explanatory value of the analysis	111
9.4	Productivity and restrictions	113
9.5	Possible words – nonce formations – institutionalized words	115
9.6	Psychological aspects of morphology	120
10	Phraseology	125
10.1	Prefabs	125
10.2	Statistically significant collocations	128
10.3	Institutionalized collocations	131
10.4	Idioms	134
10.5	The idiom principle and the mental lexicon	136
10.6	Phraseological units	138

Sentences – models of grammar

11	Syntax: traditional grammar	141
11.1	Syntax and grammar	141
11.1.1	Descriptive frameworks	141
11.1.2	Sentence and clause	142
11.1.3	Subject and predicate	144
11.2	The elements of clause structure in CGEL	147
11.2.1	Elements of clause structure as functional units	147
11.2.2	Criteria for the distinction between different elements of clause structure	148
11.2.3	CGEL's clause types	151
11.2.4	Problems of traditional terminology	152
11.3	Phrases	153
11.3.1	Types of phrase	153
11.3.2	The role of the phrase	157
11.4	Word classes	157
11.4.1	Criteria for the establishment of word classes	157
11.4.2	CGEL's word classes	160
11.4.3	Verbs	161
11.4.4	Central and peripheral members of word classes – word classes as prototypes	162
11.4.5	Multiple-class membership	164
11.4.6	The distinction between determiners and pronouns	165
11.4.7	The distinction between prepositions and subordinating conjunctions	167
11.4.8	Word classes in English	168
12	Valency theory and case grammar	171
12.1	Two types of hierarchy	171
12.1.1	Constituency	171
12.1.2	Dependency	173
12.1.3	Case grammar and valency theory	176
12.2	Case grammar: semantic roles	176
12.2.1	Basic principles of case grammar	176
12.2.2	Advantages and drawbacks of case grammar	178
12.2.3	Some useful participant roles	180
12.3	The basic principles of valency theory	183
12.3.1	Introduction	183
12.3.2	Complements and adjuncts	183
12.3.3	Qualitative and quantitative aspects of valency	185

12.3.4   Valency carriers 187
12.3.5   Components of a valency description 188
12.3.6   Valency patterns 191
12.4   A valency based approach to English syntax 192
12.4.1   Combining aspects of clause structure and valency 192
12.4.2   A modified view of phrase structure.................................194
12.4.2.1   Head complexes...194
12.4.2.2   Noun phrases, adjective phrases and adverb phrases 195
12.4.2.3   Particle phrases 197
12.4.2.4   Clauses as verb phrases 197
12.4.3   Description of units 198
12.4.4   Example 198
13   Theories of grammar and language acquisition...................200
13.1   Chomsky's approach 200
13.1.1   Basic assumptions..200
13.1.2   Transformations – deep structures and surface structures 202
13.1.3   Claims and evidence..205
13.1.4   Language acquisition 208
13.1.4.1   The language acquisition device...208
13.1.4.2   Universal grammar 209
13.2   Usage-based approaches...210
13.2.1   Construction grammar 210
13.2.2   Argument structure constructions.......................................212
13.2.3   The usage-based view of language acquisition....................215

Meaning

14   Semantics: meaning, reference and denotation....................220
14.1   Meaning..220
14.2   Meaning and reference 221
14.2.1   Bloomfield's misconception of meaning.............................221
14.2.2   Denotation 223
14.2.3   Reference 224
14.2.3.1   The general notion of reference..224
14.2.3.2   Definite and indefinite reference 226
14.3   The scope of meaning...229
15   Meaning relations 233
15.1   Polysemy and homonymy 233
15.1.1   Polysemy and homonymy in linguistic analysis..................233
15.1.2   Psycholinguistic and lexicographical implications..............237

15.2   Ambiguity 237
15.3   Problems of identification of meanings and lexical units.....238
15.4   Structural semantics..239
15.4.1   The idea of contrast 239
15.4.2   Semantic relations...240
15.4.2.1 Hyponymy: unilateral entailment 240
15.4.2.2 Synonymy: bilateral entailment..241
15.4.2.3 Semantic oppositions...243
16   Ways of describing meaning 247
16.1   Componential analysis...247
16.2   The structure of vocabulary 252
16.3   Vocabulary and conceptualization.....................................253
16.4   Prototype theory 256
16.4.1   Colour terms 256
16.4.2   Prototypes 258
16.4.3   Basic level categories 261
16.4.4   Problems of prototype theory 263

Utterances

17   Pragmatics 265
17.1   Word, sentence and utterance meaning 265
17.1.1   Sentence meaning 265
17.1.2   The meaning of utterances..266
17.2   Principles 268
17.2.1   The co-operative principle and conversational implica-
          ture 268
17.2.2   Further principles...270
17.3   Speech acts 271
17.3.1   Performatives and constatives 271
17.3.2   Locutionary, illocutionary and perlocutionary acts.............275
17.3.3   Felicity conditions 277
17.3.4   Types of speech act..278
17.3.4.1 Searle's taxonomy 278
17.3.4.2 Direct and indirect speech acts 280
17.3.4.3 Problems of classification..281
18   Texts 283
18.1   The notion of text 283
18.1.1   Cohesion and coherence 283
18.1.2   Texts as utterances...287

18.2   Cohesive relations...287
18.2.1   Explicit linking expressions.................................287
18.2.2   Grammatical aspects of relating referents and meanings......288
18.2.3   Lexical aspects of cohesion and coherence 291
18.3   Thematic structure and information structure................295
18.3.1   Theme and rheme – given and new information 295
18.3.2   End-focus and marked focus 297
18.4   Spoken and written texts....................................298

Variation

19   Variation in language.......................................302
19.1   Registers and dialects 302
19.2   Accent, dialect, standard and prestige 305
19.2.1   Standard English and its pronunciations.....................305
19.2.2   Quality judgements..307
19.3   Levels of differences between regional and social varie-
           ties..309
20   Linguistic change...315
20.1   Types of linguistic change 315
20.2   Sound change..316
20.2.1   The phoneme systems of Old English and RP...................316
20.2.2   Types of sound change 318
20.2.3   Important sound changes in the history of English 319
20.2.3.1   I-mutation 319
20.2.3.2   The Great Vowel Shift.......................................319
20.2.3.3   Quantitative changes..321
20.2.3.4   Present-day reflections.....................................321
20.3   Lexis 322
20.3.1   New words...322
20.3.2   Changes of meaning 324
20.3.3   Homonymy 325
20.4   Grammar...325
20.4.1   Differences between Old English and Modern English..........325
20.4.2   Analogy 327
20.4.3   Grammaticalization..328

Postscript...330
Bibliography...332
Index..365

Preface

English Linguistics is intended as an introduction to a field that, as such, perhaps does not even exist. The idea of this book is to introduce students of English to basic concepts of linguistics that are relevant to the description and analysis of the English language and to ideas and approaches that are relevant in this context. These, of course, apply not only to English but also to other languages.

In view of the wide range of different subjects and the great number of different theoretical and methodological approaches comprised by linguistics, it is perfectly obvious that a selection must be made with respect to the topics and approaches that can be discussed within the scope of an introductory book. Any selection of this kind will inevitably involve a personal element in the choice and treatment of particular topics. The present book has emerged from a manuscript that has been used for courses during the first year in English linguistics at the Friedrich-Alexander-Universität Erlangen-Nürnberg, which means that it also includes aspects of the analysis of English that appear particularly relevant in a foreign language context, which is why reference is occasionally made to foreign language teaching and to other languages, in particular German.

This book attempts to be a general introduction to central aspects of the academic study of the English language. In my view, this entails two equally important components:

– On the one hand, this book provides the reader with an introduction to important areas of investigation and the basic concepts as well as the terminology used for the analysis of the respective fields. Thus, the book deals with the description of sounds, words, sentences, texts etc. introducing terms such as phoneme, compound, subject or coherence that are central to their analysis.

– On the other hand, however, it is one of the main concerns of this introduction that the reader should become aware of the fact that there are no (or not many) easy answers or straightforward solutions in linguistics. It is important to realize, for instance, that although many linguists use the term object in the analysis of sentences, they do not necessarily agree on what they mean by it, or – more radically, that some linguists (or schools of linguistic thought) are firmly convinced of certain assumptions that should be made about language and principles that should be followed in the analysis of language that are strongly rejected by others.

In other words, one must recognize that in linguistics there is very little in the way of "truth", but that different linguists have developed different ideas about how we can account for language or for certain linguistic phenomena. In some cases, the best or most appropriate way of describing a particular phenomenon may depend on the purpose of the description; in other cases, it may be a matter of personal conviction. Nevertheless, it is important to understand that it is precisely this struggle between different approaches that determines the nature of this subject (as is true of any other academic subject). It is for this reason that this introduction not only tries to describe and explain central concepts of linguistics, but also to indicate that the concepts outlined represent one (possibly the most established and commonly used) way of seeing things. Of course, it would be beyond the scope of an introduction of this kind – and terribly confusing for the reader – to mention all approaches to a particular phenomenon that might deserve mentioning. In some cases, however, reference is made to alternative accounts – often in footnotes or in special sections which are then marked by grey backgrounds in the chapter headings as being intended for more advanced readers.

This means that this book does not necessarily have to be read from cover to cover in one go. It is perfectly possible for beginners to work through the chapters dealing with more introductory subjects first and then to come back to the more advanced chapters of the same sections at a later stage.

This book owes a lot to help and support from a number of colleagues and friends. I would like to thank in particular Dr. Susen Faulhaber, Dr. Katrin Götz-Votteler, David Heath, Dr. Michael Klotz, Kevin Pike, Dr. Stefan Thim and Peter Uhrig for reading the entire manuscript and for their valuable comments and suggestions, their patience and the many discussions we had on different aspects of the text. Furthermore, I owe thanks to Eva Klein, Dominic Losse, Thomas Maisel, Dr. Brigitta Mittmann, Elisabeth Reber, Dr. Christina Sanchez and many of my students for commenting on earlier versions or parts of the manuscript. Barbara Gabel-Cunningham deserves special thanks for her extremely competent work in getting the manuscript into a publishable form, and equally I would like to thank Christian Hauf and Sabine Menz for their assistance in preparing it.

I very much hope that the present introduction succeeds in demonstrating the fascination of many ideas discussed in linguistics today and the importance of knowing about linguistics for everybody who teaches language.

The English language and linguistics

1 Facts about English

1.1 English world-wide

English is spoken – in different forms or varieties – by people all over the world. At the beginning of the twenty-first century, it is the most important language used in international communication. Estimates suggest that about 1.5 billion people have some command of English today. This does not only include people who have English as their mother tongue (or first language L1), but it is more than likely that a Norwegian and an Italian or someone from Japan and someone from Belgium will make use of English as a lingua franca when communicating with one another. In fact, there are considerable differences between the functions that English has for different people and the status the language has in different countries of the world.[1]

- *English as a native language* (ENL): English is spoken as a native language by the majority of people living in North America, the British Isles, Australia or New Zealand, for example.

- *English as a second language* (ESL): in some countries people whose native language is not English use English (which they have acquired after or at the same time as another language) as a second language in some situations such as certain educational, commercial or governmental contexts. This may be the case in countries such as Canada, where many French-speaking Canadians also speak English. It is also the case

---

[1] This account is based on the approach taken in CGEL (I.4-5). For an account of the distinction between ENL, ESL and EFL in terms of "social-linguistic constellations in which English is used" see Mair (2008: 151–156). Cf. also Trudgill and Hannah (⁵2008: 4–8).

in countries such as India or Nigeria, in which several native languages co-exist.[2]

- *English as a foreign language* (EFL): the group of speakers of English as a foreign language (EFL) is very heterogeneous as far as the actual command of the language is concerned.

Estimates of the number of speakers of different languages at the beginning of the twenty-first century vary: Crystal (2006: 424) gives the following figures:[3]

L1 speakers	400 million
L2 speakers	400 million
foreign language speakers	600 – 700 million

Although English neither has the largest number of L1 speakers in the world (Chinese) nor in the European Union (German) the remarkably high figures for foreign speakers of English are an indication of its status as a world language. Another important aspect of the role of English in the world is that countries in which English is at least the main language are spread over four continents: Europe (Britain and Ireland), Australia, America (USA and parts of Canada), Africa (South Africa).[4] House (2002: 246) mentions four factors for English becoming a "truly global language": "the

---

[2]   According to CGEL (1985: 1.4) English is the only official language in Nigeria, whereas in India several languages have that status. For the situation in Nigeria compare, however, Gut (2008: 35), who points out that "currently about 20% of the population have some command of English". For the status of English in East Africa or Ghana see Schmied (2008: esp. 154–155) and Huber (2008: esp. 73) respectively, for India see Schneider (2007: 161). For Africa see Schmied (1991: esp. 23-45).

[3]   Obviously, such figures have to be treated with great caution, see e.g. Crystal (2003: 108–109), who gives an estimate of 329m L1 and 433m L2 speakers. Compare the figures given by Viereck, Viereck, and Ramisch (2002: 242): 355m L1 speakers, 100m L2 speakers and 150m speakers of English as a foreign language. For other languages see Viereck, Viereck, and Ramisch (2002: 236): Chinese 1,110m, Spanish 305m, Arabic 220m, Portuguese over 160m, Russian 160m, French 124m, German 121m, Italian 66m.

[4]   For details see Crystal (1988: 8–9). For factors contributing to the status of English as international language – such as political and economic factors, its use in advertising, as a means of communication in aviation etc. or academic publications – see Crystal (2006: 426–431) and Viereck, Viereck and Ramisch (2002: 238–245).

worldwide extension of the British Empire; the political and economic rise of the United States to world power status after the Second World War; the unprecedented developments in information and communication technologies; and the recent economic developments towards globalisation and internationalisation". It is important to realize that this kind of status a language or a variety has is entirely derived from external factors and has nothing to do with particular qualities or characteristics of the language in question. The present status of English is a reflection of historic and econmic developments but one must doubt whether it has very much to do with the way plurals or the present perfect are formed in English.

1.2   Regional and social variation

When we say that the English language is spoken by 300 or 400 million people as a mother tongue today, then this is not to say that the actual language they use is absolutely the same. Quite the opposite is true, of course. Not only does language differ from one individual to another – in linguistics the language of an individual is termed their **idiolect** –, there are also remarkable differences between the language of different groups of speakers, for which the term **dialect** – or the more neutral term **variety** (> 19.1) – is used.

One can make a distinction between

▷ **regional dialects**, which are determined by the geographical distribution of certain linguistic forms,

▷ **social dialects** (or **sociolects**), which are determined by the social group to which their speakers typically belong.

It has to be borne in mind, however, that such varieties hardly ever exist in a discrete and clearly distinguishable form.[5] Furthermore, regional variation can be described in different degrees of specificity: within the British Isles, for example, we can describe dialects such as Scottish English, Irish English, Northern English English or South-Western English or Belfast Eng-

---

[5]   Furthermore, speakers are not necessarily very consistent in their speech, in that people tend to modify the kind of language they are using depending on who they are talking to, what they are talking about, whether they are speaking or writing etc. See Chapter 19.1.

lish, Birmingham English or Cockney (a dialect spoken in London) etc.[6] Taking a world-wide perspective, one can identify varieties of English such as Canadian English, Australian English, South African English, which are sometimes called national varieties. Furthermore, the world-wide spread of English has lead to language contact with other languages, which has resulted in the emergence of new varieties of English, sometimes called New Englishes, which have become a very important area of study.[7]

It is one of the interesting facts about the English language that there is no official institution – such as the Paris Académie Française for French – that would take any decisions about how English should be used. Nevertheless there exists a type of **Standard English**, which differs from other dialects or varieties in terms of the functions it has because it is the variety that is commonly used in printing and serves as a model of foreign language teaching (> 19.1). It is possible to identify different national standards, of which **British English** and **American English** are the most important internationally.

Standard English can be pronounced with a range of different accents (the term **accent** referring to variation with respect to pronunciation). The most neutral (in the sense of least regional) pronunciations of Standard English are generally referred to as **General American** (or Network English) for American English and **BBC English** or **Received Pronunciation (RP)** for British English. RP has a special status because it shows practically no regional variation within England and Wales, but is to a very high degree associated with a particular social class (> 19.2).

1.3   Historical variation

Apart from variation according to region and social group, there is also variation in time. The extent to which English has changed over the centuries is illustrated by the following examples:[8]

---

[6]   For the dialect areas and the Survey of English Dialects see Barnickel (1980: 145–151).

[7]   For different phases in the evolution of postcolonial Englishes see Schneider (2007: 29–55).

[8]   Sources: P.G. Wodehouse: *Blandings Castle*, Harmondsworth: Penguin (1935/1954: 1). – William Shakespeare: *The Complete Works. Original-Spelling Edition*, edited by Stanley Wells and Gary Taylor, Oxford: Oxford University Press (1986: 1108). – *The Riverside Chaucer*, 3rd edition (edited

(1)   *'Beach,' said Lord Emsworth.*
        'M'lord?'
        'I've been swindled. This dashed thing doesn't work.'
        'Your lordship cannot see clearly?'
        ... 'Perhaps if I were to remove the cap at the extremity of the instru-
        ment, m'lord, more satisfactory results might be obtained.'
        ... 'Ah!' There was satisfaction in Lord Emsworth's voice. He twiddled
        and adjusted, and the satisfaction deepened. 'Yes, that's better. That's
        capital.'...

                                                P.G. Wodehouse: *Blandings Castle*

(2)   LADY MACBETH *He has almost supt: why haue you left the cham-*
        ber?
        MACBETH *Hath he ask'd for me?*
        LADY MACBETH *Know you not, he ha's?*

                                                William Shakespeare: *Macbeth*

(3)   *Whan that Aprill with his shoures soote*
        The droghte of March hath perced to the roote,
        And bathed every veyne in swich licour
        Of which vertu engendred is the flour ...

                                                Geoffrey Chaucer: *Canterbury Tales*

(4)   *þa gesette se munuc ealla þa gerecednesse an anre bec, and eft ða þa*
        seo boc com to us binnan feawum gearum, þa awende we hit on Englisc,
        swa swa hit heræfter stent.

                                                Ælfric: *King Edmund*

As one can see from these examples, like varieties of present-day English,
historical varieties differ in pronunciation, spelling, vocabulary, grammar
etc. Even the Wodehouse text, which was first published in 1935, contains
a number of expressions that one would not expect to be used today or that
one would consider old-fashioned, and the changes between the earlier
periods and today are rather dramatic. The sample from Ælfric's account of
the life of King Edmund, written more than 1000 years ago, cannot be understood by native speakers of English today. It reflects a stage of the language at which English was much closer in character to German in that, for

---

by Larry D. Benson, Oxford: Oxford University Press, 1987: 23). – Ælfric:
St. Edmund (taken from: Rolf Kaiser: *Medieval English*, Berlin, 5th impression 1961: 152).

instance, nouns, adjectives, pronouns inflected for case and number in a way that they no longer do in modern English.

The texts given here represent the four phases into which the development of the English language is generally divided:

▷ **Old English**, ca. 600 – ca. 1100, characterized by a complex system of inflexions, by a relatively homogeneous vocabulary of predominantly Germanic origin

▷ **Middle English**, ca. 1100 – ca. 1500, characterized by an increasing loss of inflexions and a tremendous change in vocabulary, with a large number of words of French origin coming into English

▷ **Early Modern English**, ca. 1500 – ca. 1750, a period in which English was subject to the Great Vowel Shift and a standard language gradually emerged

▷ **Modern English**, ca. 1750 – today. Sometimes, the term **Late Modern English** is used for the period between 1750 and 1900 and the English after 1900 is referred to as **Present-Day English**.[9]

1.4 The character of English

1.4.1 English as a Germanic language

As far as its place within the world's languages is concerned, English is a Germanic language, i.e. a member of the Indo-European family of languages.[10]

---

[9] For slightly different periodisations of English compare Brinton and Arnovick (2006: 10–11), Denison and Hogg (2006: 2–3) or Mair (2008: 189–195). For a discussion of periodisation see Lutz (2002b).

[10] Based on Denison and Hogg (2006: 5). Compare Brinton and Arnovick (2006: 94–103) and Crystal (1997: 300), also with respect to Yiddish and Flemish.

Indo-European languages									
Celtic	Germanic	Italic	Balto-Slavic	Albanian	Hellenic	Anatolian	Armenian	Indo-Iranian	Tocharian

West	North	East
English	*Icelandic*	*Gothic*
Frisian	*Faeroese*	
Low German	*Norwegian*	
Dutch	*Swedish*	
Afrikaans	*Danish*	
High German		

Although as far as its historical origins are concerned English is quite clearly to be regarded as a Germanic language, it has to be noted that the vocabulary of present-day English can be seen as a mixture of words of Germanic and Romance origin. The reasons for the development from a language with an almost entirely Germanic vocabulary to the present situation lie, at least partly, in general historical developments in England and the kind of language contact in which they resulted.

The first contact that must have taken place after the arrival of the An-glo-Saxons in England in the middle of the fifth century is that between English and the language spoken by the Celts inhabiting the island at the time. However, the Celts were driven by the Anglo-Saxons into the fringe regions of Scotland, Wales, Ireland, Cornwall and Brittany, where in some parts Celtic languages are still spoken today. Until recently, it was believed that there had been very little contact between the English and the Celts, partly because very few Celtic words can be found in English. More recent research suggests, however, that the contacts may have been more intensive and are reflected linguistically in certain peculiarities of the Old English grammatical system compared with that of other Germanic languages (> 20.1).

As far as vocabulary is concerned, the languages to which English owes most are Latin, French, Scandinavian languages and Greek.[11]

1. **Latin**: The Romans, who had occupied parts of Britain between 43 and 407, had already withdrawn from the island when the Anglo-Saxons arrived. There had been contact between the Anglo-Saxons and the Romans on the Continent, however, which had indeed resulted in borrowings such as *port* or *mile*. Furthermore, there is the possibility that the Celts living in Britain during the Roman occupation took over Latin words, which were later taken over by the Anglo-Saxons. During the Old English period, towards the end of the sixth century, the Christianization of the Anglo-Saxons set in, starting in Canterbury. Christian monasteries were established and became centres of learning. It is through translations of religious and scientific texts from Latin into English that were carried out at the monasteries that Latin words were introduced into English on a large scale (*disciple, decline*).

    Later, during the Renaissance, a great number of **Latin** and **Greek** words were taken over on a large scale during the period of Neoclassicism.

2. **Scandinavian languages**: During the ninth and tenth centuries, the North-Eastern part of England, the so-called Danelaw, was settled by Scandinavians and was politically a part of Denmark. This, in the long term, resulted in Scandinavian vocabulary being taken over by English. Although the number of Scandinavian loan words is relatively small, the Scandinavian influence is important because many highly frequent words such as *take* (which replaced Old English *niman*) and the pronouns *they, their, them* were taken over from the Scandinavian languages.

3. **French**: By far the most dramatic change in the history of England and the history of English is represented by the Norman Conquest in 1066, which resulted in a situation in which practically the whole ruling class of the country was replaced by French-speaking nobility. For three hundred years, French was an official language in England, it was the language of the courts and of government; it was as late as 1362 that the London Parliament was opened in English for the first time. Thus the

---

[11]   For a short outline of British history in this context see e.g. Denison and Hogg (2006: 8–29). For developments in vocabulary see also Chapter 20.3 and the sources given there, esp. Kastovsky (2006).

vast intake of words from French (such as *crown, government, accuse, appetite*, to give just a few examples) during that period is hardly surprising.

The result of these processes is the so-called mixed vocabulary of present-day English. There are word counts that suggest that more than 50%[12] of the vocabulary of English is Romance in character (taken over from French, Latin or Italian), although one must not overlook the fact that many (although by no means all) of these words have a considerably lower frequency than many Germanic words. More detailed research on this is certainly needed to obtain reliable data. This is one of the areas where modern corpus linguistics provides a new and much more reliable empirical basis. A first analysis of the 3600 words that according to the *Longman Dictionary of Contemporary English* (LDOCE4, 2003) make up the 3000 most frequent words of the spoken language and the 3000 most frequent words of the written language in the British National Corpus has revealed that of these words about 34% are of Germanic origin and 54% of Romance origin.[13]

It is sometimes argued that the mixed character of its vocabulary makes English particularly suitable for the status of a world language and lingua franca which it occupies today. It must be said, however, that there is no empirical evidence to support such a view and that any explanation for the emergence of English as an international language in terms of cultural and political dominance is probably more powerful.

1.4.2   Language typology

Languages cannot only be classified according to their historical origins, but, in a typological way, according to certain features they show. The following types of languages are commonly distinguished:[14]

---

[12]   Cf. Scheler (1977: 72), where a much more differentiated account is given. See also Lutz (2002a: 410).

[13]   The basis of these figures is provided by LDOCE4 (for frequency) and the *Oxford English Dictionary* (OED2) (for the etymological source). Thanks to Peter Uhrig for his help and particularly for designing a computer program to work out these figures.

[14]   This kind of classification goes back to Wilhelm von Humboldt and August Wilhelm Schlegel; cf. Crystal (1980: 367) and Bußmann ([4]2008: 664–666).

▷ **agglutinating languages** (such as Turkish, Finnish, Hungarian or Basque), in which grammatical relations are expressed by unambiguous endings, which are added to words.

▷ **inflecting languages** (such as Latin, Arabic, French or German), in which grammatical relations can be expressed by endings, which can, however, have different meanings (*Fahrzeug-e*: nominative plural and accusative plural), and by changes of the stem (*singen – sang*).

▷ **isolating languages** (such as Chinese or Vietnamese), in which words are invariable and grammatical relations are expressed by word order or separate words, but not by grammatical endings.

Although these types present prototypical descriptions and further types can be established, one can say that English has developed from a language of predominantly inflecting character to a language which shows strong characteristics of an isolating language.

1.5   The linguistic analysis of English

This short characterization of the English language opens up a large spectrum of topics which can be investigated in linguistics: questions of language typology are related to questions of language change, which in turn is related to linguistic variation. Research on how a language developed can go hand in hand with research on how speakers of different varieties or of different languages behave when they communicate with one another, etc.

In principle, such questions arise in the study of any language. Nevertheless, it has to be said that the international status of English has affected its linguistic analysis. Firstly, because the kind of language contact phenomena one encounters in the study of English are manifold in that they include its status with respect to minority languages as in Wales, for example, the status of English in countries such as India or in worldwide communication and the influence that English has on other languages through its present position. The mere power of this influence and the reactions against, say, the use of anglicisms in Germany, or, perhaps in an even more pronounced way in France, gives English a special status in this respect.

This also applies to other areas of linguistic description, of course. The mere fact that English is a or *the* world language at present has resulted in

---

See Crystal (1980) for short definitions of these and further distinctions made in language typology. For analytic and synthetic see Bußmann (⁴2008: 664).

enormous research being carried out on it, especially where commercial interests are involved. The amount of teaching materials, dictionaries or grammar books on English available in Germany, for example, by far supercedes that for any other language and, as a result, fostered by large potential sales figures and by commercial competition, a very high standard has been reached in many such publications.

English is probably the best described language in the world, partly because of the commercial aspects just mentioned, but also because a great deal of linguistic research is carried out in the United States and Britain. This has resulted in a situation in which many innovative ideas and research tools ranging from computational corpus linguistics to generative language theory, which are relevant for the study of all languages, have been developed in the context of English. In fact, many claims made about universal characteristics of language as such are made on the basis of an analysis of English so that one might argue that English has replaced Latin not only as lingua franca but also in this respect. In any case, it is probably fair to say that for these reasons English today is a particularly important language to study. At the same time it is probably equally fair to say that students of English with a different mother tongue have an important contribution to make in this enterprise because a different background of thinking and the experience of another language may make them see certain aspects of the English language in a different way from native speakers and provide insights which are equally valuable to work in applied and theoretical linguistics.

2 Principles of modern linguistics

2.1 Basic concepts of linguistic structuralism

2.1.1 Principles of linguistics since de Saussure

> *... I am more and more aware of the immense amount of work that would be required to show the linguist what he is doing ... The utter inadequacy of current terminology, the need to reform it and, in order to do that, to demonstrate what sort of object language is, continually spoils my pleasure in philology, though I have no dearer wish than not to be made to think about the nature of language in general. ...*[15] (Ferdinand de Saussure)

What we today call modern linguistics emerged at the beginning of the twentieth century and is generally associated with the name of the Swiss linguist Ferdinand de Saussure, who, in a series of lectures given in Geneva between 1907 and 1911, established important principles of language description, which were published posthumously by his pupils in the famous *Cours de linguistique générale* (1916).

Of course, the study of language has a much longer history. Its origins lie not only in Europe, but also in other parts of the world such as Arabia[16] or India.[17] In ancient Greece philosophers such as Aristotle or the Stoics were concerned with the description of the nature of language. The ideas they developed can be seen as establishing a tradition of language description which was continued by Latin grammarians such as Donatus (4th century AD) and Priscian (ca. 500 AD) and has remained influential through the Middle Ages and the Renaissance up to this day. In fact, our present system of word classes owes a lot to the discussions of Ancient Greek philosophers, particularly the ideas of Dionysius Thrax (ca. 100 BC), and ideas similar to established concepts of modern sentence analysis can be found in

---

[15] F. de Saussure: 'Letter of 4 January 1894', in 'Lettres de F. de Saussure à Antoine Meillet', *Cahier Ferdinand de Saussure* 21 (1964: 95); quoted in Culler (1976: 15).

[16] Cf. Robins (1967: 97–99) and Brekle (1985: 68–87).

[17] Cf. Robins (1967: 136–148).

the work of Apollonius Dyscolus (2nd century AD).[18] A very important source of influence, in this context, have been grammars developed for the teaching of Latin and other languages, which were based on the Latin tradition.

During the eighteenth and especially the nineteenth century a focus of interest in the history and comparison of languages developed – instigated by the study of Sanskrit. The nineteenth century is the period in which historical linguistics emerged as a scientific discipline, a development which is linked with such names as that of Jacob Grimm (1785–1863).[19] It is important to realize that de Saussure's work must be seen against this background of an established discipline of comparative philology.[20] In fact, de Saussure himself, who had studied at Leipzig, which was then a centre of the historically oriented school of the *Junggrammatiker*, had published on Indo-European and Sanskrit and taught Sanskrit and historical linguistics in Paris and Geneva before he turned to the teaching of general linguistics.[21]

What is so important about de Saussure's *Cours de linguistique générale* is that it raised a few matters of linguistic principle in a very systematic manner and addressed the general question of the task of the linguistic science as such. Considering it a milestone in the history of linguistics does not mean that all work preceding de Saussure should or could be disregarded. In fact, many ideas that are being fruitfully exploited today have their roots in pre-de Saussurian linguistics: the leading American linguist of the second half of the twentieth century, Noam Chomsky, for instance, has repeatedly related his ideas to those of the German philosopher Wilhelm von Humboldt (1767–1835).[22]

---

[18]   Cf. Robins (1967: 36–39 and 56–58).

[19]   Cf. Robins (1967: 171). For a more detailed account of the history of linguistics see Robins (1967), Helbig (1970) or Sampson (1980).

[20]   Cf. Culler (1976: 9; 13–15). For a discussion of de Saussure's view of linguistics after 1800 see Culler (1976: 53–79).

[21]   Cf. Culler (1976: 15).

[22]   For such a view see Robins (1967: 174): "Wilhelm von Humboldt was one of the most profound thinkers on general linguistic questions in the nineteenth century, and one wonders whether, if his style had been less diffuse and his ideas more worked out and exemplified than they were, and his voluminous works were better known and more widely read, he would not be accorded a position comparable to that given to de Saussure as one of the founders of modern linguistic thought."

Nevertheless, it was de Saussure who with hitherto unknown systematicity outlined principles of modern linguistics, most of which are still widely accepted today. They concern the following aspects:

▷ the character of the linguistic sign and the dichotomy between *signifié* and *signifiant* (> 2.1.2)

▷ principles of the description of language such as the distinction between the synchronic and the diachronic study of language (> 2.1.3)

▷ the distinction between langue and parole (> 3.1.3)

▷ the view of language as a system which has structure and which can be analysed in terms of the relations of the elements establishing structure (> 2.1.4)

2.1.2   The character of the linguistic sign

One of the basic units of linguistic description identified by de Saussure is the linguistic sign. The linguistic sign consists of two components, which de Saussure labelled **signifiant** and **signifié**, and for which different terms have been used: *Ausdrucks- und Inhaltsseite des sprachlichen Zeichens* in German, *signifier* and *signified*, or more commonly, *form* and *meaning* in English.[23]

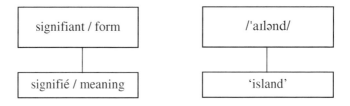

Lipka (³2002: 55) characterizes de Saussure's concept of the linguistic sign as follows:

> Saussure stresses repeatedly that the linguistic sign is a mental unit ("une entité psychique à deux faces"), and does not link a thing and a name, but a concept and a phonic image. This image is for him nothing material, physical, but a mental impression of sound. The connection of *concept* and *image*

---

[23]   Palmer (²1981: 5–6) points out that the term *sign* is often used to refer to the *signifier* in de Saussure's sense. For an outline of de Saussure's concept of the linguistic sign see Lipka (³2002: 55–56).

acoustique, of concept and sound picture, for Saussure constitutes the *signe linguistique*, the linguistic sign. The notions "concept" and "image acoustique" are later replaced by him by the terms *signifié* and *signifiant*, which have since become internationally accepted technical terms ...

The three characteristics of the linguistic sign that de Saussure emphasizes are

− the **linearity** of the *signifiant*, which means that the form of the linguistic sign consists of a chain of sounds, which is uttered and perceived in linear order,

− the **conventionality** of the linguistic sign, which means that *signifiant* and *signifié* are linked by convention within a speech community and that as a result the linguistic sign cannot be altered by an individual,

− the **arbitrariness** of the linguistic sign, which means that there is no causal relationship between form and meaning in the sense that there is a reason why a particular meaning should be expressed by a particular form in a language, i.e. why, for instance, the concept of 'island' should be expressed as *island* in English, *eiland* in Dutch, *Insel* in German, *Ailön* in Frisian, *ø* in Danish, *saari* in Finnish, *île* in French, or *isola* in Italian.[24]

The notion of arbitrariness can be extended, as Culler (1976: 21) points out, to the notion of *signifiant* as such:

It is, Saussure says, all too easy to think of language as a set of names and to make the biblical story of Adam naming the beasts an account of the very nature of language. If one says that the concept 'dog' is rendered or expressed by *dog* in English, *chien* in French and *Hund* in German, one implies that each language has an arbitrary name for a concept which exists prior to and independently of any language.

If language were simply a nomenclature for a set of universal concepts, it would be easy to translate from one language to another. One would simply replace the French name for a concept with the English name. If language were like this the task of learning a new language would also be much easier than it is. But anyone who has attempted either of these tasks has acquired, alas, a vast amount of direct proof that languages are not no-

---

[24] Onomatopoetic words like *cuckoo*, which in a way are motivated by the thing they refer to, are in de Saussure's view also arbitrary in that they differ to a certain extent in different languages and are subject to linguistic change. For a conflicting view see Lipka ([3]2002: 56). For a discussion of iconicity see Lyons (1977: 99–109) and Ungerer and Schmid ([2]2006: 300–312).

menclatures, that the concepts or signifieds of one language may radically differ from those of another. The French 'aimer' does not go directly into English; one must choose between 'to like' and 'to love'. ... Each language articulates or organizes the world differently. Languages do not simply name existing categories, they articulate their own.

Arbitrariness thus can be interpreted to mean not only that the relationship between form and meaning is not motivated, especially not motivated by any features of the objects of the real world which are covered by the meaning of a linguistic sign, but also that the way in which different languages divide up the spectrum of reality in terms of meanings differs from one language to another.

2.1.3   Synchronic and diachronic study of language

Another important distinction that was established by de Saussure which is still generally accepted in linguistics is that between the study of the system of a language at a given point in time, which de Saussure termed **synchronic**, and the study of the changes that can be observed in the course of the history of a language, which he called **diachronic.**

The importance attributed to the distinction must be seen against the background of a kind of historical linguistics prevailing at the time, which did not investigate language as a system at a particular point in time but concentrated on describing developments. It is important to realize that synchronic linguistics must not be equalled with the analysis of present-day language since a synchronic description of language can be one of a historical state of the language. The distinction between synchronic and diachronic is primarily a methodological distinction in that any diachronic study presupposes a synchronic study.[25]

---

[25]   A synchronic study of Old English is provided, for instance, by Quirk and Wrenn ([2]1957); a history of the English language that is very systematically built upon the distinction between synchronic and diachronic is that by Strang (1970).

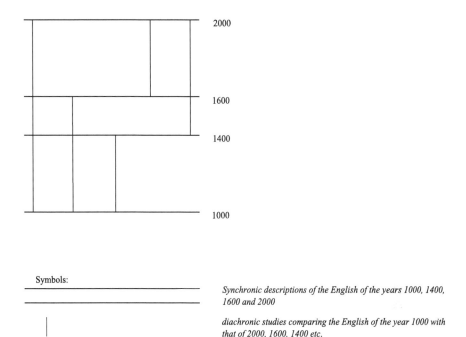

2000

1600

1400

1000

Symbols:

Synchronic descriptions of the English of the years 1000, 1400, 1600 and 2000

diachronic studies comparing the English of the year 1000 with that of 2000, 1600, 1400 etc.

Of course, one must realize that the idea of a synchronic study of a language at a given point in time is to some extent a methodological abstraction since language is always in transition and never presents a stable system as such. Nevertheless the distinction between synchronic and diachronic must not be understood as denying the essentially historical nature of language.[26]

2.1.4   The importance of relations

2.1.4.1   *The value of the linguistic sign*

One reason why de Saussure attributed so much importance to the distinction between synchronic and diachronic is that he wanted to emphasize that at any point in time the actual value of a linguistic sign is independent from its history and solely determined by its relationship to the other linguistic signs of the system at that point in time. This is no contradiction to saying

---

[26]   Cf. Culler (1976: 36).

that a particular sign and its place in the system of language as such are the result of a historical process.

Thus, for the purposes of describing the synchronic state of a language, "diachronic information is irrelevant" (Culler 1976: 36). Culler illustrates this by the example of the English second person pronoun *you*, which translates as three different forms into German, for example: *du*, *ihr* and *Sie*. Present-day English *you* is historically plural, then came to be also used as a respectful way of addressing one person until the singular form *thou* died out completely. While this is interesting in itself, it does not help you understand how present-day English *you* is used.

This kind of argument is crucial to a **structuralist approach** to the description of language, in which language is seen as a system of linguistic signs, which gain their identity or value not by some intrinsic property they possess but through their mutual relationships with each other. De Saussure (1916, English translation by Roy Harris 1983: 115) describes this as follows:

> ... The Slavic languages regularly distinguish two verbal aspects: the perfective aspect represents an action as a whole, as a single point, taking no development into account, whereas the imperfect aspect represents the same action in the process of development, taking place in time. These categories are difficult for a Frenchman, because his language does not recognise them. If they were predetermined categories, there would be no such difficulty. In all these cases what we find, instead of *ideas* given in advance, are *values* emanating from a linguistic system.

Thus it is differences and relations that matter, not substance. By the way, this irrelevance of substance also reflects the view that the linguistic sign is arbitrary (because if it were not, it would have substance) and, similarly, why the linguistic sign can be subject to diachronic change.

De Saussure's most famous analogy to illustrate this view is that with a game of chess, where the precise shape of the pieces in a particular game, their material, their size etc., i.e. all the factors contributing to substance, do not matter as long as the functional value of the different pieces – which can be recognized by relating them to each other – are clear. In the same way, to use another analogy,[27] when one identifies a train as, say, the 16.50 from Paddington, one does not mean that the same train in terms of substance (in the sense of consisting of the same engine, carriages etc.) leaves Paddington every day at that time, but one refers to a unit that has a place

---

[27]   Cf. Culler (1976: 27).

or value in the system of all trains (so that it is still the 16.50 from Paddington even if it has left Paddington late).

In a slightly different way, the example of colour terms is often mentioned to illustrate that linguistic signs do not have meaning as such but that
their meaning only exists in terms of their relationship to other linguistic
signs. The argument runs that a term such as *blue* does not mean or signify
anything as such, but that its meaning or value only becomes clear if the
other colour terms in the system are also considered and a term such as *blue*
is seen in relation to the other colour terms of the language.[28]

2.1.4.2   *Syntagmatic and paradigmatic relationships*

The crucial idea of a structuralist approach to language is to see linguistic
signs as determined by the relations they enter with other linguistic signs.
De Saussure identifies two types of such relationships: a sign enters

– a **syntagmatic relationship** with signs with which it can occur in a
  sentence (indicated by the horizontal arrow below), and

– a **paradigmatic relationship** with signs which could occur in the
  same place in the sentence (symbolized by the vertical arrow).

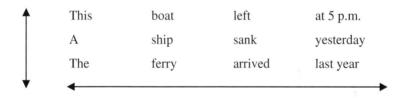

This	boat	left	at 5 p.m.
A	ship	sank	yesterday
The	ferry	arrived	last year

Such relations can be established not only between linguistic signs such as
words or grammatical elements, but also at the level of sound:

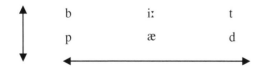

| b | iː | t |
| p | æ | d |

---

28   Compare the approach of prototype semantics described in Chapter 15. This
      has been questioned by psychologists in recent works.

Linguistic signs can thus be described in terms of the syntagmatic and paradigmatic relations they enter.

2.1.5   Schools of structuralism

The principles of structuralist linguistics were shared by various schools of linguistics, which emerged in different places of the world during the first half of the twentieth century, which can all be subsumed under the heading of **structuralism:**

-   **American structuralism**, also called **distributionalism**, which focussed on formal properties of linguistic elements, especially their distribution (associated with linguists such as Leonard Bloomfield, Charles Hockett, Zellig Harris), which provided an important basis for **generative grammar**, the kind of linguistics which was instigated by Noam Chomsky in the second half of the century and which has dominated linguistic discussion ever since, especially in the English-speaking world
-   the **Prague School**, also known as **functionalism**, which concentrated on the function of linguistic elements, particularly in the sound system of a language and in the way that sentences are organized (developing a theory called **functional sentence perspective**) (associated with linguists like Trubetzkoy, Jakobson, Mathesius, Daneš)
-   the **Copenhagen School**, also known as **glossematics**, centering on the character of the linguistic sign (founded by the Danish linguist Hjelmslev)
-   **dependency grammar** (developed by the French linguist Tesnière), which concentrates on the relationship of elements within a sentence, taking the verb as its centre, which found its most important reflection in the development of **valency theory**, a model of syntax widely used in Germany (> Chapter 17).

2.2   Linguistics and descriptivity

Although there are many differences between various modern schools of linguistics in how they approach the subject of language and which aspects of language they focus on, there is unanimous agreement with respect to one principle, namely the **descriptive** nature of linguistic research. It is generally understood that the task of linguists is

– to describe how people speak and

– not to tell them how to speak.

This has not always been so. In fact, in the past, it was quite common for grammarians to take a **normative** or **prescriptive** approach by formulating rules which did not reflect the way that the language was actually spoken but stated how, for one reason or another, it ought to be spoken.

This means that modern linguists would reject any kinds of statement that would imply value judgments about the use of particular forms. Such discussions could arise with respect to utterances like the following:[29]

(1a)$_{QE}$ *Whom did you see?*

(1b)$_{QE}$ *Who did you see?*

(2a)$_{QE}$ *It is I.*

(2b)$_{QE}$ *It is me.*

(3a)$_{QE}$ *I didn't see anybody.*

(3b)   *I didn't see nobody.*

(4a)$_{BNC}$ *Students could be given the opportunity of actively searching for information about some topic in which they are interested.*

(4b)$_{BNC}$ *That's the only thing anybody seems to be interested in.*

Normative grammarians and usage guides have used a number of different arguments to justify judgements saying that one of the forms given is to be preferred over the other and why this second form could or should be regarded as incorrect. Thus in the case of (1) *whom* is to be preferred because it is the historically older form (or because it is the objective case), (2a) is seen as preferable because it corresponds to the Latin rule of case assignment, (3b) is rejected because it is "illogical" since two negatives can be seen as cancelling each other out. However, from the point of view of descriptive linguistics the only criterion to go by is whether a particular form is used by the speakers of the variety we are describing. There is no reason

---

[29]   For an intensive discssion of these problems see Palmer (1971: 13–26), where examples (1a) – (3a) are taken from.

whatsoever why English should follow the rules of Latin grammar.[30] Furthermore, language use certainly is not logical – otherwise the response to a question such as

(5a)$_{BNC}$ *Can you tell me what time it is?*

should be *yes* or *no*, and not

(5b)$_{BNC}$ *It's nine-thirty.*

which is perfectly natural, however. Nevertheless, it has got to be said that multiple negation is not used by speakers of Standard English today, although it was a feature of earlier stages of the language. For this reason, one would not consider (3b) to be a grammatical sentence of Standard English, although, of course, it is acceptable in many dialects of English.

Example (4b) could be objected to on the basis of a normative rule that prepositions should never occur at the end of a sentence. Here, Palmer (1971: 18) quotes the famous anecdote about Winston Churchill, who, after one of his secretaries had altered a sentence to avoid it ending with a preposition, commented: "'This is the kind of pedantry up with which I will not put'".

Within a descriptive approach to the analysis of language, the only relevant criterion for calling a form acceptable is whether a form is established, i.e. used by a certain number of speakers in the variety of the language one is describing.

2.3   The principles of structuralism and foreign language teaching

While it is not necessarily to be expected that insights gained in the scientific or academic exploration of a subject are directly applicable for practical purposes, linguistics and foreign language teaching have always shown great affinity. On the one hand, theoretical and descriptive linguistics can gain important insights from investigating aspects of language (or of a spe-

---

[30]   See Palmer (1971: 20–21), who points out that double negatives are common in other languages such as Russian or Spanish and continues: "It was the same in classical Greek but not in Latin. This should be hardly surprising; if Latin had had double negatives they would have found favour, not disfavour, with English grammarians! There can, then, be no logical reason for excluding double negatives. No rules are broken by *I didn't see nobody*."

cific language) that become particularly obvious when one deals with a foreign language or problems of teaching a foreign language. In particular, many important grammars and dictionaries of English, which were written with the foreign language perspective in mind, have turned out to be valuable contributions to the description of the English language as such. On the other hand, developments in the scientific investigation of language can indeed be applied to improving teaching materials and sometimes even teaching methodology. As far as structural linguistics is concerned, two important consequences can be drawn with respect to analyses which are relevant to foreign language teaching:

– Firstly, the dichotomy of form and meaning makes it essential to keep these two levels apart in any analysis of language.

– Secondly, the recognition of great differences between languages – both with respect to the levels of form and meaning – shows the necessity that a language can only be described appropriately in terms of categories that have evolved from the analysis of that language and not by using concepts or terminology that has arisen from a different language.

It is important to note that both criteria have often been violated in the teaching of foreign languages. For a very long time foreign language teaching was carried out in the framework of so-called traditional grammar, which often used semantic criteria for the definition of formal categories such as word classes (> 11.4), for example.[31]

In the description of English one such problem arises in the identification of tenses. First of all, it is important to make a distinction between time and tense. Time is a semantic category because it relates to meaning – time being either 'past time', 'present time' or 'future time'. Tense, however, is a formal category relating to particular verb forms.[32]

As far as the tense system of English is concerned, the question is whether any kind of verbal construction that relates to time should be considered a tense or whether the term tense should be restricted to forms which can be distinguished in terms of endings (or suffixes, > 8.2) and not

---

[31]   Cf. Burgschmidt and Götz (1974: 27–30). For the weaknesses of traditional classification of word classes see 11.4 and Herbst and Schüller (2008: 12–14 and 31–35).

[32]   Note that even terms such as past tense violate the principle of keeping the levels of form and meaning strictly apart because the label 'past' is a semantic label indicating a very frequent but by no means the only meaning that can be expressed by this form.

applied to constructions involving auxiliary verbs, for instance. In this latter view, which is taken in the *Comprehensive Grammar of the English Language* by Quirk, Greenbaum, Leech, and Svartvik (CGEL 1985: 4.3), for example, English has only two tenses – a present tense and a past tense (*walks – walked*).[33]

The most important point in this respect, however, is the fact that it would be very difficult to make out a case for a category future tense in English. Both great reference grammars of English – CGEL (1985: 4.3) and the *Cambridge Grammar of the English Language* (CamG 2002: 209–210) – reject the use of this term for the description of English. First of all, there is no inflected future tense in English as in Latin (*amabo*). Secondly, there are a number of forms that can be used to refer to future time – *will* + infinitive, *be going to, be about to,* present progressive, present simple, etc. Thirdly, it is not really possible to draw a dividing line between temporal uses of the *will*-construction and modal uses of the *will*-construction.[34]

A similar case is presented by the use of the term gerund with reference to present-day English, for which there is no justification at all. While in Latin gerunds (*laudandi*) are distinguished from present participles (*laudans*) by different endings, there is no such formal distinction in English (*praising – praising*). For this reason, the standard reference grammars do not make a terminological distinction either: CGEL (1985: 17.54) merely uses the term participle and CamG (2002: 80–83) introduces the term gerund-participle. In fact, the gerund is a good example of how the teaching of English may be made unnecessarily complicated by the use of inappropriate terminology. If students are told in a pedagogic grammar that "gerund-constructions can only function as adverbials when combined with a preposition"[35], they may well be led to assume that sentences of the type

(6)~BNC~ *Knowing her children, the teacher had decided that this activity was suitable for them.*

---

[33]   CGEL (4.17) classifies forms such as *have painted* or *had painted* as realizations of a perfective aspect, whereas CamG (2002: 15) speaks of secondary tenses.

[34]   For instance, it is difficult to see why *I'll drop by sometime* and *You will come back, won't you?* should be given as examples of future tense and *We will stay here* and *I will call you when I'm ready* as examples of a modal verb *will*, as in the *Cobuild English Grammar* (1990: 4.195 and 5.53/60).

[35]   "*Gerund*-Konstruktionen können nur in Verbindung mit Präpositionen adverbiale Funktion haben" (*Englische Grammatik heute* 1999: 199).

are ungrammatical in English. Quite obviously they are not – only that this particular grammar would classify *knowing* in (6) as a participle and not as a gerund.

This example shows that traditional terminology taken over from the teaching of Latin can be quite detrimental when applied to English (and may put many students off grammar).[36] The fact that many linguists use the term gerund without finding it necessary to justify this in the light of the arguments that such a category is not appropriate to the description of present-day English is at least worrying and shows that de Saussure's qualms about "the inadequacies of current terminology" have by no means been solved a hundred years later.

2.4   Areas of investigation

The structuralist way of seeing language and of approaching its analysis has been so influential in establishing many of the categories serving for the analysis of the sound systems of languages (**phonetics** and **phonology**), the analysis of the structure of words (**morphology** and **word formation**) and sentences (**syntax**), and also the analysis of word and sentence meanings (**semantics**) that some of the chapters that follow will to a large part be based on the concepts and ideas developed by linguists working within a structuralist framework.

Apart from analysing these structural aspects of language, several subdisciplines of linguistics concentrate on different aspects of how language is used by speakers. For example, they are concerned with

– units larger than the sentence (**text linguistics, discourse analysis**)

– the social importance of language use (**sociolinguistics**)

– the analysis of language as human behaviour (**pragmatics, speech act philosophy**)

---

[36]   For questions of terminology and foreign language teaching see Schröder (2005) and Herbst (2005). Compare Palmer's (1971: 15) comments on mother tongue teaching: "Since most English grammar teaching was based upon Latin the students were often at a loss. They could not see why English had a subjunctive or a dative case, but when they learnt Latin it all became clear. Latin helped them with their English grammar, but only because English grammar was Latin grammar all the time."

− psychological aspects of language use, language acquisition, language production and perception (**psycholinguistics** and **cognitive linguistics**).

The later chapters of this book will introduce some aspects of these topics.

3 Language, intuition and corpora

3.1 Language

3.1.1 Some basic distinctions

Since modern linguistics is a descriptive discipline, one of its main tasks is to describe language (or languages) as used by native speakers. This leads to two questions:

- How do we know or find out how a language is used?
- What exactly is it that we are describing or could be aiming at describing?

The question of data will be addressed in sections 3.2 and 3.3; with respect to the second question one important aspect of the problem is whether the research carried out is primarily aiming at

- finding out about human language as such, addressing such questions as to whether there is an inborn language faculty in the mind, whether there are general principles operating in all languages (so-called universals) etc. or
- describing a particular language to show its properties, state its rules of grammar, describe its vocabulary etc., as one would, for instance, when one is writing a grammar or a dictionary of English.

This is linked, up to a point at least, with the question of whether one is aiming at a description of

- the language of an individual, which seems appropriate when one investigates questions of language and the mind,
- a language (or a variety of a language) as such, as used by a speech community, i.e. language as a social phenomenon.

That these are not identical is fairly obvious: no one would expect any individual speaker to know all the words of a language. Thus one can safely assume that most speakers of German will not be familiar with all of the following words: *Duckdalbe, Menhir, Menkenke, Hyperurbanismus, Pfahlbürger, Pfahlmuschel* – all to be found in the *Duden Universalwörterbuch* [4]2001). While it would hardly make sense to base the selection of items to be included in a general dictionary on the words known to one person, finding out which words a person knows and uses at a particular age can be highly relevant when exploring language acquisition, for example.

Thus the scope of what a descriptive linguist might aim to describe is relatively wide. A number of important distinctions have been made in linguistics which may help to clarify (or at least illustrate) the problem, some of which will be mentioned in the following sections.

3.1.2   Competence and performance: the language of the individual

One such distinction is that between **competence** and **performance**, which was introduced by the American linguist Noam Chomsky, who, in the late 1950s, instigated a theoretical framework known as generative grammar, which was to dominate linguistic theory for the second half of the twentieth century (> 13.1). In his book *Aspects of the Theory of Syntax* Chomsky (1965: 4) writes:

> We ... make a fundamental distinction between *competence* (the speaker-hearer's knowledge of his language) and *performance* (the actual use of language in concrete situations). ... A record of natural speech will show numerous false starts, deviations from rules, changes of plan in mid-course, and so on.

Elsewhere, Chomsky (1966: 9–10) describes the difference by saying that competence is "what a speaker of a language knows implicitly" and performance "what he does". It is important to emphasize the word implicitly, because native speakers very rarely are able to state rules of the grammar of their language (unless they have received some special training as teachers, for example), but they know the rules of the language in the sense that they apply them correctly.

The difference between competence and performance can be illustrated with reference to errors that people make when learning a foreign language. Performance errors are the kinds of errors that learners make but which they either put right immediately or which they would correct when looking at the text again. Competence errors cannot be corrected by the learners themselves, of course.

3.1.3   Language as a social phenomenon

One problem for the description of language is that what can be observed directly is the performance of a speaker or indeed the performance of many speakers/writers of a speech community but not their competence. However, it would be inappropriate to describe a language simply in terms of performance, i.e. in terms of the utterances its speakers produce. Rather, many linguists believe that it is possible to construct an underlying "system of rules and relations" (Lyons 1968: 52) on the basis of these utterances. De Saussure (1916) introduced the notions of *langue* and *parole* to capture this difference, which Lyons (1968: 51) describes by saying "that all those who 'speak English' (or are 'speakers of English') share a particular *langue* and that the set of utterances which they produce when they are 'speaking English' constitute instances of *parole*".[37]

De Saussure (1916, English translation by Roy Harris 1983: 13) characterizes *langue* as follows:[38]

> The individual's receptive and co-ordinating faculties build up a stock of imprints which turn out to be for all practical purposes the same as the next person's. How must we envisage this social product, so that the language itself can be seen to be clearly distinct from the rest? If we should collect the totality of word patterns stored in all those individuals, we should have the social bond which constitutes their language. It is a fund accumulated by the members of the community through the practice of speech, a grammatical system existing potentially in every brain, or more exactly in the brains of a group of individuals; for the language is never complete in any single individual, but exists perfectly only in the collectivity.

3.1.4   *System* and *Norm* – language use

Chomsky (1965: 4) draws a parallel between his own distinction of competence and performance and *langue* and *parole*, but criticizes de Saussure's

---

[37]   Compare the formulation of Chomsky (1995: 14), where an individual's *competence* is described as "knowledge and understanding" and *performance* as "what he does with that knowledge and understanding".

[38]   Cf. Culler (1976: 29): "*La langue* is the system of a language, the language as a system of forms, whereas *parole* is the actual speech, the speech acts which are made possible by the language".

concept of *langue* as being merely a systematic inventory of items.[39] This reflects a rather interesting difference of views about the nature of language as such. Chomsky (1965: 4) argues that the "problem for the linguist" or a "child learning the language, is to determine from the data of performance the underlying system of rules that has been mastered by the speaker-hearer and that he puts to use in actual performance".

This raises the question – which is one core problem of modern linguistics and will be taken up in a number of chapters of this book – to what extent language can be seen as a system of rules or not. In this respect, a distinction introduced by the Romance scholar Coseriu (1973: 44) is of interest – namely that between *System* and *Norm*. The *Norm* in Coseriu's sense[40] is the totality of traditional realizations, which Coseriu distinguishes from the *System*, which is the totality of possible realizations. The concept of *Norm* is quite useful to explain why certain forms or combinations of forms which should be possible according to the *System* nevertheless do not seem to occur: thus the fact that in present-day English there is *sensitivity* next to *sensitiveness*, while there is only *kindness* (and not **kindity*) and *idiomaticity* (and no **idiomaticness*) can be seen as a typical *Norm* phenomenon.

A similar kind of emphasis on the role of item-specific or idiomatic elements in language can be found in so-called usage-based approaches within the framework of cognitive grammar.[41] With respect to language acquisition, the basic assumption of such theories is, as Tomasello (2003: 5) puts it, "that language structure emerges from language use". The idea is that on the basis of usage events, i.e. in de Saussure's terminology instances of *parole*, children build up inventories of constructions and make certain abstractions or generalizations and that "difference between young children's inventories and those of adults" can be seen as "one of degree" (Lieven 2008: 64) (> 12.3.3). This means that grammar is no longer envis-

---

[39]   Cf. Chomsky (1965: 4): "A grammar of a language purports to be a description of the ideal speaker-hearer's intrinsic competence". See Sampson (1980: 49–50) for a discussion of competence vs. performance and langue vs. parole.

[40]   The term *Norm* must not be interpreted in the sense of prescriptive or normative grammar here.

[41]   For convention and usage see Langacker (1987: 65–66). For the importance of idioms in construction grammar cf. Croft and Cruse (2004). For item-specific knowledge and generalizations in usage-based models see Goldberg (2006: 63–65).

aged as "a fixed synchronic system", as Bybee and Hopper (2001: 3) point out:

> The notion of language as a monolithic system has had to give way to that of a language as a massive collection of heterogeneous *constructions*, each with affinities to different contexts and in constant structural adaptation to usage.

If we look upon language acquisition and the resulting linguistic competence as being usage-based,[42] then this must allow for differences in the emerging linguistic "systems" – which, up to a point, seems compatible with de Saussure's characterization of *language* in 3.1.3.[43]

3.2   Finding data: traditional methods

3.2.1   Principal options

One of the principal problems of descriptive linguistics is the question of how one can find out which forms occur or can occur within a language. Basically, there are three methods that can be used:

– relying on one's own intuition

– carrying out tests with a sufficiently large number of native speakers

– analysing authentic language material

or combining various methods of that kind.[44]

---

[42] See, for instance, Goldberg (2006: 227): "Speakers' knowledge of a language consists of systematic collections of form-function pairings that are learned on the basis of the language they hear around them".

[43] It is less compatible with Chomsky's concept of competence, which is developed with reference to the construct of the ideal speaker-hearer "in a completely homogeneous speech community" (Chomsky 1965: 3). This is, of course, a considerable abstraction, which has been criticised from a number of different perspectives. For a discussion of the distinction between competence and performance with respect to language variation see e.g. Dufter, Fleischer and Seiler (2009: 6–9). Compare also Chomsky's (1986: 20–22) discussion of I-language and E-language in this context.

[44] For a discussion of the use of attested data in different approaches see Stubbs (1996: 28–32). Compare also Mair (1997: 9–13). For the advantages and disadvantages of these methods in lexicography see Herbst and Klotz (2003: 267–280).

3.2.2   Introspection and elicitation

Many grammars and dictionaries are based on the linguistic intuitions of their authors, i.e. their own competence in that language. This involves three main dangers:

- first of all, the competence of the individual in question may not be representative of the speech community as a whole,
- secondly, linguists may be guided in their acceptability judgements by the kind of analysis they are carrying out and the kinds of claims they wish to make,[45]
- thirdly, it has been shown that acceptability judgements vary to a considerable extent.

These problems can be reduced by basing one's findings not on the intuition of a single person. This has been done, for example, in the case of the *Grammar of Contemporary English*, a large grammar published by Randolph Quirk, Sidney Greenbaum, Geoffrey Leech and Jan Svartvik in 1972. For the purposes of writing that grammar, elicitation experiments were carried out in order to clarify certain points of English grammar. The tests used involved so-called judgement tests, in which subjects were asked to rate given forms as acceptable or not etc., and so-called performance tests, in which subjects were asked to change sentences in a particular way. In order to find out whether a phrase such as *none of the children* is used with a plural or a singular verb, for instance, subjects were given a past tense sentence such as *None of the children answered the question* and required to put it into the present tense (which forces a decision as to plural or singular verb).[46] Performance tests have two advantages: they test actual behaviour (sometimes, as in this example, without subjects being aware of what is being tested) and – unlike judgement tests – they do not depend on conscious reflection about language, which is often unreliable. Still, even tests of this kind do not always lead to clear results: experience shows that it is not uncommon for the same subjects to rate the same sentences differently when the test is repeated. Furthermore, results can depend on the design of the tests: Greenbaum and Quirk (1970: 6) report that in the case of *None of the children* "a singular verb (prescribed by schoolroom precept)

---

[45]   For the problems of intuition-based linguistics see Heringer, Strecker, and Wimmer (1980: 63).

[46]   Cf. Greenbaum and Quirk (1970: 23–24).

was preferred in a judgment test more frequently than it was preferred in a selection test", which shows that people's attitude towards the acceptability of a form does not always coincide with their actual behaviour.

3.2.3 Authentic language material: citations and corpora

The alternative to relying entirely on introspection and native speaker informants is to draw upon authentic language material. In fact, there is a long tradition for dictionaries and grammars to make use of authentic examples, often drawn from literary sources.

A remarkable attempt to base linguistic description on authentic citations was the *Appeal to the English-Speaking and English-Reading Public* launched in 1879 by Murray in the process of compilation of the famous *Oxford English Dictionary*, which up to this day is the most important historical dictionary of English. By the time the first edition appeared, 5 million citations had been collected by over 1300 voluntary readers, 1.8 million of these citations were actually used in the dictionary.[47]

While the method of employing citations is based on language use in that it provides evidence for particular instances of language in use, it does not allow any kind of statistical analyses, for example. A much more comprehensive way of investigating language in use consists in the analysis of large collections of texts, so-called corpora, which will be addressed in the next section.[48]

3.3   Corpus linguistics

3.3.1   Corpora of English

Not many people outside linguistics are aware of the fact that the basis for the empirical study of English – and increasingly so, also of other languages – has changed dramatically over the last few decades. This is appar-

---

[47]   Cf. Mugglestone (2009: 243–244) and Herbst and Klotz (2003: 271–273).

[48]   For the difference between "citation of instances" and "concordancing of texts" see Sinclair (1991: 39–41). For the use of the OED as a corpus-like resource see Hoffmann (2004). Compare also Mukherjee (2009: 13 and 125–128).

ent from the introduction of a book by John Sinclair (1991: 1), where he talks about "the emergence of a new view of language" and says:

> Over the last ten years, computers have been through several generations, and the analysis of language has developed out of all recognition.
>
> The big difference has been the availability of data. The tradition of linguistics has been limited to what a single individual could experience and remember. Instrumentation was confined to the boffin end of phonetics research, and there was virtually no indirect observation or measurement. The situation was similar to that of the physical sciences some 250 years ago. ...
>
> Thirty years ago when this research started it was considered impossible to process texts of several million words in length. Twenty years ago it was considered marginally possible but lunatic. Ten years ago it was considered quite possible but still lunatic. Today it is very popular.

The main reason for this is the enormous developments in computer technology, which have resulted in possibilities of accessing, within seconds, data from linguistic databases of unprecedented size. These technological innovations have given huge impetus to the development of a corpus linguistics – a methodology[49] (or a subdiscipline of linguistics) that systematically analyses large text corpora and derives its results from the analysis of such a corpus.

Although the method of basing linguistic analysis on corpora is also characteristic of the approach taken by American structuralists in the first half of the previous century,[50] the beginnings of what we now refer to as corpus linguistics can probably be more appropriately seen in the late 1950s or early 1960s. This is the time when Randolph Quirk founded the *Survey of English Usage,* a corpus for grammatical analysis, which served as an important source of information for the 1972 *Grammar of Contemporary English.* At about the same time, the first computer corpus of American English was set up by Francis and Kucera at Brown University, and a parallel corpus for British English – the Lancaster-Oslo/Bergen (LOB)

---

[49]   See Leech (1992: 105). Cf. also Aarts (2000: 7) for the relation between corpus linguistics and theoretical linguistics. See also Leech, Hundt, Mair, and Smith. (2009: 24).

[50]   Cf. Matthews (1993: 131–133). Compare also Leech (1991: 8): "For such linguists the corpus – a sufficiently large body of naturally occurring data in the language to be investigated – was both necessary and sufficient for the task in hand, and intuitive evidence was a poor second, sometimes rejected altogether. But there is virtually a discontinuity between the corpus linguists of that era and the later variety of corpus linguists ...".

Corpus – was developed in the seventies.[51] That such important steps in corpus linguistics should have happened at this time is remarkable insofar as linguistic research, especially in the area of syntax, was dominated by the development of generative grammar with its emphasis on intuition as it had been formulated by Noam Chomsky.

In the early days of corpus linguistics corpus size was a major problem – and, in fact, it remains difficult to determine how large a corpus must be in order to be appropriate for a particular research task.[52] However, the extent of the problem has been reduced considerably by developments in computer technology. While the Brown and the LOB corpora contained 1 million words, the Cobuild Corpus established by John Sinclair at Birmingham, which can claim to be the first corpus to have been systematically exploited for the purposes of writing a general English dictionary, in 1987, when the *Cobuild Dictionary of the English Language* first appeared, already contained 7 million words. The size of corpora dramatically increased during the 1990s; Cobuild, which was then renamed the Bank of English, at one point reached up to 500 million words running text. Another equally important corpus available to us today is the British National Corpus, containing 100 million words, with a 10 per cent component of spoken English. Although the possibility that a particular form or construction does not occur in the corpus cannot be totally ruled out today, the problem quite obviously presents itself in a completely different perspective than 40 years ago.

Increasingly, corpora are being designed with the purpose of comparing different historical stages of English (such as the Helsinki Corpus of English Texts: Diachronic Part) or different varieties of English such as the In-

---

[51]   For a short survey of English corpus linguistics see Garside, Leech, and Sampson (1987), Leech (1991) and Aijmer and Altenberg (1991: appendix) and Mukherjee (2009).

[52]   Referring to a study of the negation of the verbs *need* and *dare* using the Brown Corpus, which found only 32 instances of *need* negated by *not* and only 11 of *dare*, Greenbaum (1988: 84) points at a general problem of corpus analysis: "If we are looking at syntactic data, it may be a matter of chance that a particular syntactic feature is absent or rare in our corpus. Only for very common constructions can we be certain of finding adequate evidence. We cannot know that our sampling is sufficiently large or sufficiently representative to be confident that the absence or rarity of a feature is significant."

Name	Editors	Content
Survey of English Usage	R. Quirk and S. Greenbaum (University College, London)	1 m British English (50% written – 50% spoken) from 1953–1987
Brown Corpus	W. N. Francis and H. Kucera (Brown University, Providence)	1 m American English from 1961
Lancaster-Oslo/Bergen Corpus (LOB)	G. Leech, S. Johansson and K. Hofland (Lancaster, Oslo, Bergen)	1 m British English (to match Brown) from 1961
Bank of English/ Cobuild Corpus	J. Sinclair (University of Birmingham)	in 1987: 7 million; later over 500 m British and American English, spoken and written
British National Corpus	BNC consortium[53]	100 m words of British English (90% written – 10% spoken)
Helsinki Corpus of English Texts: Diachronic and Dialectal	M. Rissanen, O. Ihalainen and M. Kytö (University of Helsinki)	diachronic corpus: 1.6 m British English from 850–1720
International Corpus of English	project initiated by S. Greenbaum (University College London)	ICE-GB, ICE-India etc. 1 million (60% spoken) texts from 1990–1993 each

Some important corpora of English

ternational Corpus of English, which is to comprise 25 subcorpora of L1-varieties such as British English, American English, New Zealand English and second language varieties such as East African, Indian or Singapore English.[54] Furthermore, FROWN and F-LOB – the Freiburg Brown and the

---

[53]   The BNC consortium includes: Oxford University Press, Addison-Wesley Longman, Larousse/Kingfisher Chambers, Oxford University Computing Services, University Centre for Computer Corpus Research on Language at Lancaster University, and the British Library's Research and Innovation Centre.

[54]   For details of ICE corpus design see Mukherjee (2009: 48–50). For Brown, LOB, Frown and F-LOB see Leech et al. (2009: 24–31).

Freiburg LOB Corpora – were designed as parallel corpora to Brown and LOB, containing texts from 1991–1992, to be paralleled by corresponding corpora with texts from 1901 and 1931 which provide a basis for research on change in English in the twentieth century.

3.3.2 What we can do with corpora

3.3.2.1 *Corpus analysis*

Corpora have become an indispensable tool for a considerable amount of research in the fields of syntax, phraseology and lexis. When Sinclair (1991: 1) speaks of a new view of language, then this is because corpus research has indeed shown the importance of phraseological units and pre-fabricated items in language use (see Chapter 12). It is not by chance that the development of corpora such as COBUILD or the BNC should have been supported by the major EFL dictionary publishers. All recent editions of English learners' dictionaries are based on extensive corpus research and can thus provide much better descriptions of the language than earlier editions. Likewise, modern grammars are based on the insights of corpus research – notably the *Longman Grammar of Spoken and Written English* by Biber, Johansson, Leech, Conrad and Finegan (1999).

Corpora provide interesting insights into the use of words or constructions. They can be used to gain information on:

▷ the frequency of words or particular constructions (in the spoken or written language or in particular types of text),

▷ whether a particular form typically occurs in particular types of texts (such as spoken texts, written texts, literary language, newspaper language),

▷ whether a particular form is typically used by particular groups of speakers (depending on factors such as age, region, sex),

▷ which other words typically occur together with a particular word (by providing collocational profiles showing the statistical significance of particular combinations),

▷ the syntactic constructions and valency patterns in which a word occurs.

For more detailed analyses of the uses of a word, the most convenient starting point is a so-called KWIC-concordance (keyword in context):

Left context	Keyword	Right context
the next eighteen years people like Hendrik Lorentz and George Fitzgerald	tried to	accommodate this observation within accepted ideas of space and time.
for the creation of the English commercial court, which has consciously	tried to	accommodate to the needs of the City of London, especially in
has written to parents after a ten-year-old girl complained that a man	tried to	accost her as she made her way to the school. Family
think that's another important thing. In fact, Marie Hoader	tried to	account for the negative consequences of unemployment in terms of five
If this is sanity, then what is madness? We	tried to	accumulate a butterfly-net catching clouds, arms taking flight in the
second source of information may be the holdings of museums which have	tried to	accumulate coins from their relevant collecting areas. The difficulty with
, saying 'both parties will fail to complete the work Hitler	tried to	achieve'. The universities mentioned in the most recent letter
study of English grammar. It was this reconciliation which the grammar	tried to	achieve. Largely because of the leadership of [gap name] , the collabora
are of interest to Lothian Highways Staff. The editorial team have	tried to	achieve a balance between matters which are of major concern to staff
and at least a proportion of the secular magnates. Tenth-century kings	tried to	achieve a balance between secular and ecclesiastical power in the localit
I would have made an oasis, and I would have er	tried to	achieve a better settlement That is accepted, and in fact we
who heads G W Run-Off, has told Gooda Walker names he	tried to	achieve a market settlement through Lloyd's, but could not reach
out in colour by the American artist Marianna Lines, who has	tried to	achieve authentic hues by using natural pigment dyes. The gem of
). The Celts loomed large in Cato's Origines. He	tried to	achieve clarity on places and names. He found a branch of
for this deed ... Miserable and degenerate criminals! The more I	tried to	achieve clarity on the monstrous event in this hour, the more
would be like taking a giant step backwards. Everything she had	tried to	achieve for herself during the last four years would have to be
have one friend, but the ideal withered as soon as he	tried to	achieve it. If he behaved normally the other boys stepped back
achieve in government what Thatcher never did — indeed, she never	tried to	achieve it. That is, the long-term view. Thatcher's
were made by several countries. Syria, Algeria and Japan all	tried to	achieve outright peace, and Sudan tried to intercede on behalf of
was determined to reduce this. Throughout the 1980s, the government	tried to	achieve this aim through a variety of measures. In 1979–80,
CL-GD5426 True Color VGA Accelerator. COMPUTER ASSOCIATES	TRIED TO	ACQUIRE NOVELL Borland International Inc chief executive officer P
balances in gold or foreign valuta. The more sophisticated provincial dealers	tried to	acquire the new denomination at the end of the year as a
repeat of Seville. And then what, Fernando?' She	tried to	act flippant by shrugging her shoulders and holding out her palms but
, look at er, George Bush in America, he's [pause]	tried to	act like forty, as I've tried to do [pause] a-- ,
go to you I'm on your side? Well she she	tried to	act like really friendly like. Yeah I know. She really
which rested casually beside him, half pointing at me. I	tried to	act unconcerned. 'Connie wasn't a big-town girl. She
in approval, no further work allowed. Action The user has	tried to	activate a DC/DCs via a package which has been submitted for QA

Left context	Keyword	Right context
WOLFCRAFT WALLCHASER Anyone who has never	tried chiselling	out a channel in a wall to accommodate electrical conduit or other
? [unclear] you choose. You choose a book. I've	tried choosing	one [pause] can't decide what I want, that's my trouble
the going was very uneven. Ahead was pure blackness; I	tried closing	my eyes, it made not the slightest difference. Suddenly,
Albert again, making for the door to the stairs. Jim	tried coaxing	him away with a glass of brandy, which Albert thought a
relief 'It was no good pleading with him. I	tried commanding	him — as if I were an angel — but he only
lead a child astray.'), and so he frequently	tried conducting	me that way. I asked him why he so dearly wished
he was not prepared to give the other woman up. Amy	tried confronting	her rival but was thrown into despair by her youth and beauty
dealer lacks sufficient knowledge to be of any help. I have	tried contacting	Olivetti by letter and telephone but they seem reluctant to deal with
slight drag, but you don't feel it. Have you	tried cycling	into a strong wind? Yeah. Especially recently? Yeah,
, or that they rarely enjoy it when they do. I	tried declaring	my own sense of dissatisfaction to a few friends and found I
ice. Printing on pure white cotton was disastrous. So Patsy	tried dipping	it in cold tea first. The experiment worked; now all
mirror. He was not pleased with what he saw. He	tried drawing	in his stomach and straightening his shoulders, as instructed by the
writings on the subject, except for those who have not yet	tried drifting	for pike (are there any?). If there are
each evening. Claire was delighted at the improvement She	tried drinking	a glass of milk, to see what would happen, and
ks in our furnishing department. She has long thick hair and	tried drying	it with three different dryers. Lorraine tested the Supersilent 2000 t
the sand. Now all I could see was spray. I	tried ducking	under broken sections, but they just ducked right down after me
what they could, which wasn't much. 'Have you	tried dusting	a brick wall for prints?' one of them had asked
the one who was behind glass and reality was theirs. I	tried eating	a sandwich with my second cup of tea and I just about
lay trips to Northern Ireland in search of cheap goods, and	tried enumerating	the benefits Ireland might receive from a Reunion with the rest of
the had difficulty in eating hers because of its hardness. She	tried exchanging	it for Fleury's but that was just as hard. The
into a hot bath in order to wind down, half have	tried exercising	as a means of relieving stress rather than simply getting fit,
he asked. 'Because when people get married,' Ellie	tried explaining	, 'it's better if they love each other.'
t letter saying it was not interested. Perhaps he should have	tried flogging	them some more marble to decorate their office. Such a tactic

Concordance from the BNCweb interface (British National Corpus)[55]

---

[55]   Cf. Hoffmann et al. (2008).

Thus, with the software currently available, it is relatively easy to find out that in the BNC (and thus, one would hope, in British English) *I suppose* is much more frequent than *I assume* (69.49 pmw versus 3.17 pmw (per million words)) or that *guilty conscience* (0.4 pmw) is more frequent than *bad conscience* (0.06 pmw).

Similarly, checking a problem such as whether *none* is used with a plural or a singular verb in a corpus such as the BNC is quicker and probably more reliable than carrying out judgment or performance tests of the type described above. Interestingly, the results show that when *none* is immediately followed by a verb, singular forms tend to occur almost twice as often as plural forms, but after phrases of the type *none of the + plural noun* plural verb forms are to be found more often (suggesting that the occurrence of a plural form in the noun may prime the use of a plural form in the verb).[56]

It is no exaggeration to say that many rules of grammar found in older grammar books or dictionaries had to be thrown overboard or modified in the light of the new evidence. For instance, it was often claimed that the difference between *try to open the window* and *try opening the window* is that the former would be used in a situation where for some reason it may be difficult to open a particular window (because it got stuck etc.) and the latter in a situation in which a window should be opened to achieve something else (such as getting fresh air into a seminar room). Corpus research shows beyond doubt, however, that this kind of rule is inadequate in that *try doing* can be used equally for both types of situation, as is shown by the concordances above.

These examples show to what extent corpus research can contribute to an accurate description of the way a language is used.[57]

---

[56] Such figures have to be treated with a certain amount of caution, however. What was calculated here was *none* and *none of the _NN2* [collocational profile + verb span R1R1 frqn (node, collocate at least 1) frqn (collocate at least 1)], but obviously more complex structures need also be taken into account.

[57] Corpora play an important role in many other areas of research as well; for first language acquisition see e.g. Behrens (2008); for a corpus-based study of gender-specific elements of language use see Grimm (2008).

3.3.2.2   *Corpora and foreign language teaching*

Corpus linguistics has of course had an immensely important impact on the quality of teaching materials such as textbooks, grammars and dictionaries. In advanced language classes, having direct access to a large corpus of the foreign language is a good way for the teacher to provide authentic information on language use, especially in areas such as collocation and phraseology (> 10.5).[58]

Furthermore, corpora can be used in research on foreign language learning. In this context the International Corpus of Learner English (ICLE) designed by Sylviane Granger, which contains subcorpora of the English used by university students with different L1-backgrounds and provides an ideal basis for finding out differences between the use of English by learners and native speakers.[59] This does not only concern the identification of errors and investigation of L1 influence, but the comparison of learner corpora with native speaker corpora has also shown overuse and underuse of particular forms to be an important characteristic of learner language: Lorenz (1999: 168–171), in a study on the intensification of adjectives, has shown that German learners of English tend to overuse high-frequency all-purpose intensifiers such as *really*, *so* and *quite* and to underuse *particularly*, *extremely* or *crucially* and *vitally*, Gilquin (2007: 288) comes to the conclusion that French learners underuse collocations with the verb *make*, and Paquot (2009: 109) provides evidence for the overuse of *for example* and *for instance* by learners with different mother tongue backgrounds.[60] It is obvious that this kind of research can be applied fruitfully to foreign language teaching: thus Granger (forthcoming) argues that "the overuse of the adjective *important* is a prompt for lexical expansion exercises aimed to raise learners' awareness of other adjectives (*major, crucial, significant*, etc.) that can be used instead".

---

[58]   For the use of corpora in the classroom see Mukherjee (2002). For the use of corpora with respect to the design of teaching materials see Mindt (1988).

[59]   See, for instance, Granger (1998 and 2009) and Gilquin (2007). For a survey of learner corpora see Nesselhauf (2004).

[60]   For the different types of chunks used by native speakers and advanced learners see de Cock (2000).

3.3.3 Corpus design and corpus size

Despite the tremendous possibilities that have been opened for linguistic research by the availability of large machine-readable corpora, one has to be aware of the problems associated with corpus linguistics, particularly those concerning corpus size and corpus design.[61]

Thus the question of how large a corpus must be for which research purpose is by no means easy to answer. One has to be aware of the fact that there is an enormous discrepancy between the 100 million words of the British National Corpus (and even larger databases used by dictionary publishers) and the size of 1 million words of the subcorpora of the ICE-project and the corpora belonging to the Brown family (like Frown and Lancaster 1931).

Equally important is the question of how representative a corpus is of the overall use of the language (Mukherjee 2009: 21), as is also pointed out by Hausser (1999: 291–292):

> The value of a corpus does not reside in the content of its texts, but in its quality as a realistic sample of a natural language. The more representative and balanced the set of samples, the higher the value of the corpus for, e.g., computing the frequency distribution of words and word forms in the language.

A very important demand to be made on a corpus today is that it should be **balanced**. This means that it should contain texts from

- different genres
- spoken and written language
- speakers of different regions, age groups, social backgrounds and genders

in an appropriate mixture.

Apart from the obvious difficulties involved in designing a balanced corpus, there are further reasons for not taking corpus evidence as unquestionable truth in any way. For instance, there is the problem that corpora, especially corpora of the spoken language, may contain errors made by native speakers or may also contain utterances by non-native speakers. Thus one would certainly not take the fact that one instance of *succeed + to*-infinitive can be found in the BNC – as opposed to 1215 examples of

---

[61] For principles of corpus design see also Mukherjee (2009: 21–23) and also Hoffmann et al. (2008).

succeed + *in* + *V-ing* – as evidence for the existence of a *to*-infinitive pattern for the verb *succeed*.

It should just be mentioned in passing that the question of not being able to verify whether an utterance was produced by a native speaker (and, if so, of which variety of English) is particularly problematic when it comes to using examples from the internet on the basis of a Google search etc. This is a particularly serious problem in the case of English because the internet contains many texts that were translated into English or written by non-native speakers, which is an important argument in favour of using carefully designed corpora.

3.4   Introspection, corpus analysis and views of language

Although there is no immediate connection between the method used to discover what the facts of language are and the particular view of language held by a researcher, it is obvious that the different tools outlined above are appropriate in different degrees for different purposes. In particular, one must be aware of the fact that corpora only contain utterances that have already been made, i.e. they are an account of usage. While this means that, up to a point, they can also be used to account for the creative potential of language, the fact that the BNC displays no instances of the verb *sneeze* of the kind discussed by Goldberg (2006: 42) with respect to a certain argument within construction grammar, namely, *She sneezed the foam off the cappuccino* cannot be taken to mean that such uses do not exist. As a consequence, it is important to bear in mind that although corpora offer fascinating possibilities they can never be the only source of linguist research, as is underlined by Johansson (1991: 313):

> In spite of the great changes in the less than three decades since the first computer corpus, there is one way in which the role of the corpus in linguistic research has not changed. The corpus remains *one* of the linguist's tools, to be used together with introspection and elicitation techniques. Wise linguists, like experienced craftsmen, sharpen their tools and recognize their appropriate uses.

Recommended further reading:

– Hoffmann ([2]2000a) and Robins (1967)
– Palmer (1971)
– Mukherjee (2009)

Sounds

4   The sounds of English: phonetics[62]

4.1   Sounds as the starting point of linguistic analysis

One can approach the systematic description of a language either from top
to bottom or from bottom to top, i.e. to begin with either the largest or the
smallest units that can be identified in the analysis. Since it is not immediately obvious what the largest unit is that can sensibly be identified for such
a purpose – the text? the sentence? – and since smaller units are perhaps of
greater relevance to the description of larger units than vice versa, the
sounds of speech will be taken as a starting point in this chapter.

The fact that it is speech sounds, and not, as one might think, letters, that
are attributed such importance in the description of language has to do with
the fact that speech precedes the written language both ontogenetically and
phylogenetically. Just as children learn to speak before they learn to write,
writing systems can be considered a kind of secondary phenomenon in the
history of the development of languages as such. For these reasons, structuralists such as de Saussure made it an important principle to base the
study of language primarily on the spoken and not on the written form.

4.2   Phones

Describing the sounds of a language presupposes knowledge of what the
sounds of a language actually are. This is by no means as obvious as it may
seem. As a rule, speakers do not produce speech sounds in isolation, but
sequences of sounds with no breaks or pauses between individual sounds,

---

[62]   The main purpose of Chapters 4 and 5 is to provide a basis for the discussion
of the phonology of English. For a more detailed account of English phonetics and phonology see, for instance, Gimson (1962/[4]1989), Arnold and Hansen (1975/[8]1992), Scherer and Wollmann (1972), Dretzke (1998), Roach
([4]2009) or Gut (2009).

or indeed words. Thus the first task of a phonetician is to identify the sound inventory of a language. This can be done by analysing stretches of sound chains and trying to find recurrent elements, i.e. units that appear repeatedly. The result of this process of **segmentation**, of dividing the continuum of a chain of sounds into small, recurrent elements, can then be represented in the form of a phonetic transcription of the following kind:

[ðɪ'ɪŋglɪʃ'hævnəʊrɪ'spektfəðeə'læŋgwɪdʒ|əndwɪɬnɒt'tʰiːtʃðeə'tʃɪɬdrəntə'spiːkɪt]

The English have no respect for their language, and will not teach their children to speak it (G.B. Shaw: *Pygmalion*).

The phonetic transcription indicates that it is possible to identify segments in a stretch of speech which are identical or at least sufficiently similar to be regarded as instances of the same speech sound or **phone**.[63] Furthermore, the transcription shows that some syllables are more prominent than others (indicated by the symbol ' preceding such a syllable). What cannot be shown in this way are features of speech that extend to larger units such as intonation. Nevertheless, the kind of segmentation procedure reflected in the transcription can be used to establish a phone inventory of a language. Thus, on the basis of the passage quoted above, it is possible to identify the following sounds as belonging to the sound inventory of English:

[ð] *the, their*

[ɪ] *the, English, English, will, it*

[ŋ] *English, language*

[g] *English, language*

[l] *English, language*

[ɬ] *will, children*

[t] *respect, it*

---

[63] This is a slightly idealized generalization. Cf. Garman (1990: 190): "Different utterances of the same word or phrase by the same speaker under the same conditions give rise to variable forms. These variables are, individually, unpredictable; but, over repeated utterances they will tend to cluster around common articulatory-acoustic centres. They can therefore be termed probabilistic variants." Garman also points at differences due to distinct vocal tracts, age and sex.

[tʰ] *teach*[64]

etc.

After segmentation, the next step is the **description** and **classification** of the phones identified for a language.

4.3 Articulatory, auditive and acoustic phonetics

Speech sounds can be described in various ways, depending on the kind of property that is taken as the focus of investigation:[65]

▷ **Articulatory phonetics** describes sounds with respect to the way in which they are produced, i.e. with respect to the speech organs involved.

▷ **Auditory phonetics** investigates the way in which speech sounds are perceived in the ear.

▷ **Acoustic phonetics** studies the physical properties of sounds such as their frequency.

Acoustic measurements are often represented in the form of so-called spectrograms, which show wave lengths and the type of vibration produced.[66]

---

[64] The symbol ʰ indicates aspiration.

[65] For an introduction to the principles of acoustic and auditory aspects of phonetics see Gut (2009: 137–195).

[66] Frequencies are shown on the vertical axis in this spectrogram. The different shades of colour refer to intensity, black areas indicating frequencies of high intensity. See Gut (2009: 147).

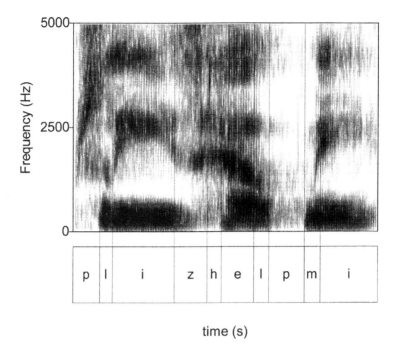

Broadband spectrogram of the utterance "Please help me".
(taken from Gut 2009: 148)

Acoustic measurements of this kind are probably the most precise method of analysing speech sounds. However, it is still customary to make use of the terminology of articulatory phonetics for most purposes of linguistic description.

One fundamental distinction that is made in the classification of speech sounds is that between **vowels** and **consonants.** This distinction can be made on the basis of the phonetic properties of the sounds or on the basis of their function in the syllable.

Phonetically, the distinction refers to the different ways in which vowels and consonants are produced: [67]

---

[67]   Cf. Gimson and Cruttenden (⁶2001: 27): "This type of definition might define vowels as median (air must escape over the middle of the tongue, thus excluding the lateral [l]), oral (... thus excluding nasals like [n]), frictionless (thus excluding fricatives like [s]), and continuant (thus excluding plosives like [p]); all sounds excluded from this definition would be consonants." Compare also the definitions given by Jones (1918/1960: 23), who draws the

▷ in the case of vowels, the air stream can pass from the lungs through the mouth across the central part of the tongue without any obstacle that would stop it or cause audible friction,

▷ whereas this is not the case with consonants.

With respect to the syllable (> 4.5), one can say that

▷ vowels have a central function in the syllable,

▷ whereas consonants have a marginal function (Gimson [4]1989: 30).

These two definitions coincide in the case of the three phones of the word *teach* in that [iː] has a central function in the syllable and shows no closure of the speech tract during its articulation and thus is clearly a vowel and [tʃ] and [tʰ] are not central in the syllable and do show such closure. However, this is less clear in the case of the [w] in *will*, which, like [j] in *yes*, is consonantal as far as its position in the syllable is concerned but phonetically is best described as a vowel glide.[68] Gimson ([4]1989: 33–34) thus describes [w] and [j] as **semi-vowels**, although more recently it has become common to include them under the class of **approximants** (Roach [4]2009: 50–52, Gimson and Cruttenden [6]2001: 211–216).[69]

---

line between vowels and consonants in such a way that "consonants ... include (i) all sounds which are not voiced (e.g. **p**, **s**, **ʃ**), (ii) all sounds in the production of which the air has an impeded passage through the mouth (e.g. **b**, **l**, rolled **r**), (iii) all sounds in the production of which the air does not pass through the mouth (e.g. **m**), (iv) all sounds in which there is audible friction (e.g. **f**, **v**, **s**, **z**, **h**)". Compare also Pike (1943: esp. 145), who distinguishes between vocoids and contoids at the phonetic level and between syllabic and non-syllabic with respect to the function of sounds within the syllable. For an elaborated discussion of different terminologies referring to phonetic quality and function in the syllable see Abercrombie (1967: 79–80).

[68]   Cf. Gimson ([4]1989: 33–44).

[69]   See also Gut (2009: 55). For [ɹ] see Gimson ([4]1989: 33) and Gimson and Cruttenden ([6]2001: 27). That the distinction between vowels and consonants is not perfectly straightforward also becomes apparent when one considers acoustic criteria, according to which consonants contain a noise component which vowels lack. This distinction does not fully coincide with that made on articulatory grounds as is pointed out by Arnold and Hansen (1975/[8]1992: 26). Arnold and Hansen ([4]1992: 32) use the term *Sonoranten* for [l] and the nasals. Compare also the classification of consonants provided by Dretzke (1998: 47). For the distinction between sonorants and obstruents see also Gimson ([4]1989: 34).

4.4   **Description of sounds in articulatory terms**

Speech sounds are produced by modifying air streams. This can be done by using organs such as the tongue, the lips and the velum (or soft palate).[70]

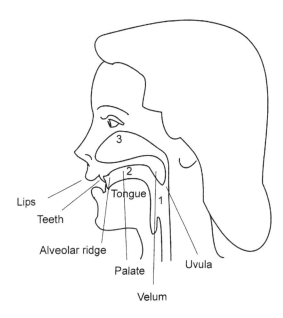

The vocal tract. The three cavities and the articulators of the articulatory system. (1= pharyngeal cavity; 2 = oral cavity; 3 = nasal cavity)
(taken from Gut 2009: 24)

Articulatory phonetics describes phones according to the way these modifications of air streams are achieved:
–   Depending upon whether the lungs are involved in producing an air stream or not, phones are classified as **pulmonic** or as **non-pulmonic**.
–   If the air stream is pushed out of the lungs, the sound is classified as **egressive**, if it is produced while breathing in, the phone is classified as

---

[70]   For a detailed description of the respiratory system, the phonatory system and the articulatory system see Gut (2009: 13–27).

ingressive. All phones of English are normally egressive, but an ingressive speech mode can be used too in some languages.[71]

– If the vocal cords are so far apart that they allow the air stream to pass without modification, the resulting sound is called **voiceless**, if they are so close together that they cause the air to vibrate the speech sound is called **voiced**.

– Depending on whether the air stream is directed through the mouth, the nose or both, sounds are classified as **oral, nasal** or **nasalized**.

These criteria are usually applied in the description of any speech sound. As far as further criteria are concerned it is usual to use separate sets of criteria for vowels and for consonants.

Consonants can be described in terms of criteria such as the following:

▷ the **place of articulation**, which indicates where the air stream is modified and which articulatory organs are involved in this modification: Since [tʰ] in English *teach* is produced by pressing the tongue against the alveolar ridge (the part of the palate behind the teeth), this sound is classified as alveolar, for example. The following places of articulation are relevant in the description of English:[72]

bilabial	lips	[pʰ] [p] [b] [m]
labio-dental	lower lip and upper teeth	[f] [v]
dental	tongue and upper teeth	[θ] [ð]
alveolar	tip and rims of the tongue and upper alveolar ridge and side teeth	[tʰ] [t] [d] [s] [z] [n] [l]

---

[71] Cf. Abercrombie (1967: 24–25): "Linguistic use of an ingressive pulmonic air-stream is certainly not common, but it can nevertheless be found in many parts of the world in a variety of circumstances. Thus in English the first part of the word *yes*, spoken in a somewhat off-hand manner, is often pronounced by many people with an ingressive pulmonic air-stream ... The quality of the voice is considerably changed when this air-stream is used ... and in a number of communities an ingressive air-stream is used as a disguise when the speaker cannot be seen and does not wish to be recognized."

[72] For a much more detailed description of manner and place of articulation of English consonants see Gimson (⁴1989: Chapter 8).

post-alveolar	tip, blade, and rims of the tongue and rear part of upper alveolar ridge	[r]
palato-alveolar	tip, blade, and rims of the tongue and upper alveolar ridge and side teeth	[ʃ] [ʒ] [tʃ] [dʒ]
velar	tongue and soft palate	[kʰ] [k] [g] [ŋ]
glottal	vocal cords	[ʔ] [h]

▷ the **manner of articulation**, which describes how the articulatory organs operate to produce this sound. In the case of [tʰ], for instance, tongue and alveolar ridge form an obstruction which is then opened so that the air stream is suddenly released. Accordingly, [tʰ] is termed plosive.

plosive / stop	articulatory organs form obstruction; air stream is held up; sudden release of air	[pʰ] [p] [tʰ] [t] [kʰ] [k] [ʔ] [b] [d] [g]
fricative	articulatory organs brought so close together that friction of air stream occurs	[f] [v] [θ] [ð] [s] [z] [ʃ] [ʒ] [h]
affricate[73]	plosive with friction during release stage	[tʃ] [dʒ]
lateral	partial closure so that air stream can escape on one or both sides of obstruction	[l]
approximant	contraction of tongue; air stream can escape without friction	[r] [w] [j]
nasal	air stream released through nose; articulatory organs form obstruction	[n] [m] [ŋ]

---

[73]   Gimson ([4]1989: 177–179) also identifies two post-alveolar affricates [tr] and [dr].

▷ the amount of **energy** involved, resulting in a distinction between **fortis** (high energy) and **lenis** (little energy).

▷ the fact whether there is **aspiration**, a short air stream following the articulation, which is the case with the [pʰ] in English *pit* but not with [p] in English *top*, for instance.

Vowels are generally described in terms of

▷ the **place of the highest point of the tongue** in the mouth during the articulation of the vowel. It can be located according to the horizontal and the vertical dimension: depending on whether the front, the central part or the back of the tongue takes the highest position, a distinction is made between **front, central** and **back vowels** whereas the degree of closeness of the highest point of the tongue towards the palate results in a distinction between **close, close-mid** (half-close), **open-mid** (half-open) and **open vowels**.

▷ the **degree of lip rounding**, where a distinction between **rounded, neutral** and **spread** is made.

▷ **length** (in terms of **long** and **short vowels**).

Furthermore, a distinction can be made between monophthongs, (i.e. relatively pure vowels such as [æ]), diphthongs and triphthongs (which involve a glide from one position to another such as [ɪə] and [aɪə]).[74]

The place of the highest point of the tongue is often indicated in the so-called vowel diagram in terms of a front-back dimension and a close-open dimension, which can be seen as an abstraction from the shape of the mouth.[75] In order to arrive at a precise description of vowel quality, reference can be made to the so-called cardinal vowels, which was outlined in detail by the famous British phonetician Daniel Jones.[76] Jones (1918/⁹1960) postulated eight primary cardinal vowels, which represent the extreme points of the possible position of the tongue and which can be located in the vowel diagram in the following way:

---

[74]   Cf. Gimson and Cruttenden (⁶2001: 129) and Gut (2009: 60).

[75]   Compare also the *English Pronouncing Dictionary* (EPD17 2006: viii) and Herbst, Stoll, and Westermayr (1991: 47).

[76]   For the history of the idea of a cardinal vowel system and references to A. M. Bell, A. J. Ellis and H. Sweet see Kohler (1977). For primary and secondary cardinal vowels see Jones (1918/⁹1960: 35–36).

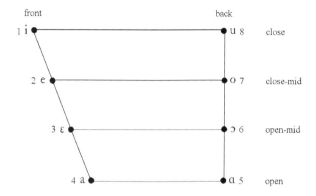

It is important to realize that the eight cardinal vowels have to be thought of as idealized realizations of particular vowel qualities and not as sounds actually occurring in any particular language. The English vowels /ɪ/ (as in *bid*) and /æ/ (as in *bad*) can be represented in this diagram in the following way:

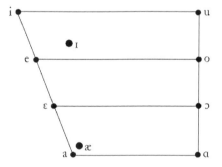

The purpose of the system of cardinal vowels is to serve as a reference grid for the exact description of vowels in real languages and to make it easier to compare vowels of different languages. So the difference between the English short [ɪ] in a word such as *bitter* and the German short [ɪ] in a word such as *bitte* can be expressed by saying that the German [ɪ] comes much closer to the position of cardinal 1 than the English one.

A phonetic description of phones of English could then take the following form:

ð	voiced	lenis	dental	fricative		oral	egressive	pulmonic
æ	voiced		front	open/open-mid		oral	egressive	pulmonic
n	voiced	lenis	alveolar	nasal		nasal	egressive	pulmonic
g	voiced	lenis	velar	plosive		oral	egressive	pulmonic
tʰ	voiceless	fortis	alveolar	plosive	aspirated	oral	egressive	pulmonic
t	voiceless	fortis	alveolar	plosive		oral	egressive	pulmonic

4.5   Syllables

Syllables are units above the individual sound segments since they can consist of one or more phones. The structure of the syllable can be described by distinguishing between onset, peak, and coda (Gimson and Cruttenden ⁶2001: 51, Crystal ²2003: 246), where the peak is the central and usually most sonorous element of the syllable, whereas onset and coda are marginal:

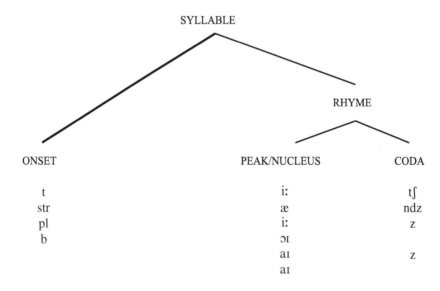

In terms of the distinction between vowels and consonants as made in 4.3, the peak of a syllable consists of a vowel, whereas the marginal elements consist of one or more consonants. The approximants [j, w, r], which phonetically are like vowels, behave like consonants in this respect. In words such as *little* or *button*, so-called syllabic [ḷ] and syllabic [ṇ] can function as the peak of the syllable.[77]

Syllables ending in a vowel (*buoy, sea*), are called **open syllables**, syllables containing a coda, i.e. ending in a consonant *(boys, girl)* are called **closed syllables**.

4.6   Suprasegmental elements

Apart from the sound segments identified in 4.4 there are a number of phonetic properties that extend to more than one segment, so-called **suprasegmental elements**.

One such element that is associated with the unit of the syllable and not with an individual sound segment is **stress**. Thus the syllable *house* is stressed in a word such as *housekeeper* but unstressed in *lighthouse*. Stress is usually associated with more energy in the pronunciation of a syllable. From the point of view of perception stressed syllables are generally described as having more **prominence**, which arises from such factors as loudness, length, pitch and vowel quality.[78]

In phonetic transcription, accented (or stressed) syllables are indicated by the symbol ' for primary stress and ˌ for secondary stress within a word:

>   *lighthouse* [ˈlaɪthaʊs]

>   *lighthousekeeper* [ˈlaɪthaʊsˌkiːpə]

Another such element is **pitch change**, where Gimson ([4]1989: 272–274) distinguishes between a falling tone, a rising tone, a falling-rising tone and a rising reinforcement of a fall.[79]

Variations of pitch and the direction of pitch within an utterance result in its **intonation**. A sentence such as

(1)$_{SP}$ *The English have no respect for their language*

---

[77]   See Gimson and Cruttenden ([6]2001: 52) and Arnold and Hansen (1992: 165–166) for a more detailed discussion.

[78]   See Roach ([4]2009: 73–74). Compare also Gimson ([4]1989: 224) and Gimson and Cruttenden ([6]2001: 272–274), where the term stress is avoided altogether.

[79]   Other linguists make different kinds of distinctions, cf. Esser (1979), Halliday (1970a) or Cruttenden (1986). Gut (2009: 118) distinguishes the following tones: fall, rise, fall-rise, rise-fall, rise-fall-rise and level.

can be pronounced with a falling or a rising intonation, for example, the former is likely to be interpreted as a statement, the latter as a question or an exclamation. Stress and pitch change can signal the prominence of a word in a sentence as in

(1a)   *The **Eng**lish have no respect for their language*

or

(1b)   *The English have no respect for their **lang**uage*

or mark a primary word **accent**.[80]

As far as **rhythm** is concerned, English, like German and unlike French or Italian, is often said to belong to the so-called **stress-timed** languages, which means that in connected speech intervals between stressed syllables tend to be of the same length, i.e. the stressed syllables are isochronous. Thus the interval of time between the stressed syllables in

(2)$_{QE}$ *'Which is the 'train for 'Crewe 'please*

is said to be roughly the same, even if the accented syllable is followed by two unaccented syllables in the case of *which*, by one in the case of *train* and by none in the case of *Crewe*. This results in a different kind of rhythmic patterning from that of **syllable-timed** languages, which require roughly the same amount of time for each syllable.[81]

---

[80]   Cf. Gimson ([4]1989: 225 and 269).

[81]   See Abercrombie (1967: 97–98) for a detailed discussion of this example. It has often been stated, though, as Cruttenden (1986: 25) points out, on a relatively poor empirical basis, that English shows **isochrony**, which is described by Gimson ([4]1989: 263–264) as follows: "It is noticeable that the rhythmic beats of an utterance occur at fairly equal intervals of time. As a result of this, the speed at which the unstressed syllables are uttered – and the length of each – will depend upon the number occurring between the strong beats." Compare also the account given in Gimson and Cruttenden ([6]2001: 251), where the lack of instrumental verification is stressed: "the occurrence of full vowels generally predicts the rhythm of English rather more usefully than any notion of stress ...".

5 Phonology

5.1 The function of speech sounds

5.1.1 Phonemes and allophones

Phonetics deals with a description of phones, i.e. with formal properties of speech sounds. A next step in the analysis of a language can be to further analyse and classify the phones identified, particularly with respect to their function within the language. Here, it must be emphasized that speech sounds as such do not have meaning. If one accepts the de Saussurean view of the linguistic sign as a combination of form and meaning, then the function of speech sounds can be described as combining with other speech sounds to make up such forms, which can be distinguished from other forms with different meanings. In those terms, the function of speech sounds is to distinguish between meanings. For instance, the phones [tʰ], [iː] and [tʃ] enter into the combination of [tʰiːtʃ], which contrasts with other linguistic forms such as the following:

[tʰiːtʃ] (*teach*) – [riːtʃ] (*reach*) – [liːtʃ] (*leach, leech*) – [pʰiːtʃ] (*peach*)

[tʰiːtʃ] (*teach*) – [tʰʌtʃ] (*touch*) – [tʰɔːtʃ] (*torch*)

[tʰiːtʃ] (*teach*) – [tʰiːk] (*teak*) – [tʰiːl] (*teal*) – [tʰiːm] (*team*) – [tʰiːn] (*teen*) – [tʰiːθ] (*teeth*)

Minimal pairs such as *teach – reach* can be taken to show that each of the three sounds in [tʰiːtʃ] is relevant to the identity of the form [tʰiːtʃ]. Thus it can be argued that one function of sounds is to contrast linguistic forms with different meanings. However, not all speech sounds in a language contrast in this way. Thus, replacing [tʰ] by [t] does not result in a form with a new meaning, not only in the case of [tʰiːtʃ] but nowhere in English. [tiːtʃ] could be considered an unusual or impeded pronunciation of *teach*, but not as a form representing a different meaning from [tʰiːtʃ].

Observations of this kind have led to the distinction between **phonemes** and **allophones**:

▷ A **phoneme** is an abstract linguistic unit at the level of sound that serves to distinguish between linguistic forms with different meanings.

▷ An **allophone** is one of several phonetic realizations of a phoneme in the form of a speech sound.

[tʰ] and [t] are thus two allophones of the phoneme /t/. These two allophones are in **complementary distribution** in that each of them can only occur in a position in which the other cannot occur. Thus, whenever the allophones of a phoneme are in complementary distribution,[82] it is predictable which allophone will realize that phoneme. For the English plosives /p/, /t/, /k/ the following distributional rule can be stated:[83]

Aspirated and non-aspirated allophones of the English phonemes /p/ /t/ /k/:		
[pʰ] [tʰ] [kʰ]	initial position in accented syllables (strong aspiration)	[pʰiːtʃ] [tʰiːtʃ] [kʰiː]
[p] [t] [k]	in all other positions (no or weak aspiration)	[spiːk] [rɪˈspekt]

According to these principles, the two speech sounds [l] (clear l) and [ɫ] (dark l), to be found in English pronunciations of *language* and *will*, for instance, can be subsumed under a single phoneme /l/. This is because [l] and [ɫ] can never serve to contrast forms with different meanings in English (although this may well be possible in other languages). Again, [l] and [ɫ] are in complementary distribution:

Distribution of allophones clear l and dark l in English:		
[l]	before vowels and /j/	[ˈlæŋgwɪdʒ] [ˈɪŋglɪʃ]
[ɫ]	before consonants at the ends of words	[bʌɫk] [wɪɫ]

---

[82] Cf. Gimson (⁴1989: 49): "No two realizations of a phoneme (its *allophones*) are the same. This is true even when the same word is repeated ... When the same speaker produces slightly different pronunciations of the word *cat*, the different realizations of the phonemes are said to be 'free variants'."

[83] For a much more detailed account of the allophones of the English plosives see Gimson (⁴1989: 152–155).

A common principle to establish the phoneme inventory of a language is the one used above, namely to find so-called **minimal pairs**, i.e. linguistic forms with different meanings which are phonetically identical with the exception of one sound such as [tʰiːtʃ] (*teach*) – [riːtʃ] (*reach*).

5.1.2   Phonetics and phonology

The difference between phonetics and phonology is basically that phonetics describes the properties of speech sounds as they occur in language, whereas phonology is concerned with the kinds of contrasts at the level of sound that can be seen as creating differences of meaning in a particular language. Phonetics thus deals with the formal or physical analysis of concrete entities, the phones, whereas phonology deals with phonemes, which have to be regarded as abstract units of linguistic analysis.[84]

5.2   The description of phonemes

5.2.1   Consonant phonemes

Phonemes are generally described with reference to the articulatory features of their phonetic realization. Since the phoneme is an abstract unit and since the idea behind the phoneme concept is one of functional contrast, it is unnecessary and inappropriate to draw upon the whole inventory of features used for the description of the sounds of a language. In phonology, only those features are used that are necessary to distinguish all the phonemes of a language from one another; features that all sounds of a language share (such as 'pulmonic' or 'egressive' in the case of English) can be ignored as can features that are not shared by all allophones of a phoneme (like aspiration in the case of the English plosives).

It is possible to establish the contrast between the consonant phonemes of English (BBC English/Received Pronunciation and General American)[85] in terms of three sets of **distinctive features**:

---

[84]   There are many different definitions of the term phoneme. Note that the famous British phonetician Daniel Jones (1944/1973: 169, 178) believed "phonemes to be undefinable" and described the phoneme as "a family of sounds in a given language ...".

[85]   Cf. EPD17 (2006: x), Gimson and Cruttenden (⁶2001: 148) and Giegerich (1992: 41). Giegerich and Gimson and Cruttenden also identify a bilabial

	Manner of articulation	**Place of articulation**	**voiceless – voiced**

/p/ /b/	plosive	bilabial	voiceless – voiced
/t/ /d/	plosive	alveolar	voiceless – voiced
/k/ /g/	plosive	velar	voiceless – voiced

/tʃ/ /dʒ/	affricate	palato-alveolar	voiceless – voiced

/f/ /v/	fricative	labio-dental	voiceless – voiced
/θ/ /ð/	fricative	dental	voiceless – voiced
/s/ /z/	fricative	alveolar	voiceless – voiced
/ʃ/ /ʒ/	fricative	palato-alveolar	voiceless – voiced
/h/	fricative	glottal	

/m/	nasal	bilabial	
/n/	nasal	alveolar	
/ŋ/	nasal	velar	

/l/	lateral (approximant)	alveolar	
/r/	approximant	post-alveolar	
/j/	approximant	palatal	
/w/	approximant	velar	

It is important to realize that, since phonemes are abstractions made in the process of linguistic analysis, the establishment of a phoneme system is dependent on a number of decisions of a relatively arbitrary nature.

---

fricative /ʍ/, which, however, does not occur in all varieties; similarly a velar fricative /x/ is listed by Giegerich and EPD17. In Gimson and Cruttenden ([6]2001) /l/ is listed as an approximant.

One such decision concerns the phoneme status of /θ/ and /ð/, which might also be treated as allophones of one phoneme since in present-day English minimal pairs are notoriously difficult to find: *thigh – thy* is unsatisfactory since *thy* is restricted in its use to archaic church language, which leaves a few minimal pairs such as *loath – loathe, mouth* (noun) *– mouth* (verb) and *wreath – wreathe.* One argument in favour of a phoneme treatment may be seen in the fact that it would not be possible to establish rules of complementary distribution for [θ] and [ð] as allophones, another is that the phonemic contrast between voiced and voiceless members can be found for all other English fricatives, which in a way makes it aesthetically tempting to postulate such a contrast in the case of [θ] and [ð], too.[86] A similar problem concerning minimal pairs is presented by /h/ and /ŋ/, which are in complementary distribution, /h/ only occurring in syllable-initial position, /ŋ/ never occurring in syllable-initial position. Here, however, lack of phonetic similarity is regarded as an argument against treating the two as allophones of the same phoneme.

A third case of possible controversy is presented by the affricates, which could also be analysed as a sequence of a plosive and a fricative. One reason mentioned by Gimson ([4]1989: 174) for treating /tʃ/ and /dʒ/ as one phoneme is that "the native speaker does not regard /tʃ, dʒ/ as composite sounds".

A problem of a slightly different kind concerns the choice of the distinctive features that characterize particular phonemes. So it is possible to use the 'voiceless' – 'voiced' contrast to establish the distinction between phonemes such as /t/ and /d/, but it is equally possible to express the opposition in terms of 'fortis' and 'lenis' since in Received Pronunciation voiceless consonants tend to be fortis and voiced ones to be lenis.[87] Which of the two types of opposition is chosen to be a distinctive feature in the phonological description is up to a point a matter of personal preference; to use both would make the description redundant, however.

5.2.2   Vowel phonemes

As with consonants, not all phonetic features of English vowel sounds have the status of distinctive features of the corresponding vowel phonemes.

---

[86]   There is a tendency for /θ/ to occur in nouns or adjectives (*thing, thick*) and for /ð/ to occur in function words such as *the* or *they.*

[87]   This is a generalization of some kind, as will be pointed out later.

Since there is no phonemic contrast between egressive and ingressive vowel articulation in English, egressiveness is not relevant to a phonological description of English. The same is true of lip rounding.

As far as vowel quality and vowel quantity are concerned, the decision as to which of these ought to be treated as a distinctive feature in phonological terms is not quite as straightforward. In some accents of English such as Received Pronunciation differences in vowel length and differences in vowel quality coincide. Thus (in identical contexts) the i- and u-vowels whose quality comes relatively close to that of the cardinal vowels 1 and 8, for instance, are longer than those which are more centered. Phonologically, this means that the difference between the vowels of *bead* and *bid* or of *pool* and *pull* can be expressed by either treating quantity or quality as a distinctive feature, which is similar to the fortis/voiceless and lenis/voiced problem outlined above. In the first case one can express the difference by a length mark, in the second by different symbols representing the quality of the sounds:

	beat	*bit*	*pool*	*pull*
phonetic realization	[biːt]	[bɪt]	[puːɫ]	[pʊɫ]
phonological representation based on quantity (used in EPD13)	/biːt/	/bit/	/puːl/	/pul/
phonological representation based on quality (used e.g. by Giegerich 1992: 45, Brown 1977: 33 or Gut 2009: 63)	/bit/	/bɪt/	/pul/	/pʊl/

While both systems are used in discussions of English phonology, many standard reference books and pronunciation dictionaries represent RP vowels in a redundant notation indicating both differences in quality and quantity.

phonological representation based on quality and quantity (used e.g. by Gimson/Cruttenden [6]2001: 91 or EPD17)	/biːt/	/bɪt/	/puːl/	/pʊl/

Thus the vowel phonemes of RP can be represented as follows (Roach, Hartman, and Setter EPD17, 2006: viii–ix):

Monophthongs:

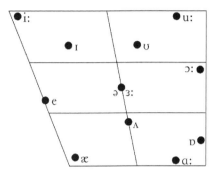

Diphthongs:

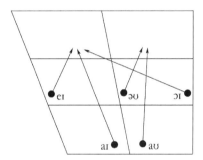
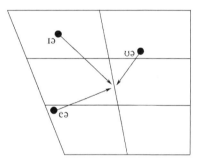

It has to be said that the number of vowel phonemes identified and the symbols used for different varieties of English vary to a certain extent.[88] The list below shows the twenty vowel phonemes identified by Roach, Hartman, and Setter (EPD17) and Gimson and Cruttenden ([6]2001: 91–93) for British English (BBC English or Received Pronunciation). For compari-

---

[88]   See, for example, Brown (1977: 33) or Giegerich (1992: 48–75). Some linguists include triphthongs such as /aɪə/ (*fire*) or /aʊə/ (*power*) for RP, see Trudgill and Hannah ([5]2008: 16) and Gut (2009: 63).

son, the symbols used for American English in EPD17 are given on the right.[89]

	RP/BBC English		**US American**
/ɪ/	*bit, bid*	/ɪ/	*bit, bid*
/e/	*bet, bed*	/e/	*bet, bed*
/æ/	*bat, bad*	/æ/	*bat, bad*
/ʌ/	*hut, putt*	/ʌ/	*hut, putt*
/ɒ/	*hot, golf*		
/ʊ/	*foot, put*	/ʊ/	*foot, put*
/ə/	*to̱mato, a̱bout*	/ə/	*to̱mato, a̱bout*
/iː/	*sea, see*	/iː/	*sea, see*
/ɑː/	*park, father*	/ɑː/	*father, golf, hot*
/ɔː/	*caught, north*	/ɔː/	*north, port*
/uː/	*cool, queue*	/uː/	*cool, queue*
/ɜː/	*bird, first*		
/eɪ/	*bay, may*	/eɪ/	*bay, may*
/aɪ/	*buy, light*	/aɪ/	*buy, light*
/ɔɪ/	*buoy, employ*	/ɔɪ/	*buoy, employ*
/aʊ/	*now, house*	/aʊ/	*now, house*

---

[89] For similar overviews see Trudgill and Hannah ([5]2008: 16 and 42) or Gut (2009: 63). Compare also the *Longman Pronunciation Dictionary* (LPD [3]2008: xvi) and the descriptions provided by Wells (1982: 118–127) or Giegerich (1992: 43–61). For the use of length marks for American English see Roach, Hartman and Setter (EPD17: ix). Compare also Wells (1982: 120), who uses length marks for RP but not for General American. See also Giegerich (1992: 72–73), who does not make use of length marks in phoneme symbols but whose phonetic description of a phonemic vowel symbol such as /ɪ/ includes the statement: "In GA and RP it is also of shorter duration than /i/ in comparable contexts."

/əʊ/	*blow, boat*		
		/oʊ/	*boat*
/ɪə/	*near*		
/eə/	*where*		
/ʊə/	*moor*		
		ɚ	"r-coloured schwa" as in *mother* (EPD17)
		ɜ˞	"r-coloured bird vowel" as in *bird* (EPD17)

5.2.3   Phonemic principle of pronunciation dictionaries

Pronunciation dictionaries such as the *Cambridge English Pronouncing Dictionary* (EPD [17]2006) or the *Longman Pronunciation Dictionary* (LPD [3]2009) generally follow the principles of a phonemic description. EPD17 (viii, xiv) mentions two exceptions to this principle – namely the use of [t̬] to show the voicing and flapping of /t/ in words such as *getting* in American English. The second exception concerns the use of the symbol [i] e.g. for the final vowel in *busy* on the grounds that in certain positions the phonological distinction between /iː/ and /ɪ/ is neutralized.[90]

   city 'sɪti   *seedy* 'siːdi   *holidaymaker* 'hɒlədiˌmeɪkə

One consequence of the generally phonemic character of the transcriptions provided by pronunciation dictionaries is that users must always be aware that the symbols used represent abstractions whose phonetic realization depends on the variety referred to. Thus both LPD and EPD provide transcriptions for the place name *Newcastle (upon Tyne)* for three different varieties of English:

---

[90]   Note, however, that Wells (LPD [3]2008: xxv) includes /i/ and /u/ under the weak vowel phonemes, whereas Roach, Hartman and Setter (EPD17: xiv) point out that /i/ "is not, strictly speaking, a phoneme symbol". Wells (LPD [3]2008: 539) points out that there are two environments in which /ɪ/ and /iː/ cannot be distinguished so that the opposition between these phonemes is "neutralized": with vowels in weak syllables at the end of a word (*happy*) or with vowels in weak syllables before another vowel (*radiation*).

British English:	'nju:ˌkɑːsᵊl
American English:	'nuːˌkæsᵊl
Northern English English:	njuː'kæsᵊl

This must not be taken to mean that the American and the local pronunciation of the vowel transcribed as /æ/ were very similar. In fact, in Northern English, it tends to be pronounced as [a], whereas the American vowel is noticeably closer – the symbol /æ/ indicates that both in American English and Northern English English *castle* has the same vowel phoneme as *bat*.

5.3   Phonotactics

There are certain restrictions on the types of combinations of phonemes that are possible in a particular language. The branch of phonology that studies the distributional and combinatorial properties of phonemes is known as **phonotactics**.

It is interesting to see, for instance, that the short vowels /e/, /æ/, /ʌ/ and /ɒ/ do not occur in word final position or that only a limited number of combinations of two consonants in word initial position are possible in English (Gimson, [4]1989: 243):[91]

/p/	+	/l/	/r/	/j/	
/t/	+		/r/	/j/	/w/
/k/	+	/l/	/r/	/j/	/w/
/b/	+	/l/	/r/	/j/	
/d/	+		/r/	/j/	/w/
/g/	+	/l/	/r/	/j/	/w/
/m/	+			/j/	
/n/	+			/j/	
/l/	+			/j/	
/f/	+	/l/	/r/	/j/	
/v/	+			/j/	
/θ/	+		/r/	/j/	/w/

---

[91]   Note that such lists of phonotactic possibilities of a language clearly depend on what one considers to be a word of that language. Cruttenden, in his sixth edition of Gimson's book ([6]2001: 240-241), adds combinations such as /vl/ or /ʃw/ on the basis of such words as *Vladivostok* and *Schweppes*, which quite clearly present borderline cases.

/s/	+	/l/		/j/	/w/	/p/	/t/	/k/	/m/	/n/	/f/
/ʃ/	+		/r/								
/h/	+			/j/							

The options for word initial clusters consisting of three consonants are even more restricted (Gimson [4]1989: 245). Interestingly enough, the first conso-nant in such a combination must always be an /s/ and it can only be fol-lowed by a fortis plosive /p/, /t/ or /k/:

/s/	+	/p/	+	/l/	/r/	/j/	
/s/	+	/t/	+		/r/	/j/	
/s/	+	/k/	+	/l/	/r/	/j/	/w/

What makes phonotactic rules of this kind interesting beyond their purely descriptive value is that one may safely assume that knowledge of such regularities may well help speakers – and especially listeners – recognize word boundaries and thus be instrumental in word recognition processes.

6   Phonetic "reality"

6.1   Problems of the phoneme concept

6.1.1   The problem

Phonetics (> Chapter 4) is concerned with the description of speech sounds
(phones), whereas phonology (> Chapter 5) investigates the function of so-
called phonemes in terms of establishing meaning distinctions in a language. The concept of the phoneme is a useful one for certain purposes of
linguistic analysis. For instance, it helps to describe certain regularities in
the area of morphology (such as phonological conditioning of allomorphs;
see 8.3.4).

It would be tempting to imagine that word recognition takes the following form:
– hearers perceive a series of sounds [a], [b], [c] etc.
– relate these to a series of corresponding phonemes /A/, /B/, /C/ etc.
– and then arrive at a meaningful unit (a morpheme or word) consisting of
  a representation of this string of phonemes and a representation of some
  meaning.
However, it seems things are more complicated than that because
– the way a phoneme is realized phonetically may depend on its position
  in the word (> 5.1.1),
– phonemes are influenced in their phonetic realization by sounds following or preceding them (> 6.2),
– one and the same phone may represent several phonemes (> 6.1),
– not all varieties of a language would necessarily be analysed as having
  identical phoneme inventories (> 19.3) even if speakers of these varieties can understand each other without any problems,
– speakers' anatomical properties influence the quality of sounds they
  produce.

It is thus an open question to what extent the notion of the phoneme is relevant to speech perception.[92]

6.1.2   Phonetic value of phonological features

The concept of the phoneme involves a good deal of abstraction from phonetic reality. This can be illustrated by looking at pairs such as /p – b/ or /t – d/ in English. At the phonemic level, the contrast between these phonemes is often described in terms of the distinctive features 'voiceless' and 'voiced'. This is misleading in so far as not every phone that realizes the 'voiced' phoneme /b/, for example, needs to be phonetically 'voiced'; in fact, RP /b d g/ seem to have full voicing only when they occur between voiced sounds (Gimson and Cruttenden [6]2001: 152).

In fact, in words such as *peat* or *bead* (i.e. when occurring in word-initial position followed by a stressed vowel) the difference between plosives such as /p/ and /b/ can best be described in terms of voice onset time, i.e. the time that passes between the release of the closure of the plosive and the voicing of the following sound. Word-initial /p/ and /b/ need not involve any voicing at all. Rather, /p/ tends to be aspirated, which means that there is a longer voice onset time than with /b/.[93] Brown (1977: 28) describes this as follows:[94]

peat	_____	,,,,,,,,,,,,,,,,,,,,,,,,,,,,? _____
	p i̩ i ? t	
bead	_____,, _____	
	b i d	

_____ closure

,,,,,,,,,,,,, voicing

---

[92] For a more detailed account of speech perception (and factors such as voice onset time) and word recognition see Gut (2009: 195–200) and Wimmer and Perner (1979: 106–119).

[93] See Catford (1988: 190–192) for details. Compare also Gimson and Cruttenden ([6]2001: 152–153).

[94] Cf. Brown (1977: 28): "Initially, the 'voiced' stops are realized by a period of voiceless closure (i.e. no vibration of the vocal cords) with, as the closure is released, immediate onset of voicing in the following segment. The difference between initial 'voiceless' and 'voiced' stops lies, then, in the timing of onset of voicing immediately following the release of the closure. The behaviour of the vocal cords during the period of closure itself is no different."

Thus the difference in the realization of the consonant phonemes /p/ (with the phonological feature 'voiceless') and /b/ (with the feature 'voiced') is created by aspiration and voice onset time, but not by any voicing of [b].

In word final position, 'voiced' phonemes such as /b d g/ can actually be realized by a partially voiced or completely voiceless lenis phone [b̥ d̥ g̊] (Gimson and Cruttenden [6]2001: 152). The problem caused by this for phonological description could perhaps be avoided by referring to the 'fortis'/'lenis'-distinction (> 4.4) instead of to the 'voiced'/'voiceless'-distinction in the description of these phonemes. What is much more important, however, is the fact that the contrast between final /p t k/ and final /b d g/ manifests itself in the length of the preceding vowel. Thus the main phonetic difference between *bat* /bæt/ and *bad* /bæd/ is not to be found in the articulation of the final consonant but in the length of the preceding vowel; the vowel in *bad* being considerably longer than that in *bat*.[95]

	bat	bad
phonological contrast	/t/	/d/
(main) phonetic contrast	[æ]	[æː]

This is not only interesting with respect to linguistic theory but also with respect to foreign language teaching. If the length contrast in the vowel is more important for perception than the voicing of the consonant, then it is important to focus on the vowel rather than the consonant in teaching. In any case, it is essential to realize that a phonological feature of one phoneme can be realized phonetically in the articulation of another phoneme.

How complicated the interaction of phonological and phonetic features can be is shown by the fact that so-called long-vowel phonemes can be shorter in articulation before 'voiceless' plosive phonemes than so-called 'short'-vowel phonemes before 'voiced' plosive phonemes.[96]

---

[95]   Cf. also Gimson and Cruttenden ([6]2001: 158): "The voiceless series /p,t,k/ will, of course, be distinguished in final positions from the voiced series /b,d,g/ either by the reduction of length of the sounds preceding /p,t,k/ or by the presence of some voicing in /b,d,g/, or by a combination of both factors. The non-release of final plosives is a feature of colloquial RP." For glottal reinforcement of final /p,t,k/ see Gimson and Cruttenden ([6]2001: 159).

[96]   Compare Brown (1977: 29): "A much more important point to dwell upon, since this is not usually stressed in manuals of English pronunciation and it is

/biːd/ [biːˑd] (*bead*) > /bɪd/ [bɪːd] (*bid*) > /biːt/ [biˑt] (*beat*) > /bɪt/ [bɪt] (*bit*)

This can be confirmed by measurements of the duration of vowels (Wiik 1965: 114):[97]

/iː/ + voiced fricative	36 csec.
/ɪ/ + voiced fricative	18.6 csec.
/iː/ + voiceless fricative	13 csec.
/ɪ/ + voiceless fricative	8.3 csec.

This means that the opposition between long and short vowel phonemes can only be interpreted phonetically as holding within the same context, but not in absolute terms. In fact, "/iː/ is typically shorter in a word such as *seat* (12.3 csec.) than /ɪ/ in a word such as *hid* (14.7 csec.)" (Gimson and Cruttenden [6]2001: 96).

What is important about these observations is the insight that the contrast between two phonemes need not necessarily be expressed in the segment that is generally regarded as the phone realizing that particular phoneme. A particularly interesting case in point is that of the pronunciation of words such as *write* – *ride* and *writer* – *rider* in U.S. English (discussed at length by Lass 1984: 30–31):[98]

– In *write* and *ride* the contrast between /d/ and /t/ is also reflected in a difference in the length of the diphthong:

phonemic	/raɪt/	/raɪd/
phonetic	[raɪt]	[rɑˑɪd]

– In intervocalic position, both phonemes /t/ and /d/ are realized by the alveolar tap [ɾ] and not by [t] or [d].

---

consequently often unknown to foreign teachers of English, is the way the word *final* distinction between 'voiceless' and 'voiced' stops is made. The main distinction is between a relatively short vowel, with 'tight' voicing and glottal stop preceding a 'voiceless' stop, and a relatively long vowel with 'full' voicing preceding a 'voiced' stop. ... The main distinction between 'voiceless' and 'voiced' stops in word final position lies in the realization of the preceding vowel – not in the articulation of the stop itself or of its release."

[97] See also Gimson and Cruttenden ([6]2001: 95–96 and 152–153).

[98] Compare Lass's (1984: 30) discussion of violations of the linearity condition, namely that "phonemic and phonetic differences must match up one-to-one in linear strings".

– The contrast between *writer* and *rider* is then expressed not by the consonant segments /t/ or /d/ but by the preceding vowel:

| phonemic | /raɪtər/ | /raɪdər/ |
| phonetic | [raɪɾər] | [rɑˑɪɾər] |

Lass (1984: 31) comes to the following conclusion regarding the role of [aɪ] and [ɑˑɪ] on the one hand and [t] and [d] on the other:

> ... two normally non-contrastive phones carry meaning difference, while two (supposedly) contrastive phones fail to contrast. There are, as it happens, perfectly respectable ways of dealing with this – but not in the framework of classical phonemics. They necessitate a fairly extensive revision of the conceptual framework, and lead to a more complex picture of what natural-language phonologies are probably like.

6.1.3 The bi-uniqueness requirement

A further element of complexity arises through the fact that there is not always one-to-one correspondence between phones and phonemes. The fact that a phoneme can be realized by different allophones is central to the theory and does not present any problems for decoding as long as each phone can be attributed to one phoneme only (which can be referred to as **bi-uniqueness**).[99] There are cases, however, where one phone is used to realize different phonemes: thus in many varieties of English the fortis plosives /p t k/ can be realized by a glottal stop [ʔ] in word-final position, as in the following examples:

/sæp/ [sæp] or [sæʔ]

/sæt/ [sæt] or [sæʔ]

/sæk/ [sæk] or [sæʔ]

It is clear that [ʔ] cannot be regarded as an allophone of just one of these phonemes. Lass (1984: 28) arrives at the following conclusion:

---

[99] Compare the description of the bi-uniqueness requirement given by Lass (1984: 27): "The idea is that the listener's 'decoding' of the speech signal is a segmentation-and-classification routine: and this is not feasible unless a given phone in a given (phonological) environment is always an allophone of one particular phoneme."

The biuniqueness solution is thus counter-intuitive and messy. The obvious solution is to permit extensive **overlapping**, giving a realization pattern like: ...

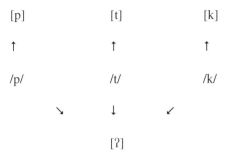

Such considerations make it clear that the concept of the phoneme is by no means uncontroversial. One can only agree with the conclusions drawn by Lass (1984: 29):

> Such situations display theoretical 'weak points': here speaker intuition vs. theoretical constraints lead to conflict. Theories have hidden consequences, which emerge only through confrontation with data; and these consequences may force us into revision or rethinking.

While this is not the place to go into alternative approaches to phonology such as the feature theory developed by Roman Jakobson or generative phonology,[100] the purpose of these few examples was to illustrate that the traditional concept of the phoneme is hardly able to cope with all problems of analysis and that perhaps much more sophisticated concepts are needed. Lass (1984: 164) argues that languages "may have different systems for different word-positions, different accentual conditions, even different morpho-syntactic or lexical categories", which is a theoretical view of language which he refers to as "at least potentially **polysystemic**, not **monosystemic** as in most classical phonological analysis."[101] In any case, the

---

[100]   Compare Jakobson, Fant, and Halle (1951) and Chomsky and Halle (1968). For features see also Lass (1984).

[101]   For psycholinguistic aspects of this problem see Garman (1990: 186–188): "Speech processing cannot be carried out initially on a phoneme-by-phoneme basis, since the rate of their arrival at the ear ... would exceed the resolving capacity of the auditory system. So there can be no question of simple 'phoneme-detectors' in speech perception. The implication is that what are detected must be much smaller than phonemes: acoustic cues, which can be processed within the time constraints, and which provide sufficient informa-

limited explanatory power of the phoneme concept should not only be borne in mind in the context of further theoretical research but especially also when it comes to questions of contrasting different languages and of teaching pronunciation.

6.2 Pronunciation in connected speech

6.2.1 Weakening of elements

The descriptive apparatus provided by phonetics and phonology can be used to describe the phonological (or phonetic) form particular lexical units have (which is what pronunciation dictionaries do, for example). It is clear, however, that using words in connected speech, especially in fast informal spoken language, means that these phonological forms can be subject to considerable modifications.

A first type of modification that can be observed is that sounds can be influenced in their quality by neighbouring sounds. This process is called **assimilation**.[102] Different degrees and directions of assimilation can be distinguished: according to whether a sound takes over some or all of the features of a neighbouring sound, there can be **partial** or **total assimilation**. Depending on whether the sound that gets modified precedes or follows the sound it assimilates to, there is **regressive** or **progressive assimilation**, and if two sounds influence each other that is a case of **reciprocal assimilation**.

dɪˈsaɪsɪfˈfæktə	v → f	decisive factor	regressive – total
ˈkɒməmwelθ	n → m	Commonwealth	regressive – partial
tʃɪkŋ	ɪn → ŋ	chicken	progressive – partial
ˈdəʊntˈmɪʃʃəˈtreɪn	sj → ʃʃ	don't miss your train	reciprocal – total

A second type of modification occurring in rapid speech is **elision**, which means that sounds get omitted altogether.

---

tion for subsequent identification of phonemes." Cf. Wimmer and Perner (1979: 111) who point out that a /d/ in syllable initial position cannot be identified if it is not followed by a vowel.

[102]   For a detailed description of the processes of assimilation and elision see Brown (1977).

Furthermore, sounds can be weakened in their articulation so that /g/ is realized by a weak [ɣ] in [sʌmˈtaɪməɣəʊ] (*some time ago*), /k/ by a weak [x] in [ˈlʊxðeː] (*look there*) or /b/ by a weak [β] in [wɪvβɪn] (*we've been*).[103] Brown (1977: 74–75) points out that this type of weakening is rather common, especially with /k/ and /t/ as long as they are not initial in an accented syllable. It is important to note that this kind of weakening may not only be reflected in the actual acoustic quality of a phone, but also in a weakening of the visual clues that accompany its articulation[104] – something which, incidentally, considerably facilitates the dubbing of foreign films.

All this shows that the actual form of a spoken utterance may differ from its phonological representation in a quite substantial way.[105] What kind of implications this has for the plausibility of the phoneme concept and for the process of understanding speech remains to be discussed.

6.2.2   Linking phenomena

The reduction of articulatory features is not the only way which characterizes the pronunciation of words in connected speech. Rather, a kind of opposite phenomenon can be observed too, namely the insertion of sounds. In English, there is a strong tendency to introduce a linking element between a word final and a word initial vowel. This can be a vowel glide in the form of a semi-vowel or the articulation of an [r]-sound:

>   to Exeter [tʊʷeksɪtə]

As far as the latter type of linking phenomenon is concerned, a terminological distinction is made between a **linking [r]**, i.e. the articulation of an [r] which is represented in the spelling of the word but not realized in other positions in those accents of English which are non-rhotic like RP, and an

---

[103]   Most of the examples in this chapter are taken from Brown (1977: 58 and 74), some from Gimson and Cruttenden (⁶2001). Note also the remark on the difficulties of transcribing weakened consonants appropriately.

[104]   See Brown (1977: 79–80) for detailed descriptions.

[105]   For the psycholinguistic implications of these facts see Garman (1990: 189): "there is an important source of potential processing difficulty, if we believe that speech processing proceeds on a segment-by-segment, syllable-by-syllable basis."

intrusive [r], which refers to the insertion of an [r] in cases where no letter <r> is present in the spelling.

more and more ['mɔːrənd'mɔː](linking [r])

idea of it [aɪ'dɪərəvɪt](intrusive [r])

6.2.3 Weak forms

Finally, one phenomenon ought to be mentioned in the context of connected speech that is very typical of the English language, namely the fact that with a number of highly frequent function words (articles, auxiliary verbs, conjunctions, prepositions, pronouns) a distinction can be made between so-called **strong forms** and **weak forms**. The weak forms are usually shorter than the strong forms and show reduction of vowel length, often reduction of the vowel to /ə/ or elision of vowels or consonants.[106]

(1)_{ZD}   *'And* [ənd] *when I'm* [m] *famous you can* [kən] *sell it and* [ən] *make your fortune.'* (weak forms)
              'So I can ['kæn].' (strong form)

(2)_{ZD}   *'We're* [ə] *living up at* [ət] *Higher Tregerthen, near Eagle's Nest. Do* [dʊ] *you know it?'* (weak forms)
              'She [ʃɪ] (weak form) *does* ['dʌz].' (strong form)

The difference between these weak forms and the weakening phenomena described in 6.2.1 is that the use of weak forms is not optional in the way that assimilation is. Assimilation and elision are processes that may or may not happen in the articulation of a particular sound sequence by a particular speaker. Weak forms, however, are always used in unstressed syllables; in fact, one might describe the occurrence of strong and weak forms by saying that it is the use of the strong form that is marked and signals particular prominence as in situations of contrast, for example.

It has often been argued that the use of weak forms is linked with the stress patterns of English and that it contributes to the tendency towards isochrony that has sometimes been claimed for English.

---

[106]   For an extensive list and a description of weak forms in English cf. Gimson (⁴1989: 265–269).

7   Contrastive aspects of phonetics and phonology

7.1   Levels of contrast

A contrastive analysis of two languages at the levels of phonetics and phonology will be concerned with similarities and differences with respect to the following aspects:[107]

- segmental phoneme and phone inventories of the two languages
- distributional properties of segmental phonemes and phones in the two languages
- suprasegmental properties of both languages.

7.2   Phoneme and phone inventories of English and German

Comparing the phoneme system(s) of English as described in 5.2 and the phoneme system of German as outlined in *Duden Aussprachewörterbuch* (⁴2000: 35 and 43) one will find that while English and German share a considerable number of, in fact, most phonemes, there are a few that occur in only one of the two languages:

consonants	only English	only German		English and German
plosives				/p//b/ /t//d/ /k//g/
fricatives	/θ/ /ð/[108]	/ç/ /x/	*ich, doch*	/f//v/ /s//z/ /ʃ//ʒ//h/
affricates		/pf/ /ts/[109]	*Pferd, Zaun*	/tʃ/ /dʒ/
nasals				/m/ /n/ /ŋ/

---

[107]   For more detailed accounts of the sound systems of English and German see Burgschmidt and Götz (1974: 196–213) and König and Gast (2007: 8–55)

[108]   For /θ/ and /ð/ in German see *Duden Aussprachewörterbuch* (⁴2000: 43).

[109]   The *Duden Aussprachewörterbuch* (⁴2000: 43) points out that the affricates are treated as two separate phonemes in other accounts of German phonology.

lateral		/l/
approxi-mant[110]		/r/
semi-vowels	/w/	/j/[111]

While in the case of consonants and semi-vowels correspondences between English and German can be established relatively easily, this is not so straightforward in the case of vowels.[112] Thus it is more appropriate to simply contrast the complete vowel systems of RP (> 5.2.2) and German *Duden Aussprachewörterbuch* ([4]2000: 35):

Monophthongs	**English (RP)**		**German**	
oral	/iː/	*bee*	/iː/	*Biene*
	/ɪ/	*middle*	/ɪ/	*Mitte*
			/eː/	*Beeren*
			/ɛː/	*Bären*
	/e/	*bed*	/ɛ/	*Bett*
	/æ/	*bank*	/a/	*Bank*
	/ɑː/	*park*	/aː/	*Tag*
	/ʌ/	*hut*		
	/ɒ/	*lot*	/ɔ/	*Tochter*

---

[110]   For /r/ in German see *Duden Aussprachewörterbuch* ([4]2000: 52–55).

[111]   /j/ is not treated as a semi-vowel in the *Duden Aussprachewörterbuch* ([4]2000: 43) but listed as a fricative; Kohler (1977: 116) calls it a semi-vowel, however.

[112]   On the one hand, one could contrast the number of phonological oppositions in the different vowel systems: Trudgill and Hannah ([5]2008: 23 and 42) identify 23 vowel phonemes for RP (including the triphthongs /aɪə/ and /aʊə/ and 15 for US English whereas the *Duden Aussprachewörterbuch* ([4]2000: 35) lists 23 vowel phonemes for German. This includes nasalized vowels such as /ɑ̃ː/ or /ɛ̃ː/ occurring in words such as *Gourmand* or *Pointe*, which play a marginal role in German. Thus one might argue that a purely numerical comparison is not particularly revealing. On the other hand, the quality of the vowel phonemes in English and German in some cases differs considerably so that it is difficult to decide whether English /ɜː/ in *heard* should be treated as in any way corresponding to German /øː/ in *hören*.

	/ɔː/	*Cornwall*	/oː/	*Sohn*
	/ʊ/	*foot*	/ʊ/	*kurz*
	/uː/	*food*	/uː/	*pusten*
	/ə/	<u>a</u>*bout*	/ə/	*all<u>e</u>*
	/ɜː/	*heard*	/øː/	*hören*
			/œ/	*Hörnum*
			/yː/	*Juist*
			/y/	*Sylt*
nasalized			/ɛ̃ː/	*P<u>oin</u>te*
			/ɑ̃ː/	*Gourm<u>an</u>d*
			/œ̃ː/	*Parf<u>um</u>*
			/õː/	*Garç<u>on</u>*
Diphthongs	/aɪ/	*ride*	/ai/	*reiten*
	/aʊ/	*house*	/au/	*Haus*
	/ɔɪ/	*employ*	/ɔy/	*t<u>äu</u>schen*
	/eə/	*there*		
	/eɪ/	*train*		
	/ʊə/	*poor*		
	/əʊ/	*low*		
	/ɪə/	*here*		

Apart from the fact that one should bear in mind that different analyses of the phoneme systems of the same language may well vary as to the number of phonemes they identify – depending, for instance, on whether particular cases are analysed as affricates, diphthongs or triphthongs or as sequences of phonemes – it must be clear that the phonological transcriptions chosen by different analysts may suggest a higher degree of similarity or difference than is actually justified. Thus the use of the symbol /æ/ for the vowel in *bank* suggests a greater difference in vowel quality to German /a/ in *Bank* than is perhaps appropriate with respect to recent developments in British

English.[113] On the other hand, the use of identical symbols in the case of such vowels as /iː/ or /ɪ/ should not be taken to signal that the actual sounds are identical; in fact, the English vowels tend to have a slightly more centralized and thus less extreme articulation. The same applies to the consonants transcribed such as /ʃ/, whose phonetic realization in English involves less lip rounding and less energy than in German.[114] In other cases, phonetic differences are already made clear in the kinds of symbols chosen for the respective phonemes, as in the case of /ɜː/ in *heard* (with no lip rounding) and /øː/ in *hören* (with strong lip rounding).

Thus inventory differences do not only concern number and character of phonological oppositions, but also the properties of the phones that realize the respective phonemes. There are, of course, significant differences in the phone inventories of two languages, which can also affect the allophones of a phoneme to be found in a particular language. Thus, for example, while both Standard German and RP have an /l/-phoneme, only RP contains the dark l allophone [ɫ].

7.3   Rule-governed differences

A further type of difference does not concern the phoneme or phone inventories of two languages, but rules which operate on the distribution of particular phonemes or phones. Thus, there are phonotactic differences of the kind that particular clusters do not occur: for example word-initial /kn/ (*knacken*) is possible in German, but not in English, whereas word-initial /sp/ (*speak*) or /st/ (*stand*) occur in English and not in German (with the exception of some Northern German dialects). Such differences can also be found with the distributional rules of the allophones of particular phonemes. Thus, whereas the English fortis plosives are realized by a non-aspirated (or weakly aspirated) allophone in word final position [hæt], German fortis plosives can have aspiration in that position [huːtʰ].[115]

---

[113]   Cf. EPD15 (1997: ix): "The quality of this vowel is now more open than it used to be, and the symbol /a/ might one day be considered preferable. We have retained the /æ/ symbol partly because it is phonetically appropriate for the corresponding American vowel."

[114]   Cf. Arnold and Hansen ([8]1992: 145).

[115]   Cf. Gimson ([4]1989: 154–155) and Kohler (1977: 160).

A very important distributional difference between English and German[116] can be found in the case of the phonemes /s/ and /z/:

	word initial		intervocalic		word final	
English	/s/	*seal*	/s/	*hissing*	/s/	*hiss*
	/z/	*zeal*	/z/	*rising*	/z/	*rise*
German			/s/	*reißen*	/s/	*Kuss*
	/z/	*sehen*	/z/	*reisen*		

Another type of a rule-governed difference between German and English is the phenomenon known as *Auslautverhärtung* in German, which results in the neutralisation of the phonological contrast between 'voiced' and 'voiceless' plosives at the ends of words in German. The phonotactic consequence of this rule is that /b/, /d/ and /g/ do not occur in word final position:

/taːk/	*Tag*	/taːgə/	*Tage*
/boːt/	*Boot*	/boːtə/	*Boote*

In contrast to that, RP shows a tendency towards "non-release of final plosives" (Gimson [4]1989: 157), which also means that the plosives cannot be distinguished by phonetic voicing. Even when this happens, there is still no neutralisation of the phonological opposition between /p t k/ and /b d g/ in English, since the opposition is then expressed by the length of the preceding vowel (> 6.1.2): /bæt/ [bæt] – /bæd/ [bæːd]. This is not the case in German, where *Rat* und *Rad* are homophones /raːt/ [raːtʰ].

7.4   Suprasegmental differences

At the suprasegmental level, one could investigate whether particular intonation contours are used to express the same meanings in both languages or not.[117] Since there is no generally accepted framework for the description of

---

[116]   This applies only to those accents of German that show an /s/-/z/ contrast. The phoneme inventories of many Southern accents of German do not possess /z/ at all.

[117]   Cf. Kohler (1977) and Esser (1979). For instance, in the case of *wh*-questions, Esser (1979: 91) distinguishes between objective *wh*-questions ("sachliche *wh*-Fragen") with a falling intonation and polite *wh*-questions

intonation (and the types of meaning expressed by different intonation patterns) this is a relatively complicated task.

In more general terms, an interesting difference between German and English at the suprasegmental level concerns the realization of pitch. In English, changes of pitch tend to be performed during the articulation of a stressed syllable, whereas in German they tend to happen between vowels, so that English can be characterized as making use of **pitch glides** whereas German typically shows **pitch jumps** (Cruttenden 1986: 54).

7.5   Pedagogical implications

A contrastive analysis may serve as a useful basis for pedagogical considerations in the teaching of pronunciation. Although it cannot necessarily serve to predict errors, it can be instrumental in explaining common errors. Thus, the common phenomenon that German native speakers substitute such phonemes as /θ/ or /w/ by /s/ or /v/ can quite easily be explained by the absence of these phonemes from the German phoneme system. Similarly, a mispronunciation of /kæt/ [kʰæt] as [kʰætʰ] can be traced back to the different distributional rules of the allophones of plosives in English and German, and the pronunciation of /bæd/ as [bæt] to the application of the German rule of *Auslautverhärtung* to English.

A question that is particularly important in this context is to what extent the distinction between the phonological and the phonetic levels of analysis is relevant to the teaching or learning of pronunciation. Initially, there is some logic behind the argument that phonological errors may result in misunderstanding (such as when [bet] could represent /bet/, /bed/ or even /bæt/ or /bæd/) and that preventing such errors should be a prime aim in the teaching of pronunciation[118] and that allophonic errors (such as [betʰ] for /bet/ or [bɔːl] for [bɔːɫ]) are relatively unimportant in comparison. At second sight, this argument must be treated with some caution. Firstly, the number of contexts in which phonological errors would actually result in misunderstandings is probably relatively limited. Secondly, it is to be doubted that listeners perceive speech so systematically that they find a clear l instead of a dark l less disturbing than a voiceless consonant instead

---

("höfliche *wh*-Fragen") with a rising intonation. Echo questions are characterized by Esser as having rising intonation in English, too. Compare Kohler (1977: 127).

[118]   Cf. Arnold and Hansen (1992: 52).

of a voiced one. Thirdly, and most importantly, in the light of the reservations made in 6.1 it must be doubted whether the phoneme concept as such provides a suitable basis for pedagogical considerations. Since the length of the preceding vowel has been shown to be much more important to distinguish between word final plosives than the quality of voicing or nonvoicing in the plosives themselves, this ought to be reflected in the teaching of pronunciation. In a different way, the convention of using /æ/ as a symbol for the vowel in *bank* should not obscure the fact that in many British accents (amongst them more recent forms of RP or BBC English) the phonetic realization of this phoneme comes very close to that of German /a/.[119] Such facts underline the importance of a phonetic (rather than a phonological) basis in the teaching of pronunciation.

A sensible starting point for weighing the goals of teaching pronunciation seems to be a perceptual approach, which does not focus on the differences between language systems, but on those features of a foreign accent that native speakers might find disturbing. In this respect, pronouncing *bad* with a short vowel might be more irritating than the voicelessness of the final consonant. From a perceptual point of view, however, it is especially suprasegmental aspects of pronunciation that will have to be considered. This means that factors such as pitch glides, rhythm (which coincides with the appropriate use of weak forms) or linking phenomena will have to be attributed high importance. An experiment carried out by Dretzke (1985) showed, for example, that English native speakers find the use of glottal stops before word initial vowels (corresponding to a rule of German) extremely irritating.[120]

Recommended further reading:

- Gimson and Cruttenden (^{6}2001)
- Lass (1984)
- Gut (2009)
- Brown (1977)
- Burgschmidt und Götz (1974), König and Gast (2007)

---

[119]   For the question of /æ/ and /a/ see also EPD17: ix.

[120]   For a justification of a perception-oriented approach towards the teaching of pronunciation see Dretzke (1985) or Herbst (1992). For the importance of pronunciation in the teaching of a foreign language see also Herbst (1994).

Meaning-carrying units

8   Morphology

8.1   The concept of the morpheme

Chapter 8, 9 and 10 will be concerned with questions such as

— how words can be analysed into smaller meaningful units (morphology)

— how new words can be formed (word formation) and

— how meanings are expressed in multi-word units (phraseology).

The discussion of these questions will be based on the following text – a short passage taken from a catalogue of an exhibition of work by the painter Patrick Heron:[121]

(1) *When he began to work again, he seemed to have listened to those*   1
who had urged him to get 'back in touch with the earth'. Justifiably,   2
Heron had always been irritated by those literal-minded critics who   3
insisted in seeking references to the Cornish landscape (which he   4
loved, and fought tirelessly to protect) in the shapes and contours of   5
his paintings. Nonetheless, as he would admit in his more philosophi-   6
cal moments, the power of the landscape to 'transmit certain rhythms   7
straight up through the soles of my shoes every minute of the day' was   8
unquestionable, and he frequently drew on it for the language he used   9
to describe the familiar elements of his compositions – the harbour   10
shapes, the boulder-like discs, the coastlines of colour-shapes. Now,   11
for the first time in quarter of a century, he picked up pencil and pa-   12
per and drew from the landscape. ... Heron had decided, as he char-   13
acteristically put it, 'to bugger things up and try something crazy';   14
completing White, Pink and Scarlet : July 1983 (cat.18) he found he   15
could no longer bring himself to fill in its final unpainted shape and   16
scribbled across it with his brush. ...   17

---

[121]   Source: James Beechey: Patrick Heron. Paintings 1970–1984, 25 February – 20 March 2004, Waddington Galleries London.

> *'Looking at something – anything', Heron once declared, 'is more*   18
> *interesting than doing anything else, ever, as a matter of fact.'*   19

After identifying the units that can distinguish meaning in a language (the phonemes), the next step in a structuralist analysis is to identify the elements that carry meaning. These are not necessarily identical with words. Thus the last clause of (1) could be divided up into the following units carrying meaning:

look | ing | at | some | thing | any | thing | Heron | once | declare | d | is | more |

interest | ing | than | do | ing | any | thing | else | as | a | matter | of | fact

In analogy to the terminology employed in phonology, such units can be called **morphs**.[122] As in phonology, where phones that show a great deal of phonetic similarity and do not distinguish meaning are classified as allophones of one phoneme, a distinction can be made between **morphemes** and **allomorphs** in morphology:

▷ A **morpheme** is the smallest abstract linguistic unit that serves to carry meaning.[123]

▷ An **allomorph** is one of several possible phonological realizations of a morpheme.

For instance, in (1) *declared* was split up into two morphs, /dɪˈkleə/ and /d/ in the phonological representation. There are two further morphs in (1) carrying the same meaning as /d/, 'past tense', which are rather similar in form to /d/:

		'past tense'	
	/pɪkt/	/t/	*picked*
	/siːmd/	/d/	*declared, seemed, used, scribbled*
	/dɪˈsaɪdɪd/	/ɪd/	*decided, insisted*

---

[122]   Cf. Lyons (1968: 180–187).

[123]   Cf. the definition provided by Hockett (1958/2000: 394): *"Morphemes are the smallest individually meaningful elements in the utterances of a language."* Bloomfield (1933/1935: 161) defines the morpheme as "a linguistic form which bears no partial phonetic-semantic resemblance to any other form." See Anderson (1988: 151). Compare Lipka ([3]2002: 85) for a critical appraisal and interpretation of the term morpheme.

The phonological representations /t/, /d/ and /ɪd/ are thus called allomorphs of the past tense morpheme {D}.[124]

A further parallel between phonology and morphology is that the allomorphs of a morpheme can be in complementary distribution. In the case of /t/, /d/ and /ɪd/ the distributional rules can be stated as follows:

{D}	'past tense'	examples
/t/	after voiceless consonants except /t/	*worked, picked*
/d/	after vowels after voiced consonants except /d/	*allowed* *seemed, loved, used, scribbled*
/ɪd/	after /t, d/	*insisted, decided*

In very much the same way, /s/, /z/ and /ɪz/ can be established as allomorphs of a plural morpheme {S} in words such as *critics, paintings* and *references* (> 8.3.4).[125]

8.2 Types of morpheme

According to whether they can occur as words on their own or not, morphemes can be classified as **free morphemes** or **bound morphemes**. Thus, {when}, {he}, {work} or {again} are free morphemes, whereas {S} 'plural' or {D} 'past tense' are bound morphemes. A further, though less clear-cut, distinction that is sometimes made is that between **lexical morphemes**, which express lexical content which is not primarily of a grammatical nature, and **grammatical** or **functional morphemes**,[126] which

---

[124] Curly brackets are used for morphemes.

[125] /s/, /z/ and /ɪz/ also occur as allomorphs of a morpheme expressing third person singular with verbs (*goes*) and a morpheme expressing genitive singular with nouns (*University's*). For the rules of distribution of the allomorphs in these cases see Schmid (2005: 63).

[126] See Lipka (³2002: 86) for the distinction, who amongst other differences mentions as distinguishing criteria that lexical morphemes "denote (particular) extralinguistic objects & states of affairs: e.g. actions, events, situations, relations" and belong to an open class, whereas grammatical morphemes "denote (general) grammatical functions, e.g. plural, tense. Syntactic relations: e.g. concord of gender, number" and belong to a closed class. Compare also Kastovsky (1982: 71–72) and Hansen et al. (1985: 15). See also Croft

serve to form particular grammatical forms or express grammatical relations:[127]

listed	{list} (free, lexical)	{D} (bound, grammatical)
composition	{compose} (free, lexical)	{-ition} (bound, lexical)
boulder-like	{boulder} (bound, lexical)	{like} (free, lexical)

The distinction between grammatical and lexical morphemes is relevant with respect to two different types of morphological process: derivation and inflection. Derivation is one way of forming new words, whereas inflection distinguishes different grammatical forms of the same word. **Inflectional morphemes** (or inflectional suffixes) are thus bound grammatical morphemes, whereas **derivational morphemes** (or derivational affixes) are bound lexical morphemes.[128]

The morpheme or combination of morphemes to which a derivational or inflectional morpheme is attached is called the **base**. Thus in the case of *coastlines* (line 11), the base is formed by *coastline*, which consists of two free lexical morphemes, and *questionable*, which consists of the free lexical morpheme *question* and the derivational suffix *-able*, is the base of *unquestionable* (line 9).

While a base can consist of several morphemes, the term **root** is used for single morphemes that are not affixes such as *question* in *unquestionable* or *coast* and *line* in *coastlines*.[129] Most roots in English consist of free

---

(2000). Compare the list of criteria given by Plag, Braun, Lappe and Schramm (2007: 88) to distinguish between inflectional and derivational affixes.

[127] See Stein (2007) for a very useful account of English affixes.

[128] As a further type of bound lexical morpheme one can identify so-called bound roots (see below).

[129] See Plag (2003: 11) and Schmid (2005: 48–49). Note that these terms are notoriously difficult to define if one wants to avoid circularity of definitions. For the distinction between root, stem and base see e.g. Bauer (1983: 20–21): "A **root** is a form which is not further analysable, either in terms of derivational or inflectional morphology. It is that part of a word-form that remains when all inflectional and derivational affixes have been removed. ... A **stem** is of concern only when dealing with inflectional morphology. It may be – but need not be – complex ... it is that part of the word-form which remains when all inflectional affixes have been removed. ... A **base** is any form to which affixes of any kind can be added." These definitions depend on the definition of affixes as "bound morphs which do NOT realize unanalysable lexemes" (Bauer 1983: 18).

morphemes, but there is also a case to be made out for bound roots[130] such as *rasp-* in *raspberry* and possibly *Corn-* in *Cornish* (line 4).

8.3   Problems of a static morpheme concept

8.3.1   The problem

The framework of morphology as outlined so far proves perfectly suitable for the analysis of the examples discussed in the previous section. What makes the concept of the morpheme rather attractive is the idea that one can split up words into different segments with identifiable meanings. So a word such as *picked* can be analysed nicely as consisting of a free lexical morpheme {pick} and a bound grammatical morpheme {D} realized by the allomorph /t/. Other words in text (1) turn out to be much more problematic:[131] in particular, *began* (line 1), *fought* (line 5), *drew* (line 9), *found* (line 15) and also *put* (line 14) do not lend themselves to a straightforward formal analysis into {begin}, {fight} etc. plus an allomorph of {D}. Similarly, *those* (line 1) cannot easily be analysed as {that} + {S} etc. There are different ways of accounting for these phenomena, all of which, however, throw some doubt on the overall validity of the morpheme concept.[132]

8.3.2   Portmanteau morphs

One concept that has been suggested to account for the problem of forms such as *had, began* or *fought* is that of a so-called **portmanteau** morph, i.e. a morph that represents two different morphemes – {begin} and {past tense} in the case of *began*. Similarly, *teeth* or *those* could be analysed as morphs combining {tooth} or {that} with the plural morpheme.[133]

---

[130]   See Plag (2003: 10) for examples such as *circul-* (in *circulate* etc.) or *hap-* (in *hapless*).

[131]   For a critical discussion of the morpheme see Anderson (1988: 153–154).

[132]   For a discussion of various problems of the traditional morpheme concept see Palmer (1971: 110–124). A very important contribution to this discussion can be seen in Hockett's (1954) distinction between *item and arrangement* and *item and process*. For this see Matthews (1974: 225–227), Anderson (1988: 157–162) or Vennemann and Jakobs (1982/2000: 409–411).

[133]   For critical remarks on this concept introduced by Hockett see Palmer (1971: 116).

An alternative approach would be to treat the relationship between *begin* and *began* or *fight* and *fought* in terms of a vowel change. Strictly speaking, this is not in line with the definition of morphemes and allomorphs given above because accounting for such relations in terms of processes "seriously weakens the idea that the morpheme is a minimal sign" (Plag 2003: 23).[134]

A similar problem is presented by forms such as *was* (line 8) or *went*, which bear no formal resemblance to forms of the "same" verbs such as *be, am, are* and *go* or *gone* respectively. Schmid (2005: 43) accounts for such cases in terms of **suppletion**.

8.3.3   Zero-morphs

The case of *put* is even more intriguing since there are good reasons for saying that *put* in line 14 expresses the meaning of 'past tense' although this is not explicitly marked (apart from the absence of third person singular {S}). The fact that some verbs in English such as *put* or *cut* have identical present tense and past tense forms (with the exception of the third person singular) or some nouns identical singular and plural forms such as *sheep* has given rise to the idea of introducing the concept of **zero-morph** or **zero-morpheme**. The argument justifying such an analysis is the obvious analogy between examples of the following kind:

present tense	past tense	singular	plural
{look}	{look} + {D}	{dog}	{dog} + {S}
{put}	{put} + {Ø}	{sheep}	{sheep} + {Ø}

Palmer (1971: 115) points out that there is a conflict between the concept of a zero-element and the definition of the morpheme given by Bloomfield:[135]

---

[134]   Cf. Palmer's (1971: 116) critique of such approaches: "… it is immediately obvious that these are very strange allomorphs; an instruction to replace one item by another can hardly be regarded as in any sense consisting of phonemes." See also Matthews (1974: 122): "A process of replacement is no more a 'morph' than zero is a 'morph'". Compare the discussion of this problem by Matthews (1974: 118–122).

[135]   Cf. Palmer (1971: 111 and 115): "It was thought reasonable that morphemes could have zero allomorphs, though with the condition that not all the allomorphs can be zero. This is an important condition since otherwise we could

The notion of the zero allomorph in *sheep* and also in *hit* (past tense) is a very useful one, but once again we are moving away from Bloomfield's conception. A zero element cannot really be said to have 'no partial phonetic-semantic resemblance to any other form'.

Similar arguments against the concept of a zero-morph have been put forward by Matthews (1974: 117–118):

> The PLURAL morpheme of *men* and the PAST PARTICIPLE of *come* can no longer be defined as 'classes of allomorphs in complementary distribution' – the reason being, quite simply, that one cannot examine one's data and determine the 'distribution' of 'zero'. One cannot say that in some forms 'nothing' is 'there' but in others it is not 'there', that the 'presence' of 'nothing' in one form 'contrasts' with the 'absence' of 'nothing' in another, and so on. ...
>
> But let us turn to a more modern conception of the morpheme. Syntactically, the *sailed* of *I have sailed* is SAIL + PAST PARTICIPLE; we are therefore justified in saying that the *come* of *I have come* is syntactically COME + PAST PARTICIPLE. Our problem is merely to specify the word-form, *come*, by which COME + PAST PARTICIPLE is represented or realised. Can we not therefore say, taking it morpheme by morpheme, that come is represented by its normal alternant *come* and PAST PARTICIPLE, quite simply, has no representation or realisation at all? This is surely quite coherent; there is all the difference in the world between saying that a grammatical element 'has zero realisation' and saying that a word-form 'contains a zero allomorph'.

8.3.4 Morphological and phonological conditioning

The discussion in the previous sections has shown that a category such as 'past tense' is expressed in different ways in English. The same is true of the category 'plural' with nouns:

- plurals can be formed by adding inflectional suffixes (*critic – critics, reference – references* but also *ox – oxen*),

---

say that CAT has a zero allomorph in the singular. (In itself, this suggestion is not altogether ridiculous: we might say it has zero in the singular and *s* in the plural; but we have then established a morpheme (zero) where there is no linguistic form anywhere in the language since English never has a formal mark in the singular.)" Looking at words such as *formula, analysis* or *curriculum*, even this statement might be subject to discussion.

- in the case of *tooth – teeth, foot – feet* the plural forms are distinguished from the singular forms by a vowel change and can thus be analysed as portmanteaux,
- *children* involves a vowel change and a suffix,[136]
- in *sheep – sheep* singular and plural are not distinguished by morphological means (or, if you prefer, by Ø) etc.

If we want to describe when these different forms occur, we are faced with the problem that generalizable rules for the distribution of these forms can only be given for the allomorphs /s/, /z/ and /ɪz/ – or in the case of the past tense /t/, /d/ and /ɪd/. The occurrence of these allomorphs is seen as being **phonologically conditioned** because the occurrence of a particular allomorph depends on the preceding phoneme:

{S}	'plural'	
/s/	after voiceless consonants except /s, ʃ, tʃ/	*critics, shapes, moments, elements, discs*
/z/	after vowels after voiced consonants except /z, ʒ, dʒ/	*contours, shoes* *paintings, rhythms, soles, compositions, coastlines*
/ɪz/	after /s, z, ʃ, ʒ, tʃ, dʒ/	*references*

However, whether a noun takes an {S}-plural at all (or whether, correspondingly, a verbs takes a {D}-past tense) is not dependent on the phonological environment, but must be seen as a property of the individual word, hence this is a matter of **lexical conditioning**. The term **morphological conditioning** is sometimes also used in this sense, sometimes it is restricted to cases where a particular derivational morpheme requires the presence of a particular allomorph as in:

compose /kəmˈpəʊz/   /kəmpəs/ + /ɪʃᵊn/ *composition*

declare /dɪˈkleəʳ/   /deklər/ + /eɪʃᵊn/ *declaration*

refer /rɪˈfɜː/   /ˈrefəʳ/ + /ᵊnts/ *reference*

---

[136]   For the notion of "empty morph" in words such as *children* see Palmer (1971: 115).

8.4 Inflectional morphology: historical background

Although it is not relevant to a strictly synchronic analysis of present-day English, it is interesting to see that quite a number of the aspects of present-day English inflectional morphology that cause problems for a synchronic analysis have their causes in earlier stages of the language and subsequent historical developments.[137]

For instance, in the description of Old English verb morphology a distinction can be made between different classes of so-called **weak verbs**, which form the past tense by a {D}-suffix and **strong verbs**, which show a regular vowel change in their paradigm known as **ablaut**. According to different types of **gradation series**, seven classes of strong verbs can be distinguished, for example:[138]

	present tense	preterite 1/3 sg	preterite pl and 2 sg	past participle	
I	rīsan	rās	rison	-risen	*rise*
II	scēōtan	scēāt	scuton	-scoten	*shoot*
III	sincan	sanc	suncon	-suncen	*sink*
IV	cuman	cōm	cōmon	-cumen	*come*
V	sprecan	spræc	sprǣcon	-sprecen	*speak*
VI	standan	stōd	stōdon	-standen	*stand*
VII	lǣtan	lēt	lēton	-lǣten	*let*

Without wanting to go into the details of the historical development here, it is easy to see that some of the vowel changes to be observed in present-day English verbs (*rise – rose – risen, sink – sank – sunk* etc.) can be related to the gradation series of different classes of strong verbs in Old English. Oth-

---

[137] For example, the morphological irregularity of plural forms such as *feet, teeth* or *mice* historically goes back to i-mutation (> 20.2.3.1), which leads to a vowel change in the dative singular and nominative and accusative plural forms in Old English (*fōt – fēt*).

[138] The following examples are taken from Quirk and Wrenn ([2]1957). The various classes show considerable variation, which is not indicated here. Class VII verbs showed reduplication in Germanic; cf. Hogg (1992: 156).

ers (such as *meet – met – met*), however, are caused by certain phonological developments (> 20.2).

Since quite a number of Old English strong verbs have become weak or regular and since a number of weak verbs have become irregular, the system has become even more obscured. Thus, there is little justification for talking about strong or weak verbs in present-day English.

8.5   Further problems of morphological analysis

The weaknesses of the morpheme concept outlined above concerned mainly inflectional morphology. However, trying to split up words into morphemes can cause a number of problems, too, particularly concerning the question of into how many morphemes a particular word should be analysed. Thus it is probably relatively uncontroversial to analyse *degree, colour* or *whole* as representing a single morpheme each, *boredom* as being made up of two, {bore} and {-dom} and *unfilled* as consisting of the three morphemes {un-}, {fill} and {D}. Even *applications* and *molecular* are relatively unproblematic if one postulates two allomorphs to account for the pronunciation differences between *apply* /ə'plaɪ/ and *application* /əplɪ/ and *molecule* /'mɒlɪkjuːl/ and *molecular* /mə'lekjʊlə/ respectively. In the same way it is possible to relate *competitive* /kəm'petɪtɪv/ to *compete* /kəm'piːt/.

Much more problematical is a synchronic analysis of words such as *suppose, ensure* or *require*, where it seems debatable whether an analysis in terms of one or two morphemes is preferable. On the one hand, one might argue that these elements are able to form series of a certain type, as in:

sup-	*suppose, support, suppress*
-pose	*expose, impose, propose*
en-	*ensure, enforce, enfranchise, engage*
-sure	*ensure, insure, assure*
re-	*require, resist, retain*
-quire	*require, acquire, enquire, inquire*

On the other hand, one might doubt whether these elements carry any identifiable meaning in English, which would be the same for all the words in a series. Furthermore, one might ask to what extent native speakers of English would consider such words as being made up of two morphemes.[139] The problem posed by such words can be accounted for by considering the historical background. In fact, all of these words are not of Germanic but of Romance origin. While these forms were morphologically transparent in Latin (e.g. *expōnere, impōnere, prōpōnere*), this transparency has become obscured in English. In the light of de Saussure's postulate that synchronic and diachronic analyses should be kept apart, such historical considerations cannot contribute to solving the analytical problem at the synchronic level. Since one would probably want to argue that native speakers of English probably are not aware of the historical origins of these words (at least not when they first encounter them in the process of language acquisition),[140] it makes sense to look for a purely synchronic solution anyway. In this particular case, however, it is probably fair to say that arguments can be found for either analysis.[141] Coates (1987: 113), discussing the analysis of words such as *dissociate* and *associate*,[142] comes to a very similar conclusion:

---

[139] One could consider analysing elements such as *-quire* in terms of bound root morphemes. A related case is presented by so-called neo-classical compounds such as *democracy, microscope* or *photograph*, which Schmid (2005: 42) analyses in terms of "combining forms" (*demo-* + *-cracy*).

[140] To what extent native speakers of English would consider such words related probably also depends on the degree of their own language awareness and to the extent to which they have been exposed to a classical education.

[141] See also Marchand ([2]1969: 5) or Lipka ([3]2002: 97).

[142] Coates (1987: 113) discusses the term formatives for recurrent patterns without a clear semantic status in this context: "On the grounds that *dis-* is relevantly and independently meaningful (cf. *trust* vs *distrust*), we could analyse DISSOCIATE as DIS-SOCIATE, and by virtue of that analysis treat – SOCIATE as a lexical element or formative recurring in ASSOCIATE and therefore AS- as a formative too. Here we have to be most careful of the criteria we use in our analysis. It is all too easy to let historical justifications support us; something similar to the above analysis is good for the Latin ancestors of the words in question, which is no sort of an argument about English. We must not be bemused by patterns, for there is prima-facie evidence that many real English speakers have not analysed the given forms in the way shown. The form /dɪsəˈsəʊsɪeɪt/ is now frequently heard, demonstrating that whilst the DIS-/AS-alternation may be perceivable it is not necessarily perceived. ASSOCIATE is clearly used as an unanalysed whole in this non-standard (but spreading) form. ..."

What, then, would be the status of … AS- in a definitive analysis of English? Is there indeed to be a boundary between it and –SOCIATE? Answer: for some, perhaps; therefore no definitive answer is possible for a *language* as opposed to a *speaker*.

A related problem is presented by words such as *blackberry, cranberry* or *raspberry*. While *blackberry* can obviously (or perhaps not quite so obviously since it is arguable whether *black* in *blackberry* means 'black') be analysed as being made up of {black} and {berry}, a corresponding analysis of *cranberry* or *raspberry* into two morphemes is problematical since *cran-* or *rasp-* only occur in the words *cranberry* or *raspberry*. On the other hand, an analysis of these words as consisting of one morpheme would obscure the fact that they contain the morpheme {berry}, which for both formal and semantic reasons would appear highly inappropriate. Such elements as *cran-* or *rasp-*, which occur only once in the language, are thus often treated as a special class of morphemes, called **unique morphemes**, **blocked morphemes**[143] or also **cranberry morphemes**.

Even if the introduction of the category of unique morphemes may be seen as solving that particular problem one can probably argue, at least from a sceptic's point of view, that quite a few analytical problems remain, especially when one believes that all occurrences of a particular morpheme should express (at least roughly) the same meaning. Whereas in the case of *blackberry* and *blackbird*, the analysis in terms of a morpheme {black} seems plausible enough, a *blackberry* is not just a 'black berry' and a *blackbird* not a 'black bird'. Similarly, a word such as *soap opera*, which at first sight easily lends itself to an analysis into two morphemes, turns out to be rather problematical when one considers the meanings of the constituents. Although such phenomena can be accounted for within a theory of word formation (> 9), they also throw light on the slightly problematical nature of the notion of morpheme.[144]

---

[143]   See, for example, Kastovsky (1982: 70) or Lipka (³2002: 87).

[144]   Compare the gradient established for typical and less typical members of the category morpheme (prototypical morpheme – bound root – combining form etc.) established by Schmid (2005: 41).

9 Word formation

9.1 Words

9.1.1 Words and lexemes

It is one of the ironical facts about language that in everyday discussions of language the term "word" plays a central role. In fact one can safely assume that it is one of the few terms an average speaker of a language will know with respect to talking about language. People ask what a particular word means, how a word is spelt, possibly whether an expression is spelt as one or two words, how many words a text contains, how a word translates into another language etc. Even in more professional contexts of looking at language one will frequently refer to words: the parts of speech are often referred to as word classes (> 11.4), dictionaries claim to contain so and so many words, and didacticians outline how many words a learner of a foreign language should know at a particular stage of learning. The irony is that linguists are slightly wary about the term and would be very hesitant to use it without explaining what they mean by it beforehand.[145]

The problem can be illustrated by a short passage taken from David Lodge's novel *Thinks*:[146]

(1) [...] *I had three hours of crucifying boredom at the Senate working*   1
     party on interfaculty modular compatibility, meaning we're supposed   2
     to come up with a formula to ensure that a course in say the School of   3
     Community Studies requires as much work and deserves the same   4
     weight as a course in say Electrical Engineering, so that the Univer-   5
     sity can put its new degree in Interdisciplinary Studies on the market .   6
     . . our Pick'n'Mix degree as the Registrar likes to refer to it, which is   7
     supposed to give us a competitive edge in the annual applications   8
     bazaar and save the University's fortunes . . . Market research has   9
     apparently established that there is an unfilled niche for a degree   10

---

[145]   For a discussion of the term "word" see e.g. Matthews (1974: 20–26) or Mair (1997: 22).

[146]   Source: David Lodge: *Thinks* (2001; Penguin edition 2002: 180–181): Harmondsworth: Penguin.

course that would allow the student to combine courses across the   11
whole university curriculum, nuclear physics with soap opera analy-   12
sis, molecular biology with medieval mystery plays . . . I daresay it   13
looks quite enticing on paper, especially the glossy, colour-illustrated   14
paper of the University's brochure, but some of these subjects are   15
harder than others and most of them can't be studied properly in   16
isolation, but I didn't make myself any friends this afternoon by point-   17
ing this out.   18

The question how many words this text contains is by no means easy to answer. While my computer program counts 198 words, I count 191.[147] With some justification, one could also arrive at a figure of 177 (or even 174), if one takes *working party, come up, Community Studies, Electrical Engineering, market research, degree course, soap opera, pointing out* as representing one word rather than two (or three in cases such as *Senate working party* or *come up with*). Furthermore, if one interprets the question in a way so that it does not refer to word **tokens**, but to **types**, this reduces the figure to something like 135: then there are 12 occurrences of *the*, 6 occurrences of *to*, 5 occurrences each of *of, in* and *a* etc. But even there, it is impossible to arrive at a precise figure: is *an* to be regarded as a different word from *a* or not? If so, what about *the* in line 1 [ðə] and *the* in line 9 [ði]? Whether *this* in *this afternoon* (line 17) is the same word as the *this* in line 18 may depend on whether one recognizes a separate word class determiner or not; it may also be seen independently from that question if you argue that a word can belong to different word classes. More importantly, however, should *University* and *University's* be considered instances of the same word? And what about *we* and *us*? Or *our*? There are probably good reasons supporting any decision regarding these questions depending on the purposes of the analysis. What this otherwise relatively insignificant word count shows, however, is that a number of terms are needed for the entities that in everyday language can be referred to as words, otherwise there is bound to be considerable confusion. For the purposes of linguistic analysis, it seems necessary to restrict the readings of the term word. Much of the discussion has centered around the definition of the word as a 'minimum free form' by the American structuralist Leonard Bloomfield (1933/1935:

---

[147]   Microsoft Word counts … as one word and ... as three words; *we're* as one word.

178), which, however, is not totally sufficient.[148] Thus, Cruse (1986: 35–36) mentions two characteristics of the word.[149]

> The first is that a word is typically the smallest element of a sentence which has positional mobility – that is the smallest that can be moved around without destroying the grammaticality of the sentence (ignoring any semantic effects).

John saw Bill.
Bill saw John.
Bill, John saw.

> By no means all words are equally mobile in this sense, but with very few exceptions, the smallest mobile units are words. ...
>   The second major characteristic is that they are typically the largest units which resist 'interruption' by the insertion of new material between their constituent parts.

Thus, in a sentence such as (2), no insertions are possible within the units separated by empty spaces, whereas insertions in those spaces seem perfectly feasible:

(2) *Some   of   these   subjects   are   harder   than   others*

                ↑   ↑   ↑

          academic   *much*   *many*

This is the reading of the term "word" in which text (1) above has 191 words. However, when it comes to talking about "different words" it seems sensible to introduce terminology to be able to express the "sameness" and the "differentness" of the words *establish, establishes, establishing, established* or *university, university's* and *universities*. This can be done by saying that *university, university's* and *universities* are different **word forms**, which can be seen as representations of the same **lexeme.** Matthews (1974: 22) describes the lexeme as a "fundamental unit (compare other terms in '-eme' such as 'phoneme' or 'morpheme') of the lexicon of the language". Thus the lexeme is an abstract unit of the language. The concept is an extremely important one since it is clear that, for instance, when one looks up a "word" such as *university* in a dictionary, one is neither interested at all in the particular token of the word printed in the dictionary (in the this-text-consists-of-191-words sense) nor just in the particular word form *university*

---

[148]   See, for instance, Palmer (1971: 50).
[149]   See also Burgschmidt (1978: 27).

but in the lexeme with all its formal and semantic properties (spelling, pronunciation, meaning etc.). Furthermore, the term lexeme is of great use in that it enables one to treat expressions such as *come up with* that consist of several words, but have one sense, as so-called multi-word lexemes. (> 10.4).

A less established, but equally useful distinction is that between lexemes and **lexical units**, which refers to the semantic or content side of the lexeme and bears witness to the fact that most words (or lexemes) have more than one meaning or sense. Cruse (1986: 80) thus describes the lexeme in the following way: "a lexeme is a family of lexical units; a lexical unit is the union of a single sense with a lexical form; a lexical form is an abstraction from a set of word forms (or alternatively – it is a family of word forms) which differ only in respect of inflections". A lexeme, then, can be seen as an abstract unit representing one or more word forms and one or more lexical units.

9.1.2　　New words

One of the obvious functions of the lexemes of a language is to enable the speakers of a language to express certain concepts or ideas. Since the world is changing constantly, both in terms of real objects and of ideas, languages must be made to accommodate new concepts. This can be done, as Leech ([2]1981: 30) points out, by "lexical innovation, which may take the form of NEOLOGISM (the invention of new words, or more precisely lexical items …) or TRANSFER OF MEANING (the derivation of new senses of established words)". Both principles can be explained referring to the previous paragraph, in which the technical terms *lexeme* and *lexicon* were used. The former is an example of a neologism, a word which was coined, in this case on the basis of existing language material, to express a certain concept, whereas in the case of *lexicon*, a word that has existed in the English language since the seventeenth century, has been used with a new sense specific to linguistics. This kind of process can also be related to the influence of another language. This is what happens, for instance, when German words take over meanings of English words which are similar in form: *kontrollieren* came to be used to mean 'have power over' alongside 'check' or, more recently, *meinen* is increasingly being used in the sense of words meaning something rather than someone having a certain opinion. It is obvious that the advantage of both types of lexical innovation is to express concepts in a more condensed and less circumspect way. Leech (^{2}1981: 31) argues "that combined with this abbreviatory function, the *word* as a lexical element has a concept-defining role", which he illustrates with examples such as *defenestration* or the use of new adjective compounds such as *ready-to-eat* in advertising.[150]

There are several possibilities speakers have for the creation of new words. They can

– use lexical material of their own language and combine or modify it in some way,

– take over words from another language (which may be integrated and modified to various degrees),

– invent new words without making use of the first two techniques.

The invention of words in this latter sense seems to be a relatively rare phenomenon, in English at least, but it does happen: the brand name *Kodak* and the technical term *quark* are relatively well-known examples. Lexical borrowing (*checken, talken* and *fighten* are recent examples from German) is a common language contact phenomenon and as such is studied widely in the context of historical linguistics (> 20.3), while the combination or modification of lexical material of the same language as in *soap opera, heliport, smog* or *temp* is studied under the headings of morphology and word formation.[151]

It is, of course, difficult to get precise figures as to which of these methods is employed how often. An estimation carried out by Bauer (1994: 35) suggests that between 1880 and 1982 75% of the new words in English are based on English, 1.6% are of unknown origin and the rest have other languages as their source (4.3% Latin, 4.0% French, 3.0% Greek, 2.5% German etc.).[152]

---

[150] Accepting Halliday's (1970b: 141) view that "the nature of language is closely related to the demands that we make on it", the fact that languages are constantly subject to lexical innovation might be taken as argument in support of Leech's claim. See also Schmid (2008).

[151] The two latter phenomena are interrelated, however, in that the influence of a donor language may result in new word material being taken over in the receptor language or in the formation of new words (or transfer of meaning) in the receptor language under the influence of the donor language. Cf. Kastovsky (1992: 299–300).

[152] Bauer (1994: 34) states a "decrease in the number of loans during the twentieth century". Compare also the figures given by Ayto (1996: 184).

9.2   Word formation

9.2.1   Introduction

Word formation (or, more precisely, lexeme formation[153]) is concerned with one of the most creative aspects of language. The field of word formation can be seen as part of morphology in the wider sense – thus, as pointed out above, excluding the inflectional properties of a word. It was defined by Marchand ([2]1969: 2) in his influential book *Categories and Types of English Word-Formation* as "that branch of the science of language which studies the patterns on which a language forms new lexical units, i.e. words."

In a more speaker-oriented view of language, it would probably be more appropriate to say that word formation studies the patterns according to which the speakers of a language can form new words; Lipka (2002: 95) thus stresses a distinction between "the analytic aspect of word-formation, i.e. the perspective of the hearer or reader who encounters already existing complex lexemes" and "the synthetic aspect, namely the perspective of the speaker/writer who creatively produces a new lexeme". This is a particularly important distinction because it is essential in any discussion of word formation to be clear about what one intends to explain. There are at least three different phenomena that one could try to describe:

- the inventory of word formations of a language at a particular point in time and the rules and mechanisms that have made these word formations possible (the study of word formation in this sense necessarily involves a diachronic component),

- the ability of native speakers to understand and interpret the word formations they encounter, i.e. the analytic aspect,

- the ability of native speakers to create new lexemes, i.e. the synthetic aspect.

The three phenomena are quite obviously related, but they are not identical, as will become apparent from the discussion below. It is also clear that the term word formation is ambiguous in that it refers to the processes by which new words can be created and to the result of such a process.[154] The fact that word formations make up a considerable proportion of probably

---

[153]   Cf. Lipka ([3]2002: 86).

[154]   See Burgschmidt's (1973: 1) distinction between *Prozeß* and *vorfindlicher Zustand* and Kastovsky's (1982: 155) remarks on "Wortbildung als Prozeß und Inventar".

any randomly chosen text of English can be seen from the following passage taken from A.S. Byatt's novel *Possession*:[155]

(3)   *When his DES grant ran out, Val became the breadwinner, whilst he*   19
      finished his PhD. She acquired an IBM golfball typewriter and did   20
      academic typing at home in the evenings and various well-paid temp-   21
      ing jobs during the day. She worked in the city and in teaching hospi-   22
      tals, in shipping firms and art galleries. She would not be drawn out to   23
      talk about her work, to which she almost never referred without the   24
      adjective 'menial'. 'I must do a few more menial things before I go to   25
      bed' or, more oddly, 'I was nearly run over on my menial way this   26
      morning'. Her voice acquired a jeering note, not unfamiliar to Roland,   27
      who wondered for the first time what his mother had been like before   28
      her disappointment, which in her case was his father and to some ex-   29
      tent himself. The typewriter clashed and harried him at night, never   30
      rhythmical enough to be ignored.   31

Whilst it is obvious that words such as *breadwinner* (line 19), *golfball* (line 20), *typewriter* (line 20) or *disappointment* (line 29) can be regarded as word formations, this is perhaps not quite so clear in cases such as *run over* (line 26), *drawn out* (line 23) or *golfball typewriter* (line 20), *academic typing* (line 21), *shipping firms* and *art galleries* (line 23). It is important to note that in English spelling is not a reliable criterion, less so than in German. It seems that in such cases the criteria listed in 9.1.1, positional mobility and uninterruptibility, are not entirely satisfactory: while they clearly identify *art galleries* as a complex lexeme (in this case, a compound)

(4a)   **art and other galleries*

(4b)   **The gallery is art*

they are not quite so clear in other cases:

(5a)   *golfball and other typewriters*

(5b)   **The typewriter is golfball*

(6a)   *academic and other typing*

(6b)   *?The typing is academic*

---

[155]   Source: A. S. Byatt, *Possession*, London: Random House (1990; Vintage edition 1991: 13–14).

(7a)   *?shipping and other firms*

(7b)   **The firm is shipping*

Thus, further criteria have been used to distinguish between compounds and noun phrases consisting of an adjective as premodifier and a noun as head:[156] Schmid (2005: 133) points out that from a cognitive point of view compounds are to be seen as new conceptual *gestalts*. Furthermore, compounds are often characterized by additional semantic features (such as 'habituality') and by a tendency of compounds to have their main stress on the first syllable.[157] Under these criteria, *art gallery* and *shipping firm* would qualify as compounds (although only the former can be found in dictionaries such as the *English Pronouncing Dictionary* (EPD15) or the *New Shorter Oxford English Dictionary* (NSOED). It is important to remember, however, that the distinction between complex lexemes (or analysable forms), which can be treated as word formations, and mere sequences of words that should not is likely to take the form of a gradient rather than to be clear-cut.

9.2.2   Formal types of word formation: a survey

Depending on the kinds of morphemes involved in the analysis of a word formation, different formal types of word formation can be distinguished. The following types are often identified for English:[158]

▷ **Compounding**: a process by which a new word is formed by combining two constituents, which are both free morphemes or contain a free morpheme[159]

---

[156]   For the terms premodifier and head in syntactic analysis see 11.3.1.

[157]   See Schmid (2005: 132–134), Kastovsky (1982: 152, 176–179) or Hansen, Hansen, Neubert and Schentke ([2]1985: 50–51). Compare also Lipka ([3]2002: 99).

[158]   The following account is based on especially Kastovsky (1982) and CGEL (1985: Appendix I). Compare also CamG (2002) and Plag (2003).

[159]   Cf. Schmid (2005: 121–122). For a detailed description of compounding in English including spelling and stress patterns of compounds see Plag (2003: 132–163). See also Plag, Braun, Lappe and Schramm (2007: 94–95) and Schmid (2005: 121–147). For a more precise definition of compounds see Plag (2003: 135): "… a compound is a word that consists of two elements, the first of which is either a root, a word or a phrase, the second of which is

breadwinner (1. 19), *typewriter* (1. 20), *teaching hospital* (1. 22–23) *shipping firm* (1. 23), *art gallery* (1. 23), *well-paid* (1. 21), *colour-illustrated* (1. 14)

Besides compounding two types of word formation can be identified, which are often subsumed under the term of **affixation**:[160]

▷ **Prefixation**: a process by which a new word is formed by combining two constituents so that a bound morpheme (prefix) precedes the second constituent

unfamiliar (1. 27), *illegal, post-modern, prearranged, non-finite, non-smoker*

▷ **Suffixation**: a process by which a new word is formed by combining two constituents so that a bound morpheme (suffix) follows the first constituent

disappointment (1. 29), *boredom* (1. 1), *compatibility* (1. 2), *application* (1. 8), *winner, writer*
crucifying (1. 1), *competitive* (1. 8), *enticing* (1. 14)

The constituents to which the affix is added are often referred to as the **base** (> 8.2).

▷ **Conversion**: a process by which a new word is formed without any formal change[161]

work (verb, 1. 22) ↔ *work* (noun, 1. 24), *talk* (verb, 1. 24) ↔ *talk* (noun), *must* (verb, 1. 26) ↔ *must* (noun), *bed* (noun, 1. 26) ↔ *bed* (verb), *clash* (verb) ↔ *clash* (noun), *this* (determiner, 1. 17) ↔ *this* (pronoun, 1. 17), *point* (verb, 1. 17) ↔ *point* (noun), *ship* (verb) ↔ *ship* (noun)

with modification of pronunciation (esp. stress shift):[162] *subject* (noun, 1. 15) /'sʌbdʒɪkt/ ↔ subject (verb) /səb'dʒekt/, research (noun, 1. 9) /'--/ or /-'-/ ↔ *research* (verb)/-'-/.

While CGEL (1985: I.43) and CamG (2002: 1640–1644), for instance, make use of the term conversion in this context, other scholars speak of

---

either a root or a word." Bauer (1983: 213–216) or Schmid (2005: 130–131) identify a category of neoclassical compounds such as *biography* or *Anglophone*, which are described as consisting of "combining forms".

[160] Cf. Lipka (³2002: 96) or CGEL (1985: Appendix I).

[161] The symbol ↔ is used here as a device to signal a relationship that could be interpreted in terms of zero-derivation. No commitment as to the direction of the process is intended at this stage. See 9.3 below.

[162] For formal modifications such as stress shift, voicing of final consonants (*advice – advise*) or spelling see CGEL (I.57).

zero-derivation, which can be described as a word formation process by which a new word is formed by the addition of a zero-morpheme.

Notice seen in Mousehole harbour

The next type of word formation can also be seen as involving affixes to a certain extent:

▷ **Back-formation**: a process by which a new word is formed by taking off a sequence of phonemes resembling a suffix from an existing word[163]

laze (< lazy), burgle (< burglar); televise (< television)

What further distinguishes back-formation from compounding, prefixation and suffixation is that it involves shortening, which is the main characteristic of the following three types:

▷ **Clipping**: a process of shortening a polysyllabic word, often to a single syllable

Val (line 19), ad, demo, prof, phone, fridge

▷ **Blending**: a process of forming a new word from two existing words by maintaining elements of both constituents[164]

heliport (helicopter + airport), smog (smoke + fog)

---

[163] Cf. Kastovsky (1982: 174).
[164] Cf. Schmid (2005: 224–225).

▷ **Acronymisation**: a process of shortening a compound by using the initial letters of the words it is made up of to form an **acronym** which is pronounced as one word

NATO (North Atlantic Treaty Organization), CARE (Cooperative for American Remittances to Europe), radar (radio detecting and ranging), LDOCE (Longman Dictionary of Contemporary English)

▷ **Abbreviation**: a process of shortening a compound by using the initial letters of the words which are pronounced separately[165]

DES (l. 19), PhD (l. 19), IBM (l. 20), U.N., U.S.A., E.U., SOED

A further type of abbreviation is that of making a word shorter and combining it with an affix to produce a **familiarity marker** such as *telly, comfy* (CGEL I.77).

One important distinguishing criterion between these word formation processes is that only affixation, conversion and back-formation lead to a change of word class.

Finally, word formation processes that are related to onomatopoetic or aesthetic features of the words have to be mentioned: Marchand (^{2}1969: 429–439) speaks of "ablaut and rime combinations", whereas CGEL (I.72) identifies a category **reduplicatives** to cover cases such as *see-saw, higgledy-piggledy, wishy-washy, teeny-weeny* etc.[166]

9.2.3   Semantic description of word formations

A semantic analysis of word formations (in the sense of lexemes formed by a word formation process) can take different forms. For instance, since the analysis of many complex lexemes involves not only one, but two or more word formation processes, whose order is not irrelevant, it is important to establish a hierarchy of immediate constituents. CamG (2002: 1626) uses the following graphic representations to make this clear:

---

[165] Sometimes abbreviations are subsumed under acronyms. Cf. however CamG (2002: 1632–1633) where the term *initialism* is used to cover both types.

[166] In terms of the distinctions made in 9.1.2 these processes might be seen as cases of inventing words rather than of word formation. While CGEL (1985: I.72) relates *din-din* to *dinner*, cases such as *tick-tock, ha ha, ping pong* seem to be different in character.

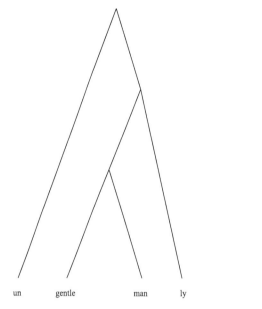

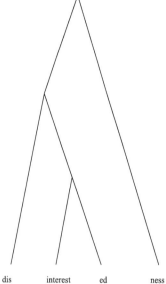

un	gentle	man	ly		dis	interest	ed	ness

This is closely related to the description of the relationship of the constituents to one another, where, following established terminology, a distinction can be made between the *determinant*, which expresses a kind of specification, and the *determinatum*, which can be characterized as representing a given category.[167] In *typewriter*, *type* specifies *write* and *typewrite* then specifies the category represented by {ER} ('machine or device').

A common device to further characterize the semantic relationship between the constituents of a word formation is to classify it according to the functional categories they have in an appropriate syntactic paraphrase: CGEL (I.61–5) uses this method to characterize compounds and arrives at types such as the following:[168]

---

[167] For determinant and determinatum see Kastovsky (2006: 229–230), see also Kastovsky (1982); for modifier and head see Plag, Braun, Lappe and Schramm (2007: 97–98).

[168] For a differentiation of these types see CGEL (I.61–5). For the historical background of the use of such paraphrases, the justification of particular paraphrases and the application of this method to various types of word formation see Kastovsky (1982: 186–195). Compare also Burgschmidt (1973: 22–67).

type		paraphrase	further examples
subject and verb	*sunrise*	*The sun rises.*	*rainfall, sound change*
verb and object	*tax-payer*	*X pays tax(es).*	*cigar smoker, song-writer*
verb and adverbial	*swimming pool*	*X swims in the pool.*	*living-room, walking stick, washing machine*
subject and object	*windmill*	*The wind powers the mill.*	*coal fire, steam engine*
subject and complement	*girlfriend*	*The friend is a girl.*	*killer shark, oak tree*

A further and probably also more appropriate semantic characterization of types of word formation can be achieved by drawing upon the model of case grammar as developed by Fillmore (> 12.2). Lipka (³2002: 107) emphasizes that the use of such case roles enables one to demonstrate the complexities of the relationship between formal and semantic aspects in word formation. Thus *breadwinner* could be described as 'AGENT', but *typewriter* as 'INSTRUMENT'.[169]

Despite such possibilities of a relatively general semantic description of certain word formation processes, further aspects of meaning may have to be taken into account. Thus, as Kastovsky (1982: 195) points out, an additional semantic feature 'profesionally' is required to characterize words such as *baker* or *shopkeeper*. Furthermore it should be noted that while such characterizations may be seen as typical of particular word formation processes, individual lexemes that have been formed through such processes may be subject to considerable semantic modification. Thus, as has already been pointed out in 8.5, *blackbird* does not mean 'black bird' but refers to a particular species of birds (50 per cent of which are brown anyway), and, similarly *breadwinner* can hardly satisfactorily be paraphrased as *someone who wins bread*. Such semantic idiosyncrasies will have to be stated individually wherever they occur. They show that word formations

---

[169] Compare also Lipka (1976) or Kastovsky (1982: 231–245) for a discussion of case grammar and word formation. For the aspect of profiling in word formation see Schmid (2005: 105–109).

can be subject to semantic processes, which can be described in terms of such concepts as lexicalization or idiomatisation (> 9.5).

It is important to point out that this kind of semantic analysis is only appropriate to certain types of word formation processes. It is obvious that in the case of acronymisation, blending and clipping, any semantic differences that one might wish to claim between base and word formation are of an entirely different character.

9.3   Word formation and morphology

9.3.1   The overlap between word formation and morphology

All of the processes outlined in 9.2.2 no doubt serve to create new words and thus fall under the scope of word formation. However, only some of them fall under the scope of morphology, if one follows the distinction as made by Schmid (2005: 14):

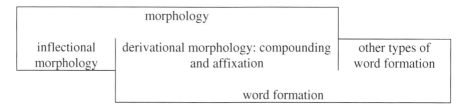

Although some linguists would subsume word formation under morphology, it is certainly true to say, as Schmid (2005: 14) does, that morpheme boundaries are not necessarily relevant to word formation processes such as clipping or acronymisation.[170] A further criterion that distinguishes compounding and affixation from other types of word formation is that only the former can be analysed in terms of a modifier-head or determinant-determinatum structure. While *art gallery* can be analysed as a particular kind of *gallery* and, with a certain sense of abstraction, *disappointment* as a particular kind of *-ment*, no such analysis seems possible in cases such as

---

[170]   See Lipka ([3]2002: 86) or Plag, Braun, Lappe and Schramm (2007: 89).

ad, LDOCE or *smog.*[171] So there are good reasons for not including word formation types such as acronymisation or clipping under morphology.

To what extent this also applies to cases such as the relationship between, say, *clean* (verb) and *clean* (adjective) is related to the question of whether one sees this relationship as conversion or as zero-derivation.[172] Lipka ([3]2002: 102) points at parallels of the kind

> *legal : legal/ize*   *clean : cleanØ 'make Adj'*
>
> *atom : atom/ize*   *cash : cashØ 'convert into N'*

and points out:

> The notion of zero-morpheme was not introduced arbitrarily in order to complicate matters. It accounts for the fact that two homonymous lexemes, which are superficially identical, are in a synchronically directed relationship. One lexeme is the base, while the other one is derived from it by means of a zero-suffix. Nevertheless, the two distinct lexemes are very closely related semantically and morphologically.

While, within a particular theoretical framework, there may be very good and well-argued reasons for postulating a unit such as zero-suffix, as was pointed out in 8.3.3, there are also very good reasons for not accepting such a concept as a sensible device in the analysis of language. Would one really want to say that in a case such as *work* Ø, for instance, the zero element represents a *determinatum*, which is specified by a *determinant work*?[173]

In any case, this is a good example of the way in which any statement about a language is determined by the theoretical framework of the analysis.[174] If one is not convinced of the idea of a zero-morpheme, then the term conversion is certainly more appropriate.

Funnily enough, although Quirk, Greenbaum, Leech and Svartvik (CGEL I.43) avoid the term zero-derivation and speak of conversion instead, they treat it as a "derivational process" within the appendix on word-formation. What is more, they apply this term not only to cases such as *ship*

---

[171]   Compare Marchand ([2]1969: 3) for a discussion of this. Back-formations and clippings also contradict Kastovsky's (1982: 153) view that only elements that can be analysed into smaller units fall under the scope of word formation.

[172]   See Kastovsky (1982: 172). Cf. also Burgschmidt (1974) or Hansen et al. ([2]1985).

[173]   Furthermore, as pointed out in CamG (2002: 1641), the fact that conversion involves a number of clearly distinct semantic properties raises the question of how many zero-morphemes would have to be identified.

[174]   For a parallel view cf. Vennemann and Jakobs (1982/2000: 409).

(noun → verb) or *answer* (verb → noun) but also to changes of what they refer to as "secondary word class" as in *coffee* (noncount noun → count noun) or *write* (transitive → intransitive). But would we really want to explain the difference between the uses of *write* in (8a) and (8b) as a change of secondary word class?

(8a)PH   *Writing for an American audience, he was, nevertheless, gently ironic about the claims already being advanced for the American influence on European art.*

(8b)BNC   *A personal friend of an artist may have a real advantage in writing criticism*

In Chapter 12, a model of grammatical analysis will be introduced – valency theory – which simply accounts for such differences between different uses of verbs by saying that certain elements they can occur with are optional (> 12.3.5). From this point of view, a description of these phenomena in terms of a word-formation process seems rather strange and counterintuitive.[175]

Again, we are faced with the theory-relatedness of statements about language. To what extent do we want to account for the fact that words can be used in different ways – "transitively" (*write something*) and "intransitively" (*write*) or as adjectives and verbs in the case of *clean* – by saying that they are different words and as such related by a word formation process? Or would it not be more appropriate to say that (8a) and (8b) are just examples of different uses of one verb *write*? But would this then also mean that we are justified in talking about one word *clean*, which can be used as an adjective or a verb?[176]

---

[175]   Equally, Bolinger ([2]1975: 116) says that "there is a sort of 'zero-derivation' every time the meaning of a word is extended" and draws attention to the fact that words affected by conversion are "new only in a grammatical sense". Compare Hansen et al. ([2]1985: 125), who seriously argue that way. For this problem see also Ayto's (1996: 183) discussion of the word *carer*.

[176]   This issue is related to the question of which word classes one thinks appropriate to identify for English (> 11.4.5–8). It is interesting to see that CGEL distinguishes between different uses of *this* in terms of the word classes pronoun and determiner, but that amongst the various categories of conversion listed in CGEL, there is no category "pronoun → determiner" or vice versa nor are such relationships between prepositions and adverbs (*round, up*) or adverbs and adjectives (*round, up*) identified as categories of conversion. For objections to this approach see Herbst and Schüller (2008) and Chapter

9.3.2 Explanatory value of the analysis

One major problem of a synchronic analysis of conversions (or zero-derivations) is that of the direction of the word formation process. Since there is no (or, if you like, only a zero) suffix, there is no morphological criterion to go by. Furthermore, within a synchronic analysis reference to the actual historical facts is ruled out for methodological reasons so that decisions about the direction of the word formation process are usually arrived at by a criterion which in CGEL (I.44) is referred to as the "semantic dependence of one item upon another". Indeed, referring to the examples from text (3) identified above, it seems more than plausible to assume that the verbs *bed, ship* and *point* are secondary to the corresponding nouns and not the other way round. But in cases such as *work, research* or *love* (noun 'feeling'; noun 'person'; verb) etc., semantic evidence is not particularly forcing in either direction. One might even ask whether there is any need to arrive at such decisions at the synchronic level.[177]

With reference to back-formation, precisely this point is made by Marchand ([2]1969: 3):

> The process called backderivation (backformation) has often diachronic relevance only. That *peddle* vb is 'derived' from *peddler* sb through reinterpretation is of historical interest. For synchronic analysis, however, the equation is *peddle : peddler = write : writer*, which means that the diachronic process of backderivation does not affect the derivative correlation for present-day speakers who do not feel any difference between the relationship *write : writer* on the one hand and *peddle : peddler* on the other.

The question is, however, if speakers of present-day English do not interpret, say, *edit* and *editor* to be related in a different way from *advise* and *advisor*, which seems plausible enough, is there then any point in identifying backformation as a word formation process at the synchronic level? And, considering how many native speakers might not be aware of the origins of *fridge, flu, plane* or *stereo* (clippings), *bit* (*binary digit*), *moped* or

---

11.4.6–7. How problematic the notion of conversion is (or, for that matter, that of zero-derivation) is also pointed out by Leisi ([5]1969: 93), who rejects the idea of conversion in a synchronic analysis and sees word classes as functional categories in present-day English.

[177] This could be seen as a consequence of Leisi's rejection of conversion at the synchronic level. See previous footnote.

telex (blends) and *e.g., i.e., laser* and *radar* (acronyms), could this argument not be extended to clipping, blending and acronymisation?[178]

The answer is probably: yes and no. Whether it is yes or no depends on what one is trying to describe. As far as the analytic aspect of word formation as identified in 9.2.1 is concerned, it probably does not matter whether speakers identify (or are able to identify) such words as results of word formation processes once these words have become part of their lexicon. With words they encounter for the first time, the situation may be different in that speakers may well be able to interpret an acronym such as *DES* or *SCR* if they are familiar with the words (or institutions) *Department of Education and Science* or *Senior Common Room*. In the case of back-formations or conversions, one is faced with a rather similar situation. A form which could be analysed as the result of either process will presumably present no difficulty of interpretation as long as the speaker is aware of the fact that such processes (back-formation, conversion from noun to verb, conversion from verb to noun) are possible in the language. The situation is probably even slightly more complicated in that there is no reason to assume that speakers (in the process which one could call a lifelong process of language acquisition) necessarily encounter the derived form after the non-derived form. In that sense, speakers might well be able to correctly interpret such items on the basis of patterns of relationship between words, but possibly without any awareness of the directions the process of conversion can take or the fact that back-formation can be identified as a separate process from suffixation.

The point of this argument is that there are certain assumptions we can make about the competence of speakers with respect to word formation, both with regard to analytic and to synthetic operations.[179] However, there does not seem to be any convincing reason that a native speaker has to be aware of the direction (suffixation or back-formation; verb→noun or noun→verb-conversion) of the process which produced a particular form. Apart from cases where there is sufficient semantic evidence that would put someone with a certain degree of linguistic awareness in a position to arrive at certain conclusions about the likelihood of the direction of a particular derivative process, there is absolutely no reason to assume that worrying

---

[178]   Examples taken from CGEL (I).

[179]   Cf. Burgschmidt's (1978: 28) view of word formation competence as the competence to analyse (known or new) word formations and produce new word formations on the basis of productive rules.

about such questions is a concern of the speakers of a language at all. This, however, raises the question of what the point of a synchronic analysis of such word formations is. Why should a linguistic description aim to arrive at any conclusions about the possible directedness of *work* and *work* or possibly even *edit* and *editor* when such directedness need not be considered part of a native speaker's competence at all?[180]

9.4 Productivity and restrictions

The situation is probably different with respect to the synthetic aspect of word formation. In this respect, speakers of course have to be aware of the fact that particular derivative processes can take place in two different directions (i.e. that suffixation as well as back-formation or conversion from verb to noun as well as from noun to verb etc. are possible in English.) As far as the competence of speakers to produce new word formations is concerned, it is obvious that it must comprise knowledge of the processes and, in some cases, also the particular word formation elements (such as affixes) that can be subject to such processes. This productive competence differs from the receptive competence required for the interpretation of existing word formations in that two factors which are irrelevant to the analytic aspect of word formation are suddenly relevant. The first of these is, as pointed out above, the questions of directedness, the second concerns the factor of productivity.

Following Aronoff and Anshen (1998: 242), **productivity** can be described as "the extent to which a particular affix" or word formation process[181] "is likely to be used in the production of new words in the language". Aronoff and Anshen (1998: 242–243) continue:

> On this view, productivity is a probabilistic continuum that predicts the use of potential words. At one end of the continuum are the dead or completely unproductive affixes, which are not likely to be used at all in coining new words. One example of this from English is the nominal suffix *-th* (as in *truth* or *growth*), which has not been used successfully to form a new word

---

[180] See also Coates's (1987: 111–112) discussion of whether morphology should be seen as "merely a historical discipline".

[181] Aronoff and Anshen (1998: 242) only use the term "affix" here, but productivity is generally seen as a feature of all word formation processes.

for 400 years, despite valiant attempts at terms like *coolth*[182] (which is attested sporadically, but which just never seems to be able to survive long). At the other end in English are ... highly productive derivational suffixes like *-ness* and *-ation*. In the middle, we find the less productive derivational suffixes like *-ity*. Some linguists treat morphological productivity as an absolute notion – a pattern is either productive or unproductive – but there is a good deal of evidence for the existence and utility of intermediate cases.

Productivity is of course extremely difficult to measure. Bauer (1994: 38), in a survey of the lexical development of English between 1880 and 1982, mentions a figure of 47.7% for suffixation, 18.5% for compounds and 10.4% for prefixation amongst the "types of formation in new words". These figures no doubt point at a high level of productivity of these word formation processes. To what extent they can be seen as representative of what happened in "the language" is of course a different matter since Bauer's data are based on lexicographical evidence, which, as Ayto (1996: 186) has convincingly demonstrated, can be misleading.[183]

To what extent productivity is related to frequency is also difficult to say. Aronoff and Anshen (1998: 245) point at interesting correlations between word frequency and productivity:

> ... the less productive a morphological pattern is, the more frequent on average its individual members will be. But frequency is also important in the selection of bases: a less productive affix is generally found attached to higher frequency-base words than a more productive affix.

Productive word formation competence involves more than simply an inventory of productive word formation processes and elements. It also comprises knowledge of a number of the distributional rules which apply to certain word formation elements. These are often dealt with in terms of restrictions: for English, Hansen, Hansen, Neubert and Schentke (1985: 33–35) distinguish between the following types:[184]

---

[182] Note, however, that *coolth* is listed in the OED and might become more and more established as it is shown by the many hits of this word on the internet.

[183] For a critical view see Ayto (1996: 186). For frequency and productivity see also Plag (2003: 53–59).

[184] For a detailed account of such restrictions see especially Hansen et al. (²1985: 33–37). Plag (2003: 59–68) distinguishes between pragmatic restrictions, structural restrictions and blocking. See also Burgschmidt (1978: 34–39) and Kastovsky (1982: 160–182). Cf. especially Neuhaus (1971).

▷ phonological restrictions of the kind that the morpheme {-ish} does not combine with nouns ending in /ʃ/ or /tʃ/ (*rubbishish, *bitchish* but: *rubbishy*),

▷ morphological restrictions of the kind that suffixations in {-ness} cannot be followed by another suffix (*kindnessless, *awkwardnessful*),

▷ semantic restrictions of the kind that suffixations in {-ess} (*stewardess*) only occur with nouns denoting human beings or higher animals,[185]

▷ etymological restrictions of the kind that the negative prefixes {in-} and {dis-} combine only with adjectives of Romance origin or that the prefix {di-} only combines with words of Latin or Greek origin.[186]

It is obvious that such distributional rules must be seen as part of a native speaker's productive word formation competence.

9.5   Possible words – nonce formations – institutionalized words

The discussion of word formation processes so far has in many ways shown that many parallels can be, and indeed have been, drawn between word formation and syntax. This is true in particular with reference to the notion of a productive word formation competence, which shows obvious similarities to how one could describe the competence of speakers to form sentences. In very simplified terms one could say that in both cases there are sets of rules which speakers can apply to what Chomsky (1957: 13) described as a finite set of elements (in the sense of lexical material such as

---

[185]   Note that Hansen, Hansen, Neubert, and Schentke (²1985: 35 and 103) use the feature <+ HUM>.

[186]   As an example of a particular type of semantic restriction Kastovsky (1982: 161) mentions that the negative prefix {un-} does not occur with adjectives with the suffix {-ish} as in (*uncleanish, *undeepish, *unplainish*) although the non-suffixed adjectives admit the prefix (*unclean, undeep, unplain*). The fact that *undeep* and *unplain* are listed neither in NSOED nor in EPD15 throws some doubt on the importance of the phenomena described. Furthermore, Kastovsky (1982: 161) identifies a type 'syntactic restriction', where the examples however also lend themselves to a semantic explanation.

morphemes or lexemes etc.) in order to produce words or sentences.[187] However, there is a significant difference as to how the result or output of this application of rules to items is judged by the language community. If, for instance, native speakers of English were asked whether

(9)$_{PH}$ *Several important painters of this generation, including William Scott, Roger Hilton, Bryan Wynter, John Wells, Peter Lanyon, Alan Davie and Terry Frost, all a few years older than Heron, were close friends, and in the post-war period his associations with these and other artists were to be consolidated by shared creative connections with West Penwith and St Ives.*

was a sentence of English, the answer would no doubt be yes. If, however, native speakers of English were asked whether

(10)$_{PH}$ *ceruleum*

(11)$_{PH}$ *juxtapositional*

(12)$_{QE}$ *psychophilatelic*

(13)$_{QE}$ *snow-cream*[188]

were words of English, the answers would be more difficult to predict: in the case of (12) and (13) it might well be no, whereas with (10) and (11) answers might differ. People might even say "I don't know" in a way that they probably would not in the case of (9).

The point is, of course, that the two questions mean different things. Judging something such as (9) as a sentence of English means that it is grammatically well-formed according to the rules of English grammar, whereas judging something such as (10–13) as a word of English would probably be understood to mean 'Does this word exist in English?'. If speakers have not encountered a word before, they might be inclined to judge it as non-existent in the language if it seems implausible to them for some reason or other. However, the fact that it had not been encountered before would not be used as a criterion to judge a sentence as not being a sentence of English. In fact, it is relatively unlikely that any reader of this text will ever have come across sentence (9) and even if someone had done, in which case it is almost 100 per cent certain that they had read Mel Good-

---

[187]   While Chomsky actually refers to phonemes and letters in this passage, the following discussion about grammaticalness allows the conclusion that this view can be extended to lexical material (> 13.1.1).

[188]   Examples (12) and (13) from CGEL (I.13).

ing's biography of Patrick Heron,[189] they probably would not remember that they had.[190]

A further difference in this respect between sentences and words is that native speakers might well expect to find the answer to the question of whether something is a word of English in a reference book and turn to a dictionary in order to find it there or not, but, even if in doubt, they would never turn to a grammar book and make their decision as to its Englishness on the basis of whether they can find that particular sentence there.

In the case of (10) – (13), only one of these words, *juxtapositional*, can be found in even a large dictionary such as NSOED. Is that sufficient evidence to claim that *ceruleum, psychophilatelic* and *snow-cream* are not words of English? Certainly not, since they all correspond to the rules of English word formation in the way that (9) corresponds to the rules of English grammar. However, the fact that a word is not contained in a dictionary, at least in a dictionary of that kind, is generally taken as an indication of its status in the language. In that respect, several distinctions can be made:

– Words such as *psychophilatelic* and *snow-cream*, according to CGEL (1985: I.13), or *policeability*, according to CamG (2002: 1624), are **possible** or **potential words** of English, i.e. words of English that correspond to the rules of English word formation. At the same time, these words are not used. There are different reasons why possible or potential words of English have not come into existence – and even *psychophilatelic* and *snow-cream* paradoxically have only been formed in order to demonstrate that they do not exist: one is that no one has seen the need to conceptualise a certain sense, as in the case of *psychophilatelic*, of which Quirk, Greenbaum, Leech and Svartvik (CGEL: I.13) say: "unused because psychological aspects of stamp collecting have not called for lexicalization". A second reason has to do with a phenomenon that Burgschmidt (1973: 124) explains in terms of an occupied slot rule and which is sometimes also referred to as **blocking** (> 9.6).[191] Thus *un-*

---

[189] Mel Gooding: *Patrick Heron*, London: Phaidon Press, 1994.
[190] Compare also the very enlightening discussion of the differences between words and sentences in this respect by Quirk et al. (CGEL I.7).
[191] See Aronoff and Anshen (1998: 238): "Because blocking is a psychological phenomenon, it is subject of the vagaries of the mind: if a person has temporarily forgotten the word *fame*, then that person may in fact use the word **famousness*, which *fame* would otherwise block. This seeming failure of

tall[192] or *Sinnvollizität* may not be used because of the existence of the words *short* and *Sinn*.

– Moving from "potential" to "established", the next status to be identified is that of a **nonce formation**.[193] A nonce formation is a word that has been formed and used by a speaker on a particular occasion but not spread any (or much) further. This is the level at which the creative potential of word formation resembles that of syntax. Numerically, nonce formations may well be a much more important phenomenon of language use than is often given credit for (especially in studies that analyse neologisms on the basis of dictionaries). Two very important areas where nonce formations might feature prominently are cases where speakers do not have a lexeme at their disposal which serves their immediate communicative needs and the language of newspaper headlines. The former can be imagined as being caused by "gaps" in the lexicon of speakers, especially perhaps in the language of children,[194] or indeed gaps in the lexicon of the language as such, for example in the field of terminology.[195] In the language of the press, nonce-formations are used consciously to achieve a certain, often humorous or ironical effect, as in the case of *Pharmaschinken*, which the *Süddeutsche Zeitung* used as a title of an article about one of the food scandals in 2002. Burgschmidt's extensive study of headlines in English papers include *Confessions of a chocaholic, In the bleak mid-winterval, Prof-lifers put MPs on the spot, Would you Adam and Eve it?* and *England's Knightmare.*[196]

---

blocking is especially common in children, who coin new words quite freely, because their vocabulary is not as entrenched as that of adults. An articulate child might use words like *famousness* and *liquidize* without hesitating." So might articulate adults, one might add, since *famousness* can be found in dictionaries such as EPD15 or NSOED. Compare also Hansen, Hansen, Neubert and Schentke (²1985: 35) for this.

[192] *Untall* is analysed in CGEL (I.13) as "unused perhaps because alternatively lexicalized".

[193] Bauer (1983: 45) defines a nonce formation as "a new complex word coined by a speaker/writer on the spur of the moment to cover some immediate need".

[194] See Kastovsky (1982: 163).

[195] Cf. CGEL's (I.15) discussion of *The scribbler of this fould message should be punished*.

[196] *The Times* (24/1/1998), *The Guardian* (23/12/1998), *The Independent* (7/2/1997 referring to anti-abortionists), *Sunday Times* (19/1/1997) and *Daily*

– Nonce formations have to be distinguished from **institutionalized** (CGEL) or **established** (CamG 2002) **words.**[197] Quirk, Greenbaum, Leech, and Svartvik (CGEL: I.7) express this distinction in terms of the contrast between "the 'made-to-measure'" and "the 'ready-made'" and say "we expect every *lexical item* we hear or read to be already 'institutionalized' ... and to have been selected from an existing stock of words, complete with its form and meaning". Consequently, it is the institutionalized words of a language that are the candidates for being entered into a dictionary. (The opposite does not hold true, of course, one could not expect a dictionary, however large, to list all the institutionalized words of the language.)

While the distinction between nonce formations and institutionalized words is probably a rather useful one, it ought to be pointed out that institutionalization is probably a matter of gradience in the sense that not all speakers may perceive a word as being institutionalized or not in the same way.

A further distinction can be made between institutionalization and lexicalization – institutionalization referring to the socio-pragmatic aspect and lexicalization to the structural aspect of word formations (Schmid 2005: 79–85). While the term institutionalization describes the fact that a word formation is known[198] and used by a large number of speakers, a word formation can be called lexicalized if it can no longer be fully related to the underlying word formation process – either at the formal or the semantic level.[199] The extreme case is to be found in so-called amalgamated compounds such as *cupboard* (loss of accent on the second element), *boatswain*

Mail (23/12/96 referring to batsman Knight). Examples collected by Ernst Burgschmidt and presented in a paper at the *Deutsch-Britische Gesellschaft* in Nürnberg in 2002.

[197] Bauer (1983: 48): "The next stage in the history of a lexeme is when the nonce formation starts to be accepted by other speakers as a known lexical item."

[198] Bauer (1983: 48) takes it as a criterion of institutionalisation "that the potential ambiguity is ignored, and only some of the possible meanings of the form are used (sometimes only one)". Compare, however, CGEL's (I.11) use of the term lexicalization in this respect. For a distinction between different types of lexicalization see Bauer (1983: 48–61).

[199] For this definition of institutionalization and a more detailed discussion of the terms lexicalization, institutionalization and concept formation see Schmid (2005: 79–85).

/ˈbəʊsᵊn/ or /ˈbəʊtsweɪn/, *breakfast, daisy, husband, neighbour* etc.[200] Less extreme cases are provided by words that have developed semantic properties that are not immediately predictable from those of their component parts such as with *blackboard* (which need not be black)[201] or *bus driver* (with stress on the first element and a component 'professionally'). Quirk, Greenbaum, Leech and Svartvik (CGEL: I.11) discuss the example of the verb *paint*, where "two verb senses have been separately lexicalized" – 'decorate with paint' and 'make pictures with paint'.

9.6 Psychological aspects of morphology

What can be concluded from the outline of morphology and word formation given in Chapters 8 and 9 is that the concept of the morpheme as defined in structuralist linguistics serves quite well to account for complex word forms such as *critics, paintings* or *coastlines* but is less convincing in other cases. With respect to psychological aspects of language use, it is the aspect of item-specific knowledge that needs to be accounted for. This concerns two slightly different phenomena. Firstly, speakers of a language know that the past tense form of *begin* is not formed by adding /d/. In traditional accounts, this sort of phenomenon is treated as an irregularity or an exception. Secondly, speakers know that words such as *kindness* and *fury* exist and seem to avoid using *kindity* or *furiousness*, which is where the aspect of institutionalization and lexicalization is relevant. We are talking

---

[200] Examples taken from Götz (1971), who discusses their historical development in detail. For a discussion of lexicalization in terms of "unrecoverability" and "unpredictability" see Quirk et al. (CGEL: I.9–10), who also discuss questions of terminology such as *fissionable* and *fissile* in this context. Compare also Brinton and Arnovick (2006: 173).

[201] See Lipka (³2002: 115). Cf. Lipka's (³2002: 113) definition of lexicalization as a "gradual, historical process, involving phonological and semantic changes and the loss of motivation". Lipka refers to semantic aspects of lexicalization as idiomatization (Lipka ³2002: 114). Cf. also Coates (1987: 116). For cognitive aspects of lexicalization see Ungerer and Schmid (²2006: 268–275). For lexicalization and grammaticalization see Hopper and Traugott (²2003: 133–135).

here about conventionalized or established ways of expressing certain meanings in a language.[202]

In fact, the question of to what extent certain types of word formation should be treated as a rule-driven or as an idiosyncractic phenomenon has been subject of much discussion in linguistics.[203]

In more recent work, the discussion of this question has focussed more on psychological issues. Coates (1987: 115) addresses the matter by asking whether it is "possible to decide whether a form is rote-learned (stored whole) or combined in usage from its constituent parts". While Coates is concerned with word formations such as *toothbrush*, there are also obvious parallels between the kind of idiosyncracy observed in word formation and irregularity in inflection. For this reason, the two aspects are often dealt with together in discussions of the mental lexicon. Jackendoff (1997: 121) translates the problem into psycholinguistic terms in the following way:[204]

> The basic psycholinguistic question about morphology is whether complex morphological forms are stored in long-term memory or composed "on-line" in working memory from stored constituents.

---

[202] This can be accounted for in terms of Coseriu's (1973) distinction between system and norm, which, as, Burgschmidt (1973 and 1977) shows, can fruitfully be applied to word formation (> 3.1.4). The rules underlying potential and actual word formations of a language can be described in terms of the system, but since not all lexical units the system would permit are actually realized in the language, the inventory of word formations in the sense of institutionalized lexical units can be considered a norm phenomenon.

[203] Within the strongly formalized models that became current in the years following the publication of Chomsky's (1957) *Syntactic Structures* the discussion took the form of asking whether certain linguistic facts ought to be placed in the syntactic component of a model of grammar or be relegated to the lexicon. It culminated in the formulation of the so-called transformational hypothesis by Lees (1960/1968), who analysed nominalizations such as *the committee's appointment of John* or *John's appointment by the committee* as "noun-like versions of sentences" of the type *The committee appoints John*. The alternative analysis was favoured by Chomsky (1970) in the form of the lexicalist hypothesis. Compare Herbst (1983: 46–54) and Kastovsky (1982: 219–229).

[204] Cf. Clark (1998: 388). See also the discussion of different approaches given by Jackendoff (1997: 121–123). Compare also McQueen and Cutler (1998: 407), who talk about "the relative importance of rule-based processing and rote-storage" in this context.

A lot of psycholinguistic research seems to be in line with the assumption made by Coates above, that "individuals may *both* store particular complex forms whole *and* have them available for analysis".[205] This *both-and-* situation seems to manifest itself in different ways:[206] one of these is represented by so-called dual-route (or dual processing) models, favoured, for instance by McQueen and Cutler (1998: 423) "where some words are morphologically parsed prior to access via their constituent morphemes and others are accessed directly via whole-word representations". This means that this model permits different processing mechanisms to be at work.[207] Similarly, Aronoff and Anshen (1998: 240) account for the blocking of inflectional forms such as *goed or lexical forms such as *furiosity* in terms of a "race between the mental lexicon and the morphology. Both operate simultaneously, and the faster one wins".

An alternative to such approaches has been developed by Bybee (1995: 428–429) in the form of the network model. She characterizes her model as being different from "structuralist models containing rules":

> The basic proposal is that morphological properties of words, paradigms and morphological patterns once described as rules emerge from associations made among related words in lexical representation. …
>
> Words entered in the lexicon are related to other words via sets of lexical connections between identical and similar phonological and semantic features. These connections among items have the effect of yielding an internal morphological analysis of complex words, as shown by Fig. 1.

---

[205] McQueen and Cutler (1998: 420), discussing a number of experiments in the field, come to the following conclusion: "In summary, the evidence for decomposition reviewed so far is stronger for inflectional than for derivational forms. Decomposition may be an optional strategy for derived words, available when normal access procedures fail. It would therefore appear that derived words have independent whole-word access representations. Inflected words may not have their own access representations, and access to the central lexicon for inflected forms may be via decomposition, leading to access representations of their component stems and affixes."

[206] For a discussion of the dual-processing model, connectionist models and the network model see Bybee (1995).

[207] Compare also Pinker (1991: 532) or Pinker and Prince (1994: 326).

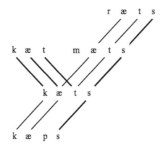

Even though the words entered in the lexicon are not broken up into their constituent morphemes, their morphological structure emerges from the connections they make with other words in the lexicon. Parallel sets of phonological and semantic connections, if they are repeated across multiple sets of words, constitute morphological relations (in Fig. 1, these are represented by heavier lines.) Note that in Fig. 1 [see above] connections between base ([kæt]) and complex form ([kæts]) exist, as well as relations among complex forms ([ræts], [mæts], [kæts], [kæps]).

Central to the model are the concepts of schemas and strength. Of the former Bybee (1995: 430) says: "Sets of words having similar patterns of semantic and phonological connections reinforce one another and create emergent generalisations describable as schemas."

When we ask how many and which elements of morphology ought to be seen as derived on the basis of morphological rules, and thus be attributed to the morphological component of a model of language, and how many or which elements ought to be treated in terms of the lexicon, the rejection of the notion of rules in Bybee's model has of course far-reaching repercussions. Whereas other models would claim that, say, all regular past tense forms are the result of applying a rule of some kind and irregular past tense forms (and only these) are stored in the lexicon, according to Bybee (1995: 450) both irregular and highly frequent regular past tense forms are stored in the lexicon. The past tense forms of low-frequency verbs are then arrived at "by applying the strongest schema to base forms".[208] This approach is of course very much in line with the finding that the verbs that have irregular past tense and participle forms tend to be amongst the most frequent verbs

---

[208] Bybee (1995: 450–451) takes phonological evidence concerning the duration of the final consonants in words such as *rapt* or *rapped* to reflect "a difference in processing type".

in English, and also that the verb *be* shows greater morphological diversity than any other verb in the language.[209]

Bybee (1995: 452) argues that morphology can be accounted for solely in terms of a "highly structured lexicon" and describes a functionalist view of the lexicon as follows:

> The distinction between storage of complex forms versus formation by schema application are based on the availability of stored items, which is determined by frequency of use, not by structural distinctions, such as the classifications into regular and irregular patterns.

What makes such an approach very interesting is that it may also offer an explanation for irregularities of the type *curriculum – curricula*, which are awkward to account for in structuralist morphology, and, in particular, that it can easily be extended to larger phraseological units.[210]

---

[209] One particularly interesting aspect of this is the phenomenon that in a certain stage of language acquisition children seem to overgeneralize *-ed*-past tense forms. This is often explained in terms of children having acquired the rule of past tense formation at this stage. Bybee (1995: 449) explains this in terms of children having understood the obligatory nature of tense marking. See Tomasello (2003: 232–235).

[210] Cf. Bybee (2007: 281–292). Thus usage-based approaches play an increasingly important role in cognitive linguistics – not only in morphology, but also in other areas of linguistics such as syntax (> 13.2), and in particular in models of language acquisition (Tomasello 2003). It is interesting to see that the concept of pre-emption can be used for morphology as well as syntactic constructions, see Tomasello (2003: 178–182 and 234).

10   Phraseology

10.1   Prefabs

Institutionalized lexemes can be seen as prefabricated items which speakers can make use of when conceptualizing ideas and forming sentences. It would be a mistake, however, to suppose that prefabrication stops at the word boundary. While some aspects of this phenomenon have always raised scholarly attention, especially as far as collocations (> 10.2–3) and idioms (> 10.4) are concerned, the full dimension of this phenomenon has only become apparent through the results of the machine-supported analysis of large text corpora. These findings are related to statistical data and it is thus of particular interest that frequency is also taken as a highly relevant factor of language description in some recent models of the mental lexicon in psycholinguistics (> 9.6).

There is a lot of experimental and corpus evidence to illustrate the role prefabricated material plays in language production.

- For instance, sentence completion tests carried out by Greenbaum (1974/1988: 118–119) demonstrate the high association between particular lexical items. The following table lists the percentages of the verbs that were given frequently by British and American speakers for the sentence beginnings in the left-hand column:[211]

I badly	*UK*: need 65% – want 28%
	US: need 48% – want 17%
Your friend very much	*UK*: like 29% – want 18%
	US: like 19% – want 10%
I entirely	*UK*: agree 82%
	US: agree 27% – forget 13%
I completely	*UK*: forget 50%
	US: forget 46%

---

[211]   For the results of these tests with German students of English cf. Herbst (1996: 389–391).

– Mittmann (2004) points out that in two large corpora of American and British spoken English, all occurrences of *beg your* were followed by *pardon*, while all occurrences of *your pardon* were preceded by *beg* or that *should think* is almost always preceded by *I*.

– Sinclair (2004: 45–47) has shown that if one finds the phrase *naked eye* at the beginning of a sentence, it is very likely to be preceded by *the*, which again is likely to be preceded by *with* or *to*, *with* is preceded by a form of *see*, which in turn tends to be preceded by a modal verb, *to* tends to be preceded by *visible* or *invisible*.

– The following extract from the British National Corpus illustrates that the phrase *would you* is followed by the verb *like* in 25% of all occurrences.

What else	**would you**	expect after the rotten day I'd had?
"What	**would you**	know?" demanded Thomas, the under-footman, jealous that it had been she who had found the
"You wouldn't expect them to paint it pretty pink,	**would you**	?"
	Would you	like to come round for a cup of tea?"
	Would you	like some more tea?"
	Would you	mind desperately if just this once I paid at the other end?"
	Would you	like some tea?"
I'll check to see what's on offer and in the meantime, how	**would you**	like a day's pay here?"
	Would you	like to come and sit out the back with me for a minute?"
	Would you	mind if I bought you a coffee or something?"
"	**Would you**	take the flat now, then?
"Where	**would you**	like to live?"
Do you want to check into a hostel just in case it rains or	**would you**	rather have another night in the park?"
"Where	**would you**	like to eat?" she asked me.
I paused for a moment, then added, "	**Would you**	mind if I had some pudding?"
	Would you	mind if I made a few housing enquiries for you?
	Would you	like some tea?"
If you were given "carte blanche" so to speak, what	**would you**	go for?"
"	**Would you**	like some newspapers to read on your journey?"
	Would you	like Jenny to go along as well?"
Which	**would you**	rather have in your garden --; sticky clay or thin, hungry sand?
	Would you	do something for me?
If you did not burn chemicals like PCBs, what else	**would you**	do with them?
"If the people in Hong Kong were white," he asked,"	**would you**	be taking the same view?"

	Would you	care to hear my analogy?"
"Right," said Marina, "Dionne, what kind of animal	**would you**	be?"
And now, she thought in the blessed silence, my dear Jay, what	**would you**	like to do?
"	**Would you**	do that, Donald?
	Would you	Hide if you had to?"
"Well, where else	**would you**	go to meet up with the Duke and his followers?"
Donald came down two hours ago, and	**would you**	believe it, Bisset will not come to marry them."
"Well --; Donald asked me to ask you --;	**would you**	do the honours?"
If you were Atholl, who	**would you**	come for first?
ands and said eagerly, "Don --; we could live here --; it is right for us --;	**would you**	like that, Don?"
"If a deadly beast was coming for you, what	**would you**	do?
	Would you	lie low, if it came to it?"
"	**Would you**	talk to me for a few minutes?"
"	**Would you**	sit closer?" he asked, smoothing the sand.
	Would you	, I wonder, would you walk with me?
Would you, I wonder,	**would you**	Walk with me?
Take my situation; you'd never be able to handle that,	**would you**	?

It is facts like these which point at the relevance of units higher than the individual word or the individual lexeme in linguistic analysis. What is particularly interesting to observe is that prefabrication does not necessarily coincide with units of syntactic analysis such as phrase, clause or sentence (> 11.1.2 and 11.3). This was demonstrated by Altenberg (1998: 120):

> What is perhaps the most striking impression that emerges from the material is the pervasive and varied character of conventionalized language in spoken discourse. The use of routinized and more or less prefabricated expressions is evident at all levels of linguistic organization and affects all kinds of structures, from entire utterances operating at discourse level to smaller units acting as single words and phrases.

Altenberg (1998) identifies the following types of recurrent word-combinations:

full independent clauses	*it's all right, that's all right, well I don't know*
full dependent clauses	*if you like, that is to say, I should think*
multiple clause constituents	*and you know, there is, and then I, because I mean*

| single clause constituents | *on the whole, at the moment, the whole thing, in this country, and so on* |
| incomplete phrases | *a sort of, a kind of, part of the, one of the* |

The enormous amount of variation reflected in this material demonstrates the problems of classification in this field.[212] Altenberg (1998: 121) concludes:

> The picture that emerges ... emphasizes rather than clarifies the fuzzy character of phraseology. Speakers engaged in spontaneous interaction are in constant need of easily retrieved expressions to convey their intentions and reactions in discourse. At their disposal they have a large stock of recurrent word-combinations that are seldom completely fixed but can be described as 'preferred' ways of saying things – more or less conventionalized building blocks that are used as convenient routines in language production.

10.2   Statistically significant collocations

That certain affinities hold between particular words can be demonstrated by looking at almost any text.[213]

(1)   *I shall never forget the immense sensation of space the first moment*   1
        we entered that room, at the end of our journey from London: it was   2
        an October night and a full moon was rising over Godrevy. ... I   3
        probably painted more St Ives harbour window paintings in London   4
        than in Cornwall. ... Also established at the time I painted it was my   5
        habit of applying only one coat of colour over the white ground,   6
        which seems to be responsible for the brilliance of hue – there are one   7
        or two areas, very noticeably, where I have applied more than one   8
        colour ...   9

This short passage contains quite a number of co-occurrences of words which one might consider typical in one way or another: *I shall never forget, enter – room, full – moon, moon – rise, apply – colour.* Following the

---

[212]   See, for instance, Gläser (^{2}1990).

[213]   From a letter by Patrick Heron to the Tate Gallery, quoted in Mel Gooding: *Patrick Heron*, London: Phaidon Press, 1994, 74.

terminology established by the British contextualist John Rupert Firth, who emphasized the "mutual expectancy of words"[214] such combinations are generally referred to as **collocations**.[215] Sinclair (1991: 170) defines collocation in a very general way as "the occurrence of two or more words within a short space of each other in a text". This mutual expectancy can be demonstrated very nicely by looking at the likelihood of co-occurrence on the basis of corpus material (which, of course, has to be treated with some caution but nevertheless can be taken as some indication of the facts). For instance, the BNC contains 148 instances of the cluster *I shall never*. These are followed by the following words:[216]

forget 48; *know* 17, *be* 13, *see* 9, *go* 5, *marry* 4, *forgive* 4, *get* 4, *go* 4, *let* 3, *understand* 3, *regret* 2 and words which occur only once.

Corpus analysis enables us not only to find out the absolute frequencies of words occurring together within a certain span (the number of words to the left and to the right from a particular key word), but to determine so-called **statistically significant collocations**, which are "collocations that occur more frequently than would be expected on the basis of the frequency of occurrence of individual items" (Herbst 1996: 382). The statistical significance of collocations can be represented in the form of log-likelihood values, T-scores or Z-scores, which are different ways of relating the frequency of occurrence of a collocation to the probability of the two elements of the collocation co-occurring in that corpus. Thus a lemma query (covering all morphological forms) of the verb *paint* in the BNC lists the following among the 50 most frequent nouns occurring within a span of +1 to +3, i.e. within the next three words:

---

[214]   Cf. Firth (1957/1968: 181).

[215]   For a discussion of Firth's ideas on collocation and the distinction between a text oriented, a statistically oriented and a significance oriented approach to collocation see Herbst (1996). For discussions of different approaches to collocation see Nesselhauf (2005: 11–40) or Siepmann (2007: 236–237 and 2008: 186–187).

[216]   All figures in this chapter are based on BNC World Edition queried through BNCweb (described by Lehmann, Hoffmann, and Schneider 2000).

lemma	collocate (noun)	number of co-occurrences	log-likelihood value
paint (verb)	*picture*	178	1824.9
	portrait	39	420.9
	pictures	38	321.1
	colours	32	272.0
	portraits	19	208.9
	house	30	109.9
	boats	7	49.6

Similarly, a lemma query for the noun *moon* within a span of -3 to -1 includes the following collocates:

lemma	collocate	number of co-occurrences	log-likelihood value
moon (noun)	*the*	2074	8534.2
	full	209	1951.2
	sun	88	829.4
	over	102	494.4
	phases	23	265.7
	blue	31	233.3

These figures show that there is not necessarily a direct correlation between the absolute frequency and the statistical significance of a combination. Thus *I shall never see* appears more significant in terms of its log-likelihood value (56.1) than *I shall never be* (47.2).

Furthermore, statistically significant collocations may of course be the result of a number of factors, not all of which are linguistically interesting. If, for instance, it is found that *house* frequently collocates with *sell* in a corpus of British English, this may be an indication of certain elements of British culture (such as that British people tend to talk about selling houses quite often), but it is not necessarily something that would affect the linguistic description of *house* or *sell*. Nevertheless, the statistically oriented approach to collocation can make an important contribution to, for example, foreign language teaching, for instance, as far as the selection of typical and natural examples is concerned. Furthermore, irrespective of the degree in which they are caused by cultural factors, the phenomenon of statistically significant collocations opens up an important field of psycholinguistic research in that a tendency of co-occurrence of particular words can be surely seen as an important factor in the planning and perception of speech.

10.3   Institutionalized collocations

There is a further type of collocations to be distinguished from statistically significant collocations, which can also be characterized in terms of the significance of the co-occurrence of two or more lexical items, which however is not related to frequency. Such collocations, as Sinclair (1991: 170) puts it, "can be dramatic and interesting because unexpected". Indeed, it is the unexpectedness or unpredictability at the semantic level that characterizes such collocations. Thus there is no particular reason why *white wine* should be called *white wine* and not **yellow wine*, why *weak tea* should not be **feeble tea* or why *a conscience* should be *clear* and not **clean*. Collocations of this kind are norm phenomena in very much the same way as word formations, where there is also no reason why *blackbird* should not be **brownbird* or *dishwasher* should not be **washing-up machine*.

Nevertheless, the term unpredictability is very problematical as a criterion for determining the status of a collocation. Firstly, as Palmer (²1981: 77) points out, whether a combination is semantically predictable or not depends on the meanings one assigns to the items involved.

> It would ... be a mistake to draw a clear distinguishing line between those collocations that are predictable from the meanings of the words that co-occur and those that are not. ... For one can, with varying degrees of plausibility, provide a semantic explanation for even the more restricted collocations, by assigning very particular meanings to the individual words. ... We can thus explain *white coffee, white wine* ... by suggesting that *white* means something like 'with the lightest of normal colours associated with the entity'.

Indeed, if one argues that it is part of the (or one) meaning of *white* that it can refer to wine or part of the meaning of the lexeme *coat* that it can refer to paint, then the combinations *white wine* and *coat of paint*[217] are highly predictable. In fact, sentences of the type

(2)   *Do you prefer white or black?*

strongly support such an analysis since (2), quite obviously, will be taken to refer to coffee (as an extralinguistic entity), while – and that is the crucial point – the use of *white* and *black* is not dependent on the presence of the word *coffee.*[218] Nevertheless, an element of unpredictability remains in that within such an analysis of the meaning of *white* it is difficult to explain why tea with milk is not generally referred to as **white tea* (although *tea whitener* seems to exist as a word).[219]

The second problem with the criterion of unpredictability is that unpredictabiliy entails the question of "unpredictable for whom". Thus, to take a simple example, *make coffee* is a common collocation in English, whereas **boil coffee* or **cook coffee* are not. From a semantic, intra-English point of view, *make coffee* does not seem to be a case of great unpredictability. This is different for users of English with a different language background, however. Germans who tend to say *Kaffee kochen* have to learn that it is *make coffee* in English, Germans who say *Kaffee machen* are not confronted with a collocational difficulty. Similarly, it may depend on a foreign user's language background whether *apply colour* and *coat of colour* present a problem or not. While such considerations lead to the conclusion that the ideal place for dealing with collocations is the bilingual and not the monolingual dictionary, as Klotz[220] has argued, the contrastive approach can of course only be seen as a methodological device for discovering collocations of this kind in a language. Nevertheless, it highlights two characteristics of collocations of this kind: firstly, that they are norm phenomena (> 3.1.4), and secondly, that they have to do with choice. Thus one might argue that one could postulate a theoretical choice between, say, *good, clear,* and *clean* in the case of *conscience,* but only *clear conscience* seems to be an estab-

---

[217]   *Coat of colour* as used in text (1), however, seems to be rather unusual as a collocation and restricted to the artistic context.

[218]   Cf. Herbst (1996: 386–389).

[219]   This may be an instance of language change: occasionally, the combination *white tea* can be found in coffee shops etc.; the BNC has three instances of *white tea*, one of which is an example of coordination *a cup of white tea or coffee*, the other two referring to instant tea.

[220]   I owe these examples and this line of argument to Michael Klotz (personal communication). See Herbst and Klotz (2003).

lished collocation, and *good* is used in the phrase *in good conscience*. This arbitrariness of the combination features prominently in Hausmann's (1985: 118) definition of collocations as "typical, specific and characteristic relations between two words".[221]

In fact, one could approach a definition of this type of collocation by saying it occurs in cases where on semantic grounds there would seem to be a lexical choice in the language but where the combination of two (or more) particular lexemes is so established that it is the only combination possible or at least the preferred combination. Nevertheless, the frequency factor should not be overlooked. Thus, looking at three possible collocates of the words *gale(s)*, *storm(s)* and *wind(s)* one finds:

	gale	*gales*	*storm*	*storms*	*wind*	*winds*
heavy	1	0	2	4	3	2
severe	4	6	6	9	1	1
strong	4	0	0	0	85	144

As far as these figures can be regarded as representative at all, apart from *strong storm(s)* all combinations have been used, while at the same time there is a strong tendency for *gale(s)* and *storm(s)* to co-occur with *severe* and for *wind(s)* to be used together with *strong*.[222] This can be represented in the following way:

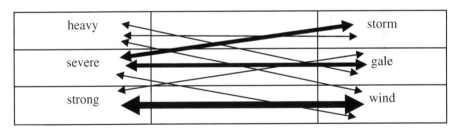

In a way, collocations of this type can be compared to institutionalized word formations. They are institutionalized in the sense that they are pre-fabricated items, "Halbfertigprodukte der Sprache" in Hausmann's (1984: 398) words, and not productively created on the spur of the moment. Up to a point, institutionalization in this case also entails limiting the choices available to a speaker at the formal level.[223] One important difference, however, is that in a collocation, as opposed to word formation, the semantic independence of the constituents is not affected, even if this criterion clearly admits for a considerable amount of gradience.[224]

10.4   Idioms

This transparency of meaning is also often taken to be the distinguishing criterion between collocations and idioms. An **idiom** can be defined as "a combination of two or more words which function as a unit of meaning" (Cowie and Mackin 1974: viii–ix) or as "a lexical complex which is semantically simplex" (Cruse 1986: 37).[225] As such, idioms are multi-word lexemes.[226]

Idioms can take different forms, for instance:

– noun phrases: *the wind of change, bad blood, a nervous wreck*

– predicates: *have a frog in one's throat, have second thoughts, pull strings, scream blue murder*

– sentences: *the early bird catches the worm, don't cry over spilt milk*

---

[223]   This type of collocation has, of course, received considerable attention in the fields of foreign language teaching and lexicography. See Cowie (1981), Hausmann (1984, 1985), Alexander (1992), Bahns (1996), Herbst (1996), Siepmann (2005, 2007, 2008) and Lea (2007).

[224]   Cf. Cruse (1986: 40): "The term **collocation** will be used to refer to sequences of lexical items which habitually co-occur, but which are nonetheless fully transparent in the sense that each lexical constituent is also a semantic constituent."

[225]   Cruse (1986: 37) criticizes definitions of idioms which characterize them as expressions "whose meanings cannot be inferred from its parts" and arrives at the following conclusion: "We shall require two things of an idiom: first, that it be lexically complex – i.e. it should consist of more than one lexical constituent; second, that it should be a single minimal semantic constituent."

[226]   It could be argued that idioms are word formations and should have been dealt with in Chapter 9.

– phrasal verbs (combinations of verb and adverbial particle): *look up,*
 come up with.

The area of idioms is subject to gradience in various respects. First of all,
idioms are lexically stable to various degrees. So *have a screw loose* is
paralleled by *got a screw loose* and *with a screw loose*, similarly one finds
get a good press as well as *get a bad press, get a fair deal* and *get a square*
deal etc. Secondly, idioms can be used in a shortened form, so, for instance,
the early bird catches the worm can be reduced to *early bird* etc. Thirdly,
the extent to which idioms allow syntactic modification also differs considerably, so *scratch one's head* can also be found in a sentence such as

(3)$_{QE}$ *This caused a bit of head-scratching at the BBC.*[227]

whereas passives

(4)   *?*Blue murder was screamed*

(5)   *?*The wood was not seen for the trees*

or correspondence to the general rule of concord are often subject to restrictions:[228]

(6)   **They all had frogs in their throats*

(7a)   **They cannot have their cakes and eat them too.*

(7b)$_{BNC}$ *As it stands the districts seem to be wanting their cake and eat it in that*
            they would like er a policy restricting development in the open country-
            side but they don't want it to come with baggage that is specific which
            says what the exceptions should be.

Furthermore, of course, different degrees of idiomaticity can be distinguished, as Cowie and Mackin (1974: x) also point out: "the boundary between highly idiomatic items and the rest is not sharply drawn but hazy and
imprecise. We shall do better to think in terms of a *scale* of idiomaticity".
This can be illustrated by looking at examples containing the particle *up*:

(8a)   *They pulled the flag up.*

(8b)   *They pulled the flag.*

---

[227] Example taken from the *Oxford Dictionary of Current Idiomatic English*
      (ODCIE), volume 2.
[228] Since idioms are often used in informal contexts, generalizations of this kind
      are difficult to make since jocular uses might easily occur. See also Götz
      (1976: 63–65).

(8c)   *The flag was up.*

(9a)   *They ate the cake up.*

(9b)   *They ate the cake.*

(9c)   **The cake was up.*

(10a)   *They gave up smoking.*

(10b)   **They gave smoking.*

(10c)   **Smoking was up.*

Pull up is a perfectly transparent combination of the verb *pull* and the particle *up*, which has no idiom status at all; in *eat up* the particle *up* does not have a locative, but a terminative meaning (in the sense 'bring to an end' as in *finish up*), whereas in *give up* neither the verb nor the particle contain the meanings they have in other contexts, so *give up* is best analysed as one unit of meaning.

10.5   The idiom principle and the mental lexicon

Whereas idioms, as has been pointed out in 10.4, clearly have lexeme status and thus have to be stored in the mental lexicon, the status of other prefabricated items such as collocations (in either interpretation of the term) is less clear. Corpus linguists like Sinclair and linguists concerned with foreign language teaching certainly emphasize the importance of these elements for the production of sentences. Psychologically, this raises the issue of how much weight ought to be given to rule-governed aspects and how much to rote-learned aspects in the sense of prefabricated items.[229]

Sinclair (1991: 109–110) contrasts the open-choice and the idiom principle in this context. Of the open-choice principle he says:

> This is a way of seeing language text as the result of a very large number of complex choices. At each point where a unit is completed (a word or a phrase or a clause), a large range of choices opens up and the only restraint is grammaticalness.
>
> This is probably the normal way of seeing and describing language. It is often called a 'slot-and-filler' model, envisaging texts as a series of slots which have to be filled from a lexicon which satisfies local restraints. At

---

[229] Compare the controversy between the lexicalist and transformationalist hypotheses in word formation (> 9.6).

each slot, virtually any word can occur. Since language is believed to operate simultaneously on several levels, there is a very complex pattern of choices in progress at any moment, but the underlying principle is simple enough.

Any segmental approach to description which deals with progressive choices is of this type. Any tree structure shows it clearly: the nodes on the tree are the choice points. Virtually all grammars are constructed on the open-choice principle.

This open-choice principle Sinclair (1991: 110) contrasts with the principle of idiom (which does not refer to idioms in the sense identified above but to idiomaticity):

> The principle of idiom is that a language user has available to him or her a large number of semi-preconstructed phrases that constitute single choices, even though they might appear to be analysable into segments. To some extent, this may reflect the recurrence of similar situations in human affairs; it may illustrate a natural tendency to economy of effort; or it may be motivated in part by the exigencies of real-time conversation. However it arises, it has been relegated to an inferior position in most current linguistics, because it does not fit the open-choice model.

One very obvious type of evidence emphasizing the importance of the idiom principle comes from advanced foreign language teaching, where a common comment of native speakers marking translations or essays is of the type "it is not wrong but it does not sound English". Experimental evidence confirms this: for instance, Greenbaum's sentence completion experiments described in 10.1 were repeated with German students of English. Whereas 82% of Greenbaum's native speaker subjects continued a sentence beginning *I entirely* using the verb *agree*, only 23% of the German students did so; in the case of *I badly need* the figures are 65% versus 11% (Herbst 1996: 390). The same point can be made on the basis of the study of learner corpora (> 3.3.2.2); Guilquin (2007: 286) found collocational errors such as the following in a corpus of French-speaking learners of English:

(11)$_{QE}$ *They wanted to make an end to these conflicts ... (mettre fin)*

(12)$_{QE}$ *Children are often unable to make the difference between fiction and reality (faire la différence).*

Detailed research of the valency structures of English verbs can be taken as another source of evidence in favour of the idiom principle. Thus Klotz (2000: 210) points out that there can be a correlation between the lexical realizations of a valency slot and the valency patterns in which the slot occurs. This often takes the form of tendencies such as *ride a bike* being more common than *ride on a bike.*[230]

If one takes these ideas to the extreme one could argue that the idiom principle as described by Sinclair should not only be taken to cover the use of prefabricated items such as idioms, institutionalized collocations or significant collocations, but that it might also comprise the idea that certain concepts are more likely to be formulated one way rather than another in a particular language. One indication of this is the fact that bilingual dictionaries very often give an equivalent for a word such as *zerquetschen* in the case of *grind* and then list certain 'phrases' or contexts in which another equivalent would be more appropriate:

> **grind** ... **❶** *v.t.* ... **◖C** (rub harshly) *zerquetschen*; **~ a cigarette end into the ground** einen Zigarettenstummel austreten[231]

Such equivalents, for which Herbst and Klotz (2003) introduce the term **probabemes**, are not necessarily identical with any of the phraseological units above but also contribute to the idiomatic character of language.[232]

10.6   Phraseological units

It can be said that the importance of multi-word units has been recognized not only by linguists working within the traditional discipline of phraseology, which put a strong focus on idioms, but also by corpus linguists, foreign language linguists and construction grammarians.[233] However, it is relatively difficult to identify classes of units that are relevant in this context since phraseological units are subject to gradience in several respects. In some cases, semantic transparency (or, rather, lack of semantic transparency) may be the defining criterion, others may be recognized as units on the basis of frequency, some can be seen as extremely fixed, while others

---

[230]   Compare also Klotz (2000: 220–230). For the correlation of patterns and nouns see also the collostructional approach developed by Stefanowitsch and Gries (2003).

[231]   *Duden Oxford Großwörterbuch Englisch* ²1999.

[232]   For a definition of probabemes and a discussion of *faintest* (or *foggiest*) *idea* and German *keine Ahnung* see Herbst and Klotz (2003: 145–146).

[233]   For the role of multi-word units in construction grammar see e.g. Fillmore, Kay, and O'Connor (1988) and Croft and Cruse (2004: 226–256) (> 13.2).

show a higher degree of variation.[234] Thus it is not surprising that many classifications should have been suggested in the literature. The following is a list of the categories (and examples) given by Granger and Paquot (2008: 43–44):

1. Categories of referential phrasemes:
– lexical collocations (in the sense of institutionalized collocations as described above): *heavy rain, closely linked, apologize profusely*
– idioms (*to spill the beans, to let the cat out of the bag, to bark up the wrong tree*)
– irreversible bi- and trinominals (*bed and breakfast, kith and kin, left, right and centre*)
– similes (*as old as the hills, to swear like a trooper*)
– compounds (*black hole, goldfish, blow-dry*)
– grammatical collocations (*depend on, cope with, a contribution to, afraid of, angry at, interested in*), to which other valency relations (such as *manage to_INF* etc) could be added[235]
– phrasal verbs (*blow up, make out, crop up*)

2. Categories of textual phrasemes
– complex prepositions (*with respect to, in addition to, apart from, irrespective of*)
– complex conjunctions (*so that, as if, even though, as soon as, given that*)
– linking adverbials (*in other words, last but not least, more accurately, what is more, to conclude*)

---

[234] Compare Handl (2008), who makes a distinction between a semantic, a lexical and a statistical dimension in the analysis of collocation. For a survey of approaches to phraseology see Gries (2008), Granger and Paquot (2008) and also Gläser (^{2}1990).

[235] Granger and Paquot (2008: 43) use the term grammatical collocations. Within a construction grammar approach, there is very little point in distinguishing between lexical expressions of valency patterns and more abstract categories such as infinitives or clauses so that a category valency patterns might seem more appropriate.

- textual sentence stems (*the final point is ..., another thing is ..., it will be shown that ..., I will discuss ...*)

3. Categories of communicative phrasemes

- speech act formulae (*good morning!, take care!, happy birthday!, you're welcome, how do you do?*)

- attitudinal formulae (*in fact, to be honest, it is clear that, I think that*)

- commonplaces (*Enough is enough, We only live once, It's a small world*)

- proverbs (*A bird in the hand is worth two in the bush, When in Rome*)

- slogans (*Make love, not war*).

Recommended further reading:

- Schmid (forthc.)
- Gries (2008), Granger and Paquot (2008)
- Sinclair (2004)

Sentences – models of grammar

11   Syntax: traditional grammar

11.1   Syntax and grammar

11.1.1   Descriptive frameworks

Syntax, the analysis of the structure of sentences, has been one of the main points of interest in the study of language since the ancient Greeks. As a result, we are faced with an enormous number of different approaches towards the description of sentences. The frameworks developed by the American structuralists during the first half of the twentieth century, the version of Chomsky's transformational grammar which dominated linguistics during the sixties and seventies, Chomsky's (1995) *Minimalist Program*, theories such as lexical functional grammar,[236] Hudson's (1984) word grammar, construction grammar (> 13.2) or dependency and valency theory (> 12.3), to name just a few, all propose different ideas for the description of sentence structure.

Alongside the development of such syntactic theories, there is also the very strong tradition of describing the "rules" of a particular language which is commonly associated with the word grammar. This is the kind of description usually found in the grammar books used at schools or that is referred to in statements about grammatical properties of words in dictionaries. Much of this framework has emerged from the analysis and the teaching of languages such as ancient Greek and Latin over the centuries. It is obvious (to linguists) that many of the categories established by traditional grammar – such as the well-known distinction between transitive and intransitive verbs, the terms gerund or future tense – really appear to be inappropriate for the description of present-day English or German (> 2.3). Nevertheless, one should be aware of the fact that up to this day traditional

---

[236]   Cf. Kaplan and Bresnan (1982). See also Sells (1985: 132–190).

grammar determines linguistic thought to a considerable degree: all the theories mentioned above identify word classes such as noun and verb or make use of a category subject and indeed most would use the term object. This is not to say, of course, that all representatives of these theories would have exactly the same concept of an object; quite the contrary.

While models of syntax such as the Minimalist Program or dependency theory, for which the term grammar is also sometimes used (in the sense of 'model'), are usually concerned with principles of syntactic organization in general, grammars in the more traditional sense aim at a more or less comprehensive description of a particular language.[237] Modern descriptive grammars of this kind can be seen as being firmly rooted in the tradition of grammar writing, while however incorporating insights, concepts and terminology of various approaches of modern linguistics and avoiding the inadequacies and pitfalls of traditional grammar.

The most important descriptive grammar of English at the beginning of the twenty-first century is probably the *Comprehensive Grammar of the English Language*, abbreviated as CGEL, which was published by Randolph Quirk, Sidney Greenbaum, Geoffrey Leech and Jan Svartvik in 1985. It is the largest and most detailed of a number of grammars by this team of researchers, who were all involved in the Survey of English Usage (> 3.3.1) and are sometimes referred to as the London School. A grammar of comparable size and complexity with contributions of thirteen authors was published in 2002 under the title of *Cambridge Grammar of the English Language* (CamG), edited by Rodney Huddleston and Geoffrey Pullum.

Since the London School has influenced linguistic research and the teaching of English all over the world, the terminology and the categories employed in CGEL will be outlined in this chapter.

11.1.2   Sentence and clause

Syntax is concerned with the way in which words combine to form larger units such as sentences. Although texts or utterances often consist of more

---

[237] For a highly interesting discussion of different uses of the term *grammar* see Greenbaum (1988: 20–26), who distinguishes senses such as: (i) "a general theory of language description", (ii) "a theory for describing one language", (iii) "a book about English grammar", (iv) "the contents of the books ('a grammar is a book about grammar')" etc.

than one sentence, it makes sense, for certain purposes of analysis at least, to consider the sentence the largest unit of description.[238] Basically, all theories of syntax, i.e. traditional grammar, structuralist syntax, or generative approaches, although recognizing the fact that sentences can link with each other to form texts, treat the sentence as the basic unit of investigation. One reason that is often given to justify the sentence as the highest unit of analysis is that the formation of sentences is rule-governed in a way that the formation of texts is not (> 18).

However, the situation with the term sentence is not unlike that with the term word described in 9.1 in that sentence is a linguistic term used in everyday language but linguists do not necessarily find it easy to define. While in the written language sentences are divided by full stops, the notion of sentence is very difficult to define when we consider spoken language (cf. CGEL 2.11), as can be seen from the following extract from a corpus of spoken language:[239]

(1)_{QE} *Well I had some people to lunch on Sunday and – they turned up half an hour early – ... – I mean you know what [g] getting up Sunday's like anyway and – I'd – I was behind in any case – and I'd said to them one o'clock – and I almost phoned them up and said come a bit later – and then I thought oh they've probably left by now – so I didn't – and – twelve thirty – now that can't be them – and it was – ....*

As will become clear in this chapter, sentences can be described as consisting of clauses and phrases: if we proceed from top to bottom, a hierarchy of the following kind can be established:

$$\text{sentence} \supseteq \text{clause / phrase} \supseteq \text{word} \supseteq \text{morpheme}$$

This means: a sentence can consist of one or more clauses, a clause can consist of one or more phrases, a phrase can consist of one or more words, and a word can consist of one or more morphemes.

As is pointed out by Quirk, Greenbaum, Leech and Svartvik (CGEL 2.11), the clause is a much more clearly definable unit of linguistic analysis than the sentence. A **clause** can occur as

▷ a **dependent** (or **subordinate**) **clause** if it forms a constituent of a larger clause as in

(2)_{PW} *Barbara Hepworth had also begun <u>to work in metal</u>.*

---

[238]   For problems connected with the definition of sentence see CGEL 2.11.
[239]   Cf. Leech and Svartvik (²1994: 11).

▷ an **independent clause** if it is not a constituent of a larger clause as in

(3)PH   *We shall now watch New York as eagerly as Paris for new develop-*
         ments.

The term **sentence** will be used

▷ for a single independent clause that is not co-ordinated with another clause as in (3).

▷ for a combination of two or more independent clauses in co-ordination as in

(4)PH   *It was an October night and a full moon was rising over Godrevy.*

11.1.3   Subject and predicate

When it comes to analysing clauses, the most immediate distinction that can be made is that between **subject** and **predicate**. In a way, one can consider those two elements as essential parts of an active declarative clause such as

(2)PW   *Barbara Hepworth had also begun to work in metal.*

The distinction between subject and predicate was already established in traditional grammar. However, it is also perfectly in line with structuralist principles: firstly, *Barbara Hepworth* and *had also begun to work in metal* represent the **immediate constituents** of the clause, i.e. if asked to divide the clause into two parts one would draw the boundary between *Hepworth* and *had* and not anywhere else:[240]

         Barbara Hepworth | *had also begun to work in metal*

not: *Barbara* | *Hepworth had also begun to work in metal*

not: *Barbara Hepworth had* | *also begun to work in metal*

not: *Barbara Hepworth had also* | *begun to work in metal*

etc.

Secondly, from a purely formal point of view, i.e. disregarding aspects of meaning, both *Barbara Hepworth* and *had also begun to work in metal* can be exchanged for other elements (with which they stand in the relation of

---

[240]   See Matthews (1981: 73–74). See also Hockett (1958).

commutation) without affecting the acceptability of the sentence. Structurally, (2) can be reduced to

(2a)   *She* | *worked.*

or expanded to

(2b)   *Barbara Hepworth, whose former studio in St. Ives is now open to the public,* | *had also begun to work in metal.*

In a way, the distinction between subject and predicate reflects the fact that subject and predicate represent the structural minimum of active declarative clauses, and, indeed, many other types of clause in languages such as English or German.

Of course, the analysis is not always as straightforward as in the case of (2). For instance, a sentence such as

(5)$_{PW}$ *At this time Ben Nicholson and Barbara Hepworth identified completely with the European avantgarde.*

does not lend itself so easily to a division into two parts: one would obviously hesitate to take *at this time* as a part of the subject since *At this time Ben Nicholson and Barbara Hepworth* do not commute with any other single element. At the same time, for positional reasons alone it would not be particularly satisfactory to regard it as a part of the predicate. Thus, one might find it preferable to separate (5) into three parts:

> *At this time* | *Ben Nicholson and Barbara Hepworth* | *identified completely with the European avantgarde.*

Unfortunately, there is no general agreement about the use of the term predicate in linguistics: while Robins (^{2}1971: 240) says that "predicate may be used to refer to the rest of the sentence apart from the subject", Lyons (1968: 334) takes a narrower view of the predicate and arrives at a threefold distinction of the parts of the sentence:[241]

> It is a fundamental principle of traditional grammar, and also of much modern syntactic theory, that every simple, declarative sentence consists of two

---

[241]   Note that this definition is in line with the use of the term predicate in CGEL (2.47), where *buys her vegetables in the market* and *arrived late today* are given as examples of predicates. However, Matthews (1981: 97–99) identifies three types of predicate: those consisting of a verb and an object, those consisting of a copula and a predicative, and those consisting merely of an intransitive verb.

obligatory major constituents, a *subject* and a *predicate*; and that it may contain, in addition, one or more *adjuncts*. Adjuncts (of place, time, manner, reason, etc. ...) are optional, or structurally dispensable, constituents of the sentence: they may be removed without affecting the remainder of the sentence.

A distinction between what Lyons (1968: 334) calls the "nucleus" of the sentence, the part of the sentence that consists of subject and predicate, and the extranuclear part or parts made up of adjuncts, seems more useful for many purposes of analysis. This approach to the analysis of clauses is taken by Aarts and Aarts (1982/²1988) and in certain versions of valency theory.[242] Within this terminology, the following elements of a clause can be identified:[243]

Subject: a clause constituent

▷ which is obligatory in an active declarative clause

▷ which is realized by a noun phrase (> 11.3.1) or can be replaced by a noun phrase

▷ which shows **concord** (i.e. the same value with respect to singular or plural) with the verb of the predicate.

Predicate: a clause constituent

▷ which is obligatory in an active declarative clause

▷ contains a verb (and possibly further elements) with the verb showing concord (i.e. the same value with respect to singular or plural) with the subject.

Adjunct: a clause constituent which is optional from a structural point of view.

Within this framework, which will be expanded below, the following clause constituents can be identified for sentences (6), (2), and (7):

---

[242] Cf. Herbst et al. (2004) and 12.3.

[243] Note that these definitions are to some extent prototypical in character, see Herbst and Schüller (2008: 4–9 and 18–21). For a more precise characterization of adjuncts see 11.2.2 and 12.3.2.

(6)_{PH}	*We*	*were*	*actually*	*in St. Ives*	*when I painted them*
	SUBJECT	PREDICATE →⎸	ADJUNCT 1	PREDICATE ⎸←	ADJUNCT 2

(2)_{PW}	*Barbara Hepworth*	*had*	*also*	*begun to work in metal*
	SUBJECT	PREDICATE →⎸	ADJUNCT	⎸← PREDICATE

(7)_{TS}	*Following Ben Nicholson's first visit to St. Ives*	*he*	*painted a number of land-scapes and sea paintings of Porthmeor beach.*
	ADJUNCT	SUBJECT	PREDICATE

11.2   The elements of clause structure in CGEL

11.2.1   Elements of clause structure as functional units

Despite the advantages of an analysis of clauses in terms of subject, predi-cate and adjuncts as outlined above, CGEL employs a slightly different framework. In this grammar, clauses are analysed in terms of the following five elements of clause structure:

▷ subject

▷ verb (which here is a functional term not identical with the word class verb)

▷ object: direct object and indirect object

▷ complement: subject complement and object complement

▷ adverbial

Since, with the exception of the subject, these elements of clause structure can be used to further analyse the predicate into smaller constituents, for example, the two approaches are highly compatible.

What is important to realize about these elements of clause structure is that they are functional categories. This can easily be demonstrated by showing that the same formal element – such as *colour* in

(8a)_{PH}   *<u>Colour</u> exists in itself, has its own beauty.*

and

(8b)_{PH}   *I used <u>colour</u> as a means of expressing my emotion and not as a transcription of nature.*

can fulfil different functions in different clauses (such as that of subject in (8a) and object in (8b)). Looking at the word *colour* in isolation (i.e. taken out of context) it could not be attributed any function, whereas its formal properties such as that it is a noun consisting of six letters can be determined irrespective of any particular occurrence.

11.2.2   Criteria for the distinction between different elements of clause structure

Whereas in a language such as German case plays a very important role in determining the elements of clause structure, this is a very problematic criterion for a language such as modern English, where most inflexional endings have vanished. This is why other criteria have to be used for distinguishing between different elements of clause structure, as is outlined in detail by Quirk, Greenbaum, Leech and Svartvik (CGEL 10.6).

CGEL, in each case, draws upon criteria from different levels of linguistic analysis. In the case of the **subject**, these are, for instance:[244]

▷ morphological in that pronouns functioning as subjects take subjective case (*he, she, they* etc.)

▷ positional in that subjects normally precede the verb

▷ semantic in that subject status often coincides with a semantic role such as AGENTIVE

In contrast, **objects** and **complements** (called **predicatives** in CamG 2002: 251–253) usually follow the verb and, if realized by pronouns, take

---

[244]   See CamG (2002: 236–239).

objective case (*him, her, them* etc.).[245] The distinction between objects and complements is made on the basis of two main criteria:

▷ objects can become the subjects of passive clauses, complements cannot

▷ complements refer in some way to the subject or object of the clause (hence the distinction between **subject complements** and **object complements**), objects do not.

Thus, *one of the leading artists of his generation* in (9a) refers to the subject of the clause, *Patrick Heron*, and thus is a subject complement.

(9a)_{PH}   *Patrick Heron is <u>one of the leading artists of his generation</u>.*

It cannot become the subject of a passive clause such as

(9b)   **One of the leading artists of his generation was been by Patrick Heron.*

This is different in the case of an object such as *a number of landscapes and sea paintings of Porthmeor beach* in

(7a)_{TS}   *Following Ben Nicholson's first visit to St. Ives, he painted <u>a number of landscapes and sea paintings of Porthmeor beach</u>.*

where a passive is possible:

(7b)_{PH}   *They are painted in a variety of methods.*

Furthermore, complements can also be realized by adjectives, whereas objects cannot:

(10)_{PH}   *That period at St Ives was <u>idyllic</u>.*

The two criteria distinguishing objects and complements can also be illustrated by looking at a sentence such as (11), which contains an object (*him*) and an object complement (*the best art critic to have emerged in London since Roger Fry*):

(11a)_{PH}   *I considered <u>him</u> then <u>the best art critic to have emerged in London since Roger Fry</u>.*

Only the object can be made a subject in a passive clause such as

(11b)   *He was considered the best art critic to have emerged in London since Roger Fry,*

---

[245]   In CamG (2002: 455–456) the traditional terms nominative and accusative are used for forms such as *I* and *me*.

but only the object complement can be replaced by an adjective:

(11c)   *I considered him excellent.*

If two objects occur, the first is the **indirect object**, the second the **direct object**. Both are also characterized semantically in CGEL (10.7). Direct objects are described as typically referring to an 'entity that is affected by the action denoted in the clause', whereas indirect objects are characterized as realizing 'an animate being that is the recipient of the action'.

(12)$_{PH}$ *Mrs. van der Straeten has written me (indirect object) a very nice letter ... (direct object).*

Finally, **adverbials**, which in CGEL (2.15) are described as "a heterogeneous category", are defined by a number of criteria, such as a tendency towards general mobility within the sentence, a tendency to provide information about temporal, spatial or other circumstances etc.:

(13)$_{PH}$ *A full moon was rising over Godrevy.*

(14)$_{PH}$ *I shall never forget the immense sensation of space the first moment we entered that room, at the end of our journey from London.*

(15)$_{PH}$ *Also established at the time I painted it was my habit of applying one coat of colour over the white ground.*

(16)$_{PH}$ *Ben Nicholson and Barbara Hepworth had been living in Carbis Bay, a little to the East of the town ...*

It is important to understand that the classification provided by CGEL is very much in line with the categories and also the principles of traditional grammar. In particular, one should note that the distinctions are not made on the basis of a single level of linguistic analysis but that both formal and semantic criteria are being used. As a result, the categories established must be seen as exemplifying prototypes and not as clear-cut entities separated by rigorous boundaries. Thus, for instance, *a long tradition as an artists' community* in

(17)$_{PW}$ *By 1918 St Ives had a long tradition as an artists' community*

would be analysed as an object according to CGEL, since, although the sentence cannot be passivized, the semantic relationship between *tradition* and *have* meets the description of an object and not that of a complement.[246]

---

[246]   For a very similar treatment see CamG (2002: 246). See also 11.2.4.

11.2.3   CGEL's clause types

Quirk, Greenbaum, Leech and Svartvik (CGEL 2.16) draw upon the elements of clause structure identified in order to establish seven clause types in English.[247]

clause type		verb class (CGEL)	valency (> 12.3)
SV	*She is reading*	intransitive	1
SVC	*This is an island*	copula	2
SVA	*She was there*	copula	2
SVO	*She is reading a book*	monotransitive	2
SVOO	*He gave her the book*	ditransitive	3
SVOC	*She called him a fool*	complex transitive	3
SVOA	*She put the book on the table*	complex transitive	3

These clause types are then taken as the basis for classifying verbs as

▷ intransitive

▷ transitive   ▷ monotransitive
                    ▷ ditransitive
                    ▷ complex transitive or

▷ copular.

This classification is based on a traditional and well-established distinction: the term transitive indicates that a verb takes an object. It is subclassified here into three different types of transitivity, depending on whether it occurs in an SVO, a SVOO or an SVOA structure.[248]

---

[247]   See CamG (2002: 218–219) for the distinction between intransitive, complex intransitive, monotransitive, ditransitive and complex (mono)transitive and their relation to valency.

[248]   It is worth noting, however, that the distinction between the seven clause types results in a classification of only five types of verb, since copular verbs represent clause types SVA and SVC and complex transitive verbs represent types SVOC and SVOA respectively.

It is important to note that Quirk, Greenbaum, Leech and Svartvik (CGEL 2.16) only subsume a clause containing an adverbial under the SVA or SVOA type if that adverbial is obligatory. As a consequence,

(13)_{PH}   *A full moon was rising over Godrevy*

belongs to clause type SV since the adverbial is optional, whereas

(16)_{PH}   *Ben Nicholson and Barbara Hepworth had been living in Carbis Bay, a little to the East of the town*

is an example of SVA since the adverbial cannot be left out (at least not without changing the meaning of the verb).[249]

11.2.4   Problems of traditional terminology

Categories such as object or subject complement or transitive and intransitive verb are widely used in traditional grammar, lexicography and also more recent theories. Nevertheless, it should be pointed out that these categories are by no means unproblematic because their use varies considerably. For instance, Aarts and Aarts (1988: 131–132, 138) take passivization as a defining criterion of the category direct object, which, however, contradicts the use of the term in CGEL (16.26–27), where

(18)_{QE}   *They have a nice house.*

is given as an example of a "monotransitive verb" with "a noun phrase as direct object" although it does not "normally" have a passive.[250] The difficulty of applying the term object to such cases arises from the fact that in CGEL these categories are defined by formal and semantic criteria (> 11.2.2), which do not always coincide.

A further example of this is presented by sentences such as

(19)_{BNC}   *He's in a good mood.*

---

[249]   Making this distinction between obligatory and optional adverbials introduces a distinction which has the same effect as that between predicate and adjuncts established in 11.1.3. What is referred to as an optional adverbial in CGEL is classified as an adjunct if one wishes to make the predicate-adjunct distinction, whereas CGEL's obligatory adverbials are part of the predicate.

[250]   For a discussion of so-called middle verbs such as *have, possess, resemble* see also CGEL 10.14. See also 11.2.2.

Semantically, *in a good mood* meets the description of subject complements given in CGEL (10.8), but it hardly fits the formal characteristics
listed there: "normally a noun phrase or an adjective phrase, but it may also
be a nominal clause".[251] It is for this reason that some approaches avoid the
use of terms such as object (cf. Halliday 1994: 26, Herbst and Schüller
2008) and replace them by terminology which keeps the levels of form and
meaning more strictly apart (> 12.4).[252]

11.3   Phrases

11.3.1   Types of phrase

The next question to address is which formal elements of a sentence can
actually function as an element of clause structure, i.e. occur as subjects,
objects, etc. In the terminology employed in traditional approaches such as
CGEL, this can either be another clause, as in:

(20)_{PW}   *Peter Lanyon felt strongly that figuration and abstraction were not
incompatible* [that-clause as direct object]

(21)_{PW}   *When he moved to St Ives* [wh-clause as adverbial]*, Nicholson acquired
one of the large Porthmeor studios.*

(22)_{PW}   *Still living in Carbis Bay* [-ing-clause functioning as adverbial] *... for a
time Barbara Hepworth came each day to the studio by taxi, and then
she started to live there during the week* [infinitive clause as direct ob-
ject]

or a unit generally identified as a phrase:

(23)_{PW}   *The town of St Ives* [noun phrase] *stands* [verb phrase] *on the Atlantic
coast of the Penwith district of west Cornwall* [prepositional phrase]

(24)_{AE}   *During the summer* [prepositional phrase as adverbial] *St. Ives* [noun
phrase as subject] *has attracted* [verb phrase as verb] *many visitors*
[noun phrase as direct object]

---

[251]   Compare, however, CGEL (10.11)'s discussion of "prepositional phrases
[that] are semantically similar to adjective or noun phrases functioning as
complement" and of cases such as *They are in love* as subject complements.
[252]   Compare also the classification proposed by Meyer (2009).

A **phrase** is characterized by the fact that it can take a particular slot in the structure of a sentence. Most types of phrase, the so-called endocentric phrases, can be realized by a single word, which on its own can fulfil the same syntactic function in a sentence:

(25a)	*Painters*	
(25b)	*Many painters*	*felt attracted to the place*
(25c)	*The painters who moved to St Ives after the war*	

A word which can stand for a phrase on its own is called its **head**, endocentric phrases are also called **headed phrases**. Such headed phrases can contain a number of other elements, which are structurally dependent on the head, and which are known as **modifiers**.

For English, the following types of phrase are often identified, the first four are headed, the fifth type is non-headed (or exocentric).[253]

1. Noun phrases

determi-native	premodifier	head: noun or pronoun	postmodifier
the		*town*	*of St Ives*
many	*very interesting*	*paintings*	*showing St Ives Bay*
a	*spectacular*	*view*	*over the bay*
the		*one*	*that I mean*
		St Ives	*which is an artists' community*
		they	
this	*fascinating*	*book*	*on linguistics*

---

[253] It should be noted that the account of phrase structure terminology employed here is not always generally accepted. Within a dependency framework, for instance, it is more convincing to see the relations holding between the elements making up a phrase as dependency relations. Also, the distinction between headed and non-headed phrases is by no means uncontroversial. See, for instance, Hudson (1993) and 12.4.2.1.

The head of a noun phrase is a noun or a pronoun. It can be modified by adjective phrases, prepositional phrases, relative clauses, adverb phrases, etc. Apart from modifiers, noun phrases can also contain **determinatives** (for which the term determiner is also often used). Although there is a certain overlap between modification and determination, the typical function of modifiers is to further describe what is expressed by the head, whereas the sole function of determiners is to establish reference, i.e. to identify the elements in the real world to which the phrase can be applied. Thus, in the case of a phrase such as *this fascinating book on linguistics*, the function of *this* can be seen as pointing out or identifying which of all the possible books is referred to in a particular context; *this* thus fulfils a determinative function, whereas *fascinating* and *on linguistics* describe the book more closely and are thus classified as modifiers.

2. Verb phrases

The term verb phrase is used in different ways in linguistics (sometimes to refer to the whole predicate). In the more traditional approach of CGEL, for instance, what is meant by verb phrase is the complex of a verb and the auxiliary verbs that are used to express such grammatical categories as aspect (simple/progressive; non-perfective/perfective), modality (possibility, obligation, etc.) or voice (active/passive). In CGEL, the terms **main verb** and **auxiliary verb** are used to describe the functions of head and premodifier in the case of the verb phrase:

auxiliary verbs	main verb
	paints
is	*painting*
has been	*painted*
may have been	*painted*

3. Adjective phrases

premodifier	head: adjective	postmodifier
	beautiful	
very	*nice*	
	friendly	*to him*
too	*far*	*to walk*

In some cases, as in *too far to walk*, pre- and postmodifier have to be seen as one complex modifier, which can then be called a discontinuous modifier (Aarts and Aarts [2]1988: 63).

4. Adverb phrases

premodifier	head: adverb	postmodifier
	beautifully	*indeed*
very	*well*	
much more	*slowly*	*than they had expected*

5. Prepositional phrases

Prepositional phrases consist of a preposition and a prepositional complement. Both these elements are obligatory in the sense that neither can represent a prepositional phrase on its own. Prepositional phrases are thus non-headed.

preposition	prepositional complement
to	*the island*
on	*going there*

Except for the rather special use of the term verb phrase, these categories outlined above or similar categories are fairly established in linguistics, although a number of alternative views have also been suggested (> 12.4.2).

11.3.2   The role of the phrase

While categories such as sentence or word also play an important role in general and non-academic discussions of language, the phrase does not. Nevertheless, the phrase is to be seen as a central unit of linguistic description. In particular, it must be borne in mind that it is through noun phrases – and not through nouns as words – that speakers can refer to concrete people or objects of the real world (> 14.2). A word such as *book* in itself evokes a certain idea about the kind of object a speaker is talking about in the hearer's mind, but it does not enable them to identify a concrete object in the particular situation of communication. This is quite clearly different in the case of a noun phrase such as *this book*, which in the present context enables you to identify the object referred to as the one you are just reading. Thus the notion of the phrase is highly relevant to syntactic and semantic analysis.

There is also psycholinguistic evidence to suggest that phrases are an important unit of language perception, for instance. Experiments were carried out in which people were asked to listen to recorded sentences, into which distorting signals called clicks were inserted. The test subjects were then asked to locate the clicks in the sentence.[254] Interestingly, subjects were able to identify the location of all clicks at phrase boundaries correctly, while there was a tendency to move the location of clicks within a phrase towards a phrase boundary.

11.4   Word classes

11.4.1   Criteria for the establishment of word classes

If one aims at describing the way words combine to form sentences it is desirable to be able to make generalizations. Thus, little is gained by saying that a word such as *the* can be followed by the word *professor* or the word *book* or the word *scheme* or the word *island* etc. It seems more satisfactory to state that a word such as *the* can be followed by words belonging to a particular class, namely nouns.

Such labels also play a major role in language teaching and in dictionaries: if, for example, a word such as *flight attendant* is classified as a noun, this can be taken as a shortcut for listing a number of properties such as the

---

[254]   See Clark and Clark (1977: 53–55) and Wimmer and Perner (1979: 126).

fact that it can be preceded (a) by words such as *the* or (b) by an adjective
and (c) that it can take a plural form:

(26a)   *the flight attendant*

(26b)   *a friendly flight attendant*

(26c)   *flight attendants*

However, it is important to realize that some features commonly associated
with a particular word class do not apply to all members. Thus, for example, words such as *advice* or *psychiatry* are marked as uncountable nouns in
the *Longman Dictionary of Contemporary English* (LDOCE5) or the *Oxford Advanced Learners' Dictionary* (OALD7) to indicate that they do not
have plural forms. It is thus essential to know how a word class label is to
be interpreted in a particular framework: it can either mean – in a kind of
prototype approach – to indicate that a particular word shares more features
with other members of this class than with members of any other class, or it
can mean that the word has all the features listed for this particular class.

In the history of linguistics, different types of criteria have been used for
the establishment of different word classes. Semantic criteria, which were
often used in traditional approaches, have turned out not to be particularly
suitable.[255] If one tries to distinguish between nouns and verbs, for instance,
by saying that nouns refer to 'persons, things or ideas' and verbs denote
'actions', one is immediately faced with problem cases such as nouns denoting actions such as *arrival, birth, development* or verbs not denoting
actions such as *be, belong, resemble*.[256] It is obvious that even a modifica-

---

[255]   Cf. CGEL (2.43), Palmer (1971), Huddleston (1984). For problems of the
         traditional classification of word classes see Robins (1971: 218–219). Com-
         pare Herbst and Schüller (2008: 30–36). Compare also Behrens (2005: esp.
         182–183), also with respect to the role of word classes in cognitive linguis-
         tics.

[256]   Cf. Allerton (1990: 89): "... the noun *hesitation*, the verb *hesitate* and the
         adjective *hesitant* show clearly that different word classes can be endowed
         with the same basic meaning; and yet in traditional grammar we are given
         mainly semantic definitions of the 'parts of speech' (= Latin 'partes ora-
         tionis', as word classes are usually termed). This is mainly due to the influ-
         ence of the Roman grammarians Palaemon and Priscian, who (unlike their
         more enlightened predecessor Varro) not only insisted on finding eight word
         classes, just because Greek had eight ... but also defined their classes on a
         purely semantic basis. This is unfortunate, because, for instance, although
         verbs, e.g. *hesitate*, are meant to be the words that designate an activity,

tion of the semantic descriptions provided for nouns or verbs will not solve the problem but only result in different borderline cases.

It thus seems reasonable to draw the distinction between different word classes on formal criteria such as the distribution of words or their morphological properties. In the case of present-day English, morphological criteria are less useful in that respect than in the case of inflected languages such as Latin, Russian, Old English or even German. Nevertheless, the criterion of which kinds of endings particular words take can be usefully applied in present-day English to the definition of verbs, nouns, and also adjectives.[257] It is interesting to see that different models tend to agree with respect to the identification of these three classes, whereas there are remarkable differences as far as number and character of the other word classes are concerned.

---

nouns like *hesitation* do so just as much, and even if the adjective *hesitant* does, as required, denote a quality, the derived noun *hesitancy* does so equally. It is true that prototypical nouns (such as *author, town, word*) designate a person, place or thing (or more generally an 'entity'), that verbs (like *abscond, write* and *sit*) designate an event, process or state, and that most adjectives denote qualities. The difficulty is with the large number of abstract nouns, verbs and adjectives." Cf. also Robins (1966/2000) and Pullum (2009).

[257] Interestingly enough, in attempts at automatic classification of words with respect to their word classes in computational linguistics, the morphological criterion can be extended to cover certain orthographic regularities. Thus, Garside (1987: 37), describing the probabilistic approach to parsing developed at the University of Lancaster, describes as one factor relevant to machine-based classification of word classes the so-called suffixlist: "The suffixlist contains sequences of up to five letters, including 'suffixes' in the ordinary sense, such as -*ness* (noun), but also any word endings which are associated invariably (or at least with high frequency) with certain word classes, for example -*mp* (noun or verb) – the letters -*mp* do not constitute a morphological suffix but it is a fact that almost all words ending with these letters are either nouns or verbs (the few exceptions such as *damp* or *limp* are listed in the lexicon). The suffixlist is searched for the longest matching word-ending. Thus there are entries in the list for -*able* (adjective), -*ble* (noun or verb), and -*le* (noun), and these will be tested for in that order; exceptions (such as cable or enable) are in the lexicon."

11.4.2   CGEL's word classes

One established model of word class categorization is that of the *Comprehensive Grammar of the English Language* by Quirk, Greenbaum, Leech and Svartvik (1985: 2.34), where the following word classes – or parts of speech – are distinguished:[258]

I	NOUN	*John, room, answer, play* (> 11.4.1)
II	ADJECTIVE	*happy, steady, new, large, round* (> 11.4.4)
III	FULL VERB	*search, grow, play* (> 11.4.3)
IV	ADVERB	*steadily, completely, really*
V	PREPOSITION	*of, at, in, without, in spite of* (> 11.4.7)
VI	PRONOUN	*he, they, anybody, one, which* (> 11.4.6)
VII	DETERMINER	*the, a, that, every, some* (> 11.4.6.)
VIII	CONJUNCTION	*and, that, when, although* (> 11.4.7)
IX	MODAL VERB	*can, must, will, would* (>11.4.3)
X	PRIMARY VERB	*be, have, do* (> 11.4.3)
XI	NUMERAL	*one, two, three; first, second, third*
XII	INTERJECTION	*oh, ah, ugh, phew*
words of unique function		*not* (negative particle), *to* (infinitive marker)

The first four of these word classes – nouns, full verbs, adjectives and adverbs – are often referred to as **open classes** because the number of words they comprise is not restricted and new members can constantly be added. The number of prepositions, pronouns, determiners, conjunctions, modal and primary verbs, however, is limited and not easily subject to change. These word classes are thus called **closed classes**.[259]

---

[258]   Criteria for the definition of these word classes are discussed in the sections listed in the table. See also the relevant chapters in CGEL or CamG. For a detailed discussion of the properties of different word classes see Herbst and Schüller (2008: 30–75).

[259]   For the distinction between autosemantic and synsemantic words see Mair (2008: 73).

11.4.3   Verbs

Morphological criteria serve rather well to define a word class full verbs
(CGEL 1985) – or lexical verbs (CamG 2002; Herbst and Schüller 2008) –
in present-day English. A full verb or lexical verb can be characterized by
the following properties:

▷ It has a base form (*speak*) which can occur on its own (used in the infinitive and all present tense forms with the exception of the third person
singular).

▷ It has a specific form for third person singular present tense; marked by
the suffix {S} (*speaks*).

▷ It is tensed in that it is morphologically marked for present tense or past
tense and shows tense distinctions, i.e. it possesses a past tense form
(*spoke*).

▷ It can form a present participle with the morpheme {-ing} (*speaking*).

▷ It can form a past participle (*spoken*).

For some lexical verbs, some of these forms coincide: thus, in the case of
paint, the past tense form (*painted*) is identical with the past participle form
(*painted*); similarly, verbs such as *put* or *cut* do not show a contrast between the two tenses except in the third person singular.

The following forms can thus be identified for lexical verbs:[260]

base form	*paint, put, speak, write*	
{S}-form	*paints, puts, speaks, writes*	finite
past tense form	*painted, put, spoke, wrote*	finite
-*ing*-participle/present part.	*painting, putting, speaking, writing*	non-finite
-*ed*-participle/past participle	*painted, put, spoken, written*	non-finite

---

[260]   See Herbst and Schüller (2008: 39). For a discussion of finite and non-finite
see CamG (2002: 1173) and CGEL (1985: 3.52). The base form is often analysed as a finite form in declarative-'statement'-constructions such as *This
does not mean that they put themselves into the hands of an absolute author-
ity.*BNC and as non-finite when used in imperative-'directive'-constructions
such *as Put them in now, before autumn gales and winter blasts make the
plants rock at their roots.*BNC This is not entirely unproblematic since there is
no morphological difference between these forms. Compare also: *The arguments put forward can be interesting in themselves.*BNC

It seems appropriate to distinguish two further types of verb from the class of lexical (or full) verbs (CGEL 3.21), namely

▷ **modal verbs** (*can, may, shall, will, could, might, should, would* and *must*), which are characterized by the fact that they do not admit suffixation by {S} and do not have participle forms, and

▷ the **primary verbs** *be* (which, by the way, has eight different morphological forms), *do* and *have*, which can occur as auxiliaries or main verbs in the verb phrase.

11.4.4   Central and peripheral members of word classes – word classes as prototypes

It is important to realize that no single criterion seems to suffice to define a word class. Although the {ing}-suffix can be used for the characterization of verbs, this does not mean that any form containing –*ing* could or should necessarily be classified as a verb:

(27a)$_{BNC}$ *That bloody bird has been <u>annoying</u> me for days.*

(27b)$_{BNC}$ *And she knew she was <u>annoying</u> them whenever she questioned their assumptions.*

(27c)$_{BNC}$ *This was extremely <u>annoying</u>.*

(27d)$_{BNC}$ *The most <u>annoying</u> fact was that it could and should have been a masterpiece.*

In (27c) and (27d) *annoying* should be classified as an adjective rather than a verb because it occurs in positions that are typical of adjectives (such as *clever*):

(27e)$_{BNC}$ *Coleridge had developed an apparently relaxed, but in fact extremely clever style of blank verse.*

Adjectives can generally be characterized by the following four criteria:[261]

▷ attributive use (I)   *annoying questions, clever girl*

▷ predicative use (after *seem* etc.) (II)   *This was extremely annoying, this seems clever ...*

---

[261]   See Herbst and Schüller (2008: 58), CGEL (1985: 7.3) and CamG (2002: 526–542).

▷ premodification by adverbs such as   *extremely annoying, very clever*
   very (III)

▷ comparative and superlative forms (IV)   *darker, most annoying*

Again, it is important to point out that these four criteria do not apply to all adjectives alike, as can be seen from the following examples:

(28)   *an afraid person/state*

(29)   *The fool/failure seems utter*

(30)   *These two expressions are very synonymous*

(31)   *These two words are more homophonous than those two.*

CGEL (7.3) establishes a gradient of the following kind to illustrate this phenomenon:

	I	II	III	IV	
hungry	+	+	+	+	central adjectives
infinite	+	+	-	-	
old (as in *old friend*)	+	-	+	+	peripheral adjectives
afraid	?	+	+	+	
utter	+	-	-	-	
asleep	-	+	-	-	
soon	-	-	+	+	adverbs
abroad	-	-	-	-	

Adjectives that can occur in attributive and predicative position are considered central adjectives in CGEL; adjectives that occur only in one of these positions peripheral adjectives. In terms of prototype theory (> 16.4), one could say that the prototypical adjective shows all four criteria whereas more marginal members of the category do not have all these features. If a word does not meet all the criteria that characterize the prototypical members of that word class, it may be necessary to determine its word class with respect to the greatest similarity to any prototype it may show.

11.4.5   Multiple-class membership

In other cases, of course, it may also be convenient to attribute a word or, to be precise, a particular word form, dual or multiple class membership. Thus, there would be little controversy about the question that the form *painting* in

(32a)_{PH}   *… his paintings of the room and window at St Ives had been done from the experience of a sea-level interior in a town*

can be regarded as a noun, whereas in

(32b)_{PW}   *It came as a great shock, so much so that I actually stopped painting myself*

it can be considered a verb. In fact, it is quite common to assign dual word class membership to particular word forms:

(27a)_{BNC}	*That bloody bird has been annoying me for days.*	verb
(27b)_{BNC}	*This was extremely annoying.*	adjective
(33a)_{BNC}	*It was the car that annoyed her.*	verb
(33b)_{BNC}	*We are very annoyed.*	adjective
(8a)_{PH}	*Colour exists in itself, has its own beauty.*	noun
(8b)_{BNC}	*Brushes may also be used to colour larger areas such as the blue ribbon of this design.*	verb
(34a)_{BNC}	*Come in!*	adverb
(34b)_{BNC}	*the Barbara Hepworth Museum in St Ives*	preposition

A particularly interesting example of multiple class membership is presented by *round*, which can be analysed as belonging to no less than five word classes:

(35a)_{BNC}	*Would you like to come round for a cup of tea?*	adverb
(35b)_{BNC}	*It's just round the corner.*	preposition
(35c)_{BNC}	*They'd have their round hat boxes…*	adjective
(35d)_{BNC}	*He enjoyed a round of golf and playing cricket …*	noun
(35e)_{BNC}	*You round the Point to make your way south to Douglas — first on beaches, then on cliff and meadow paths.*	verb

11.4.6   The distinction between determiners and pronouns

How many word classes a word belongs to is not just a question of the properties of the word as such but also depends on how one analyses the word or the language in question. Thus, while it is probably relatively un-controversial that a word such as *interest* has two clearly distinct uses – one corresponding to a prototypical verb and one corresponding to a prototypi-cal noun – this is not quite so obvious with words such as *this, these, those, each* or *all*.

(36a)_{WG}   *<u>This</u> was followed in the 1960s by a series of paintings ...*

(37a)_{WG}   *<u>These</u> were necessary to ensure that there was no overlap where two colour-areas touched ...*

(38a)_{WG}   *It is impossible to discuss Heron's paintings, particularly <u>those</u> of the 1970s, without drawing on his own writings about them.*

(39a)_{WG}   *Each new period ... seemed to involve an abandonment of <u>all</u> that had gone before, so that <u>each</u> could be said to mark a true beginning again.*

In these uses, the words underlined fall under the category of pronoun, even in terms of the most traditional definition of a pronoun "substituting a noun". *This* in (36a), like *these* in (37a) and the second *each* in (39a), rep-resent a whole noun phrase, *those* in (38a) and *all* in (39a) function as heads of noun phrases. This is different with the following uses of the same words:

(36b)_{PW}   *The prehistoric standing stones of the Penwith peninsula were the cata-lyst for <u>this</u> transformation.*

(37b)_{PW}   *<u>These</u> years brought artistic success for Wood.*

(38b)_{WG}   *... Heron had always been irritated by <u>those</u> literal-minded critics who insisted in seeking references to the Cornish landscape (...) in the shapes and contours of his paintings.*

(39a)_{WG}   *<u>Each</u> new period ... seemed to involve an abandonment of all that had gone before, so that each could be said to mark a true beginning again.*

(39b)_{WG}   *<u>All</u> Heron's canvasses of the 1970s were painted using small, delicate Japanese watercolour brushes.*

(39c)_{WG}   *His work of <u>all</u> periods retains a remarkable freshness.*

Here, *this, these* etc. do not represent the heads of noun phrases (as defined above) but rather they have a determinative function within those noun phrases in the sense that it is *these* which determines the range of referents of the noun phrase *these years*. This function is identical to that of the words that in traditional grammar were called articles:

(36b)$_{PW}$ *The prehistoric standing stones of the Penwith peninsula were the cata-*
           lyst for this transformation.

Words such as *all, each* or *this* can thus function as heads of noun phrases, as in the first group of examples, or occur as determinatives within a noun phrase, as in the second group. There are two ways of dealing with this: either one takes the fact that these words can occur in different functions in a noun phrase as a property of the word classes under which these words were traditionally treated or one establishes a separate word class **determiner** and argues that when a word such as *these* occurs in a sentence such as (37a), it is a demonstrative pronoun, whereas in a use of the type exemplified by (37b), it is a determiner. Many modern grammars of English, amongst them CGEL, have opted for this second approach[262] and established determiners as a word class. Allerton (1990: 90) justifies this on the following grounds:

> In languages like English, it is worth distinguishing a class of 'determiners', embracing the articles and words such as *any* and its possible replacements ..., i.e. words such as *the, a, any, some, all, my, your, this, that*. The words *my, your*, etc. are traditionally called either pronouns or adjectives: but they differ from true pronouns like *mine, yours* (which stand for a whole noun phrase) in that they occur with a noun: equally they differ from adjectives ...

This means that most words which fall under the category of determiner actually have to be assigned dual class membership, as indicated above.[263]

The alternative option in terms of a classification of these words is not to assign multiple class membership to such words. Thus Aarts and Aarts (1982/1988: 51) classify *this, that, these* and *those* as demonstrative pronouns and say that they "function as constituents of the sentence or in the structure of the noun phrase". Herbst and Schüller (2008) go a step further and make a three-fold distinction between

---

[262]   Compare, however, the approach taken by Aarts and Aarts (^{2}1988), who use the term determiner to refer to the function within the noun phrase that CGEL calls determinative.

[263]   For a subclassification of determiners see, for instance: Leech and Svartvik (^{2}1994: 269).

▷ pure pronouns (which comprise all words which are classified as pronouns but not as determiners in CGEL, i.e. words such as *someone, everybody* or *you* that can function as the head of a noun phrase)

▷ pure determiners (which comprise the words *a, an, little, no,* which can only occur as determiners but not as pronouns) and

▷ determiner-pronouns (which like *this, that, each* show both uses).

11.4.7   The distinction between prepositions and subordinating conjunctions

The concept of multiple class membership is used in CGEL and many other models to account for the different uses of words such as *before* in examples of the following kind:

(40a)ₚₕ   *Several years before this Heron had adopted the practice of giving his paintings titles almost factually descriptive ...*

(40b)ₚw   *St Just is the last town in England before you reach Land's End.*

(40c)wₑ   *In 1967, two years before he embarked on this series, Heron broke a leg in an accident ...*

(40d)wₑ   *He was using a fuller palette of colours, too, with the introduction of paler tints ... that he had never before dared attempt.*

Traditionally, these three uses of the word *before* are analysed as representing three different word classes:

– in (40a) *before* is classified as a preposition because it is followed by a noun phrase,

– in (40b) and (40c) it is seen as a subordinating conjunction because it introduces a clause, and

– in (40d), in which it is neither followed by a noun phrase nor a clause, it is classified as an adverb.[264]

Again, the alternative is to simply see (40a–d) as different uses of one word and assign it to one word class. In fact, one can argue that the differences displayed by these examples find a direct parallel in verb complementation, where quite a large number of verbs show transitive and intransitive uses.

---

[264]   Note that *before* also allows premodification, e.g. by *two years* in (40c) and *never* in (40d).

For these reasons, CamG (2002: 612–617) subsumes all uses of words such as *since* and *before* under one word class label, namely that of prepositions. This means that most subordinating conjunctions and a number of words that have traditionally been categorized as adverbs are classified as prepositions in CamG.[265] Following a similar line of argument, Herbst and Schüller (2008) introduce a word class particle as a cover term for all words that traditionally are classified as prepositions or subordinating conjunctions as well as some adverbs.[266] Particles are seen as valency carriers (> 12.3.4) in this model so that the different uses exemplified by (40a–d) are described as valency properties of these particles.

11.4.8   Word classes in English

It follows from what was said above that there is no obvious and not only one answer to the question of how many word classes a language has and how they ought to be distinguished. This is caused in part by the prototypical nature of word classes, i.e. the fact that it is not always possible to draw clear dividing lines between different classes, but it also has to do with the fact that different analysts come to different conclusions as to what is to be considered the most appropriate way of analysing particular facts.

---

[265]   See CamG (2002: 600) for the parallels between *She was eating an apple. – She was eating.* and *I haven't seen her since the war. – I haven't seen her since.* For a discussion of this cf. also Pullum (2009).

[266]   Note that in this approach words such as *up* and *here* are excluded from the adverb category because they can function as valency complements (> 12.3.2) of verbs such as *be, place* or *put* if they cannot function as premodifiers of adjectives or adverbs (Herbst and Schüller 2008: 59). This is based on the approach taken in CamG (2002: 602, 612–617). See Herbst and Schüller (2008: 59–60) for a definition of adverbs in terms of criteria such as that they can function as premodifiers of adjectives (*very* interested), other adverbs (*however* slightly), that they can occur immediately before verbs (*I was just explaining* ...), etc. Furthermore, words derived from adjectives by {-ly} count as adverbs.

CGEL (1985)	CamG (2002)	Herbst and Schüller (2008)	
full verb	lexical verb	lexical verb	*write, say ...*
primary verb	auxiliary verb: non-modal	primary verb	*be, have, do*
modal verb	auxiliary verb: modal	modal verb	*can, could, may, might, shall, should, will, would, must*
noun	noun	lexical noun	*conference, idea, pancake ...*
determiner/ article	determinative/ article	determiner	*the, a*
determiner	determinative	determiner-pronoun	*every*
			some (as pre-head of NP)
pronoun	pronoun		*some* (as head of NP)
adjectives	adjectives	adjectives	*clever, intelligent, friendly, ...*
adverb	adverb	adverb	*furiously, very, well*
	pronoun	pronoun	*yesterday, today*
	preposition	particle	*here, somewhere*
			since
preposition			*since* + noun phrase
			since + finite clause
(subordinating) conjunction	subordinator		*that/whether* + finite clause
infinitive marker	infinitival subordinator		*to* + infinitive clause
(coordinating) conjunction	coordinator	(coordinating) conjunction	*and, but, or, nor*
interjection	interjection	interjection	*oh, ...*

It is important to remember that word classes provide useful labels for some purposes of linguistic description, but that they "tend in fact to be rather heterogeneous, if not problematic categories" (CGEL 2.41). In fact, it may be doubted whether the relevant aspects of the use of all words can be described appropriately by assigning them membership of a particular word class.

Nevertheless, word class labels are widely used in linguistic description. In many dictionaries, for instance, word classes are taken as one of the prime principles of structure because it is assumed that it speeds up the looking-up process considerably if the noun uses of a word such as *interest* are kept apart from the verb uses of *interest*, for example. Again, however, it is debatable whether this applies to all word class distinctions in the same way. It is interesting to see that with respect to words such as *each* or *this* the more recent editions of English learners' dictionaries such as *Longman Dictionary of Contemporary English* (LDOCE5) or the *Oxford Advanced Learner's Dictionary* (OALD7) tend not to make a systematic distinction between e.g. a pronoun *this* and a determiner *this* but simply give both word class labels without indicating which word class label applies to which example.[267]

This of course raises the question to what extent word classes represent concepts that are psychologically relevant. Garman (1990: 140) comes to the following tentative conclusion:[268]

> ... if word class turns out to be a determinant of lexical accessibility, it will be likely to prove a highly indirect one – a conclusion which in no way runs from the apparent fact that words like *a* are very different from those like *match*. One respect in which they are different is frequency of occurrence: is this likely to be a factor? ... If frequency of a word has anything to do with its accessibility, it may completely obscure the distinction between open and closed classes.

---

[267]   LDOCE5 gives "determiner, pron, adv" for *each* and distinguishes between *this*[1] ("determiner, pron") and *this*[2] (adverb). *This* is treated similarly in OALD7, where, however, *They lost 40 each* is subsumed under "*det, pron*".

[268]   For aspects of language acquisition see Behrens (1999) and (2005). Compare in this context Tomasello (2003: 45): "... virtually no one believes that adult part-of-speech categories are relevant to children just beginning to learn language". It would be interesting to see to what extent this is also true of some of the distinctions discussed in 11.4.6. and 11.4.7.

12   Valency theory and case grammar

12.1   Two types of hierarchy

12.1.1   Constituency

One way of analysing a sentence is to establish a hierarchy of elements that takes the complete sentence or clause as the highest element and finishes at the level of the word. For a sentence such as

(1)_{PW}   *By 1918 St Ives had a long tradition as an artists' community*

this kind of a hierarchy can be represented in the following form of a structural tree:

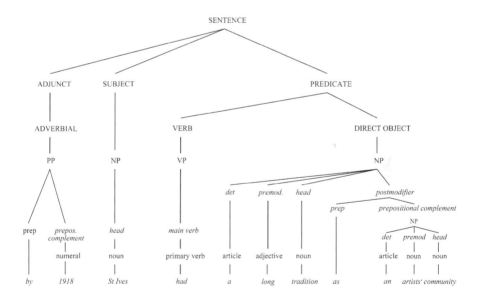

This kind of tree structure, which represents the analysis of a sentence into its constituents, represents a part-whole relationship. Grammars based on this kind of analysis are known as **phrase structure grammars** or **constituency grammars**. In various forms, mostly based on the principle of binary divisions, such phrase structure analyses are characteristic of American structuralism, but also of early phases of generative transformational grammar.[269] For instance, in *Syntactic Structures*, Chomsky (1957: 26) formulates a phrase structure grammar in terms of so-called rewrite rules:

(i)   *Sentence* → NP + VP

(ii)   NP → T + N

(iii) VP → *Verb* + NP

(iv) T → *the*

(v)   N → *man, ball*, etc.

(vi) *Verb* → *hit, took*, etc.

This can be seen as a description of the sentence

(2)$_\text{QE}$ *The man hit the ball*

which can also be represented in the form of a tree diagram:[270]

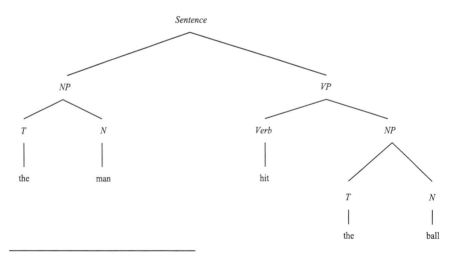

---

[269] For the principles of phrase structure trees cf. Matthews (1981: 73–78) and Vennemann (1977).

[270] Cf. Chomsky (1957: 27) and Allen and van Buren (1971: 24–25). For a discussion of the limitations of pure phrase structure grammars and their status

12.1.2   Dependency

The principle of constituency is not the only one that can be employed in the analysis of sentences, however. An alternative is to establish a hierarchy of elements that are at the same level of a constituency analysis by looking at the way in which they depend on one another.[271] Matthews (1981: 78) describes the principles underlying dependency theory by referring to the traditional notion of government:

> In the traditional language of grammarians, many constructions are described in terms of a subordination of one element to another. A verb is said to 'govern' its object ... A preposition is also said to govern the noun which follows.

This notion of government can perhaps more convincingly be demonstrated in languages where it manifests itself in terms of case marking. Thus, in the case of

(3)_{NF}   *Am 17. Mai 1797* **beschlossen** *die ostfriesischen Stände unter ihrem Vorsitzenden, dem Grafen Edzard Mauritz zu Inn- und Knyphausen, die Errichtung einer Seebadeanstalt auf Norderney.*[272]

one could argue that the object *die Errichtung einer Seebadeanstalt auf Norderney* is governed by the verb *beschließen* in that it determines its form, in this case requiring the object to be in the accusative case. A verb such as *zustimmen* would govern a dative, for example:

(3a)   *Am 17. Mai 1797* **stimmten** *die ostfriesischen Stände unter ihrem Vorsitzenden, dem Grafen Edzard Mauritz zu Inn- und Knyphausen, der Errichtung einer Seebadeanstalt auf Norderney zu.*

---

within early transformational models see Chomsky (1957). See also Lyons (³1991: 56–65).

[271]   Hudson (1976: 197) points out that the constituency approach is "typically American" and "underlies all the main American schools of syntactic theory (so-called immediate constituent analysis, transformational grammar, stratificational grammar and tagmemics) – and, also, incidentally, other versions of 'systemic' grammar", whereas the dependency approach is "typically European".

[272]   Translation: (3) *On the 17th of May 1797, the East Frisian estates, under the leadership of Count Edzard Mauritz zu Inn- und Knyphausen decided to establish a seaside spa on Norderney./* (3a) *... agreed to establishing ...*

In the same way one could see *ihrem Vorsitzenden* as governed by the preposition *unter*, which requires a dative. Despite the limited amount of case marking in present-day English, the notion of government is appropriate to describe whether a verb can be followed by a noun phrase, an *-ing*-clause or a *to*-infinitive-clause or to describe the relationship between nouns, adjectives and verbs and the prepositions which they allow for their complementation patterns:

(4)_PH   *This is the true **significance** of his **preference** for the earlier of the Rothkos in the ICA show.*

(5)_PH   *In spite of **misgivings** about his 'muted' colour, he now **seemed** to Heron to be 'the best of living Americans …'.*

Such "forms of subordination", as Matthews (1981: 79) points out, are often dealt with under the name of **dependency**, because this kind of analysis reveals how the elements of a sentence depend on one another.[273] The first main representative of a model of grammar based on dependency relations, **dependency grammar** or **dependency theory**, Lucien Tesnière (1959), introduced so-called stemmata to illustrate these relationships:[274]

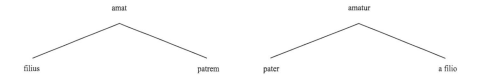

A dependency stemma is different from a phrase structure tree in that it does not represent a part-whole relationship and does not attribute the highest rank to the whole clause or sentence. Rather, it is the governing word that takes the highest place in the hierarchy. One important characteristic of many dependency approaches distinguishing them from a constituency type of analysis is that they do not attribute any special status to the subject. Since the verb is generally seen as the highest element of the sentence, the value of the traditional distinction of subject and predicate, which is also reflected in an immediate constituents analysis, is rejected, as, by the way,

---

[273]   For the relationship between *Rektion* and *Dependenz* see also Ágel (2000: 47–79).

[274]   Cf. Tesnière (1959/²2000: 526).

is the principle of binary division underlying the principles of immediate constituent analysis (> 11.1.3).[275]

There has been considerable discussion in linguistics as to whether constituency analysis and dependency analysis are to be seen as competing or complementary models of analysis. On the one hand, a dependency stemma is superior to a constituency tree because it reveals relationships between the elements of a clause which are not brought out at all in the constituency analysis. On the other hand, it must not be overlooked that a dependency analysis presupposes an analysis into constituents because it is precisely those constituents whose relationships with each other it describes. For this reason, many linguists today would argue that the two approaches complement rather than exclude each other.[276]

If one accepts the view that dependency relations hold between elements which belong to the same hierarchical level of a constituency analysis, the dependency relationships holding between the phrases of a sentence such as

(1)_PW   *By 1918 St Ives had a long tradition as an artists' community.*

could be represented as follows:

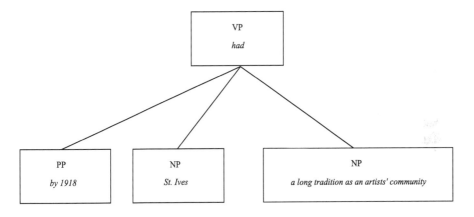

---

[275]   Cf., for instance, Tesnière (1959/²2000: 525–526).
[276]   Cf. Matthews (1981: 84–93), Herbst, Heath, and Dederding (1980: 44–45), Brinker (1977: 91), Vennemann (1977), Hudson (1976: 197–206), Baumgärtner (1970), Heringer (1970 and 1993).

12.1.3   Case grammar and valency theory

This chapter will deal with two approaches to syntax which combine elements of dependency and constituency and which attribute a central role to
the verb in the structure of the sentence – case grammar and valency theory. Whereas case grammar was originally formulated by Charles Fillmore
in a famous article called 'The case for case' (1968) in the general framework of generative linguistics, valency theory, which features very strongly
in the analysis of German, is strongly related to dependency theory and the
ideas of Tesnière (1959). Despite the different theoretical backgrounds of
the two theories there are many parallels between them: in fact, they deal
with the same aspect of linguistic structure from different perspectives in
that the main concern of case grammar is semantic, whereas the starting
point of (most approaches to) valency theory is formal. In a way, both theories can be related to Tesnière's (1959/2000: 522) comparison of the verbal
core to a play on the stage, where he makes a distinction between *verb,
actants* and *circonstants* – the verb corresponding to the action, *actants* to
the actors and *circonstants* to the circumstances.[277]

12.2   Case grammar: semantic roles

12.2.1   Basic principles of case grammar

The basic idea of case grammar as proposed by Fillmore (1968) can be
illustrated by considering sentences such as

(6a)$_{QE}$ *John opened the door.*

(6b)$_{QE}$ *John opened the door with the key.*

(6c)$_{QE}$ *The key opened the door.*

(6d)$_{QE}$ *The door opened.*

What is interesting about these sentences is that it can be argued that the
elements showing the same type of underlining make the same semantic
contribution to the overall meaning of the sentence irrespective of whether
they occur as the subject, the object or as a prepositional phrase. This has

---

[277]   For a discussion of different types of valency such as semantic or syntactic
         valency see Helbig (1992: 7–10).

led Fillmore (1968: 24) to establish a system of what he (misleadingly)[278] called case relationships:

> The case notions comprise a set of universal, presumably innate, concepts which identify certain types of judgments human beings are capable of making about the events that are going on around them, judgments about such matters as who did it, who it happened to, and what got changed.

In 'The Case for Case', Fillmore (1968: 24–25) identifies six such **cases**:

AGENTIVE (A)	the case of the typically animate perceived instigator of the action identified by the verb
INSTRUMENTAL (I)	the case of the inanimate force or object causally involved in the action or state identified by the verb
DATIVE (D)	the case of the animate being affected by the state or action identified by the verb
FACTITIVE (F)	the case of the object or being resulting from the action or state identified by the verb, or understood as a part of the meaning of the verb
LOCATIVE (L)	the case identifies the location or spatial orientation of the state or action identified by the verb
OBJECTIVE (O)	the semantically most neutral case, the case of anything representable by a noun whose role in the action or state identified by the verb is identified by the semantic interpretation of the verb itself; conceivably the concept should be limited to things which are affected by the action or state identified by the verb.

In (6ab), *John* could be described as realizing the semantic case of AGENT, *the door* that of OBJECTIVE and *the key* that of INSTRUMENT. A verb such as *open* can thus be characterized as having a case frame of the following kind (Fillmore 1968: 27):

+ [____ O (I)(A)]

This means that if only the OBJECTIVE case is realized, it becomes the subject, if the INSTRUMENTAL is also realized, it becomes the subject and if the AGENTIVE is realized, it becomes the subject of the clause.[279]

---

[278] The term case is usually used for morphological case such as nominative, accusative etc.

[279] Compare Fillmore's (1968: 33) rule for "'unmarked' subject choice".

12.2.2   Advantages and drawbacks of case grammar

Although case grammar was originally developed within the framework of Chomsky's generative transformational grammar (> 13.1), the idea of deep cases was adopted in many other models, for instance in valency theory (> 12.3 and 12.4), often under the more appropriate names of **semantic cases, semantic roles** or **participant roles** (as well as **theta roles/θ-roles** in generative work). This is not surprising since the model is rather attractive in a number of respects:

- Semantic roles provide a relatively satisfactory labelling system for the description of certain semantic properties of valency complements.

- The model is able to formally relate sentences such as (7a – 7d):

(7a)$_{BNC}$ *I (A) nearly broke a chair (O) with my hands (I) as I listened.*

(7b)$_{BNC}$ *If we (A) broke a window (O), it was accidental.*

(7c)$_{BNC}$ *One tankard hit the ceiling, another (I) broke a window (O).*

(7d)$_{BNC}$ *The window (O) broke because John threw a ball at it.*

- The model can account for restrictions in coordination of the type:

(6e)   **Mr Davey (A) and the key (I) opened the case.*

(7e)   **Mary Yellan (A) and the rock (I) broke the window.*

- The meanings of different verbs can be related:

(8a)   *He (A) showed them (D) Jamaica Inn (O).*

(8b)   *They (D) saw Jamaica Inn (O).*

On the other hand, the model also suffers from a number of problems. First of all, the correspondences outlined above cannot necessarily be generalized. Thus

(7f)$_{BNC}$ *... they were breaking the law and prepared to face the consequences.*

(7g)$_{BNC}$ *... these people broke the agreement ...*

are not paralleled by

(7h)   **The law broke.*

(7i)   **The agreement broke.*

Furthermore, not all restrictions on coordination can be explained by means of different semantic roles. Palmer (^{2}1981: 148) points out that

(9)$_{QE}$ **I saw Helen and a football match.*

"is a very strange sentence, yet both *Helen* and *a football match* are here in the object case." On the other hand, coordination of noun phrases representing different semantic roles can be found:

(7j)$_{BNC}$ *Someone (or something) has broken the kitchen window.*

What is perhaps more important is that it is by no means always clear which semantic role to assign to a particular valency complement in a clause. Thus while the *with*-complements in

(10a)$_{BNC}$ *Severe forearm bruising may be covered with both a crêpe bandage and a shin pad ....*

(10b)$_{BNC}$ *Once dug and left to dry, potatoes can be sorted and stored in teachests, thick paper sacks or shallow boxes covered with sacking to keep the light from turning them green.*

can clearly be assigned the semantic role of INSTRUMENT, this is far less clear in cases such as

(10c)$_{BNC}$ *The walls are covered with posters illustrative of various radical causes – nuclear disarmament, women's liberation, the protection of whales ....*

(10d)$_{BNC}$ *... her kitchen cupboard is covered with postcards, love letters from old boyfriends and local newspaper articles.*

(10e)$_{BNC}$ *Dorothy said her lawn was covered with snow when she arrived yesterday morning.*

The main problem of any case grammar or semantic role approach is the difficulty of clearly delimiting semantic categories, which is also described by Palmer (^{2}1981: 148–149):

> ... case grammar runs into the familiar difficulty of the vagueness of semantic categories. Often it will be difficult to decide, on semantic grounds, what is the case of a particular noun phrase. Fillmore sees *the smoke* as object in *The smoke rose*, and the same would be true of *the wind* in *The wind blew*. But what, then, shall we say of *The smoke rose and blotted out the sun, The wind blew and opened the door*?

How justified Palmer's objections are can be seen by the fact that even almost forty years after the publication of Fillmore's (1968: 25) article, in which he said that "additional cases will surely be needed", various models with varying numbers and kinds of semantic role have been suggested.[280] It would certainly be naive to expect that there could ever be anything such as a finite inventory of such roles. Despite these apparent difficulties one must not overlook the fact that semantic roles, especially when taken to be prototypes rather than clearly distinct categories, present a useful concept for the analysis of certain syntactic problems.

12.2.3   Some useful participant roles

One way of avoiding the problems that inevitably arise with general semantic roles is to make use of much more specific roles which only apply to one particular verb or a limited number of verbs. Thus within Fillmore's FrameNet project verbs are attributed to certain frames, which are characterized by frame elements resembling semantic roles. FrameNet (framenet.icsi.berkeley.edu) includes a verb such as *paint* in a frame Create_physical_artwork:[281]

(11)_{PH}   *I probably painted more St Ives harbour window paintings in London than in Cornwall.*

This frame is then described as having as core frame elements Creator (*I*) and Representation (*more harbour window paintings*). While such specific descriptions may be useful for certain purposes of linguistic description, it has to be said that they do not provide the kind of generalization which is desirable for other purposes. It may thus be advisable to apply rather specific role labels whenever general role labels do not seem to be appropriate but to make use of more general labels whenever they seem unproblematic. Thus in the case of example (11), a case can be made out for using a label such as 'AGENT' and 'EFFECTED'. Herbst and Schüller (2008) list a number of participant roles which can be applied fairly generally, for instance:

▷ **'BENREC'**: someone or something that benefits from the action expressed by the verb or is the intended recipient of the action described by the verb:

---

[280]   See for instance CGEL (1985), CamG (2002), Dirven and Radden (1977) or Haegeman (1991).
[281]   Compare Fillmore (2007) for an outline of the FrameNet project, in which much more specific frame elements are used.

(12)_{PW}   *It gave Ben ('BENREC') a reasonable studio and Barbara ('BENREC') one near the kitchen, filled with light.*

Whenever this seems appropriate for the purposes of the description, a distinction can be made between **'BENEFICIARY'** and **'RECIPIENT'**:

(13)_{NW}   *I'll write you ('BENEFICIARY') a glowing reference ...*

(14)_{PH}   *Zennor, he wrote to Middleton Murray and Katherine Mansfield ('RECIPIENT') in the spring of 1916, 'is a most beautiful place: ...'.*

▷ **'ÆFFECTED'**: something (or someone) that is affected by or is the outcome or result of the action described by the verb

(15)_{PH}   *Once there, Heron had immediately started work on a series of small vertical paintings ...*

If appropriate, the more specific labels **'AFFECTED'** and **'EFFECTED'** can be employed:

(16)_{PH}   *At Zennor one sees infinite Atlantic ('AFFECTED') ...*

(17)_{PH}   *The house ('AFFECTED') has been neglected ...*

(11)_{PH}   *I probably painted more St Ives harbour window paintings ('EFFECTED') in London than in Cornwall.*

(18)_{PH}   *Red Ground ('EFFECTED') was painted in May 1957 ...*

▷ **'PREDICATIVE'**: identification, equation, characterization or description (which could be seen as subroles of 'PREDICATIVE'):

(19)_{PH}   *Heron has never been a programmatic artist ...*

▷ **'LOCATIVE: STATIVE'**:

(16)_{PH}   *At Zennor one sees infinite Atlantic ...*

▷ **'LOCATIVE: GOAL'**:

(20)_{PH}   *... Heron moved beyond the rapid summary strokes and washes of the 'stripe' and 'horizon' paintings towards what he described as a 'true spontaneity' ...*

(21)_{PH}   *Exactly forty years before D.H. Lawrence had moved into Higher Tregerthen, the tiny group of cottages at the bottom of the hill below Eagles Nest ...*

▷ **'LOCATIVE: SOURCE':**

(22)_{PH}   *... Heron moved <u>beyond the rapid summary strokes and washes of the</u>*
    <u>'stripe' and 'horizon' paintings</u> towards what he described as a 'true
    spontaneity' ...

(23)_{PH}   *... the change <u>from London</u> to Zennor was registered immediately in the*
    bright colour, loose structures and atmospheric translucencies of the
    'garden' paintings ...

▷ **'TIME':**

(21)_{PH}   *<u>Exactly forty years before</u> D.H. Lawrence had moved into Higher Tre-*
    gerthen, the tiny group of cottages at the bottom of the hill below Eagles
    Nest ...

▷ **'PURPOSE':**

(24)_{PW}   *<u>In order to realize the subject emotionally and to further his under-</u>*
    <u>standing of the composition,</u> Lanyon made use of his practical skills in a
    number of three-dimensional constructions.

▷ **'TOPIC':**

(25)_{PH}   *Heron had, of course, been thinking and writing <u>about the nature of</u>*
    <u>abstraction</u> since his very first published article in 1945 ...

▷ **'AGENT':** someone that carries out an action[282]

(25)_{PH}   *<u>Heron</u> had, of course, been thinking and writing about the nature of*
    abstraction since his very first published article in 1945 ...

While these participant roles can be used in the description of quite a few
cases, this list is not intended to provide a complete framework for all participant roles required for the description of English verbs. Rather, the idea
is that these roles must be supplemented by other possibly more specific
roles in many cases.

---

[282]   The notion of AGENT is rather problematic. CamG (2002: 230–231) treats
    'AGENT' as a "subtype of causer". Compare Palmer (1994: 25) and also Gold-
    berg (2006: 184–186).

12.3   The basic principles of valency theory

12.3.1   Introduction

While valency theory, as was pointed out above, is probably the most widely used approach in the analysis of German (see Helbig 1992 or Ágel 2000), there are only relatively few attempts to use it as a descriptive framework for English. It has to be said that no generally accepted version of the theory has emerged as yet as the first two models that offer a fairly comprehensive treatment of English verb valency – Emons (1974, 1978) and Allerton (1982) – differ in many respects. For this reason, the following outline will be mainly based on the version of valency theory that provides the basis of the *Valency Dictionary of English* (2004) (VDE) and the approach taken by Herbst and Schüller (2008).

12.3.2   Complements and adjuncts

Like case grammar, valency theory attributes a central role to the verb in determining the structure of clauses but takes formal considerations as its starting point. Valency analysis concentrates on the relationships that hold between a valency carrier (sometimes also called predicator) and those elements whose occurrence in a sentence is related to the presence of that valency carrier, i.e. those elements which can be considered to be governed by it. With reference to a sentence such as

(1)$_{PW}$ *By 1918 St Ives had a long tradition as an artists' community.*

this means that the verb *have* is to be seen as the valency carrier because the occurrence of *St Ives* and *a long tradition as an artists' community* can be regarded as being dependent on the verb. This can be shown by a deletion test:

(1a)   **By 1918 St Ives had.*

(1b)   **By 1918 had a long tradition as an artists' community.*

By 1918, however, is independent of the verb *have* and can be deleted:

(1c)   *St Ives had a long tradition as an artists' community.*

This difference is reflected terminologically in the distinction between complements and adjuncts:

Complements (*Ergänzungen*)[283] are constituents of a clause

▷ that are either required by the valency of the governing predicator

▷ or determined in their form by the predicator.

Adjuncts (*freie Angaben*) are constituents of a clause

▷ that are neither required by the valency of the governing predicator

▷ nor determined by it in their form.

To indicate the different kinds of dependency relation holding between complements and adjuncts and the governing element, different types of line might be used in the stemma representing (1) (cf. p. 175):

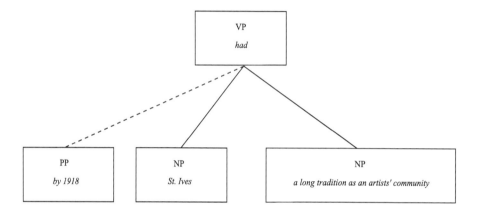

While the notion of adjunct largely corresponds to that of adjunct in other frameworks (or to that of "optional adverbials" in CGEL), the term complement is used in valency theory to cover all constituents that are dependent on a valency carrier (i.e., for instance, CGEL's subject, object, obligatory adverbial etc.).

Finding tests to establish the distinction between complements and adjuncts has played a major role in the development of German valency the-

---

[283] The German terms are given here because the German terminology is much more established than the English. Matthews (1981: 123) draws a distinction between *complements* and *peripheral elements* while Allerton (1982) uses the term *verb elaborator* for *Ergänzung*. The term complement in valency theory must not be confused with complements in other theories, especially the subject and object complements of CGEL.

ory.[284] On the whole, it has to be said that there is no one single criterion on which the distinction can be based and that it must probably be seen in terms of gradience. However, adjuncts typically meet the following criteria:

▷ Adjuncts tend to show greater positional mobility than complements.

(1d)   *St Ives had a long tradition as an artists' community by 1918.*

▷ Adjuncts can often be left out without the remaining sentence being ungrammatical.

(1e)   *St Ives had a long tradition as an artists' community.*

It is important to note that deletability is not a reliable criterion for adjunct status since adjuncts, like complements, can be necessary from a communicative point of view. Thus it would not be possible to delete the adjuncts in (16) or (18) in the contexts of (16a) or (18a) (> 12.3.5):

(16)PH   *At Zennor one sees infinite Atlantic...*

(16a)   *Where does one see infinite Atlantic?*

(18)PH   *Red Ground was painted in May 1957 ...*

(18a)   *When was Red Ground painted?*

A further criterion of adjunct status that is sometimes discussed is that of free addibility, meaning that (as long as they are semantically compatible) adjuncts can be added to sentences irrespective of the valency of the verb.[285]

12.3.3   Qualitative and quantitative aspects of valency

One of the reasons why valency theory (and dependency theory in general) attributes a central role to the verb in syntactic analysis is that the form of a clause is largely determined by the verb in that it depends on the verb as to how many and which complements can occur in a clause. Thus a verb such as *enjoy* can be followed by a noun phrase complement and a [V-ing]-clause-complement but not by a [to_INF]-complement:

---

[284] For a discussion of tests to distinguish between complements and adjuncts see e.g. Helbig and Schenkel ([2]1973: 31–40), Helbig (1992: 72–87), Emons (1974: 65–105), Somers (1987: 11–18) and Herbst and Schüller (2008: 113–116).

[285] See Heringer (1996: 195).

(26a)   *She enjoyed the book.*

(26b)   *She enjoyed going to the theatre.*

(26c)   **She enjoyed to go to the theatre.*

In this respect, which can be referred to as qualitative valency, *enjoy* differs from a verb such as *want*, for example:

(27a)   *She wanted the book.*

(27b)   **She wanted going to the theatre.*

(27c)   *She wanted to go to the theatre.*

Which type of complement can be used with a particular verb can thus be seen as an item-specific property of the verb. There are similar differences with respect to the number of complements that can occur with a particular verb are concerned. One can make a distinction between

▷ monovalent uses

(28a)$_{PH}$ <u>*Christmas Eve*</u> *was **painted** at the invitation of the Arts Council for the Festival of Britain Exhibition 60 Paintings for 51.*

(28b)$_{PH}$ *Abstract art never interested me.* <u>*I*</u> *have always **painted** realistically.*

▷ divalent uses

(11)$_{PH}$ <u>*I*</u> *probably **painted*** <u>*more St Ives harbour window paintings*</u> *in London than in Cornwall.*

(29)$_{PH}$ *Heron has said that he stopped making the 'stripe' paintings when he realized that* <u>*they*</u> ***resembled*** <u>*the sunset skies over the sea at Zennor.*</u>

▷ trivalent uses

(30)$_{PW}$ *For two years* <u>*this*</u> ***gave*** <u>*him*</u> <u>*studio facilities and a small stipend.*</u>

▷ tetravalent uses

(31)$_{SP}$ <u>*I*</u>*'ll **bet*** <u>*you*</u> <u>*all the expenses of the experiment*</u> <u>*you cant do it.*</u>

Abstracting from such uses, statements can be made about the maximum number of complements a lexical unit can occur with.[286] Thus verbs such as

---

[286]   VDE furthermore contains statements about the minimum valency of verbs in active and passive uses.

give and *show* can be said to have a maximum valency of 3 as illustrated by (30) or

(32)_{PW} *Mondrian* **showed** *us how completely possible it was to find a personal equation.*

whereas *realize* has a maximum valency of 2:

(29)_{PH} *Heron has said that he stopped making the 'stripe' paintings when he* **realized** *that they* **resembled** *the sunset skies over the sea at Zennor.*

and *malfunction* one of 1:

(33)_{BNC} *But the rocket* **malfunctioned.**

This aspect of valency, **quantitative valency**, makes clear why the term valency was chosen to describe this linguistic phenomenon since the role of predicators in (nuclear) sentences can be compared to the capability of an atom to combine with one or more other atoms to form a molecule.

12.3.4   Valency carriers

The property of valency cannot only be attributed to verbs, but also to other word classes such as adjectives or nouns: in

(34)_{PH} *This is* **true** *of his* **writings** *about his own paintings.*

the phrase *of his writings about his own paintings* can be analysed as a complement of the adjective *true*, and *about his own paintings* as a complement of *writings*.

The elements underlined can be regarded as complements of the words in bold type because the possibility of the occurrence of these phrases can be seen as item-specific properties of these words. This is not the case with modifiers, which are not determined by the valency of the governing word:

(35)_{PH} *This, as we have seen, is not entirely* **true** *of Heron's production in that period* ...

(36)_{PH} *It goes without saying that the immediacy of sensational* **impact** *of which he is writing is only possible in the actual relation of spectator to painting.*

The notion of verb, adjective and noun valency is generally accepted. Herbst and Schüller (2008), following the extension of the word class

preposition in CamG (2002), also apply it to the word class particle (>
11.4.7):

(37a)_{PW}   *St Just is the last town in England **before** you reach Land's End.*

Irrespective of word class it is important to realize that valency is not a
property of words, but a property of lexical units, i.e. combinations of word
forms and senses (> 9.1.1): thus, in the case of *deny*, for instance, VDE
makes a distinction between two lexical units 'say that something is not
true' and 'refuse', which differ in the kinds of complements they allow.

(38)_{VDE}   *He **denied** that the country was facing an economic crisis.* ('not true')

(39)_{VDE}   *This means courts can obtain important evidence which previously
would have been **denied** to them.* ('refuse')

12.3.5   Components of a valency description

On the basis of these considerations, valency can be defined as follows
(Herbst and Schüller 2008: 108):

> A lexical unit has the property of valency if it opens up one or more
> valency slots which can or must be realised by a complement.

A valency description of a lexical unit can then comprise the following
components:

▷ level of form: specification of the complements that can fill a valency
  slot – a complement being any formal realization of a valency slot (e.g.
  a phrase or a clause)

▷ level of semantics: specification of the participants or participant roles,
  which characterize the semantic function of the complement in the
  clause (> 12.2.3)

▷ level of optionality: specification of whether (or under which contextual
  conditions) a valency slot must or can be realized by a complement

Like Fillmore's (1968) case frames, valency descriptions of this kind are to
be seen as an account of the syntactic potential of a lexical unit. For instance, (in a simplified account of the verb's valency structures) one can
identify two valency slots for a verb such as *paint*, which can be attributed
the participant roles of I 'AGENT' and II 'ÆFFECTED'.

As far as the description of the complements is concerned, one would
have to say that valency slot I can be expressed by a noun phrase [NP] in

active clauses and by a [by_NP]-complement in passive clauses, whereas valency slot II can be realized by an [NP] in the predicate in active clauses and a subject [NP] in passives:

(11)$_\text{PH}$ *I probably* **painted** *more St Ives harbour window paintings in London than in Cornwall.*

(28a)$_\text{PH}$ *Christmas Eve was* **painted** *at the invitation of the Arts Council for the Festival of Britain Exhibition 60 Paintings for 51.*

In the case of *watch*, valency slot II ('AFFECTED') can be realized by a range of different complements such as

[NP]   *During the week I can watch all the soaps on TV*$_\text{VDE}$

[*how*-CL] *If you can spare the time, spend a day watching how the light changes in strength and direction.*$_\text{VDE}$

[NP INF] *Today you can watch the catch come in (approx 7:30–8 am) at Hayle, St Ives, Newlyn and Mousehole, as fishing boats bring back dover sole and haddock.*$_\text{VDE}$

in active clauses and by [NP]s in passives:

[NP]   *We are being watched.*$_\text{VDE}$

It is remarkable that in English the fact whether a complement can function as the subject of a clause or is realized in the predicate is an important part of its description.[287] In a language such as German, in which morphological case plays a much more prominent role than in English, terms such as *Akkusativergänzung* or *Nominativergänzung* can be used, which implicitly contains information about possible subjects. It is for this reason that the description of complements provided in the complement inventories of verbs in the VDE combine information about morphological form such as [NP], [to-INF] with information about the possibility of occurrence as a subject in active and passive clauses.[288]

---

[287]   Herbst and Schüller (2008: 117) use a subscript $_\text{act-subj}$ for complements that occur as subjects of active clauses and a subscript $_\text{pass-subj}$ for complements that occur as subjects of passive clauses.

[288]   For a more detailed description of the approach indicated here see VDE (2004: xxiii–xxxiii) or Herbst and Schüller (2008). For an alternative account of the description of different types of complement in English see Emons (1974 and 1978). See in particular Emons (1978: 26–27) for the principle of *Kommutationsklassen*: *A man/He sees a child.*

With respect to the level of optionality, a distinction can be made between

▷ obligatory valency slots, which have to be realized by a complement whenever the valency carrier is used,

▷ contextually optional valency slots, which can but need not be realized by a complement as long as the referent of the corresponding participant can be identified from the context,

▷ optional valency slots, which need not be realized by a complement.[289]

In this terminology, both valency slots of a verb such as *paint* realized in (11) can be classified as optional

(11)_{PH}   *I probably* painted *more St Ives harbour window paintings in London than in Cornwall.*

(28a)_{PH}   *Christmas Eve was **painted** at the invitation of the Arts Council for the Festival of Britain Exhibition 60 Paintings for 51.*

(28b)_{PH}   *Abstract art never interested me. I have always **painted** realistically.*

Valency slot II of *watch*, however, is contextually optional since sentences such as

(40)_{VDE}   *The men just watched and laughed.*

(41)_{AE}   *I've always wanted to know.*

only occur if it is clear what is being watched or known. Finally, valency slot II of *put* – realized by *her soiled breakfast things* is an example of an obligatory valency slot:

(42)_{NW}   *She puts her soiled breakfast things into the sink ...*

It is important to realize, however, that the fact that an element is optional from the point of view of valency does not mean that it could be deleted from a sentence. The level of valency is only one factor with respect to the optionality of an element in a sentence. It can be supplemented by the lev-

---

[289]   Allerton (1982: 68–69) makes a distinction between indefinite and contextual deletion on which the distinction between optional and contextually optional complements is based. For a discussion of very similar concepts in the FrameNet context see Fillmore (2007: 144–151). Compare also Goldberg's (2006: 39) description of lexically profiled roles as those which are "obligatorily expressed, or, if unexpressed, must receive a definite interpretation" – as argument roles.

els of structural and communicative necessity. **Structural necessity** refers to the influence of sentence structure in this respect: thus imperative constructions do not have subjects, whereas declarative and interrogative constructions usually have subjects.[290] **Communicative necessity** finally refers to the fact that in a given situation any element of a sentence can be necessary from a communicative point of view, as pointed out in 12.3.2.

12.3.6 Valency patterns

The complementation properties of lexical units can either be described in terms of valency slots that are realized by complements expressing particular participant roles or in terms of patterns in which a valency carrier can occur.[291] This is the approach taken in the model of Pattern Grammar developed by Hunston and Francis (2000)[292] or the Erlangen Valency Patternbank (www.patternbank.uni-erlangen.de), for example.

Within a valency-driven approach, it may make sense to distinguish between three types of patterning:

▷ valency patterns as patterns of formal valency complements

▷ participant patterns as patterns of the same participant roles

▷ valency constructions as patterns of valency complements expressing the same participant roles.

Thus, at a purely formal level, *be* and *reach* in (37a) can be seen as representing the same valency pattern: NP – VHC$_2$ – NP.[293]

(37a)$_{PW}$ *St Just is the last town in England before you reach Land's End.*

---

[290]   See Herbst and Schüller (2008: 148–156) for a description of different sentence types such as the imperative-'directive'-construction or the declarative-'statement'-construction. It must be recognized that there is a certain overlap between the levels of structural necessity and valency because the ability of a complement to occur as subject entails certain facts about its optionality.

[291]   For reasons to regard these two perspectives as complementary see Herbst (2007). Compare also Herbst and Faulhaber (forthcoming). For the role of patterns in German valency theory and a distinction between *Satzmuster* and *Satzbauplan* see VALBU (2004: 46–47) and Engel (1977: 180–181).

[292]   For parallels between pattern grammar and construction grammar see Stubbs (2009: 27).

[293]   VHC stands for verbal head complex, 2 for the valency of the verb (> 12.4).

They represent different valency constructions, however, because the NPs have different semantic roles – such as 'PREDICATIVE' (*the last town in England*) and 'ÆFFECTED' (*Land's End*). (32) and (43), on the other hand, display the same cluster of participant roles (possibly to be described as 'AGENT' – 'BENREC' – 'ÆFFECTED') with different formal realizations:

(32)_{PW}   *Mondrian showed us how completely possible it was to find a personal equation.*

(43)_{TI}   *This is the first work by Barbara Hepworth to which she gave a title referring directly to landscape.*

Examples (11), (44) and (45) can be attributed to the same valency construction in that they represent the same valency pattern $NP - VHC_2 - NP$ and the same participant roles ('AGENT' – 'EFFECTED'):[294]

(11)_{PH}   *I probably painted more St Ives harbour window paintings in London than in Cornwall.*

(44)_{TS}   *In the early 1950s, Nicholson produced a series of paintings which show him at the height of his powers.*

(45)_{TI}   *Lanyon made numerous versions of this composition …*

12.4   A valency based approach to English syntax

12.4.1   Combining aspects of clause structure and valency

Although valency properties of individual words, in particular verbs, have a determining influence on the structure of a sentence, a number of other factors will also have to be taken into account.

In what follows we will introduce an approach towards the analysis of English sentences that combines the aspect of clause structure and valency. This seems appropriate since

(a) valency properties of governing verbs have an influence on the structure of the clause, in particular the predicate,

---

[294]   It would be interesting to find out to what extent these different types of patterning are cognitively relevant. The concept of valency constructions bears close resemblance to Goldberg's (2006) argument structure constructions (> 13.3.2), cf. also Herbst (2010).

(b) properties of the clause (active, passive or declarative, interrogative, imperative) have an influence on the form and degree of optionality of complements.

The approach developed by Herbst and Schüller (2008) combines the terminologies of traditional grammar and valency theory and introduces the following terms for different kinds of unit:

▷ **subject complement unit (SCU)**, which consists of the subject of the clause, which is realized by a complement of the governing verb

▷ **predicate complement unit (PCU)**, which is any complement of the governing verb which occurs in the predicate, i.e. any complement other than the subject

▷ **predicate head unit (PHU)**, which contains the governing verb of the clause plus any other elements in the predicate (auxiliaries, modifiers) that are not complements

▷ **adjunct unit (AU)**

▷ **linking unit (LU)**.[295]

(1)$_{AE}$ *By 1918 St Ives had a long tradition as an artists' community.*

By 1918	*St Ives*	*had*	*a long tradition as an artists' community*
AU	SCU	PHU	PCU

(30)$_{AE}$ *For two years this gave him studio facilities and a small stipend.*

For two years	*this*	*gave*	*him*	*studio facilities and a small stipend*
AU	SCU	PHU	PCU1	PCU2

---

[295]   An example of a linking unit would be *and* in ... *it was an October night and a full moon was rising over Godrevy*$_{PH}$, which links two independent clauses (> 11.1.2).

12.4.2   A modified view of phrase structure

12.4.2.1   Head complexes

One problem of the traditional definition of phrases as given in CGEL (1985: 2.26), for example, is that in the case of endocentric phrases (> 11.3.1) the head of a phrase is defined as that element of a phrase that can stand for the phrase on its own. This criterion works in cases such as:

(46)ₚₕ   *Once there Heron had immediately started work on a series of <u>small</u> <u>vertical</u> **paintings** <u>that carried forward a programme of radically ab-</u> <u>stract experimentation that had begun in earnest in late 1955</u> ...*

(46a)   *Once there Heron had immediately started work on a series of **paintings**   ...*

However, in many cases, a noun phrase cannot be replaced by the head in this way: [296]

(47)ₜₛ   *Barbara Hepworth's situation was very different at this time.*

(47a)   **Situation was different at this time.*

(48)ₚₕ   *For Heron it was a dream realized ...*

(48a)   **For Heron it was dream realized ...*

One possible way of tackling this problem is to identify a nominal head-complex within the noun phrase, which can consist of a number of so-called pre-heads and a head: the right-most constituent of the head-complex is the head. The head can be preceded by up to three pre-heads.

---

[296]   It is for this reason that some theories consider it more appropriate to speak of determiner phrases (with determiners as heads) than of noun phrases. While this works in the case of *a dream* in (48), an analysis in terms of determiner phrases is problematic in cases where there is no determiner as with *Heron* or *paintings* in (46). See Hudson (1984: 90–92) and Matthews (2007). Cf. also Radford's (1993) proposal of co-headedness.

pre-head(s)	head
	book
a	*book*
his second	*book*
all these	*books*

In the terminology introduced by Herbst and Schüller (2008) (> 11.4.6),

▷ determiners (*the*), determiner-pronouns (*this*) or genitives of pronouns (*their*) or nouns (*John's*) can function as pre-heads of noun phrases, and

▷ determiner-pronouns (*this*), pronouns (*they*) or nouns (*John, book*) can function as heads of noun phrases.

In very much the same way, the distinction of pre-head and head can be used to describe the verbal head-complex:

pre-head(s)	head
was	*going*
	went
has been	*laughing*

In the verbal head-complex,

▷ modal verbs and primary verbs can function as pre-heads or (if they are the right-most constituent of the verbal head-complex) as heads, whereas

▷ lexical verbs always function as heads.

12.4.2.2   Noun phrases, adjective phrases and adverb phrases

A further difference in the account of phrase structure in a valency-based model is that a distinction is made between the valency complements of the head and modifiers, which are not dependent on the valency of the head.

The structure of the noun phrase can then be described as follows (pre-heads and head forming the nominal head-complex):

Noun phrase				
pre-head(s)	premodifier(s)	head	postmodifier(s)	complement(s)
		they		
all the		boys		
		books		on linguistics
these	lovely	paintings	made in St Ives	
no		idea		where to go

Adjective and adverb phrases only have single heads:

Adjective phrase			
premodifier(s)	head	postmodifier(s)	complement(s)
very	clever		
extremely	good		at mathematics
	interesting	enough	

Adverb phrase			
premodifier(s)	head	postmodifier(s)	complement(s)
	cleverly		
rather	stupidly		
	independently		of the outcome
very	well	indeed	

Apart from pre- and postmodifiers, there are also discontinuous modifiers (Aarts and Aarts 1988), where the second constituent is dependent on the first constituent:

(49)_{PH}   *I thought I was making the most extreme paintings in the world.*

12.4.2.3   *Particle phrases*

If one follows the word class distinctions suggested by Herbst and Schüller (2008) and subsumes subordinating conjunctions, prepositions and some adverbs under a single category of particles which has the property of valency (> 11.4.7), then one can also identify a category particle phrase. Particle phrases can be analysed as being headed because the minimum realization of any particle phrase consists of the particle and its valency complements.

Particle phrase			
	premodifier(s)	head	complement(s)
1		here	
2	not long	after	Robyn's arrival
		on	the table
3		whether	she wanted to stay
		to	go
	three years	after	they first met

In traditional accounts, these phrases would be classified as adverb phrases (1), prepositional phrases (2) and subordinate clauses (3).

12.4.2.4   *Clauses as verb phrases*

Within such a valency-oriented model of phrase structure, it does not really make sense to distinguish between clauses and verb phrases, which is a point of view also taken by Fillmore (1988: 43), for example. CGEL's (1985: 2.27) verb phrases correspond to the verbal head-complex as described here. The verbal head-complex can be seen as being central to the clause in very much the same way as the nominal head-complex is central to the noun phrase.

In the description of the clause, the verbal head-complex will be specified in two ways:

▷ as active or passive

▷ in terms of the number of complements dependent on its head in the sentence.

(50)   *She received* [VHC$_{act: 3}$] *a letter from him.*

(51)   *She was given* [VHC$_{pass: 2}$] *a letter yesterday.*

12.4.3   Description of units

In the model proposed by Herbst and Schüller (2008), the different types of unit identified are further specified as follows:

▷ **predicate head units** (PHUs) are described in terms of the type of verbal head-complex by which they are realized

▷ **subject complement units** (SCUs), **predicate complement units** (PCUs) and **adjunct units** (AUs) are described in terms of their formal realizations, i.e. in terms of phrases or clauses

▷ **predicate complement units** realized by noun phrases are assigned a semantic role (> 12.2.3)

▷ **linking units** are specified in terms of word class only.

(52)	She	had given	him	a book	yesterday
	SCU:	PHU:	PCU1:	PCU2:	AU: AdvP
	NP	VHC$_{act:3}$	NP$_{BENREC}$	NP$_{ÆFFECTED}$	

It is obvious that a comprehensive description of the sentence should comprise an indication of the semantic roles for all predicate complement units as well as for SCUs and AUs. For practical purposes, this can be restricted to noun phrase PCUs, where roles serve to make clear the difference between sentences such as (52) and (53):

(53)	She	had called	him	a fool	yesterday
	SCU:	PHU:	PCU1:	PCU2:	AU: AdvP
	NP	VHC$_{act:3}$	NP$_{ÆFFECTED}$	NP$_{PREDICATIVE}$	

12.4.4   Example

This model can be used to analyse a sentence such as

(52)$_{PH}$ *I shall never forget the immense sensation of space the first moment we entered that room ...: it was an October night and a full moon was rising over Godrevy.*

in the following way:[297]

sentence_{<I>}: declarative-'statement'

⌐ SCU: NP ——————— h: pron		*I*
├ PHU: VHC_{act2} ┬ preh: modal		*shall*
├ AU: AdvP ─────┬─ h: adv		*never*
	└ h: lv		*forget*
└ PCU: NP_{ÆFFECTED} ┬ preh: det		*the*
	├ prem: AdjP— h: adj		*immense*
	├ h: ln		*sensation*
	├ c: of_NP ┬ h: part		*of*
		└ c: NP —— h: ln		*space*
	└ postm: NP ┬ preh: det		*the*
		├ preh: det-pron		*first*
		├ h: ln		*moment*
		└ postm: cl ┬ SCU: NP —— h: pron		*we*
			├ PHU: VHC_{act2}— h: lv		*entered*
			└ PCU: NP_{ÆFF} ┬ preh: det-pron		*that*
			└ h: ln		*room:*

sentence_{<II>}: declarative-'statement'

⌐ SCU: NP ——————— h: pron		*it*
├ PHU: VHC_{act2} ——————— h: pv		*was*
└ PCU: NP_{PREDICATIVE} ┬ preh: det		*an*
	├ prem: ln		*October*
	└ h: ln		*night*
── LU ─────────── conj		*and*

sentence_{<III>}: declarative-'statement'

⌐ SCU: NP —————— ┬ preh: det		*a*
	├ prem: adj		*full*
	└ h: ln		*moon*
├ PHU: VHC_{act1} ——————— ┬ preh: pv		*was*
	└ h: lv		*rising*
└ AU: PartP ——————— ┬ h: part		*over*
	└ c: ln		*Godrevy.*

---

[297] For an approach towards the analysis of English sentences in eight steps and more examples see Herbst and Schüller (2008: 173–193).

13   Theories of grammar and language acquisition

13.1   Chomsky's approach

13.1.1   Basic assumptions

A radically different approach towards the description of syntactic structures is taken by Noam Chomsky, whose ideas can no doubt be said to have dominated much of the linguistic and particularly syntactic research in the second half of the twentieth century all over the world. It is probably fair to say that for many researchers in the field his theories presented not only a new and in many ways interesting way of looking at language, but the only conceivable framework for linguistic analysis. From a slightly more cautious perspective, this phenomenon is difficult to explain. The enormous appeal of Chomsky's theories may have a number of reasons, such as

- the high degree of formalization characteristic of his theories,
- the precise formulation of the aims of linguistic theory connected with a clearly defined view of language,
- his interest in language universals, i.e. properties that are common to all languages,
- certain psychological implications of his theories.

For instance, the crucial distinctions introduced by Chomsky between competence and performance (> 3.1.2) and his own concentration on competence as the object of research have resulted in a view of language and sentence analysis that to a very large extent abstracts from (and thus ignores) sociolinguistic and situational factors. This becomes particularly apparent in Chomsky's (1965: 3) notion of the ideal speaker/hearer, which forms the basis of his theory:

> Linguistic theory is concerned primarily with an ideal speaker-listener, in a completely homogeneous speech community, who knows its language perfectly and is unaffected by such grammatically irrelevant conditions as memory limitations, distractions, shifts of attention and interest, and errors

(random or characteristic) in applying his knowledge of the language in actual performance.

This abstraction from social factors of communication also shows in the following definition of language provided by Chomsky in *Syntactic Structures* (1957: 13):

> I will consider a *language* to be a set (finite or infinite) of sentences, each finite in length and constructed out of a finite set of elements. All natural languages in their spoken or written form are languages in this sense, since each natural language has a finite number of phonemes ... and each sentence is representable as a finite sequence of these phonemes ..., though there are infinitely many sentences.

The task of linguistics then is to describe which combinations of elements can be sentences of a language. This is strongly linked with the notion of generative grammar, which Chomsky (1965: 8) describes as follows:[298]

> ... by a generative grammar I mean simply a system of rules that in some explicit and well-defined way assigns structural descriptions to sentences. Obviously, every speaker of a language has mastered and internalized a generative grammar that expresses his knowledge of the language. This is not to say that he is aware of the rules of the grammar or even that he can become aware of them, or that his statements about his intuitive knowledge of the language are necessarily accurate. Any interesting generative grammar will be dealing, for the most part, with mental processes that are far beyond the level of actual or even potential consciousness.

Within such a generative grammar, it is not only the rules that operate in any particular language that are of interest to the linguist but rules or principles which apply to all languages and can thus be subsumed under the heading of universal grammar. In *Aspects of the Theory of Syntax*, Chomsky (1965: 6) emphasizes the need for research into the nature of universal grammar, which has characterized his approach ever since:

---

[298] While the use of the phrase "mental processes" might be taken as an indication of certain psychological or cognitive aims of the theory, Chomsky (1965: 9) also says: "When we speak of a grammar as generating a sentence with a certain structural description, we mean simply that the grammar assigns this structural description to the sentence. When we say that a sentence has a certain derivation with respect to a particular generative grammar, we say nothing about how the speaker or hearer might proceed, in some practical or efficient way, to construct such a derivation."

> Within traditional linguistic theory … it was clearly understood that one of
> the qualities that all languages have in common is their "creative" aspect.
> Thus an essential property of language is that it provides the means for ex-
> pressing indefinitely many thoughts and for reacting appropriately in an in-
> definite range of new situations (…). The grammar of a particular language,
> then, is to be supplemented by a universal grammar that accommodates the
> creative aspect of language use and expresses the deep-seated regularities
> which, being universal, are omitted from the grammar itself.

Thus one could argue that what made Chomsky's approach towards the
study of language so attractive to many scholars was that he emphasized
different perspectives in the study of language from, say, the ones addressed by structuralism. The model of generative grammar as promoted by
Chomsky has given rise to an enormous number of different theories based
to a greater or lesser degree on the ideas outlined by Chomsky. Chomsky's
own version of generative grammar has also gone through a number of
rather radical modifications, represented by publications such as *Syntactic
Structures* (1957), *Aspects of the Theory of Syntax* (1965), *Lectures on
Government and Binding* (1981) and *The Minimalist Program* (1995).

13.1.2   Transformations – deep structures and surface structures

One of the key notions of the early versions of Chomsky's generative
grammar is that of transformation. It can be described as an operation between two levels of syntactic structure identified – deep structure and surface structure. The distinction between two such levels of structure can be
justified through examples of syntactic ambiguity in sentences such as[299]

(1)$_{QE}$ *Flying planes can be dangerous.*

It is argued that the surface structure of (1) represents two deep structures
representing the different readings of these sentences as

(1a)   *The flying of planes can be dangerous.*

(1b)   *Planes that fly can be dangerous.*

---

[299] For a discussion of constructional homonymy see Matthews (1993:149–153)
and Palmer (1971: 141–150).

On the other hand, there are cases which can be explained as representing different surface structures such as actives and passives that are derived from the same deep structure.[300]

(2a)$_{QE}$ *John plays golf.*

(2b)$_{QE}$ *Golf is played by John.*

The deep structure as envisaged by Chomsky in *Aspects* can be imagined as an unambiguous conceptual syntactic structure, in which the elements are ordered according to certain principles. The deep structure as such is based on the constituency or phrase structure analysis frequently employed in American structuralism (> 12.1.1). In early versions of the model such as *Syntactic Structures*, such deep structures are then subject to a process of transformations, which maps them into surface structures, i.e. grammatical sequences of the language.[301] The passive transformation can be represented as follows: [302]

$$NP_1 + Aux + V + NP_2 \rightarrow NP_2 + Aux + be + en + V + by\ NP_1$$

which then leads to the corresponding surface structure. In *Aspects of the Theory of Syntax* and related models, particular transformations required for the generation of sentences in a language – such as the passive transformation, deletion, substitution, relative transformation – were specified. In later versions of the theory, this is no longer the case. In the 1981 *Gov-*

---

[300]   Cf. Chomsky (1965: 21). For the passive transformation see Chomsky (1957: 77–81). Similarly, declarative and different types of interrogative sentences (*John ate an apple – Did John eat an apple*) are seen as being derived by different transformations from one underlying string "*John – C – eat + an + apple*"; see also Chomsky (1957: 91). See also Palmer (1971: 135–141).

[301]   Chomsky (1965: 141) describes the *Aspects* model as follows: "The syntactic component consists of a base and a transformational component. The base, in turn, consists of a categorical subcomponent and a lexicon. The base generates deep structures. A deep structure enters the semantic component and receives a semantic interpretation; it is mapped by the transformational rules into a surface structure, which is then given a phonetic interpretation by the rules of the phonological component. ... The categorical subcomponent of the base consists of context-free rewriting rules."

[302]   Compare Chomsky (1957: 43) and Chomsky (1965: esp. 131–132). For a description of active and passive in terms of transformations see Harris (1957/1981: 194–197). For the contribution of Harris see Matthews (1993: 160–162). For a discussion of the inadequacy of phrase structure grammars see Chomsky (1957: 34–48).

ernment and Binding model[303] a general operation called *move α* is introduced instead, which relates the levels of s- and d-structure (as they are called in this model), and restrictions on *move α* are defined.[304] Apart from the levels of s-structure and d-structure, Chomsky identifies the levels of phonetic form and logical form referring to output in terms of sound and meaning. In the *Minimalist Program*, Chomsky (1995: 219) abolishes the levels of d-structure and s-structure.

Looking at the overall development of generative grammar one aspect to be noted is the increasing specification of syntactically relevant lexical properties in determining sentence structure, which results in a closer similarity to valency and dependency approaches. Thus, integrating notions of case grammar (> 12.2), the lexical entry for a verb such as *defeat* is specified in the following form:

defeat [__NP] <Agent, Patient>

This description contains a formal statement that the verb *defeat* needs to be followed by a noun phrase (as its object, in this case) and that subject and object represent the semantic roles (called theta-roles in this model) of AGENT and PATIENT.[305]

Despite considerable changes in the formalizations proposed, two basic convictions can be identified as remaining relatively constant in Chomsky's approach. First of all, there is a strong focus on general principles, which is also reflected in his view of the lexicon given in the *Minimalist Program* (1995: 235):[306]

---

[303]   For introductory accounts of the model see Cook (1988), Haegeman (1991) and Sells (1985). See also Matthews (1990), Lyons (1991) or Maclay (1971).

[304]   Cf. Chomsky (1995: 20): "We assume that the language (the generative procedure, the I-language) has two components: a computational system and a lexicon. The first generates the form of SDs; the second characterizes the lexical items that appear in them. ... We will assume that one aspect of an SD is a system of representation, called *D-Structure*, at which lexical items are inserted. D-Structure expresses lexical properties in a form accessible to the computational system." (SD = structural description) In addition to d-structure and s-structure, Government-Binding Theory introduces phonetic form and logical form (referring to meaning), cf. Sells (1985: 19–20).

[305]   See Cook (1988: 122) for this and the notions of s-selection, c-selection and the Projection Principle. For the passive compare also Sells (1985: esp. 43). For a discussion of s-selection and c-selection cf. Chomsky (1986: 86–90).

[306]   See Chomsky (1965: 164–170) for an earlier description of the lexicon involving strict subcategorization features and selectional restrictions.

I understand the lexicon in a rather traditional sense: as a list of "exceptions", whatever does not follow from general principles. These principles fall into two categories: those of UG, and those of a specific language. The latter cover aspects of phonology and morphology, choice of parametric options, and whatever else may enter into language variation. Assume further that the lexicon provides an "optimal coding" of such idiosyncrasies.

A second principle underlying the various versions of the theory is the idea of deriving syntactic structures, as is obvious from Chomsky's (1995: 219) description of language: "The language L determines a set of *derivations*". Both of these ideas have been challenged by construction grammar (> 13.2).

13.1.3   Claims and evidence

It was said in 13.1.1 that generative transformational grammar constitutes one of the most important research paradigms in the history of linguistics. Indeed it would be difficult to deny the great intellectual appeal of the model and the value of an enormous number of contributions to descriptive linguistics carried out within the Chomskyan framework. Furthermore, it is an indication of the outstanding importance of Chomsky's work that it is not only referred to by people working within the framework or frameworks outlined by him, but that many who work within alternative frameworks also refer to Chomsky's work in order to demonstrate in what way their approach differs from his.

One of the main points of criticism raised against Chomsky's approach concerns the question of evidence. Thus Sampson (2001: 141) speaks of "Noam Chomsky's fairly unempirical theory of 'Transformational Grammar'" and criticizes that[307]

> ... the existence of linguistic universals is, for Chomsky and his followers, not so much a finding that has emerged from their research despite their expectations, but rather a guiding assumption which determines the nature of the hypotheses they propose in order to account for data. (Sampson 1980: 148)

Similarly, as far as data are concerned, the fact that judgments about the grammaticality or ambiguity of sentences were largely based on the intuition of the linguist, is highly problematic, as Matthews (1990: 124) points

---

[307]   For a similar view see Matthews (1990: 16).

out.[308] The focus on the rather abstract notion of an ideal speaker-hearer and the question of what is possible in a language provides good reasons for considering introspection as superior to the analysis of corpora: firstly, corpora represent instances of performance, and, secondly, the fact that a particular form does not occur in a corpus does not mean that it does not exist in the language. However, the total rejection of the use of corpora and the methodology of corpus linguistics by Chomsky – culminating in the statement that corpus linguistics "doesn't exist" (Aarts 2000: 5) – means a neglect of certain aspects of language use for which (given the size of to-day's corpora) there is less justification today than there was in the 1950s and 1960s.[309] A similar type of limitation can be seen in the focus of attention to what Chomsky (1995: 19–20) calls core language in the exploration of universal grammar (UG):[310]

> For working purposes (and nothing more than that), we may make a rough and tentative distinction between the *core* of a language and its *periphery*, where the core consists of what we tentatively assume to be pure instantiations of UG and the periphery consists of marked exceptions (irregular verbs, etc.). Note that the periphery will also exhibit properties of UG (e.g., ablaut phenomena), though less transparently. A reasonable approach would be to focus attention on the core system, putting aside phenomena that result from historical accident, dialect mixture, personal idiosyncracies, and the like.

Such an approach entails two dangers: from a methodological point of view one could argue that it is relatively easy to observe regularity in core grammar when all elements of irregularity can be relegated to the periphery. Furthermore, one might ask whether it is not an essential part of language, and thus of any comprehensive description of language, that it is the result of a historical process and whether the amount of irregularity to be observed in language is something that can be relegated to the periphery so easily. In fact, study of such phenomena as collocation and valency might

---

[308] For a more conciliatory view compare Matthews (1993: 33).

[309] See 3.2.3. Of course, the (by today's standards) small size of corpora available during the early stages of transformational grammar meant considerable limitations. Cf. Leech (1991: 13) for this: "... Chomsky, in his turn, could not have conceived, in the 1950s, of a corpus of 500 million words capable of being searched in a matter of minutes or hours. ... it is unlikely that foreknowledge of such a phenomenon would have changed Chomsky's view of corpora at that time."

[310] Compare also Matthews (1990: 136).

lead one to assume that the opposite is the case and that a considerable amount of item-specific information will have to be accounted for in any theory of language, as has been done by the formulation of the idiom prin- ciple by Sinclair (> 10.5) and in particular in construction grammar (> 13.2).

Critics might also object to the general tenor of some of the claims made within the theory.[311] Thus, there is a certain discrepancy between Chom- sky's (1995: 7) describing the principles and parameters model outlined in the *Minimalist Program* as "in part a bold speculation rather than a specific hypothesis" and at the same time claiming that it "constituted a radical break from the rich tradition of thousands of years of linguistic enquiry, far more so than early generative grammar, which could be seen as a revival of traditional concerns and approaches to them" (1995: 5). Similarly, a state- ment of the type

> Generative grammar can be regarded as a kind of confluence of long- forgotten concerns of the study of language and mind, and new understand- ing provided by the formal sciences.
> The first efforts to approach these problems quickly revealed that tradi- tional grammatical and lexical studies do not begin to describe, let alone explain, the most elementary facts about even the best-studied of languages. (1995: 4)

is hardly reconcilable in tone with saying

> The end result is a picture of language that differs considerably from even its immediate precursors. Whether these steps are on the right track or not, of course, only time will tell. (1995: 10)

However, in this respect Chomsky seems to agree with one of his critics, Peter Matthews (1993: 252), who says:

---

[311] Matthews (1982: 22–23) deplores "never-ending reformulation" and speaks of the challenge of "demystification". Compare Chomsky's introduction to the *Minimalist Program* (1995: 10): "The field is changing rapidly under the impact of new empirical materials and theoretical ideas. What looks reason- able today is likely to take a different form tomorrow." Compare also Chom- sky's (2004: 152) statement in an interview given in 2002: "... I think the minimalist critique of the past ten years has given substantial reasons to sup- pose that none of these things exist: d-structure, s-structure, and LF just don't exist. There is no X-bar Theory forming d-structure."

Faith is a beautiful thing, which a non-believer can only regard with awe. ... There are many who share Chomsky's faith, and for them 'The research program of modern linguistics' (Chomsky 1988: Ch. 2) must without arrogance be his programme. Others cannot bring themselves to accept that it has empirical content. 'C'est magnifique, mais peut être n'est pas la linguistique'. But all they can do is watch and wait.

13.1.4   Language acquisition

13.1.4.1   *The language acquisition device*

One of the main attractions of Chomsky's approach is perhaps to be seen in the fact that right from the beginning it had been linked with questions of language acquisition. In his famous review of Skinner's book *Verbal Behavior*, Chomsky (1959: 57) rejects the behaviourist approach to language acquisition and argues for a mentalistic approach:

> The fact that all normal children acquire essentially comparable grammars of great complexity with remarkable rapidity suggests that human beings are somehow specially designed to do this, with data-handling or 'hypothesis-formulating' ability of unknown character and complexity.

The key points in this statement are "great complexity" and "remarkable rapidity". The idea is that since language acquisition is such a highly complex task and takes place relatively quickly, humans must be equipped with special genetically determined properties which enable them to acquire language.[312] In the 1965 *Aspects* model, this takes the form of an innate language acquisition device (LAD), which means that "the child has an innate theory of potential structural descriptions" (Chomsky 1965: 32). The job of the LAD is to select the appropriate type of grammar on the basis of the data the child is exposed to during the language acquisition process:

> This device must search through the set of possible hypotheses *G1, G2* ..., which are available to it ... and must select grammars that are compatible

---

[312]   Note, however, that Steinberg (1982: 100) points out that one "basic underlying premise on which this argument rests is that four or five years (or whatever length of time it takes the child to acquire a grammar) is not a long time." Cf. Steinberg (1982: 96–100). See also Klann-Delius (1999: 51–52), who criticizes the concept of the LAD as remaining rather vague.

with the primary linguistic data. ... The theory that the device has now selected and internally represented specifies its [the child's] tacit competence,
its knowledge of the language. The child who acquires a language in this
way, of course, knows a great deal more than he has 'learned'. His knowledge of the language ... goes far beyond the presented primary linguistic
data and is in no sense an 'inductive generalization' from these data.
(Chomsky 1965: 32–33)

13.1.4.2   Universal grammar

In later models, the idea of a language acquisition device is given up in
favour of the principles and parameters approach. According to this model,
a child is genetically equipped with universal grammar, which Chomsky
(1986: 24) describes as "a characterization of these innate, biologically
determined principles, which constitute one component of the human mind
– the language faculty". The UG contains principles and parameters, which
Chomsky (1986: 146) describes as follows:

> ... UG consists of various subsystems of principles; it has the modular struc-
> ture that we regularly discover in investigation of cognitive systems. Many
> of these principles are associated with parameters that must be fixed by ex-
> perience. The parameters must have the property that can be fixed by quite
> simple evidence, because this is what is available to the child. ... Once the
> values of the parameters are set, the whole system is operative. ... The sys-
> tem is associated with a finite set of switches, each of which has a finite
> number of positions (perhaps two). Experience is required to set the
> switches. When they are set, the system functions.
>   The transition from the initial state S_0 to the steady state S_s is a matter of
> setting the switches.

Language acquisition is then a matter of parameter setting. This setting of
parameters takes place on the basis of the input data and eventually leads to
the acquisition of the core grammar of the language.[313]
   In a way, the same types of objections that applied to the earlier versions
of the grammar can be raised against the principles and parameters approach. Firstly, as was already pointed out above, the concentration on core
grammar, which is an essential element of the theory, may well mean that
important aspects of language are totally ignored. Secondly, as Klann-
Delius (1999: 53) points out, the model still does not offer an outline of the

---

[313]   Cf. Klann-Delius (1999: 52–53).

process of language acquisition as such. Factors such as the interaction of children with their parents and other people or the special kind of language parents use when talking to very young children – known as child-directed speech (> 13.2.3) – are totally ignored. Thirdly, this model lacks empirical evidence. With the exception of cases such as clitic climbing in Italian, discussed by Fanselow and Felix (1987: 15–20), there does not seem to be overwhelming evidence to show that the setting of one parameter affects a significantly large number of grammatical features of a language – which, however, would be essential for the model to be attractive. In other words, there may be good reasons to suspect, as Peter Matthews (1990: 137) does, that "yet again, we posit that something is innate not because we have found it to be universal, but because we see no way by which it can be learned".[314]

13.2   Usage-based approaches

13.2.1   Construction grammar

Of the many models of grammar that exist alongside or as modifications of or alternatives to the Chomskyan version of generative grammar, the approach of construction grammar is perhaps particularly interesting. On the one hand, it offers an opportunity of accommodating the findings of corpus linguists and foreign language linguistics with respect to the item-specific nature of some linguistic phenomena. On the other hand, construction grammar and related approaches have had considerable impact on models of first language acquisition (> 13.2.3).[315]

Construction grammar must not be perceived as one unified theory. In fact, Charles Fillmore (1988: 35) speaks of "a set of moving targets with the same name." Fischer and Stefanowitsch (2006: 3–4) distinguish three main approaches – that of the Berkeley constructionists such as Fillmore, that developed in a cognitive linguistics framework by Lakoff (1987) and Goldberg (1995, 2006), and that of Radical Construction Grammar, which, however, share a number of important assumptions:[316]

---

[314]   Compare also Goldberg (2006: 72).
[315]   For a slightly more sceptical view see Stubbs (2009: 27), Sinclair and Mauranen (2006: 31). Cf. also Herbst (2007: 49–53).
[316]   For an account of these different models see Fischer and Stefanowitsch (2006) and Croft and Cruse (2004: 257–290).

The key notion of the model is the term construction, which is defined as a "form-meaning pair" (Lakoff 1987: 467).[317] At first sight, the range of elements subsumed under the term construction may seem rather wide. Goldberg (2006: 5), for example, lists elements such as the following as constructions:[318]

- morphemes   *this, paint, pre-, -ing, -s*
- idioms (filled)   *give the Devil his due*
- idioms (partially filled)   *jog <someone's> memory*
- covariational conditional   *the Xer the Yer*
- ditransitive   Subj V Obj1 Obj2
- passive   SUBj aux VP_{pp} (PP_{by})

This means that a sentence such as

(3)$_{WG}$ *Justifiably, Heron had always been irritated by those literal-minded critics who insisted in seeking references to the Cornish landscape (…) in the shapes and contours of his paintings.*

is analysed as a combination of different constructions such as the passive construction, the past perfect construction etc.; furthermore words such as *Heron, always* or *–ly* would be identified as constructions occurring in this sentence.

The advantage of subsuming all these under the term construction – despite the different degrees of concreteness or abstraction of the whole or parts of the construction – concerns the fundamental hypothesis of construction grammar, namely the idea of "**a uniform representation of all grammatical knowledge** in the speaker's mind" (Croft and Cruse 2004: 255). In other words, the basic idea of the theory is that language can be described as a structured inventory of constructions, which can be combined to form utterances, as formulated by Fillmore (1988: 37):

---

[317]   Whereas Goldberg (1995: 4) argues in favour of a non-compositional view, a later formulation by Goldberg (2006: 5) is weaker in this respect: "In addition, patterns are stored as constructions even if they are fully predictable as long as they occur with sufficient frequency …". For the discussion whether constructions can be compositional or not see Fischer and Stefanowitsch (2006: 5–6). Compare also Croft and Cruse (2004: 247).

[318]   Examples taken from Goldberg (2006: 5). Compare Croft and Cruse (2004: 255–256) and Fischer and Stefanowitsch (2006: 6).

The grammar of a language can be seen as a repertory of constructions, plus a set of principles which govern the nesting and superimposition of constructions into or upon one another.

In this respect, construction grammar differs fundamentally from the generative approach outlined in 13.1 since it does not posit "underlying syntactic or semantic forms" or transformations (Goldberg 1995: 7).[319] Also, of course, it is interesting to see that construction grammars do not make a distinction between core and periphery, but rather regard integrating the idiomatic component of language as central to the model. There is a striking parallel between Sinclair's (1991) idiom principle (> 10.5) and the insight formulated by Fillmore, Kay, and O'Connor (1988: 534) that "in the construction of a grammar, more is needed than a system of general grammatical rules and a lexicon of fixed words and phrases". They demonstrate the appropriateness of the concept of constructions by providing evidence for the idiosyncratic and productive properties of constructions such as the *the X-er the Y-er* construction

(4a)$_\text{QE}$ *The more carefully you do your work, the easier it will get.*

(4b)$_\text{QE}$ *The bigger they come, the harder they fall.*

or the *let alone* construction

(5a)$_\text{QE}$ *Max won't eat SHRIMP, let alone SQUID.*

(5b)$_\text{QE}$ *John hardly speaks RUSSIAN let alone BULGARIAN.*

The fact that in this framework of thinking no sharp distinction between syntax and lexis is made is a further parallel to Sinclair (2004: 164).[320]

13.2.2   Argument structure constructions

The notion of argument structure constructions as developed by Goldberg (1995, 2006) provides an interesting framework for discussing certain aspects of verb valency and clause structure. Goldberg (1995: 43) makes a distinction between participant roles – which she describes as frame-specific roles – and more general argument roles such as agent or patient (>

---

[319]   Note that Goldberg (1995: 7) nevertheless sees construction grammar as a form of generative grammar.

[320]   See also Bybee (2007: 284–292).

12.2–3).[321] Participant roles and argument roles can be fused under certain conditions. One of these is the Semantic Coherence Principle according to which the participant roles of the verb and the argument roles of the construction must be compatible.[322]

Goldberg (2006: 41) identifies the participant roles loader, loaded-theme and container for the verb *load*, which can then be related to the Caused motion construction and a combination of the causative construction and a *with*-construction in the following way:

Caused motion

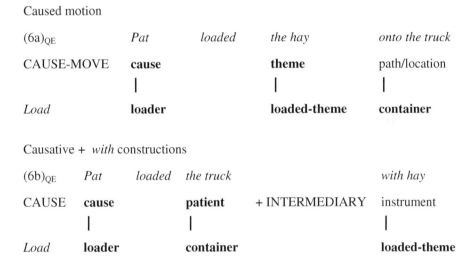

(6a)QE	*Pat*	*loaded*	*the hay*	*onto the truck*
CAUSE-MOVE	**cause**		**theme**	path/location
	|		|	|
Load	**loader**		**loaded-theme**	**container**

Causative + *with* constructions

(6b)QE	*Pat*	*loaded*	*the truck*		*with hay*
CAUSE	**cause**		**patient**	+ INTERMEDIARY	instrument
	|		|		|
Load	**loader**		**container**		**loaded-theme**

Assigning (6a) and (6b) to two different constructional analyses is one way of doing justice to the subtle differences in meaning between the two sen-

---

[321] Goldberg (2006: 20) makes no claims as to the universal nature of the labels for argument roles.

[322] For the Correspondence Principle see Goldberg (2006: 40): "… profiled participant roles of the verb must be encoded by profiled argument roles of the construction, with the exception that if a verb has three profiled roles, one can be represented by an unprofiled argument role (and realized as an oblique argument)". See Herbst (2010) for a discussion from the point of view of valency theory.

tences – such as the element in direct object position being presented as being affected in some special way.[323]

Furthermore, positing argument structure constructions of this sort may help to explain aspects of linguistic creativity concerning sentences of the type

(7)$_{QE}$ *She sneezed the foam off the cappuccino.*

or, to use a German example,

(8)$_{AM}$ *Den letzten habe ich dann wirklich noch daneben zittert.*[324]

The explanation offered by Goldberg (2006: 6 and 94–98) is that the 'caused-motion'-interpretation of such sentences must be due to the construction since one would not want to argue that the locative complement *off the cappuccino* or *daneben* really represent a valency slot or a separate meaning of the corresponding verb.[325] From that point of view the concept of argument structure constructions seems quite attractive.

Argument structure constructions are defined in terms of form and meaning, as illustrated by the following examples (Goldberg 2006: 73):

Form/Example	Meaning	Construction Label
1. Subj V Obl$_{path/loc}$	X moves Y$_{path/loc}$	**Intransitive Motion**
e.g. The fly buzzed into the room.		
2. Subj V Obj Obl-$_{path/loc}$	X causes Y to move Z$_{path/loc}$	**Caused Motion**
e.g. Pat sneezed the foam off the cappuccino.		
3. Subj V Obj Obj2	X causes Y to receive Z	**Ditransitive**
e.g. She faxed him a letter.		
4. Subj V Obj RP	X causes Y to become Z$_{state}$	**Resultative**
e.g. She kissed him unconscious.		

---

[323]   For an account of this in terms of clausal roles see Herbst and Schüller (2008) and Herbst (2010). See Goldberg (2006: 33–38) for arguments for not treating such alternations in terms of derivation.

[324]   Said by Magdalena Neuner on the occasion of winning the gold medal in the Olympic biathlon race describing her last shot: *I really trembled my last shot wide of the mark.*

[325]   For an account in terms of "nonce applications of the pattern" see Kay (2005).

The "formal" categories used such as Obj (object) and RP (resultative phrase) are determined semantically to a certain degree and thus different from the complement classes identified in valency theory (> 12.3).[326] Semantically, some of these argument structure constructions show a considerable amount of polysemy. Thus for the ditransitive construction, Goldberg (1995: 38) identifies a central sense "Agent successfully causes recipient to receive patient", which applies to verbs such as *give, pass, throw, bring, take* and five further senses such as "Agent enables recipient to receive patient" (*permit, allow*) etc.[327]

Since so far the discussion of argument structure constructions has focused on a relatively small number of constructions such as the ones listed above, it is difficult to say whether all verb uses (or all valency patterns) could be related to argument structure constructions or whether these should be imagined as prototypical centres in a continuum.

13.2.3   The usage-based view of language acquisition

Construction grammar and other usage-based approaches are closely related to questions of the representation of language in the mind and offer very promising alternatives to the Chomskyan approach to language acquisition. In particular, followers of these theories argue that language can be learnt and that there is no need to make the special kinds of assumptions about innate properties of the mind that Chomsky made. Ellis (2003: 64–65) characterizes the usage-based perspective on language as follows:[328]

> They hold that structural regularities of language emerge from learners' lifetime analysis of the distributional characteristics of language input and, thus, that the knowledge of a speaker/hearer cannot be understood as an innate grammar, but rather as a statistical ensemble of language experiences that changes slightly every time a new utterance is processed.

Thus the idea of storage plays an important role in such accounts, which also has important consequences for the role of memory. Bybee (2007:

---

[326] For the question of to what extent correlations between verb meaning and use in particular argument structure constructions are concerned see Faulhaber (forthcoming). Compare Herbst (2009ab) and Herbst and Faulhaber (2010).

[327] Cf. Gries and Stefanowitsch (forthc.) for polysemy of constructions and collexeme classes.

[328] Compare Hopper's (1987) notion of Emergent Grammar.

291) describes the brain as "a powerful categorization device for the efficient sorting and storing of the pieces of our experience, including the units of language use". On the one hand, this accounts for item-specific knowledge relating to the phraseological aspects of language, where Bybee stresses that it is "easier to access, produce, and comprehend a precompiled chunk". On the other hand, it is assumed that shared features can be discovered and more abstract schemata will be developed on the basis of stored examples of a similar nature.[329] In *Constructing a Language*, Tomasello (2003: 140 and 142) describes this as follows:

> In the initial stages ... children's linguistic competence is most accurately characterized not as a "grammar", but rather as an inventory of relatively isolated, item-based constructional islands. Development after these initial stages, typically at 2–3 years of age, then proceeds gradually and in piecemeal fashion, with some constructions becoming abstract more rapidly than others – mainly depending on the type and the token frequency with which children hear particular constructions, since this is what provides the raw material for the schematization process. ... Regardless of details, under no circumstances does this development look like an instantaneous setting of parameters in which all verbs and other lexical items immediately participate in a totally abstract construction.

Abstraction, identification of constituents and formation of schemata are recognized as important parts of the language acquisition process. At the same time it is important to note that even in adult language "there is solid evidence that both item-specific knowledge and generalizations coexist" (Goldberg 2006: 63). This means that all types of constructions (> 13.2.1) can be acquired through the same processes of acquisition, which Tomasello (2003: 6) describes as intention-reading and pattern-finding.

There seems to be a considerable amount of evidence for Tomasello's (2003: 6) claim that "children's early language is largely item-based".[330] For instance, in a study by Lieven, Behrens, Speares and Tomasello (2003)

---

[329]   For the nature of storage compare cf. Behrens (2007): "It is as of yet unknown whether we simply store more and more tokens upon repeated usage, or whether we store more repeated information on a more general and abstract level when available, or whether we do both." See also Bybee (2005: 7) and Goldberg (2006: 62). For the role of the memory and access to memory see Bybee (2007: 291).

[330]   Behrens (2009: 394) considers it an "as of yet open issue ... where item-based formulas are the starting point for each aspect of language development".

the linguistic development of a 2-year old child learning English was moni-
tored relatively closely over a period of 6 weeks and the utterances produced on the last day were compared with the recordings of the period before:[331]

- 79 percent of the things the child said on the target day (and 63 percent
  of the multi-word utterances), she had said in exactly the same form before

- 74 percent of the novel multi-word utterances modified a previously
  made utterance only in one place (*Where is the butter?* on the basis of
  Where is the ___?)

This is hardly surprising when one considers that the input children get also
seems to be highly repetitive and item-based. A very important factor in
this context is that child-directed speech, sometimes referred to as
motherese, i.e. the language that adults use when talking to very young
children shows certain characteristics which may facilitate the language
acquisition process. Tomasello (2003: 111–113) reports on a study of 12
English-speaking mothers interacting with 2-year old children, which
showed that the majority "of the utterances children hear are grounded in
highly repetitive item-based frames that they experience dozens, in some
cases hundreds, of times every day".[332]

What these examples show is that child language can also be imagined
as an inventory of constructions of the same type as construction grammar
posits for adult language.[333] Tomasello (2003: 99) points out that children
under the age of 2 have inventories consisting of words (such as *bird*),
some bound morphemes (plural *–s*), "frozen phrases" (*I-wanna-do-it*) and a
variety of item-based mixed constructions (*Where's-the X? I-wanna X*) and
comes to the conclusion that "children do not first learn words and then
combine them into sentences via contentless syntactic 'rules'".

---

[331] For a more detailed discussion of these results see Tomasello (2003: 307–
308) and Lieven, Behrens, Speares and Tomasello (2003). See also Ellis
(2003: 70), who talks about "a developing set of slot-and-frame patterns" in
this respect.

[332] See Cameron-Faulkner, Lieven and Tomasello (2003) for details. For the role
of motherese see also Klann-Delius (1999: 142–146). For the verb-island hypothesis see Tomasello (2003: 117–118).

[333] See Tomasello (2003: 105–108) for chunks and analysability in adult language.

The idea of usage-based approaches to language acquisition is that linguistic structure can be accounted for in terms of a few basic psychological processes such as entrenchment and categorization, as pointed out by Behrens (2009: 386):[334]

> A central cognitive phenomenon is entrenchment, the fact that repeated encounter of a unit leaves memory traces that stabilize the more often this unit recurs. ... However, repetition alone does not lead to the abstraction of more general information. In order to generalize and form categories, the mind must recognize similarities as well as dissimilarities. It filters out aspects that do not recur, and registers communalities by comparing stored with new units. New units are categorized along those dimensions where similarities with stored units are detected. Through abstraction and generalization, schemas are formed.

With respect to generalizations about argument structure constructions or valency properties of verbs, entrenchment seems to play an important role, but so does the factor of pre-emption. While it is relatively obvious that if children hear a verb frequently used in a particular construction this use will become entrenched, it is not quite so clear how children find out that sentences such as

(9)   *He explained them the situation.*[335]

(10)_{QE}   *He disappeared the rabbit.*

(11)_{QE}   *She giggled me.*

(12)_{QE}   *Dad said Sue something nice.*

do not seem to occur. Tomasello (2003: 178) argues that if one pattern is established for a verb, children will not use it in another construction in which they have not experienced it. Furthermore, hearing *He made the rabbit disappear* or *She made you giggle* may pre-empt sentences such as (10) or (11).[336] With respect to example (12), Stefanowitsch (2008: 527)

---

[334]   For the concept of entrenchment see Langacker (1987: 59), Ungerer and Schmid (2006) or Stefanowitsch (2008).

[335]   See Stefanowitsch (2007: 67–68) for an analysis of examples of *explain me this* and a discussion of the notion of grammaticality.

[336]   For a discussion of pre-emption compare also Goldberg (2006: 96–98), who points out that *She sneezed the foam off the cappuccino* would not be pre-empted by the more frequent intransitive use of *sneeze* for semantic reasons. Tomasello (2003: 180) also draws attention to the role of child-parent-interaction in this context.

introduces the concept of negative entrenchment, which is based on hypotheses about the expected frequency of co-occurrence of linguistic features.[337] Constraints such as the ones illustrated by (9) – (12) can thus be explained in a way which is compatible with a view of language acquisition in terms of learning.

There thus seems to be considerable empirical evidence for a usage-based view of language acquisition in which the grammar of a language appears as an emergent phenomenon, although of course it would be wrong to assume that all scholars would necessarily interpret all the data in the same way or that all data would point in the same direction.[338] Nevertheless, there is a large body of evidence to suggest that linguistic competence can be explained entirely as the result of a learning process and that no assumptions about a special genetic predisposition of human beings that would exclusively serve the purpose of language acquisition need to be made.

Recommended further reading:

– CGEL (1985), CamG (2002)
– Sampson (1980), Sells (1985)
– Herbst and Schüller (2008)
– Palmer (1971)
– Tomasello (2003), Fischer and Stefanowitsch (2006), Behrens (2009)

---

[337] For the hypothesis that "*degrees* of significant absence correlate with *degrees* of unacceptability" see Stefanowitsch (2008: 527).

[338] Compare for instance Tomasello's (2003: 121–122) and Goldberg's (2006: 77–79) discussions of the role of high-frequency verbs in the acquisition of argument structure constructions. See also the connectionist model suggested by MacWhinney (1998). For an account of different theories of language acquisition within the usage-based approach see Ellis (2003) and Behrens (2009).

Meaning

14 Semantics: meaning, reference and denotation

14.1 Meaning

One of the basic ideas about language which is shared by practically all schools of modern linguistics is de Saussure's characterization of the linguistic sign as consisting of two components – *signifiant* (form) and *signifié* (meaning). Although many of the aspects of language discussed in chapters 4–16 focus on the form-component of the sign (at least in taking form as the starting point of analysis), reference to meaning was repeatedly made. For instance, the phoneme was defined as a linguistic unit that has the function to "distinguish between forms with different meanings" (5.1), and the morpheme was described as a "unit that serves to carry meaning" (8.1). It is remarkable – although hopefully it escaped the notice of most readers – that no precise definition or characterization of the term *meaning* was given in these contexts. Similarly, there is nothing unusual about statements of the sort that *talk* has a different meaning in English and in German or that the meaning of the word *nice* has changed since Jane Austen's time. In the same way, speakers of a language (who have had no training in linguistics) are perfectly able to make statements about meanings of words, for instance, to the effect that *good* means the opposite of *bad*. Speakers, in very many situations, are also able to describe the meanings of words to children or even argue about the meaning of a word (in the sense that there can be disagreement what words such as *democracy* or *freedom* really mean or whether there can be such a thing as a *third alternative* or whether the meaning of *alternative* is 'one of two possibilities').[339] It thus seems that, contrary to the word *word* (> 9.1.1), the way the word *meaning*

---

[339] Compare the definitions of *alternative* in NSOED, LDOCE5 and OALD7.

is used in everyday language does not differ greatly from its use in linguistics.

The fact that most linguists would probably not object to any of the uses of *meaning* above does not necessarily mean that all linguists would have the same ideas about what *meaning* actually is. In science, one is sometimes confronted with a situation in which it is easier to talk about a particular phenomenon or to describe some of its properties than to state what the phenomenon actually is. Thus, physicists, for instance, have been perfectly able to measure certain qualities of quarks and to distinguish between several types of quarks (which they have labelled red, green, etc.), without necessarily fully understanding as yet the exact nature of quarks. In the same way, it is easier to make statements about meaning in language than to describe the character of the phenomenon that we call meaning. As a consequence, various approaches towards the character of meaning have been taken, which can perhaps be subsumed under the following three headings:

- meaning as a purely linguistic phenomenon, a property of the linguistic sign, which, according to the principles of Saussurean and post-Saussurean structuralism, can be determined on the basis of the place of a sign in the system of a language and its relationship to other signs;

- meaning as a psychological phenomenon, i.e. the ideas or concepts speakers associate with a particular linguistic form; and

- meaning as a phenomenon of use, i.e. a property that can be determined on the basis of how a word form is actually used by the speakers of a speech community.

14.2   Meaning and reference

14.2.1   Bloomfield's misconception of meaning

While it may be relatively difficult to arrive at a precise definition of meaning, it is at least relatively clear what meaning is not. It is accepted today that the meaning of a word must not be equated with the objects, people, ideas etc. of the real world to which this word can apply. In fact, it can be seen as one of the great weaknesses of the approach taken by the most influential scholar of American structuralism, Leonard Bloomfield, that he did not make this distinction as rigorously as appropriate. He seemed to think that the description of the meaning of a word benefits from scientific knowledge of the object described (such as its chemical composition). Since such knowledge is not available for most objects one can describe using words, the study of meaning was considered particularly difficult by American structuralists. It is for this reason – not, as is often maintained in the literature, that they considered it unimportant – that the study of meaning was widely ignored in American structuralism. The point about this argument is, however, that it is misguided, as is pointed out by Palmer (²1981: 22):

> Bloomfield (1933: 139) argued that *salt* could be clearly defined as sodium chloride, or NaCl. He was wrong to do so. *Salt*, for ordinary language, is the substance that appears on our table. It is no less salt if its chemical composition is not precisely that of the chemist's definition. *Salt*, for most of us belongs with pepper and mustard, which do not lend themselves to any simple scientific specification – and neither should *salt* in its everyday use.

Also, one could object, as Leech (1981: 2) does, that "Bloomfield's argument implies a vision of an eventual period when everything would be capable of authoritative scientific definition, or in simpler words, when everything there was to be known would be known about everything."

A further argument against Bloomfield's conviction that scientific knowledge about an object is necessary for the description of meaning is that it ignores the fact that such knowledge may not be available to the majority of language users and one does not have to know that salt is NaCl in order to use the word *salt* correctly.[340] In fact, it is more than likely that children acquire a perfectly appropriate use of the word *salt* long before they learn that salt is sodium chloride.[341]

Whatever the relationship between knowledge about objects and their properties and knowledge about word meanings may be – and some more recent psycholinguistic approaches suggest that the two should not be seen as entirely independent from one another – it is clear that knowledge about objects (in terms of precise and scientifically accurate chemical, physical properties etc.) is no prerequisite for mastering the meaning of a word that can be used for that object.

---

[340]   Cf. Ullmann (1972: 59): "… one may wonder whether this is really the meaning of the word for the average speaker who probably has no idea of the chemical composition of salt".

[341]   For an account of Bloomfield's views see also Sampson (1980: 68–69).

14.2.2 Denotation

In order to describe the relationship between the various entities involved it makes sense to distinguish between the linguistic sign – with its two components form and meaning – on the one hand, and entities of the extra-linguistic world (which includes the possible worlds of our imagination) to which linguistic signs can be applied on the other. Thus, on the one hand, there is a word such as *island* – consisting of a form, namely /ˈaɪlənd/ or <island>, and a meaning, which can be described as 'a piece of land completely surrounded by water'.[342] On the other hand, there are objects to which this definition applies in the sense that if speakers of English talk about such things, they can use the word *island*.

The set of objects, people etc. of the world to which a word can be applied is often called its **denotatum**. Thus the denotatum of the word *island* is identical with the set of all islands which exist in the reality of the world or in the imagination of the speakers. The relationship between a linguistic sign and its denotatum is its **denotation**.

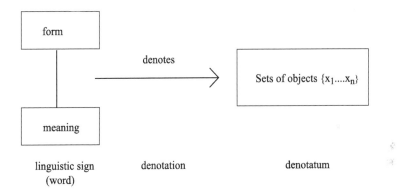

form		
	denotes →	Sets of objects $\{x_1....x_n\}$
meaning		

| linguistic sign (word) | denotation | denotatum |

---

[342] LDOCE5.

14.2.3 Reference

14.2.3.1 The general notion of reference

What is important to note is that the denotation is a property of a word which is independent of its use in any concrete speech situation. However, when speakers use words they do not necessarily want to talk about the whole class of objects, persons, etc. which the word denotes but rather they often wish to identify one particular object, person etc. in order to say something about them. In the context of Searle's speech act theory (1969), the act which speakers perform in such situations has been called **refer-ring**. A speaker can refer to an object, person etc. by using a linguistic expression, usually a phrase, through which it is possible to identify a par-ticular member of the set comprising the denotatum. The member of the set referred to is called the **referent**, the relationship between the respective phrase and the referent is called **reference**.[343]

---

[343] Compare Searle (1969: 26–29), Lyons (1977: 174–215) and Lipka (³2002: 74–77). It should also be pointed out at this stage that, especially in research prior to Searle (1969) and Lyons (1977), the distinction between denotation and reference is not made in the same way. Thus, Ogden and Richards (1923/¹⁰1956: 11) use the model of a semiotic triangle to describe the rela-tionship of linguistic signs and extralinguistic objects:

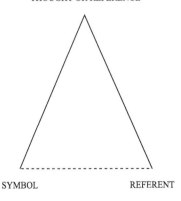

THOUGHT OR REFERENCE

SYMBOL   REFERENT

Ullmann (1972: 55–56) describes this model as follows: "On this reading, there is no direct relation between words and the things they 'stand for': the word 'symbolizes' a 'thought or reference' which in its turn 'refers' to the feature or event we are talking about. There is nothing fundamentally new in

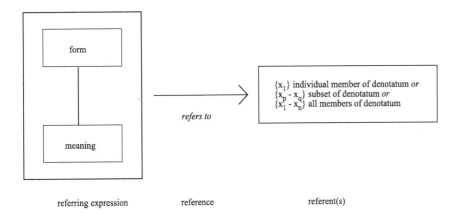

Two things are worth noting here: firstly, a word as such does not have reference nor does it have a referent. Reference only holds with respect to a particular speech situation. This can easily be demonstrated by considering sentences such as the following:[344]

(1a)$_{AE}$ *The cultural landscape of Jersey – its Norman style farmhouses, the narrow winding lanes and small fields, the French street names – reflect a fascinating and complex history that has entwined <u>the island</u> in the fate of two great nations: Britain and France for over one thousand years.*

(1b)$_{AE}$ *Situated in the Bay of St. Malo <u>the islands</u> enjoy approximately over 2,000 hours of sunshine per annum.*

---

this analysis of meaning; the mediaeval schoolmen already knew that 'vox significat mediantibus conceptibus' (the word signifies through the medium of concepts)." For a critique of this model see Ullmann (1972: 54–58). For an outline of the Ogden and Richards model against its behaviourist background see Lyons (1977: 96–99).

[344] Sources of examples in this section: http://www.jersey.com/index.asp, http://www.gov.gg/, http://www.visitorkney.com/island.html, http://www.tate.org.uk/stives/default.htm and Munisha Underhill, Perry Green 2000, http://www.henry-moore.org/pg/henry-moore-research/henry-moores-life/1898–1925 (last accessed 14 April 2010); and Tom Cross: *Painting the Warmth of the Sun,* Tiverton/Cambridge: Westcountry Books/The Lutterworth Press (1995).

(1c)_{AE}   *The warmth of the welcome and the beauty of <u>the islands</u> will restore your appetite and your joie de vivre, and enrich your visit to Orkney.*

(1d)_{PW}   *Thus in complete readiness to land he sat looking back at <u>the island</u>.*

In all four sentences, the word *island* is used with the same meaning. Thus the denotatum of the word, which is independent of its use in any particular context, is identical with the set of all islands in the world. The referents of the four uses of the word *island* are different, however. In (1a) the phrase *the island* refers to Jersey, the phrase *the islands* refers to the islands belonging to the Bailwick of Guernsey in (1b) and to the Orkney islands in (1c). *The island* in (1d) finally refers to the fictional island where the lighthouse in Virginia Woolf's *To the Lighthouse* is situated.

Secondly, the linguistic unit that carries reference is not the word but what Searle (1969: 26–27) has described as a referring expression:

> Any expression which serves to identify any thing, process, event, action, or any other kind of 'individual' or 'particular' I shall call a referring expression. Referring expressions point to particular things; they answer the questions "Who?" "What?" "Which?"

From a grammatical point of view it could be argued that it is the phrase (not the word) that has the ability to function as a referring expression (> 11.3). It is quite obvious that it is one of the main functions of the determiners (or pre-heads) in a noun phrase, for example, to establish which elements of the denotatum of the head of the noun phrase are being referred to in a concrete situation:

(2a)_{PW}   *The long window in four sections of the large, sunfilled sitting room overlooking the sea wall and the harbour became the principal subjects of <u>Patrick Heron's paintings</u> from 1947 onwards.*

(2b)_{PW}   *Heron made <u>many paintings</u> from St Ives subjects which responded to the zestful enjoyment of freely applied colour.*

(2c)_{PW}   *In 1950 Patrick Heron was commissioned by the Arts Council to make <u>a large painting</u> for the Festival exhibition '60 paintings for '51'.*

14.2.3.2   Definite and indefinite reference

Nevertheless, the notion of referring expression is not totally clear-cut. First of all, Searle (1969: 27) recognizes a need to distinguish between definite and indefinite referring expressions:

Expressions beginning with the indefinite article, such as "a man", as it occurs in the utterance of the sentence, "A man came", might be said to refer
to a particular man, but they do not serve to identify or to indicate the
speaker's intention to identify an object in the manner of some uses of expressions with the definite article, such as "the man".

The problem of the degree of definiteness of the kind of reference established is also apparent from the sentences under (2). The reference of the
phrase *Patrick Heron* in (2a) is no doubt definite, as is probably also that of
Patrick Heron's paintings. This is perhaps less clear in the case of *many
paintings* in (2b). In any case, the referential character of *a large painting*
in (2c) might be considered questionable in that it is not apparent from the
text at this point whether Heron actually painted this painting or not.

What is perhaps more important is that Searle (1969: 27), as later Lyons
(1977: 185),[345] finds it necessary to speak of

non-referring uses of expressions formed with the indefinite article: e.g., the
occurrence of "a man" in the utterance of "A man came" is to be distinguished from its occurrence in the utterance of "John is a man". The first is
referential, the second predicative.

Similarly, while *this great twentieth-century sculptor* in

(3)_{AE}   *The Gallery also manages the Barbara Hepworth Museum and Sculpture Garden, which gives a remarkable insight into the work of <u>this
great twentieth-century sculptor</u>.*

is clearly referential in character (which has Barbara Hepworth as its referent), this is not so clear in the case of *a Penzance girl* in

(4)_{PW}   *Margo Maeckelberghe was <u>a Penzance girl</u>.*

The same applies to *as a painter and draughtsman* and *as a schoolboy* in

(5)_{PW}   *Patrick showed early talent <u>as a painter and draughtsman</u>. <u>As a school-
boy</u> he was aware of the work of Cézanne and Sickert ...*

or *a sculptor* in[346]

---

[345]   Cf. Lyons (1977: 185): "A definite noun-phrase may occur as the complement of the verb 'to be' and it may then have a predicative, rather than a referential, function."

[346]   Examples (6) and (7a) taken from   http://www.henry-moore.org/pg/henry-
moore-research/henry-moores-life/1898–1925 (last accessed 14 April 2010).

(6)_{HM}   *During these years Moore began carving in wood and modelling clay, and he consciously decided to become a sculptor, ...*

where one could argue that these noun phrases do not contribute to the identification of an element of the denotatum and thus are not referential. However, Searle (1969: 27) points out that Russell (1919: 172) treats such cases as (4) as identity statements. (5) and (6) could be analysed in a similar way, attributing indefinite reference to *painter, draughtsman, schoolboy* and *sculptor*. Otherwise, the analysis would result in a rather contradictory treatment of similar noun phrases such as

(7a)_{HM}   *Henry Moore went to infant and elementary schools in his home town, and then in 1910, like several of his brothers and sisters he won a scholarship to Castleford Secondary School, which later became a Grammar School under subsequent reforms and administrative developments.*

(7b)_{BNC} *Joanne works at a grammar school and almost all her teaching experience has been at this school.*

If, as would be in line with the view held by Searle and Lyons, one were to analyse *a grammar school* in (7b) as an instance of a singular indefinite referring expression, and, possibly, in (7a) as a non-referring use, then presumably only because the school had already been mentioned previously in the text in (7a) but not in (7b). Since the whole question of reference has been subject to considerable debate in linguistics and philosophy, it may suffice at this point to point out that there are differences as to the referential character of certain phrases in certain contexts. Whether there is any great descriptive advantage in either solution is perhaps to be doubted. In any case, it has become obvious that if one makes a distinction between denotation and reference in the way suggested by Lyons (1977), reference is a speaker- and utterance-oriented notion, which, strictly speaking, is only of relatively marginal interest to semantics. The act of referring is appropriately seen by Searle as part of performing a speech act and thus falls under the scope of pragmatics and speech act theory (> 17.3), whereas referential relations also constitute an important subject in the analysis of texts and textual structure (> 18.2). What is more important to semantics is the relationship between a linguistic sign and its denotatum, where, of course, the denotatum can be seen as the set of all possible referents.

14.3 The scope of meaning

Up to a point, meaning and denotatum can be seen as complementary notions. Thus, the word with the meaning 'a boat etc. for transporting people, vehicles or goods across a stretch of water' (NSOED) can be applied to any member of the set of ferries in the real world, which make up its denotatum. Likewise, any ferry can be referred to by the word *ferry*. This parallel only holds to a certain extent, however.

One of the most famous examples to illustrate the fact that meaning may comprise more than the relationship of denotation was introduced by the German philosopher Frege, who pointed out that the words *Morgenstern* and *Abendstern* (as well as the word *Venus*) have the same denotatum but still would not be considered to be synonymous.[347]

In a similar way, one could argue that words such as *autumn* and *fall* or *child* and *kid* do not differ with the respect to their respective denotata but rather with respect to who uses them (*autumn* being a typically British, *fall* a typically American use) or in which situation they are being used (*kid* being typical of an informal style). They thus contain information which goes beyond the identification of their denotatum. Such considerations have led many linguists to talk about different types of meaning. Leech ([2]1981: 23), for instance, introduces a category of social meaning to cover regional, social and stylistic differences between words.[348] Whether these should be treated as differences of meaning is by no means uncontroversial, however. Referring to *autumn* and *fall*, Palmer ([2]1981: 89) argues:

> The works of dialectologists are full of examples like these. They are especially interested in words to do with farming; depending where you live you will say *cowshed, cowhouse* or *byre, haystack, hayrick* or *haymow*. ... But these groups of words are of no interest at all for semantics. Their status is no different from the translation-equivalents of, say, English and French. It is simply a matter of people speaking different forms of the language having different vocabulary items.

Thus, while *autumn* and *fall* clearly provide a reader or hearer with information about the speaker's or writer's background, this kind of information need not necessarily be seen as one of meaning. Similarly, the stylistic

---

[347] Cf. Frege (1906/2000: 685).

[348] Leech ([2]1981: 9–23) distinguishes between the following seven types of meaning: conceptual meaning, connotative meaning, social meaning, affective meaning, reflected meaning, collocative meaning and thematic meaning.

value of a word can be seen as part of its meaning, as in Leech's (^{2}1981) model, or as separate property of words independent from meaning.

A further element of meaning that is sometimes seen as a separate level of meaning is that of "emotive or evaluative" meaning, as Palmer (^{2}1981: 90) points out:

> Some semanticists have made great play with the emotive difference be-tween *politician* and *statesman*, *hide* and *conceal*, *liberty* and *freedom*, each implying approval or disapproval. The function of such words in language is, of course, to influence attitudes. ... Nevertheless, it is a mistake to sepa-rate such emotive or evaluative meaning from the 'basic' 'cognitive' mean-ing of words for three reasons: First, it is not easy to establish precisely what cognitive meaning is, and certainly not reasonable to attempt to define it in terms of reference to physical properties. On such a definition, most verbs and adjectives would have little or no cognitive meaning. Secondly, there are words in English that are used PURELY for evaluative purposes, most obviously the adjectives *good* and *bad*, but it is not normally assumed that they have no cognitive meaning. Such words are of interest to moral philosophers, but should not, I believe, have any special place in linguistics. Thirdly, we make all kinds of judgments and do not merely judge in terms of 'good' and 'bad'. We judge size and use the appropriate terms – *gi-ant/dwarf, mountain/hill,* etc., and we make other kinds of judgments in our choice of words. The meaning of words is not simply a matter of objective facts; a great deal of it is subjective and we cannot clearly distinguish be-tween the two.

As far as word meaning is concerned, there is probably a lot to be said in favour of Palmer's rejection of different types of meaning.[349] Nevertheless, what we consider to be part of the meaning is yet another case of a rela-tively arbitrary decision made by the investigating linguist, the appropriate-ness of which must be judged against the overall purpose of investigation.

---

[349]   Note, however, that some of Leech's seven types of meaning explicitly refer to sentence meaning. This applies in particular to his categories of thematic meaning, and also to affective meaning: "Factors such as intonation and voice-timbre ... are also important here. ... Affective meaning is largely a parasitic category in the sense that to express our emotions we rely upon the mediation of other categories of meaning – conceptual, connotative, or stylis-tic. Emotional expression through style comes about, for instance, when we adopt an impolite tone to express displeasure ..., or when we adopt a casual tone to express friendliness." (Leech ^{2}1981: 16)

This is also true of another type of meaning that is often identified – **connotation**.[350] In this case, the argument is not so much about whether a particular feature of a word – such as its stylistic value – is to be seen as part of its meaning or as a category of its own. Rather, the question is whether connotation is a linguistic property at all. Connotations of words can be characterized by three properties:

- Connotations are associations speakers have with a word beyond its (denotative or conceptual) meaning.

- Connotations arise from the properties of (elements of) the denotatum.

- Connotations are not necessarily shared by the whole speech community and "they vary considerably ... according to culture, historical period and the experience of the individual" (Leech [2]1981: 13).

Thus it is quite possible that, with a word such as *nuclear power station*, some speakers connote positive attributes such as 'modern technology' whereas others may connote negative properties such as 'danger', 'threat to health or environment' etc. Similarly, Palmer ([2]1981: 92)[351] points out that "*woman* has the connotation 'gentle' and *pig* the connotation 'dirty'" and argues that "... this is not a matter of the meaning of words or even of meaning in general. It rather indicates that people (or some people) believe that women are gentle and pigs dirty". While in these cases one might indeed argue that associations of this kind are related to the denotata, i.e. that they are clichés attributed to women or pigs by particular groups of speakers, the negative connotations of words such as *vergasen* or *Führer* in German cannot be explained away quite so easily as a purely extralinguistic phenomenon. In any case, the study of connotations (whether one considers them part of semantics or not) touches upon the question of whether one can (should or must) make a distinction between linguistic and extra-linguistic knowledge or not. This is also emphasized by Leech ([2]1981: 12–13):

> It will be clear that in talking about connotation, I am in fact talking about the 'real world' experience one associates with an expression when one uses or hears it. Therefore the boundary between conceptual and connota-

---

[350] The term connotation is often contrasted with denotative or conceptual meaning (Leech [2]1981: 9) but this must not be confused with the term denotation as defined above.

[351] Compare also Leech's ([2]1981: 12–13) discussion of the connotations of *woman*.

tive meaning is coincident with that nebulous but crucial distinction … between 'language' and the 'real world'. This accounts for the feeling that connotation is somehow incidental to language rather than an essential part of it, and we may notice, in confirmation, that connotative meaning is not specific to language, but is shared by other communicative systems, such as visual art and music. Whatever connotations the word *baby* has can be conjured up … by a drawing of a baby, or an imitation of a baby's cry.

15   Meaning relations

15.1   Polysemy and homonymy

15.1.1   Polysemy and homonymy in linguistic analysis

Irrespective of how meaning is defined or how the description of meaning is approached, there is consensus in linguistics that meaning is one of the components of the linguistic sign that is firmly connected with its form. In 9.1.1 it was pointed out that it may make sense to distinguish between lexemes and lexical units. In the terminology employed by Cruse (1986: 80), "a lexical unit is the union of a single sense with a lexical form", whereas "a lexeme is a family of lexical units". This distinction presupposes that it is possible for a lexeme to have more than one meaning and that it is possible to distinguish between these.

That the same word form can occur with different meanings can easily be demonstrated: One would not expect there to be any disagreement amongst speakers that *bank, ear, press* and *royalty* are not always used in the same meanings in the following sentences:

(1a)_{BNC}   *In that same year I was posted to South Shields on the south <u>bank</u> of the River Tyne.*

(1b)_{BNC}   *I will not accept Eurocheques because when I pay them into the <u>bank</u> I am losing money because of the transaction charges.*

(2a)_{BNC}   *"You are not at all satisfied", Susan said softly into the President's <u>ear</u>.*

(2b)_{BNC}   *If you crush an <u>ear</u> of barley, however, you will not get beer.*

(3a)_{BNC}   *Does freedom of the <u>press</u> mean freedom to choose its own standards?*

(3b)_{BNC}   *I was not to answer the phone; above all I was not to speak to the <u>press</u>.*

(3c)_{BNC}   *The technology of printing now has virtually nothing in common with the wooden <u>presses</u> and lead type of 15th-century pioneers like Johannes Gutenberg or Nicolas Jensen.*

(3d)_{BNC}   *Two types of <u>presses</u> are used, the horizontal press and the traditional Champagne press.*

(4a)$_{BNC}$ *Apart from demonstrating one of the unwavering laws of British jour-*
nalism, that nothing sells newspapers like <u>royalty</u>, and nothing makes a
better editorial column than declamations of simple patriotism, the cu-
rious thing about these assaults is how much they belong to a period.

(4b)$_{BNC}$ *And contact with <u>royalty</u> gives the lord lieutenants real influence.*

(4c)$_{BNC}$ *But then Michael gets an even bigger <u>royalty</u> rate than Madonna.*

(4d)$_{BNC}$ *This <u>royalty</u> is divided between the writer and the publishing company.*

On the basis of such sentences, one could argue that, for instance, (4a-b)
and (4c-d) represent two different meanings of the lexical form *royalty* and
thus establish the following two lexical units:[352]

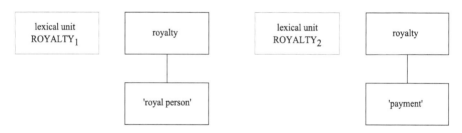

Similarly, two lexical units can be established for *ear*.

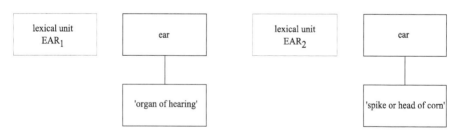

This does not necessarily mean, however, that these lexical units can necessarily be subsumed under one lexeme. In many approaches to semantics, a
distinction is made between polysemy and homonymy:

▷ A lexeme is **polysemous** when it has more than one meaning, i.e. when
it comprises more than one lexical unit.

▷ Two lexemes (each consisting of one or more lexical units) are **ho-
monymous** if their forms are identical.[353]

---

[352] Cf. NSOED.

Polysemy: Homonymy:

The problem with the distinction between homonymy and polysemy is that it can only be made reliably in diachronic linguistics. If one takes the history of the language into account, then the criterion to distinguish between polysemy and homonymy is the etymology of the word forms in question: it makes sense to say that if two lexical units have the same etymological root, they can be considered as belonging to the same lexeme (which then must be regarded as polysemous) and if they have different roots they belong to two different lexemes (that are homonyms).

On the basis of this criterion, *bank* and *ear* present cases of homonymy, whereas *press* and *royalty* are to be classified as polysemous lexemes. Thus *bank*$_1$ ('sloping margin of a river etc.') is related to Old Icelandic *bakki*, whereas *bank*$_2$ ('financial institution') is derived from French *banque* or its Italian source *banca*. Similarly, *ear*$_1$ ('organ of hearing') is derived from Old English *ēare* and related to German *Ohr*, whereas *ear*$_2$ ('spike or head of corn') is derived from Old English *ēar* and related to the German word *Ähre*. Sound changes operative since Old English have led to a situation in which two forms which originally were distinct from one another have become identical. In contrast to *bank* and *ear*, *press*$_1$ and *press*$_2$ and *royalty*$_1$ and *royalty*$_2$ cannot be traced back to different forms in the history of the language. Rather, one meaning developed out of another meaning of the lexeme. Thus it is easy to see how the following meanings identified in the *New Shorter Oxford English Dictionary* (NSOED) are related: "10a ... a machine for printing", "10b a place or business of which the printing-press is the centre ..." and "11a ... newspapers, journals ... generally". In the case of *royalty*, the relationship between the two meanings illustrated above is perhaps not quite so obvious, but again the meanings identified in the

---

[353] Note that lexemes that are only identical in the phonological form are called homophones, whereas lexemes that are identical in spelling are called homographs.

NSOED suggest a plausible semantic development: "A prerogative or right granted by a monarch, esp. in respect of jurisdiction or over minerals", "A payment made by a person working on a mine, obtaining oil, etc., to the owner of the site or the mineral rights over it; a payment made for the use of a patent or a technical process; a payment made to an author, editor or composer for each copy of a work sold or performed ...".

Synchronically, of course, etymological considerations do not provide a criterion to establish a distinction between homonymy and polysemy. It has thus been suggested that within a synchronic approach homonymy can be distinguished from polysemy by arguing that only in the latter case "two meanings are psychologically related" in the sense that "present-day users of the language feel intuitively that they are related, and therefore tend to assume that they are 'different uses of the same word'" (Leech [2]1981: 227).[354] Leech ([2]1981: 228) points out that etymological relatedness and psychological relatedness need not coincide and argues that in cases such as *ear*[1] and *ear*[2], which on the basis of their etymological development are clearly instances of homonymy, "people often see a metaphorical connection between them, and adjust their understanding of the words accordingly".[355] In the same way one might argue that the historical relatedness of the meanings of *press*[1] and *press*[2] or *royalty*[1] and *royalty*[2] is not necessarily something that the (or all) speakers of the language today would be aware of when using these words.

Since, as Bloomfield (1933/1935: 436) points out, "the degree of nearness of the meanings is not subject to precise measurement", a synchronic distinction between homonymy and polysemy is "bound to be subjective and to some extent arbitrary" (Ullmann 1972: 178) and as such not particularly useful.[356]

---

[354] In a more precise form, Leech ([2]1981: 228) states: "We may, in fact, say that two lexical meanings are 'psychologically related' if a user of the language is able to postulate a connection between them by lexical rules, e.g. by the rule of metaphoric transfer."

[355] Compare also Ullmann's (1972: 164–165) discussion of such examples.

[356] Compare Lyons (1968: 405–407), Lipka ([3]2002: 153–157) or Kastovsky (1982: 121–124).

15.1.2   Psycholinguistic and lexicographical implications

It has to be said that for the purposes of a synchronic semantic analysis the distinction between homonymy and polysemy can be regarded as pretty irrelevant anyway since its subject is the analysis of meanings (or lexical units).[357] It is highly relevant, however, as soon as one tries to investigate the organization of the mental lexicon and tries to discover how people access meaning.

This question is closely related to the way that multiple meaning ought to be treated in dictionaries. Historical dictionaries such as the OED or the NSOED can obviously draw upon the etymological criterion and provide two separate entries for *bank₁* and *bank₂* or *ear₁* and *ear₂* respectively and deal with the different meanings of *press* or *royalty* under a single entry. But such a principle of organization would hardly be appropriate in a synchronic dictionary, especially in a foreign learners' dictionary. For this reason, such dictionaries often make use of the criterion of psychological relatedness so that *sole₁* ('bottom surface of the foot') and *sole₂* ('fish'), which historically present a case of polysemy, are treated as homonyms in OALD2 (1963) and LDOCE1 (1978). Because of the inevitable arbitrariness of such decisions outlined above, there is an increasing tendency in such dictionaries to generally only provide one entry for one lexical form belonging to a particular word class, thus making polysemy a general principle of lexicographical organization.[358]

15.2   Ambiguity

The use of polysemous lexemes or homonyms in sentences can result in **ambiguity**. For instance, a sentence such as

(1c)ᴮᴺᶜ   *How sweet the moonlight sleeps upon this bank!*

is at least potentially ambiguous in that it is not clear which of the meanings of *bank* is being referred to.[359] Usually, ambiguity can be resolved by the (linguistic or extralinguistic) context, however, as in

---

[357]   Cf. Kastovsky (1982: 122).
[358]   For a discussion of polysemy and homonymy as organizational principles in dictionaries see Herbst and Klotz (2003).
[359]   For a discussion of intended ambiguity compare Ullmann (1972: 188–192).

(2c)_{BNC} *If the subject is instructed to attend to one <u>ear</u> and ignore the sounds coming into the other <u>ear</u>, all the sounds in the attended <u>ear</u> will produce an enhanced N100 component in the ERP.*

where *ear* quite clearly illustrates the same meaning of *ear* as in (2a).

15.3   Problems of identification of meanings and lexical units

Irrespective of the question of homonymy and polysemy, it can be considered fairly uncontroversial that *bank₁* and *bank₂* or *press₁* and *press₂* represent different meanings of *bank* and *press*, i.e. different lexical units. However, this is not always as straightforward. For instance, it is far less clear how many meanings one would associate with the different occurrences of the lexical form *meet* in the following sentences:

(5a)_{BNC} *Let's <u>meet</u> for lunch tomorrow.*

(5b)_{BNC} *But the pound will face another test on Thursday when the Bundesbank council <u>meets</u>.*

(5c)_{BNC} *She first <u>met</u> him when she studied at Trinity College, Dublin, as he neared the end of his degree course.*

(5d)_{BNC} *Sampdoria and Barcelona will <u>meet</u> in the European Cup final at Wembley on May 20.*

(5e)_{BNC} *The stack emission comfortably <u>meets</u> the American standard for breathing air.*

One could argue that the kind of meeting that takes place between two sports clubs as in (5d) is sufficiently different from that of (5a), for instance, that it might be justified to talk of two different meanings in this case. Similarly, a case could be made out for treating (5c), which would be translated by *kennenlernen* into German, as a separate meaning, while it could also be said that meeting a person for the first time is getting to know them. One could establish a difference on the basis of arranged meetings and meetings by chance, for instance. Similarly, the use in (5e) could be treated as a different meaning on the grounds that it does not describe a meeting between two people or groups of people. On the other hand, it could be argued that in all five cases the verb describes more or less the same phenomenon, the coming together of two entities, and that whatever differences between these types of meeting exist they are obvious from the nature of these meetings and not caused by the verb meaning. This is the kind of problem that any lexicographical description of words is faced with. The fact that the number of meanings established for words such as *meet* hardly ever coincide between different dictionaries can be taken as an indication of the fact that no clear decision is possible in such cases.[360]

15.4　Structural semantics

15.4.1　The idea of contrast

The first approach to the description of meaning to be discussed here is known as structural semantics. It can be characterized as a purely language-internal approach in that it attempts to discover semantic properties of lexical units without taking psychological or extralinguistic factors (such as the denotatum of a lexical unit) into account.

De Saussure's conviction (> 2.1.4) that the value of a linguistic sign can be determined by its relationship to other linguistic signs in the system is reflected in structural semantics by the idea that word meanings or elements of word meanings can be elicited by contrasting them with other word meanings within the same system. One method that has been frequently employed in this context is that of word fields or lexical fields (> 16.1). It is an illustration of one of the basic assumptions of a structuralist approach to semantics, namely that the vocabulary of a language (at least in parts) displays structure,[361] as is expressed by Lyons (1968: 443):

> Acceptance of the structural approach in semantics has the advantage that it enables the linguist to avoid commitment on the controversial question of the philosophical and psychological status of 'concepts' or 'ideas' … As far as the empirical investigation of the structure of language is concerned, the sense of a lexical item may be defined to be, not only dependent upon, but identical with, the set of relations which hold between the items in question and other items in the same lexical system.

---

[360]　Palmer (²1981: 105–106) points out the limited usefulness of tests to establish different meanings of a lexeme: "It has been suggested that one test of ambiguity is the 'co-ordination test'. … But these tests do not help, for judgments about co-ordination depend upon judgments about sameness of meaning, and the doubtful cases remain. If we judge that *Mary cried and so did Ruth* is acceptable in the sense that Mary wept and Ruth shouted, it will be because we do not regard *cry* as ambiguous."

[361]　Cf. Coseriu (1973: 10–11) and Wotjak (1971: 54–59).

15.4.2   Semantic relations

15.4.2.1   Hyponymy: unilateral entailment

One of the central semantic relations that can be taken as an indication of the structuredness of vocabulary is that of hyponymy, which can be described in terms of unilateral entailment (Cruse 1986: 88–89), where **entailment** is defined as follows: "A proposition P is said to entail another proposition Q when the truth of Q is a logically necessary consequence of the truth of P (and the falsity of P is a logically necessary consequence of the falsity of Q)" (Cruse 1986: 14). Thus

(6a)   *This is a <u>seal</u>.*

entails

(6b)   *This is an <u>animal</u>.*

(7a)$_{BNC}$ *Set in the dipping wooded hills of Lambton Park, through which the wide and tidal Wear cuts a deep valley, this grandest of early Georgian houses looks south down a long wide avenue, smothered solid with <u>daffodils</u> in the spring.*

entails

(7b)   *Set in the dipping wooded hills of Lambton Park, through which the wide and tidal Wear cuts a deep valley, this grandest of early Georgian houses looks south down a long wide avenue, smothered solid with <u>flowers</u> in the spring.*

whereas (6b) and (7b) do not entail (6a) or (7a) respectively. **Hyponymy** can then be defined as the relationship between a hyperonym and a hyponym:[362]

▷ A lexical unit X is a **hyperonym** (or **superordinate**) of a lexical unit Y if the meaning of Y entails the meaning of X.

▷ A lexical unit Y is a **hyponym** (or **subordinate**) of a lexical unit X if the meaning of Y entails the meaning of X.

▷ Two lexical units Y and Z are **co-hyponyms** if they are hyponyms of the same hyperonym X.

Thus one can identify *fly*, *drive* and *walk* as co-hyponyms of the hyperonym *go*, because

---

[362]   See Cruse (1986: 88–89).

(8a)   We *flew* to Kirkwall.

(8b)   We *drove* to Kirkwall.

(8c)   We *walked* to Kirkwall.

all entail

(8d)   We *went* to Kirkwall.

without (8d) entailing (8a), (8b) or (8c). The logical relation of unilateral entailment can thus be used to establish a particular type of lexical relation. However, this must be seen as no more than a methodological device that can be fruitfully applied in structural semantics. In particular, this does not mean that this kind of test would work in all natural language contexts. Thus, Cruse (1986: 90) points out that while

(9a)$_{QE}$ *Flowers* are prohibited.

entails

(9b)$_{QE}$ *Dandelions* are prohibited.

(10a)$_{QE}$ *Flowers* make an acceptable present.

does not entail

(10b)$_{QE}$ *Dandelions* make an acceptable present.

Furthermore, *fly* could not be replaced by its hyperonym *go* in a sentence such as

(8e)$_{BNC}$ We *flew* to Kirkwall with British Airways, which flies to Orkney and Shetland regularly, from Glasgow and Edinburgh via Inverness.

15.4.2.2   *Synonymy: bilateral entailment*

The method of investigating entailment relationships can also be used to define the notion of synonymy,[363] which can then be defined as

---

[363]   Compare Cruse (1986: 88), who provides the following definition of cognitive synonymy: "X is a cognitive synonym of Y if (i) X and Y are syntactically identical, and (ii) any grammatical declarative sentence S containing X has equivalent truth-conditions to another sentence S[1], which is identical to S except that X is replaced by Y." For a detailed discussion of synonymy see Cruse (1986: 265–294).

▷ Two lexical units are **synonymous** if they entail each other.

If one considers *purchase* and *buy* to be synonyms, then one could argue that

(11a)_{BNC} *Saatchi is known to have <u>purchased</u> five major Warhols in the last six months, for extremely high prices, which few would argue is the action of someone dispersing their collection.*

entails

(11b) *Saatchi is known to have <u>bought</u> five major Warhols in the last six months, for extremely high prices, which few would argue is the action of someone dispersing their collection.*

and that (11b) also entails (11a). The same holds true in the case of (11c) and (11d):

(11c)_{BNC} *The Association has recently <u>purchased</u> a large, detached house in a residential area of Melton Mowbray, Leicestershire.*

(11d) *The Association has recently <u>bought</u> a large, detached house in a residential area of Melton Mowbray, Leicestershire.*

Nevertheless it has to be said that mutual entailment is a definition and not a test of synonymy. The analysis of sentences such as (11a) and (11b) is based on the assumption that *buy* and *purchase* have the same meaning, otherwise the relationship of mutual entailment would not hold. In fact, there are many linguists who consider true synonymy an extremely rare phenomenon in language. Palmer (²1981: 89), for instance, maintains "that there are no real synonyms, that no two words have exactly the same meaning" and points out that even in pairs such as *brotherly/fraternal*, *buy/purchase* and *world/universe* the "'native' words are often ... less learned".[364] In particular, when one considers meaning from the point of view of use, it makes sense to argue that while in particular sentences or contexts there is no difference between the contribution that two words that can be interchanged in a particular position make to the meaning of a sentence, this does not mean that the lexical units as such are really synonymous.

---

[364] For a discussion of synonymy see e.g. Palmer (²1981: 88–93).

15.4.2.3   Semantic oppositions

The logical relation of entailment, which was drawn upon in the definition of hyperonymy and synonymy, can also be used to identify a type of semantic opposition which is exemplified by such pairs as *male : female* and *good : bad*. Thus, for instance,

(12a)$_{BNC}$ *Her evidence about being telephoned late at night on 11 January 1987 (...) was that the caller was <u>female</u> and that the call lasted three to five minutes.*

entails

(12b)   *... that the caller was not <u>male</u>.*

just as

(12c)$_{BNC}$ *The shape was close enough for Henry to see that it was <u>male</u>.*

entails

(12d)   *The shape was close enough for Henry to see that it was <u>not female</u>.*

In the same way one could argue that

(13a)$_{BNC}$ *For once the forecast was <u>good</u>.*

entails

(13b)   *For once the forecast was <u>not bad</u>.*

and

(13c)$_{BNC}$ *Subjectivity in this field is <u>bad</u>.*

entails

(13d)   *Subjectivity in this field is <u>not good</u>.*

Nevertheless there is an important difference between the two cases since (12b) entails (12a) whereas (13b) does not entail (13a). This is due to the fact that meanings such as those of the lexical units *good* or *bad* are gradable in a way in which this is not true of pairs such as *male* and *female*.[365]

---

[365]   Compare Lyons's (1977: 272) discussion of these differences in terms of the traditional logical distinction between contradictories and contraries, which he however considers insufficient to cover linguistic differences of this kind. See also Leech (^{2}1981), Palmer (^{2}1981) or Cruse (1986). Note, however, that corpus evidence suggests that the distinction between gradable and non-

(13e)_{BNC} *The pollution was <u>pretty bad</u> up there.*

(13f)_{BNC} *One of the great unanswered questions in my life is why Mrs Spence was going to antenatal classes that afternoon when, as she had already had one child, she presumably had a <u>pretty good</u> idea of what to expect.*

A further characteristic of pairs such as *good* and *bad* or *far* and *near* is that one of the two terms can be considered to be marked and the other unmarked. The unmarked member of the pair is the one that is used in neutral questions for example:

(13g)_{BNC} *How <u>good</u> is your photographic memory?*

(14a)_{BNC} *How <u>far</u> are money and the media responsible for the misbehaviour of football supporters?*

Questions with the marked term are somehow presupposing part of the answer:

(13h)_{BNC} *The police will have put out checks on every hospital for miles. How <u>bad</u> is it?*

(14b)_{BNC} *How <u>near</u> is your proposed venue to airports (if it involves international visitors), and the road and rail links?*

In the case of pairs such as *male* and *female* no such distinction between marked and unmarked members of the pair can be made. Because of these differences it may seem appropriate to distinguish between different types of oppositeness and to refer to pairs such as *good : bad, far : near* as **antonyms** and to pairs such as *male : female* as **complementaries**.[366] According to Cruse (1986: 204) antonyms in this sense share the following characteristics:

---

gradable adjectives is by no means as clear as is sometimes suggested: *Lewis's debate in the Preface with other Milton critics with Saurat, Eliot, I. A. Richards or Leavis all seems <u>pretty dead</u> to us now, since not many people would read any of the aforementioned critics nowadays as critics unless they were interested in the history of criticism for its own sake.*_{BNC} *Many provincial towns in the United States have lost almost all their shops to suburban shopping malls and have become <u>very dead</u> places as a result.*_{BNC} *He was <u>very dead</u>, and there was blood all over the floor.*_{BNC} *It remained <u>very male</u>, in its content, and in its style.*_{BNC}

[366] See Lyons (1977: 279), who however also points at the arbitrary nature of the distinction: "Opinions will differ on the advisability of drawing a terminological distinction in one way rather than another."

(i)   they are fully gradable (...)
(ii)   members of a pair denote degrees of some variable property such as
       length, speed, weight, accuracy, etc.
(iii) when more strongly intensified, the members of a pair move, as it were, in
       opposite directions along the scale representing degrees of the relevant
       variable property. Thus, *very happy* and *very light*, for instance, are more
       widely separated on the scale of weight than *fairly heavy* and *fairly light*.
(iv)   the terms of a pair do not strictly bisect a domain: there is a range of val-
       ues of the variable property, lying between those covered by the opposed
       terms, which cannot be properly referred to by either term.

Complementaries, on the other hand, are characterized by Cruse (1986:
198) as follows:

> The essence of a pair of complementaries is that between them they exhaus-
> tively divide some conceptual domain into two mutually exclusive com-
> partments, so that what does not fall into one of the compartments must
> necessarily fall into the other. There is no 'no-man's land', no neutral
> ground, no possibility of a third term lying between them. Examples of
> complementaries are: *true : false, dead : alive, open : shut, hit : miss* (a tar-
> get), *pass : fail* (an examination).

This is illustrated by sentences such as

(12e)_{BNC} *He couldn't say whether the person was male or female, because the
       curtain was drawn halfway across.*

It is interesting to see that differences in the entailment relations holding
between antonyms and complementaries can be used to illustrate the differences between them but that they do not suffice to characterize them fully,
since, as Palmer ([2]1981: 97) points out, in "both cases we must also show
that they belong to the same semantic system or field". In the case of complementaries "it is not true to say that, if something is not male, it is female,
since it could also be inanimate". In the same way

(15a)   *The milk is sour.*

entails

(15b)   *The milk is not fresh.*

but (15b) does not entail (15a) since the lexical relationship between *sour*
and *fresh* is far too complex to be established on a scale of antonymy.
   Apart from antonymy and complementarity, a third type of oppositeness
can be established, for which Lyons (1977: 279) uses the term **converse-**

ness but which is more commonly treated as **relational opposition**.[367] This type of oppositeness is characterized by the fact that the members of the opposition pair express the same relation between two entities, but do so from a different perspective (which is why **perspectival opposition** might be an even more appropriate term to use). This type of opposition can be exemplified by pairs such as *buy : sell, teacher : pupil* or *husband : wife*.

(16a)_{BNC} *They belonged to Hammersmith Council who had <u>bought</u> them from the BBC for something like three million pounds.*

(16b) *... the BBC <u>sold</u> them to Hammersmith Council for something like three million pounds.*

(16c)_{BNC} *The group did not exercise its rights but <u>sold</u> them to a third party for £200,000.*

(16d) *... the third party <u>bought</u> them for £200,000.*

(17a)_{BNC} *By far the most important of the Venetian composers, after Monteverdi, was his <u>pupil</u> Francesco Cavalli.*

(17b) *Monteverdi was Francesco Cavalli's <u>teacher</u>.*

(17c)_{BNC} *Miller is a friend of Pringle's: he was her <u>teacher</u> at University College.*

(17d) *Pringle was Miller's <u>pupil</u> at University College.*

The distinction between antonymy, complementarity and converseness shows that oppositeness can be expressed in different ways in the vocabulary of a language.[368]

---

[367] See Leech ([2]1981: 102–106), Palmer ([2]1981: 98–100), Cruse (1986).

[368] For further types see Lyons (1977: 281–287), Leech (1981: 96–108) or Cruse (1986: 223–264). For oppositeness see also Kastovsky (1982: 131–139). Compare also the critical discussion by Lipka ([3]2002: 163–165).

16   Ways of describing meaning

16.1   Componential analysis

In the previous chapter it was demonstrated that a number of relations between lexical units can be established such as hyponymy, different types of
oppositeness and possibly synonymy. This can be taken as a confirmation
of the basic conviction of structural semantics, that the lexical units of a
language form a system and that the meanings of the lexical units can be
determined on the basis of the relations which they enter into with the other
lexical units in that system. While establishing or revealing such relations
between lexical items does not describe the meaning of the lexical units as
such, such relations can be used to contrast the meanings of lexical items
and to discover elements of their meaning on this basis. As pointed out
above, one approach that has been widely used in this context, especially
within the European tradition of structuralist semantics, is that of the analysis of word fields or lexical fields. A **lexical field** can be defined as a set
of lexical units that belong to the same word class and have at least one
specific semantic component in common.[369] This semantic component can
exist as a lexical unit in a language, in which case it is the hyperonym of all
members of the lexical field. Thus, *house, cottage, palace, castle, railway
station* can be seen as members of a lexical field with *building* being the
hyperonym of all the members of this field. Kastovsky (1982: 84) points
out, however, that the field of adjectives denoting temperature in English
(of which *hot, warm, cool, cold* etc. are members) lacks such a hyperonym,

---

[369]   See Lipka (^{3}2002: 167–168), who uses the further criterion that "field-
membership must be established by objective procedures". For a detailed
treatment of the history of field theory see Lyons (1977: 250–261). For differences in terminology see Lipka (^{3}2002: 168), who uses the term lexical
field for fields "consisting of simple or complex lexemes" and word field for
fields "exclusively containing morphologically simple items". For a critical
account compare Leisi (1973). See also Coseriu (1973: 53). For a discussion
of various approaches and definitions see also Kastovsky (1982: 124–128).

for example.[370] In any case, lexical fields provide a suitable basis for establishing contrasts of meaning in different lexical units.

Leech ([2]1981: 89), who argues that the "analysis of word-meanings is often seen as a process of breaking down the sense of a word into its minimal components", illustrates this approach by contrasting the meanings of *man, woman, boy, girl*.

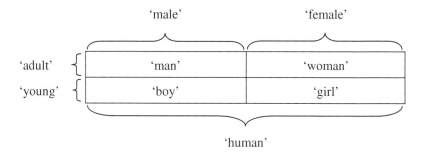

The diagram shows two dimensions of meaning: that of 'sex' and that of 'adulthood'; a third dimension is presupposed by the isolation of the field as a whole: that between 'human' and 'non-human' species.

In a slightly more abstract form, these components can be represented as:[371]

man:	+ HUMAN	+ ADULT	+ MALE
woman:	+ HUMAN	+ ADULT	− MALE
boy:	+ HUMAN	− ADULT	+ MALE
girl:	+ HUMAN	− ADULT	− MALE

The method of analysing meanings in terms of semantic components which are gained through contrasting meanings of lexical units (in a lexical field) is known as **componential analysis**.[372]

---

[370]   Coseriu uses the term **Archisemem** to characterize the semantic features common to all members of a word field, and **Archilexem** for cases of lexical units representing such features. Cf. Coseriu (1973: 54) and also Kastovsky (1982: 84).

[371]   See Leech ([2]1981: 90).

[372]   While it has been frequently employed by European structural semanticists, often in connection with lexical field analysis, the theory has also received an important impetus by proposals made within an early generative framework, especially by Katz and Fodor (1963). For detailed accounts of this approach

One aim of componential analysis in semantics is to draw up an inventory of semantic components similar to that of the distinctive features in phonology.[373] Some proponents of the theory hoped that within this approach it would be possible to describe any word meaning as a combination of semantic components (similar to the way that any phoneme in any language can be described with a very limited set of distinctive features), which would make descriptions of this kind particularly suitable for machine translation, for example. For this to be possible, semantic components would have to meet four conditions, namely that they should be

- atomic, i.e. it should be impossible to split them up into further semantic components,
- recurrent, i.e. not just be designed to cover the meaning (or part of the meaning) of only one lexical unit,
- binary, i.e. describable in terms of ± values, and
- universal, i.e. applicable to all languages.[374]

It is relatively easy to show that achieving this goal is very problematic. It is true that semantic components such as the ones identified above are recurrent (and probably also universal) in that they can fruitfully be applied to other lexical units such as *stallion, mare, filly* etc. As to atomicity, it has to be noted that there is considerable disagreement in this respect. While, for instance, Kastovsky (1982: 88) regards the features "MALE : FEMALE" as minimal, Lyons (1977: 330) says that "most of the sense-components that have been postulated by linguists (e.g. MALE, ALIVE, FOR

---

[373]   see Kastovsky (1982: 80–150) and Leech ([2]1981: 89–122). See also Palmer ([2]1981: 108–117) and Lyons (1977: 317–335). Compare also Kastovsky's (1982: 80) discussion of this parallel. Cf. also Hjelmslev (1943/1974: 69–71). Compare also Coseriu's (1973: 58–67) comparison of the analysis of lexis and phonology. For this see also Herbst, Heath, and Dederding (1980: 82–84).

[374]   Cf. Lyons (1977: 331): "The most extreme form of the thesis of universalism would combine at least the following three distinguishable sub-theses: (i) that there is a fixed set of semantic components which are universal in that they are lexicalized in all languages; (ii) that the formal principles by which these sense-components are combined to yield as their products the meanings of lexemes are universal (and presumably innate); and (iii) that the sense of all lexemes of all languages is decomposable, without residue, into variable combinations of (homogeneous) sense-components." For a discussion of the idea of universalism see Palmer ([2]1981: 114–117).

SITTING UPON) are not atomic in this sense".[375] However, Kastovsky (1982: 89) also argues that atomicity is not a necessary condition for a semantic component when he points out that words such as *grocer* and *haberdasher* are to be distinguished with respect to the dimension SOLD OBJECT in terms of the meanings of the lexeme *food* or the phrase *small articles of dress*. Using *food* and *small articles of dress* as semantic components, however, raises the problem of the recurrent character of such components.

There are two ways of approaching this problem: one is to give up the claim that all components to be used in a semantic analysis should be expected to be recurrent and atomic.[376] The other way out of the problem is to give up the claim that componential analysis would provide a suitable basis for the description of word meanings as a whole. It is indeed difficult to imagine a component which is atomic and recurrent that could distinguish *daffodil* from *tulip* or *dandelion*. Lyons (1977: 334) points at a different problem:[377]

> For example, if the meaning of the lexemes 'man', 'woman', 'adult', 'girl', 'boy' and 'child' are analysed in terms of the sense-components HUMAN, ADULT and FEMALE, we can readily explain the fact that phrases like 'adult child' or 'male girl' are semantically anomalous. In doing so, we must assume (and it is more often assumed than stated explicitly in treatments of componential analysis) that "male" (i.e. the sense of the English lexeme 'male') contains and is exhausted by the sense-component – FEMALE, that "adult" contains and is exhausted by ADULT, and so on. On this assumption, however, 'male child' should be synonymous with 'boy'. But it is not.

Taking up this argument, Leech ([2]1981: 121) comes to the conclusion that "… componential analysis is not the whole story; but that it is part of the

---

[375] Lyons (1977: 330) refers to the ideas of the German philosopher Leibniz in this context.

[376] Note the distinction between so-called markers and distinguishers made in an early model of componential analysis, developed by Katz and Fodor (1963) in the context of transformational grammar: in the analysis of one meaning of *bachelor*, they identify HUMAN and MALE as markers and as a distinguisher 'who has never married'. For a critical account of this approach see Kastovsky (1982: 82 and 251).

[377] For the problem of semantic notation see, for instance, Leech's ([2]1981: 94–97) concept of "signese".

story, and a significant part, need not be doubted".[378] Indeed, the insight that componential analysis alone is probably not an appropriate means of describing the meanings of lexical units should not be taken as an argument for rejecting the approach altogether. For instance, componential analysis is ideally suited to describe semantic relations as the ones identified in 15.4.2:

- The relationship between a hyperonym and its hyponyms can be stated in componential terms by saying that the hyperonym lacks the semantic component which distinguishes its hyponyms.
- Synonymy can be described as a total identity of components and their + or – values.
- Antonymy, complementarity and converseness can be described as an identity of all components with the value of one component being different in a pair.

Furthermore, componential analysis serves perfectly well to explain certain syntagmatic relationships, above all the oddity of a sentence such as

(1a)   *Wood*   *swims.*

         – ANIMATE   + ANIMATE

on the basis of the **incompatibility** of the features – ANIMATE (of *wood*) and + ANIMATE (required of a subject of the lexical unit *swim*)[379] as opposed to

(1b)_{BNC}   *Wood*   *floats.*

         – ANIMATE   – ANIMATE

It should just be mentioned in passing that the relationship of incompatibility played an important role in the discussion of the grammaticalness of sentences in Chomsky's (1965: 149) *Aspects* model of generative transformational syntax, where he described "sentences that break selectional

---

[378] See Leech (²1981: 121): "There have emerged three different levels at which word-meaning may be analysed. Firstly, the word-sense as an entirety may be seen as a conceptual unit in its own right ...; secondly, this unit may be subdivided into components or features, by CA; and thirdly, both word-senses and features, representing prototypic categories, can be broken down into fuzzy sets of attributes. If this is more complex than the view of word-meaning with which we started, it is of a similar order of complexity to that of systems studied in natural science."

[379] Cf. Coseriu's (1973: 78) concept of *Klasseme* and the role of such features in stating selectional restrictions in transformational grammar.

rules" such as *colourless green ideas sleep furiously* as "deviant". Semantic components were introduced in the form of selectional features to prevent the generation of such sentences.[380]

16.2   The structure of vocabulary

While the various approaches that can be subsumed under the heading of structural semantics have succeeded in revealing and formalizing certain relations between the lexical units of a language, the overall question as to what extent the vocabulary of a language can or should be regarded as being organized in this way is still open.[381] There is evidence to suggest that the relationship between the various lexical units of a language is much more complex than is suggested by accounts such as the one given above. For instance, on the basis of the phrase *old man* one would be inclined to take *young* as an antonym of the lexical unit *old*. However, *new* would be the appropriate antonym in cases such as *an old manuscript* or *an old program*. It is certainly debatable whether this is a sufficient reason to argue that the *old* in *old man* represents a different meaning of *old* than the *old* in *old manuscript*. Similarly, *sell* can be seen as the opposite of *buy* (in terms of converseness; > 15.4.2.3), but, in other contexts, *steal* could also be regarded as expressing the opposite of *buy*. This suggests that statements about oppositeness, like statements about sameness of meaning, are to a large extent dependent on the context in which a lexical unit occurs.

The same point can be made about linguistic hierarchies. Thus *fly* and *walk* were established as hyponyms of *go* on the basis of sentences such as

(1)_{BNC}   We _flew_ to Kirkwall with British Airways, which flies to Orkney and Shetland regularly, from Glasgow and Edinburgh via Inverness.

but this leaves open the question of the status of a verb such as *travel* in the hierarchy. Lyons (1977: 295, 297–298) also rejects a model of a hierarchically organized vocabulary of the following form:

---

[380]   It may just be noted that the combination *green ideas* is no longer unusual: … *they no more held a patent on green ideas than feminists did on equal rights for women.*_{BNC} *A great many green ideas were produced by Labour that summer.*_{BNC}

[381]   Compare Lipka's (³2002: 148) description of the lexicon "as the structured word-store of a language".

... If we take the most common adjectives in English we will see that there are no superordinate adjectives at all of which particular subsets are hyponyms. There are no lexemes of which adjectives, denoting differences of colour, are all hyponyms. We do not say *Was it red or coloured in some other way?*; but rather *Was it red or (of) some colour?* Similarly for subclasses of adjectives denoting shape, texture, taste, sound, age, size, state of mind, etc.

What is perhaps particularly problematic is a view of vocabulary as expressed by Coseriu (1973: 53) in his characterization of word field:[382]

> Word fields contain ... units that divide up amongst themselves a conceptual area on the basis of immediate oppositions. An immediate opposition exists if no third term can be inserted between two terms.

There are two rather interesting claims involved in this statement, namely (i) that there is a clear delimitation of the meaning of a lexical unit in the sense that one can identify (or at least assume) clear boundaries between the meanings of two lexical items and (ii) that all possible meanings or concepts (within a certain field) are actually expressed by lexical units. Both claims are more than doubtful. The first has come under attack in prototype theory (> 16.4) and the second can be shown to be wrong by the existence of lexical gaps such as the one concerning a neutral colour adjective outlined above. Furthermore, the contextual view of meaning created in multi-word expressions as propagated by John Sinclair (> 10.5) contradicts such a structuralist view of vocabulary.

16.3   Vocabulary and conceptualization

The questions addressed in the previous section are closely related to the way the conceptualization process is imagined. It was pointed out in 2.1.2 that de Saussure's view of the arbitrariness of the linguistic sign can also be interpreted as referring to the way that languages divide up or conceptualize the world.[383] In other words, the world (or at least parts of it) is imag-

---

[382] Original: "Wortfelder enthalten ... Einheiten, die eine Bedeutungszone auf Grund unmittelbarer Oppositionen unter sich aufteilen. Eine unmittelbare Opposition besteht dann, wenn zwischen zwei Termen kein dritter mehr eingeschoben werden kann."

[383] For a more recent discussion of the notion of arbitrariness see Leech ([2]1981: 26): "This leads on to the question of the partial 'arbitrariness' of the catego-

ined as a (relatively) unstructured continuum, which is broken up by a language. This is apparent from the writings of the Danish linguist Hjelmslev (1943/1961: 52),[384] one of the founders of structuralism, who says:

> A paradigm in one language and a corresponding paradigm in another language can be said to cover one and the same zone of purport, which, abstracted from those languages, is an unanalyzed, amorphous continuum, on which boundaries are laid by the formative action of the languages.

In this context it was argued by Hjelmslev (1943/1961: 53) – mistakenly, as will be shown in 16.4 – that the colour spectrum is a good example of such a continuum. Using the example of the Welsh colour terms *gwyrdd*, *glas* and *llywd*, he pointed out that Welsh does not draw a boundary in the same place as Danish does between *grøn* and *blaa*. The English translation of Hjelmslev's text represents this in the following way:[385]

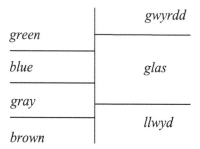

The American structuralist Gleason (1961: 4) also points out differences in the vocabulary denoting colours, referring to English, Shona (spoken in Zimbabwe) and Bassa (spoken in Liberia):[386]

---

ries language provides for us. By 'arbitrariness', I mean, firstly, that conceptual boundaries often vary from language to language in a way that defies principled explanation. A second kind of arbitrariness, presupposed by the first, is the arbitrariness of language with respect to experienced reality: languages have a tendency to 'impose structure upon the real world' by treating some distinctions as crucial, and ignoring others."

[384] Hjelmslev: /jel'msleu/

[385] The translators of the German version point out that Hjelmslev's basis are Danish colour terms such as *grøn* and *blaa*; see Hjelmslev (1943/1974: 57).

[386] See Sampson (1980: 95).

English	purple	blue		green	yel-low	orange	red
Shona	cips^{w}uka	citema		cicena		cips^{w}uka	
Bassa	hui				zĩza		

Colour terms were also addressed in the work of the German scholar Trier (1934), who is known for his work on word fields. His ideas are interpreted by Lyons (1977: 253) in the following way:

> Considered as a continuum, the substance of colour is (...) a conceptual area (Sinnbezirk); it becomes a conceptual field (Sinnfeld) by virtue of its structural organization, or articulation, by particular language systems.

While colours may be a particularly good example to demonstrate the structuralist conviction that the vocabulary of a language gives structure to reality, this view is by no means restricted to colour terminology.[387]

From such considerations it is only a small way towards raising the question of the relationship between language and thought. If human beings perceive the world through the conceptual system of their mother tongue and if the conceptual systems imposed on reality by different languages differ, then, one might argue, perception and thought are influenced by language. While such a statement is relatively uncontroversial still today, the extent to which this is the case has been the subject of much debate.

A particularly extreme form of the claim that human thought is shaped by language is the so-called **Sapir-Whorf-hypothesis**, which is based on ideas of the American anthroplogists and linguists Edward Sapir[388] and Benjamin Lee Whorf, which they developed in the study of the American Indian languages. One of the most important claims made about one such language, Hopi, is that it does not have tenses, but uses different verb forms "according to whether the speaker is reporting a situation or expecting it, and according to an event's duration, intensity, or other characteristics" (Trudgill ³1995: 13).[389] Such observations on Indian languages led Whorf

---

[387] For a discussion of further differences between languages in the field of lexis or with respect to tense systems see Hjelmslev (1943/1961: 53–54).

[388] Sapir: /sə'pɪə/ /seɪ'pɪə/

[389] For a detailed discussion of the Sapir-Whorf-hypothesis see Sampson (1980). Sampson (1980: 86) describes the situation in Hopi as follows: "... the language does not recognize time as a linear dimension which can be measured

to claim that the world is perceived in a different way by speakers of different languages.

Many objections can be raised against these ideas: for instance, that there is no proof that such differences between languages result in different perceptions of the world, in fact, there seems to be counterevidence that this is not the case.[390] Also, one has to bear in mind that it is apparently possible to translate from one language into another and that new ideas going beyond the concepts provided by a language at any given point in its history can quite obviously be shaped and put into words, as is obvious from the study of word formation. Furthermore, quite important differences can also be observed between European languages (such as the absence of a distinction between simple and progressive aspect in German). For these reasons, any kind of strong form of the hypothesis is rejected by semanticists and sociolinguists today.[391] Still, the Sapir-Whorf-hypothesis has provided an important impetus for the study of the relationship of language and thought.

16.4   Prototype theory

16.4.1   Colour terms

The analysis of colour terms has played a central role in semantics. As was pointed out in 16.3, structuralist semanticists assume that the spectrum of colours that the human eye can identify takes the form of a continuum that is divided up in different ways by different languages. Colour terms thus present one example of the arbitrariness of the linguistic sign in de Saussure's sense.

Approaching colour terms from a psychological point of view, however, there is evidence to suggest that the colour spectrum is not perceived as a

---

and divided into units like spatial dimensions, so that for instance Hopi never borrows spatial terms to refer to temporal phenomena in the way so common in European languages …, nor does Hopi permit phrases such as *five days* since daytime is not a thing like an apple of which one can have one or several. … And since there is no concept of time, there can be no concept of speed …".

[390]   Cf. Steinberg (1982: 109), who points out that "knowing word forms (spoken or written) may aid memory". See also 16.4.1.

[391]   Compare Trudgill (^{3}1995: 14–15) or Leech (^{2}1981: 26–27).

continuum by human beings. In a famous study, Berlin and Kay (1969) compared different languages as to their basic colour terms. Basic terms are words such as *red, yellow, orange* or *green*, i.e. terms that cannot be subsumed under any other term (as is the case with *crimson*), that are morphologically simple (like *blue*, but not *bluish* or *dunkelblau*), frequent and not restricted to technical language. The remarkable insight provided through the experiments carried out by Berlin and Kay is that there are shades of a particular colour which are better examples of that colour than others, in other words, that some greens are greener than others. Experiments have shown that speakers differ considerably when asked to indicate the boundaries between different colour terms. This holds both within one language and across different languages. There is a great deal of agreement, however, when it comes to picking a particularly good example of a particular colour. Taylor (³2003: 9) summarizes this as follows:

> Although the range of colours that are designated by *red* (or its equivalent in other languages) might vary from person to person, there is a remarkable unanimity on what constitutes a 'good red'.

The special status of focal colours is confirmed by a number of experiments. For instance, people seem to be able to name samples of focal colours more easily than samples of non-focal colours.[392] The conclusion that can be drawn from evidence such as this is that cognitively colour categories "have a centre and a periphery" (Taylor ³2003: 14).

This view is different from the structuralist account of colour terms in two important ways:

- Colour terms do not seem to present a very good example of the arbitrariness of linguistic classification. If the colour spectrum contains certain focal colours which are particularly prominent for human percep-

---

[392] See especially Rosch Heider (1971, 1972) and also Taylor (³2003: 10-11). For the more far-reaching claims made by Berlin and Kay (1969) see also Clark and Clark (1977: 524–527), Taylor (³2003) or Leech (1981: 235–236), who comes to the following conclusion: "But however much opinions may vary, psycholinguistic evidence ... points strongly to the conclusion that the relative uniformity of colour semantics in different languages has much to do with the uniformity of the human apparatus of visual perception. Whatever language a person speaks, he will tend to perceive certain focal colour stimuli as more salient than others; and his language, too, will tend to discriminate colours on the basis of these perceptionally salient areas." See also Ungerer and Schmid (²2006: 7-14).

tion and if it is for these focal colours that languages have basic colour terms, then the colour spectrum is not divided up by language.

- If focal colours can be named and identified more quickly than non-focal colours, then category membership cannot be seen in terms of a yes/no-decision but is rather a matter of gradience.

16.4.2   Prototypes

The question is to what extent the prototypical nature of categories such as colour terms can be applied to the description of word meanings. If some greens are greener than others in the sense that some shades of green are seen as better examples of the meaning of *green* than others, then perhaps some types of bird can be regarded as birdier than others or some pieces of furniture as better examples of the category furniture than others.[393]

And indeed, so-called goodness-of-example rankings suggest precisely this. For instance, Rosch (1975: esp. 229) asked American college students to judge elements of a list of household items as to their membership in the category furniture on a scale ranging from 1 (very good example) to 7 (very bad example; not an example at all). The result is a clear gradient: *chair* (1.04), *sofa* (1.04), *couch* (1.10), *table* (1.10), ... *desk* (1.54), *bed* (1.58), ... *piano* (3.64), ... *cupboard* (4.27), *stereo* (4.32) ... *ashtray* (6.35), *fan* (6.49) or *telephone* (6.68).

In a similar way, ratings for different types of birds were established, which Aitchison ([3]2003: 56) presents in a kind of hierarchy in which the robin is the most central member and the penguin and the ostrich the most marginal members.

---

[393]   For a more detailed discussion of Rosch's approach see Taylor ([3]2003), Aitchison ([3]2003: 53–58).

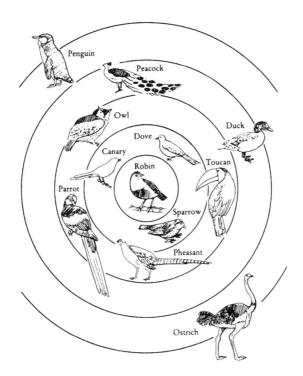

Birdiness rankings
(taken from Aitchison [3]2003: 56)

From a psychological point of view, these rankings are certainly relevant. Rosch (1973) found that usually people (especially children) are quicker to verify a sentence of the type *A pear is a fruit* if the test item was a good example of the category.

To what extent these psychological findings can be applied to the description of word meaning may be a matter of debate.[394] What is certainly true is that the marginal status of certain members of a category is reflected by their ability to occur in sentences containing so-called hedges such as

(2a)   *Strictly speaking, a penguin is a bird.*

---

[394] Compare the discussion of the relationship between goodness-of-example ratings and degree of membership outlined by Croft and Cruse (2004: 79), where it is pointed out that it could be argued "that an ostrich is a fully paid-up member of the BIRD category" despite its low goodness-of-example-rating.

(3a)$_{\text{QE}}$ *Strictly speaking, rhubarb is a vegetable.*[395]

which central members of the category cannot

(2b)   *?Strictly speaking, a seagull/a guillemot is a bird.*

(3b)$_{\text{QE}}$ *?Strictly speaking, beans are vegetables.*

Following a similar line of thought, Cruse (1986: 16–18) points out that a feature such as 'can bark' is an expected trait of a category such as dog since a sentence such as

(4a)$_{\text{QE}}$ *It's a dog, but it can bark.*

is judged as odd, whereas a sentence such as

(4b)$_{\text{QE}}$ *It's a dog, but it can't bark.*

is perfectly normal. On the other hand, a sentence such as

(4c)$_{\text{QE}}$ *It's a dog, but it can't sing.*

is odd because 'can sing' is an unexpected trait of *dog*. The fact that both

(4d)$_{\text{QE}}$ *It's a dog, but it's brown.*

(4e)$_{\text{QE}}$ *It's a dog, but it isn't brown.*

are judged as odd shows that 'is brown' is a possible trait of dogs, which is why a sentence such as

(4f)$_{\text{QE}}$ *It's a dog and it's brown.*

is normal.

The crucial difference between such observations and the structuralist approach to meaning is that all components employed in a componential analysis of a word such as *bird* would have equal status and be supposed to apply to all members of the category. Thus 'can fly' cannot be used as a semantic feature of *bird* in a structuralist approach. On the other hand, one could argue that if speakers of a language see the ability to fly as a core characteristic of the category *bird*, they will also consider it to be an important feature for the description of the meaning of the word *bird*.

That this is indeed the case is shown by the definitions of words such as *bird*, *seagull* or *penguin* in the *Longman Dictionary of Contemporary English* (LDOCE4):

---

[395]   Example taken from Taylor (^{3}2003: 80).

bird ...   **1** a creature with wings and feathers that can usually fly. Many birds sing and build nests, and female birds lay eggs.: *wild birds* | *The dawn was filled with the sound of birds.* | *a **flock of birds*** (= a group of birds flying together) | *a wooden bird cage*

seagull ... a large common grey or white bird that lives near the sea

penguin ...a large black and white Antarctic sea bird, which cannot fly but uses its wings for swimming ...

Whereas structural semanticists insist that the linguistic analysis of word meaning and knowledge of extralinguistic categories should be kept apart, from a cognitive point of view this does not seem to make sense. Cruse (1986: 19) would argue "that any attempt to draw a line between the meaning of a word and 'encyclopaedic' facts concerning the extra-linguistic referents of the word would be quite arbitrary".

As Croft and Cruse (2004: 81–82) point out, prototypes can be defined in two different ways:[396]

– in terms of a list of attributes or features: "The centrality of an item in the category depends on how many of the relevant set of features it possesses: the more it possesses, the better an example of the category it will be. A feature is justified if, other things being equal, its presence leads to a higher GOE [goodness-of-example] rating" (Croft and Cruse 2004: 81).

– on the basis of similarity: "A concept can be thought of as represented by an ideal exemplar, and membership and centrality of other items can be defined in terms of their similarity to the prototype" (Croft and Cruse 2004: 82).

16.4.3   Basic level categories

One central concept of prototype theory aims at an explanation for the fact that words of a particular level of specificity tend to be used rather frequently to refer to certain objects in the world rather than others. Thus it would be odd to replace *chair* by *a piece of furniture* in sentences such as

(5a)$_{BNC/NW}$*Robyn sank down on a chair.*

---

[396]   See Ungerer and Schmid (²2006: 7–45) for attributes, family resemblances and gestalts with respect to prototypes.

(5b)_{BNC/NW}*Looking at Philip Swallow now, as he seats himself in a low, uphol-
stered chair facing her, Robyn has difficulty in recognising the jet-set
philander of Rupert Sutcliffe's description.*

Similarly, in most situations, it would seem more natural to say

(6a)_{BNC}   *I'll get the car out.*

than

(6b)   *I'll get the vehicle out.*

(6c)   *I'll get the VW out.*

Interestingly, there are 33942 instances of *car* in the BNC but only 7201 of
vehicle and 150 of *VW* (and 200 of Volkswagen). Although any car can
also be referred to as a *vehicle*, this is quite obviously not done very often.
There seems to be a level of specificity which is convenient for many purposes of communication. Thus, for instance,

(7a)   *I'll go by car.*

contrasts with

(7b)   *I'll go by bus.*

(7c)   *I'll go by train.*

or

(7d)   *I'll go by bike.*

Terms such as *car, bus* (6666 instances in BNC), *train* (8164), *bike* (2212),
lorry (1980) are referred to as basic level terms. This level is described by
Croft and Cruse (2004: 83–84) by the following characteristics:[397]

(i)   It is the most inclusive level at which there are characteristic patterns of
       behavioral interaction. ...
(ii)   The most inclusive level for which a clear visual image can be formed. ...
(iii) The most inclusive level at which part-whole information is represented.
       ...
(iv)   The level used for everyday neutral reference. ...
(v)   Individual items are more rapidly categorized as members of basic level
       categories than as members of superordinate or subordinate categories.

---

[397]   Cf. Croft and Cruse (2004: 82–92). For a discussion of basic level terms see
        also Taylor ([3]2003: 48–55) and Ungerer and Schmid ([2]2006: 64–76).

16.4.4   Problems of prototype theory

It is obvious that prototype theory has an important contribution to make to
the analysis and understanding of meaning. However, there are also a number of problems.[398] One is that many of the prototype effects that have been
observed experimentally depend very strongly on the cultural and situational environment. Whether or not a seagull is named as a very good
example of the category *bird* may depend on whether the informants live
close by the sea or not.[399] Whether a word is a useful basic level term may
depend on the degree of expertise of a group of speakers. While *train* is a
useful basic level term in everyday discourse, it probably is not for people
designing railway time tables or responsible for the organization of the
railway network of a country. These, however, are not principal objections
to the approach but only indications of the fact that we are dealing with a
great number of subsystems.

What is more difficult to account for is the fact that prototype effects
can be observed even with clearly defined categories such as odd and even
numbers. Apparently, informants were happy to name a good example of a
category such as *odd number*, 3 getting a high degree of membership, 91 a
low one (Taylor [3]2003: 73; Armstrong, Gleitman and Gleitman 1999: 241).
This contradicts the common understanding of odd and even numbers as
categories that on the mere basis of their defining criteria do not allow for
any gradience of category membership.[400]

The most important deficit of prototype theory, as Croft and Cruse
(2004) point out, is that it does not offer a satisfactory explanation for category boundaries. Although the notion of fuzzy category boundaries is justified on the grounds that different subjects locate category boundaries, such
as those between different colours, in different places, "it should be pointed
out that even a fuzzy boundary has a location" (Croft and Cruse 2004: 91).

Furthermore, one could argue that while it is tempting to analyse the
uses of a colour term such as *white* in combinations such as *white coffee*,

---

[398] For some objections to prototype theory see Leech (1981: 84–86).

[399] Compare Croft and Cruse (2004: 79) on priming effects: "The priming effect
correlates with the GOE score of the category member, that is, for Britons,
FRUIT will speed up the response to APPLE to a greater degree than the response to, for instance, DATE." See also Ungerer and Schmid ([2]2006: 45–58,
esp. 53), who draw attention to the fact "that cultural models are not static but
changing" [GOE = goodness of example].

[400] See Croft and Cruse (2004: 88) for a discussion.

white skin or *white wine* as uses which are not central to the category, that in itself does not explain why the combination *white wine* rather than *yellow wine* is used in the language.

Recommended further reading:

- Leech ([2]1981), Palmer ([2]1981), Cruse (1986)
- Ungerer and Schmid ([2]2006)
- Croft and Cruse (2004)

Utterances

17   Pragmatics

17.1   Word, sentence and utterance meaning

17.1.1   Sentence meaning

As was shown in Chapter 16, it is extremely difficult to answer a question such as *What does such and such a word mean?* In fact, from a linguistic point of view one might argue that this is not a sensible question to ask. Nevertheless, questions about the meanings of words do get asked, especially perhaps in foreign language contexts. Questions of the type *What is the German word for "chair"?* are by no means uncommon. In the case of *chair* and *Stuhl* most people who know both languages would probably not hesitate to answer the question. A question such as *What does the word "chair" mean?* is probably slightly more problematic because one might have to think about such attributes as to whether a chair can have arms or not, whether it has to have four legs or not etc. Even if we accept that word meanings are often perceived and explained in terms of prototypes, it is remarkable that speakers feel able to answer such questions at all.

In the case of *chair*, the kind of meaning that speakers would probably think of is that used in sentences such as

(1a)$_{VDE}$ *He relaxed back into his chair, letting his pipe burn itself out in his hand.*

(1b)$_{VDE}$ *A padded chair covered with green velvet was the only article of furniture in the room.*

and not

(1c)$_{VDE}$ *You could apply for a personal chair.*

(1d)$_{VDE}$ *Hawking, inheritor of Sir Isaac Newton's chair at Cambridge, originally played with the idea that time might run backwards if the universe stopped expanding and collapsed in on itself.*

It is obvious that in semantics one would tend to treat this as a case of polysemy as far as the meaning of the word *chair* is concerned. On the other hand, it is unlikely that anyone would consider sentences such as (1a), (1b), (1d) or even (1c) ambiguous. The reason for this must be that speakers are able to select the appropriate meaning of a polysemous word on the basis of information provided by the (linguistic or extralinguistic) context. Although psycholinguists seem to disagree as to whether all meanings of a word are activated when a particular sound chain or string of letters is perceived or not, there can be no doubt that some kind of disambiguation process must take place.

The guiding principle behind the process of working out the meaning of a sentence seems to be to look for sense. This may sound trivial, but at the same time it is probably a fact essential to the understanding of human communication that hearers or readers assume that a particular utterance is meaningful. It is for this reason that one would immediately rule out the reading of 'university chair' as the appropriate meaning of *chair* in a sentence such as

(1e)$_{VDE}$　　*Each chair will vary, so you'll have to measure up and make a paper pattern before cutting out the fabric.*

17.1.2　　The meaning of utterances

The principle of assuming utterances to be meaningful – which has been termed the "no-nonsense-principle" or the "reality principle"[401] – has wider consequences than merely selecting the appropriate sense of a word in a given context. It can equally be applied to the interpretation of an utterance in a particular context of situation. For instance, a sentence such as

(2)$_{VDE}$　　*A visit to the site is truly memorable.*

can be interpreted as a characterization of a particular site which stresses its significance or impressiveness. In the appropriate context, however, it can also be interpreted as a piece of advice to the effect that it is worthwhile visiting this particular site. The descriptive or advisory character of the utterance can also be seen as part of its meaning, but one which is not captured in a semantic description. In the same way, an utterance such as

(1c)$_{VDE}$　　*You could apply for a personal chair*

---

[401]　　See Clark and Clark (1977: 72–73).

can be meant as a piece of advice or as consolation or as information about a possible course of action to take. This kind of meaning can only be arrived at in the concrete situation of an utterance or by imagining situations in which a sentence such as (2) or (1c) could be uttered.

In linguistics, a distinction is made between semantic meaning or, in the terminology employed by Leech (1983: 17), **sense** and pragmatic meaning or **force**.[402] While **semantics** deals with sense, **pragmatics**, which Leech (1983: 6) defines as "the study of meaning in relation to speech situations", deals with force. If, like Leech (1983: 14), one reserves "terms like *sentence* or *question* for grammatical entities derived from the language system … and the term *utterance* for *instances* of such entities, identified by their use in a particular situation", then one can say that semantics deals with the meanings of words and sentences, whereas pragmatics deals with the meaning of utterances.

What makes the study of pragmatics so interesting is that there can be rather interesting discrepancies between semantic and pragmatic meaning. Thus all four of the following sentences

(3a)$_{VDE}$ *Can you clear the feathers off the mattress?*

(3b)$_{VDE}$ *Can you give me an example?*

(3c)$_{VDE}$ *Can you delay him in some way?*

(3d)$_{VDE}$ *Can you dismiss the management company if they fall down on the job?*

can be classified as questions, more precisely even as 'ability questions'. From a pragmatic point of view, however, it is arguable whether they all are interrogative in character. Whereas this is (relatively) clearly the case in (3d) and (3c), utterances such as (3a) or *Can you open the window?* tend to be requests rather than ability questions in that by uttering them a speaker as a rule wants the hearer to do something rather than merely find out about the hearer's ability to do something.

There is of course considerable overlap between the various pragmatic interpretations. (3b), for instance, might be said by an examiner and thus be a request also testing ability. In fact, it seems that the interpretation of utterances in terms of their force is also dependent on the assumption that an utterance is meaningful. Since it would hardly make sense to ask an adult person whether they are able to open a window (provided it is not some sort of special window or a window that has caused other people trouble), one

---

[402]   Compare also Bublitz (^{2}2009: 19–24).

would tend to interpret the utterance *Can you open the window?* as a request or a command. This is different, of course, when one is talking to a small child who might not be able to open the window, and where, as a consequence, asking an ability question does make sense.[403]

In the same way, of course, a sentence such as

(1c)$_{VDE}$ *You could apply for a personal chair*

could receive the 'furniture' interpretation in a context where the existence of personal chairs in this sense might appear plausible. Thus it is probably arguable whether the distinction between semantics and pragmatics can be drawn as clearly as is sometimes suggested.

17.2   Principles

17.2.1   The co-operative principle and conversational implicature

In order to describe how human communication works, Paul Grice (1975: 45) established the so-called **co-operative principle**, which comprises four maxims:[404]

QUANTITY: Make your contribution as informative as is required (for the current purposes of the exchange). Do not make your contribution more informative than is required.

QUALITY: Do not say what you believe to be false. Do not say that for which you lack adequate evidence.

RELATION: Be relevant.

MANNER: Be perspicuous.
Avoid obscurity of expression.
Avoid ambiguity.
Be brief (avoid unnecessary prolixity).
Be orderly.

---

[403]   The question is, of course, whether we should interpret these facts to say that the interpretation of an utterance such as (3a) relies on certain inferences to be made by the hearer or whether one could see such questions as prefabricated phraseological units. For a discussion of idiom theory and inference theory see Levinson (1983: 268–270). Compare also Leech (^{2}1981: 338–339). See also 17.3.4.2.

[404]   Cf. Levinson (1983: 97–166) and Bublitz (^{2}2009: 197–214).

It is rather unfortunate that Grice phrased the co-operative principle in terms of imperatives because thus it can easily be misinterpreted as a list of instructions or a style guide. Hence it is important to point out that the idea behind the co-operative principle is purely descriptive in that it claims that when people communicate they follow these principles. In this context it must be understood that, as Leech (1983: 8) points out, Grice's principles and maxims differ from rules in a number of important ways:

(a) Principles/maxims apply variably to different contexts of language use.

(b) Principles/maxims apply in variable degrees, rather than in an all-or-nothing way.

(c) Principles/maxims can conflict with one another.

(d) Principles/maxims can be contravened without abnegation of the kind of activity which they control.

The co-operative principle helps to explain how hearers interpret utterances beyond their explicitly stated content. For instance, a dialogue such as

(4)   A: *I have to be home by 5.*
         B: *There is a bus at 4.20.*

can be interpreted to mean that if A gets that bus A will be home by 5 – otherwise B's utterance would not be relevant. Similarly, in the case of

(5)₍QE₎   A: *When is Aunt Rose's birthday?*
          B: *It's sometime in April.*

B's response at first sight appears like a violation of the quantity maxim. Since there is no reason to assume that B is uncooperative in making that response, the only explanation for the vagueness of the response is that B does not wish to violate the quality maxim. Thus A can infer that B does not know the exact date of Aunt Rose's birthday. Leech (1983: 31) describes this process as follows:

> The three stages of this inference are (i) rejection of the face-value interpretation as inconsistent with the CP; (ii) search for a new interpretation consistent with the CP; (iii) finding a new interpretation, and checking that it is consistent with the CP. The new interpretation includes an implicature ...

This implicature (in this case that B does not know the precise date of Aunt Rose's birthday) is necessary in order to make B's utterance consistent with the co-operative principle. Of course, one could also have come to the conclusion that B does not want to co-operate and deliberately does not tell A when Aunt Rose's birthday is. Such **conversational implicatures** differ from semantic inferences in that they are, as Levinson (1983: 104) says, "inferences based on both the content of what has been said and some specific assumptions about the co-operative nature of ordinary verbal interaction".

The co-operative principle thus enables hearers to infer meaning elements in utterances that are not necessarily compatible with an analysis in terms of semantics or logic. For instance, an utterance such as

(6a)$_{QE}$ *Many of the delegates opposed the motion*

will normally be interpreted to mean

(6b)$_{QE}$ *Not all delegates opposed the motion*

although it is not inconsistent with

(6c)$_{QE}$ *All the delegates opposed the motion.*

The reason for this is, as Leech (1983: 9) explains, "that if the speaker knew that all of the delegates opposed the motion, the first Maxim of Quantity … would have obliged him to be informative enough to say so." (6b) thus is a conversational implicature of (6a).[405]

17.2.2   Further principles

While Grice's account of how people use and interpret utterances is restricted to the co-operative principle, Leech argues that further principles should be introduced such as the Irony principle, the Banter principle or the Pollyanna principle to account for particular instances of language use. The most important of these is the **Politeness principle**: 'Minimize (other things being equal) the expression of impolite beliefs' (Leech 1983: 81). Thus, for instance, in

(7)$_{QE}$ A: *We'll all miss Bill and Agatha, won't we.*
             B: *Well, we'll all miss Bill.*

or

(8)$_{QE}$ P: *Someone's eaten the icing off the cake.*
             C: *It wasn't ME.*

---

[405]   See Levinson (1983: 102–103), Brown and Yule (1983: 31–33) and especially Bublitz ([2]2009: 218–236).

impolite beliefs such as "We won't miss Agatha" or "You have eaten the icing off the cake" are not expressed explicitly. One of the maxims within the politeness principle is the tact maxim – 'Minimize the cost to *h*' and 'Maximize the benefit to *h*',[406] which enables Leech (1983: 107–109) to establish different scales of politeness:

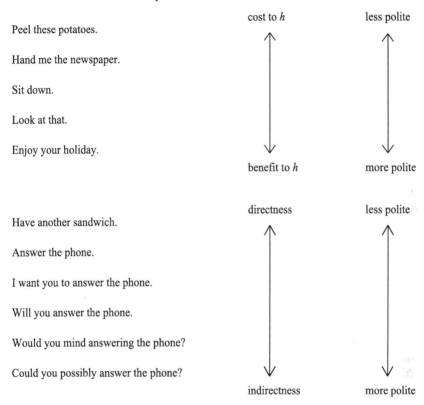

17.3 Speech acts

17.3.1 Performatives and constatives

Speech act theory, which is mainly associated with the British philosopher J.L. Austin and the American philosopher J.R. Searle, focusses on describing the use of language as the performing of actions. The starting point of speech act theory is the observation – made by Austin in a famous book

---

[406] *h* = hearer.

entitled *How to do things with Words*[407] – of the special character of utterances such as

(9)_{QE}   '*I name this ship the* Queen Elizabeth' – as uttered when smashing the
          bottle against the stem.

(10)_{QE}   '*I do (sc. take this woman to be my lawful wedded wife)*' – as uttered in
          the course of a marriage ceremony.

Austin (1962: 6) introduces the term **performative** for utterances of this
kind and distinguishes them from other utterances, which he calls **constatives**, by saying that performatives do "not 'describe' or 'report' or constate
anything at all" (1962: 5). In particular, Austin points out that constative
utterances such as

(11)_{BNC}   *The functionalist approach to the study of mind characterizes much of
          the work currently being done in cognitive psychology, artificial intelli-
          gence and linguistics.*

(12)_{BNC}   *I come to the beach every week.*

can be assigned a truth value, i.e. they can be said to be true or false in a
particular situation, whereas performative utterances such as (9) or (10)
cannot be true or false in the same way. The reason for this is that by saying something such as *I name this ship the Queen Elizabeth*, the person
does not describe an event or a fact, but carries out an action or performs an
integral part of an action, or, in Austin's (1962: 5) words,

> the uttering of the sentence is, or is part of, the doing of an action, which
> again would not *normally* be described as saying something.

In fact, it is difficult to imagine the naming of a ship taking place without
such words being uttered – just as certain other ceremonial actions will
have to be performed as well. Similarly, the making of a promise is carried
out by uttering the words *I promise* and a wedding ceremony involves certain linguistic utterances (*I will – I hereby pronounce you man and wife*) as
well as non-linguistic actions (exchanging rings – kissing the bride etc.).

Performative utterances typically exhibit certain grammatical or lexical
features such as the use of present tense verbs, the use of the pronouns *I*
and *we* or the presence of *hereby*: thus

---

[407]   *How to do things with Words* is a series of lectures given in Harvard by Aus-
        tin in 1955, which were published posthumously in 1962. See Austin (1962:
        5).

(13)$_{SP}$ *PICKERING: ... Never mind crying a little, Miss Doolittle: you are doing very well; and the lessons won't hurt. I promise you I wont let him drag you round the room by your hair.*

can certainly be interpreted as the making of a promise, whereas

(14)$_{SP}$ *MRS PEARCE: ... I had to promise her not to burn it; but I had better put it in the oven for a while.*

(15)$_{SP}$ *MRS HIGGINS: ... Henry! ... What are you doing here today? It is my at-home day: you promised not to come.*

(16)$_{BNC}$ *So I promised I wouldn't go out with him again.*

are constative utterances that make a statement about a promise being given. However, performative utterances do not have to meet these criteria, as is shown by the following examples:[408]

(17)$_{SP}$ *MRS HIGGINS: If you promise to behave yourself, Henry, I'll ask her to come down. If not, go home; for you have taken up quite enough of my time.*
HIGGINS: Oh, all right. Very well. Pick: you behave yourself. Let us put on our best Sunday manners for the creature that we picked out of the mud.
...
MRS HIGGINS: Remember your promise, Henry.

(18)$_{BNC}$ *The Artist hereby authorizes the Publisher to pay all fees due to her agents ...*

(19)$_{BNC}$ *Readers are reminded that the term "United Kingdom" (UK) includes Northern Ireland, whereas "Great Britain" (GB) does not.*

(20)$_{BNC}$ *You are fired.*

Furthermore, it is apparent also from Austin's discussion of the distinction between performatives and constatives that the view of utterances as actions need not be restricted to performatives: when one makes a constative utterance, one also performs an action, namely the action of making a statement. This is why Bublitz (^{2}2009: 85–86), who also points out that it is

---

[408]   See Austin (1962: 53–66). For an outline and a critical discussion of the features of performatives see Bublitz (^{2}2009: 71–86). See also Levinson (1983: 229–236). Compare also Austin's (1962: 32–33) distinction between explicit (such as *I order you to* go) and implicit performatives (such as *go*).

difficult to draw a clear dividing line between constatives and performatives, still considers the distinction to be a milestone in the development of pragmatics:[409]

> We owe the following insights to Austin's discussion of these two types of utterance:
> - that we use language to act, in particular to act in a goal-oriented way,
> - that there are various types of linguistic actions,
> - that there are verbs whose use counts as the performance of the action they denote,
> - that in some cases – apart from the use of a performative verb – further (non-linguistic) conditions have to apply for the action to count as performed
> - that performative verbs are used predominantly for particular types of institutionalized action (BAPTIZING, CONVICTING or DECLARING OPEN)
> - that speech acts are usually implicit, but (almost always) can be made explicit,
> - that speech acts can go wrong in different ways, but can only be true or false under certain conditions.

---

[409] Original text: "Wir verdanken Austins Überlegungen zu diesen beiden Äußerungstypen die Erkenntnisse,
- dass wir mit Sprache handeln, und zwar zielgerichtet handeln,
- dass es mehrere Arten von sprachlichen Handlungen gibt,
- dass es Verben gibt, deren Gebrauch als Vollzug der von ihnen denotierten Handlung gilt,
- dass in manchen Fällen zusätzlich zu den performativen Verben andere Bedingungen erfüllt sein müssen, damit die genannte Handlung auch vollzogen werden kann (sprechhandlungsunterstützende nicht-sprachliche Bedingungen)
- dass performative Verben vor allem für den Vollzug bestimmter institutionalisierter Handlungen explizit verwendet werden (TAUFEN, VERURTEILEN oder ERÖFFNEN)
- dass Sprechhandlungen gewöhnlich implizit sind, aber (meist) explizit gemacht werden können
- dass Sprechhandlungen in verschiedener Hinsicht misslingen, aber nur unter bestimmten Bedingungen wahr oder falsch sein können."

17.3.2   Locutionary, illocutionary and perlocutionary acts

Producing an utterance can be seen not only as one single act but as a number of different acts: in Austin's (1962) theory, three types of act are distinguished which a speaker performs when making an utterance:[410]

▷ a **locutionary act** by formulating and pronouncing a grammatical and
   meaningful utterance,[411]

▷ an **illocutionary act** by expressing the communicative intention of the
   speaker, i.e. "asking or answering a question, giving some information
   or an assurance or a warning, announcing a verdict or an intention, pronouncing sentence, making an appointment or an appeal or a criticism,
   making an identification or giving a description, and the numerous like"
   (Austin 1962: 98-99),

▷ a **perlocutionary act** by producing certain effects in the hearer.[412]

Leech (1983: 199) illustrates this with the following example:

LOCUTION:*s* says to *h* that *X*.
(*X* being certain words spoken with a certain sense and reference)
ILLOCUTION:In saying *X*, *s* ASSERTS that *P*.[413]
PERLOCUTION:By saying *X*, s CONVINCES that *P*.

Searle (1969), in his model, splits up Austin's locutionary act and emphasizes the act-character of referring (> 14.2.3) and predicating as being distinct from the mere uttering of words. Consequently, the following four
kinds of acts are identified by Searle (1969: 24–25):

▷ **utterance acts**: "uttering words (morphemes, sentences)"

▷ **propositional acts**: "referring and predicating"[414]

▷ **illocutionary acts**: "stating, questioning, commanding, promising, etc."

to which he adds

---

[410]   Cf. Bublitz (²2009: 87–100).
[411]   Austin (1962: 95) describes the locutionary act in terms of "the phonetic act,
        the phatic act, and the rhetic act".
[412]   Austin (1962: 117) makes a distinction between perlocutionary object and
        perlocutionary sequel, which Coulthard (²1985: 19) describes as "intended re-
        sult of the illocutionary act" and "an unintended or secondary result".
[413]   P stands for proposition.
[414]   Cf. Bublitz (²2009: 101–103).

▷ **perlocutionary acts**: "... the consequences or *effects* such [illocution-ary] acts have on the actions, thoughts, or beliefs etc. of hearers."

This can be demonstrated by looking at the following passage taken from P.G. Wodehouse's novel *Blandings Castle*:[415]

(21)_{AE}　*'Beach,' said Lord Emsworth.*
　　　　'M'lord?'
　　　　'I've been swindled. <u>This dashed thing doesn't work</u>.'
　　　　'Your lordship cannot see clearly?'
　　　　'I can't see at all, dash it. It's all black.'
　　　　The butler was an observant man.
　　　　'Perhaps if I were to remove the cap at the extremity of the instrument,
　　　　m'lord, more satisfactory results might be obtained.'
　　　　'Eh? Cap? Is there a cap? So there is. Take it off, Beach.'
　　　　'Very good, m'lord.'
　　　　'Ah!' There was satisfaction in Lord Emsworth's voice. He twiddled and
　　　　adjusted, and the satisfaction deepened. 'Yes, that's better. That's capi-
　　　　tal.'...

If we take the sentence *This dashed thing doesn't work* as an utterance of (the fictional character of) Lord Emsworth, then we can say that Lord Emsworth performs an utterance act by saying these words. The proposi-tional act involves establishing reference to the binoculars he is trying to use by the noun phrase *this dashed thing* and by making a predication about it. The illocutionary act can probably be described as a statement, while the perlocutionary act can be seen as prompting a question as a response.

It is important to realize that these acts should not be seen as unrelated actions taking place simultaneously. Leech (1983: 201) points out that this would be like describing an event in a football match as "The centre-forward has kicked the ball; moreover, he has scored a goal; and further-more, he has won the match." Searle (1969: 24) also makes this perfectly clear when he outlines the relation between utterance acts, propositional acts and illocutionary acts:

> I am not saying, of course, that these are separate things that speakers do, as it happens, simultaneously, as one might smoke, read and scratch one's head simultaneously, but rather that in performing an illocutionary act one characteristically performs propositional acts and utterance acts. Nor should it be thought from this that utterance acts and propositional acts stand to il-

---

[415]　P.G. Wodehouse: *Blandings Castle*, Harmondsworth: Penguin (1954: 9).

locutionary acts in the way buying a ticket and getting on a train stand to taking a railroad trip. They are not means to ends; rather, utterance acts stand to propositional and illocutionary acts in the way in which, e.g., making an "X" on a ballot paper stands to voting.

17.3.3   Felicity conditions

Although only certain utterances can be true or false, performatives of the type

(9)$_{QE}$ *I name this ship the* Queen Elizabeth.

(22)$_{BNC}$ *I declare you man and wife.*

can go wrong or be non-felicitous[416] – for instance, if the person making the utterance is not authorized to do so, if there is no ship or no couple present, etc., then the conventionalized speech acts of naming or of marriage will not have been carried out. Searle (1969) suggests a distinction between different types of felicity conditions for the performance of illocutionary acts from which he derives four different types of rule, which can be exemplified rather well describing the speech act of promising as in (13) *I promise you I wont let him drag you round the room by your hair*:[417]

(1) propositional content rules:

- A promise can only be uttered "in the context of a sentence (or larger stretch of discourse) *T*, the utterance of which predicates some future act *A* of the speaker *S*" (Searle 1969: 63), in the case of (13) not allowing Higgins to drag Eliza round the room.

(2) preparatory rules:

- A promise can only be uttered if the hearer would prefer the speaker's carrying out the act *A* to the speaker's not carrying it out and if the speaker believes that this is so.

---

[416]   For infelicities see Austin (1962: 14–24).

[417]   For the character of these "rules for the use of the illocutionary force indicating device" see Searle (1969: 54–56). For a more detailed discussion of the felicity conditions of promising compare Searle (1969: 57–64) and Searle (1971: 46–53). For a description of different types of illocutionary act in these terms see Searle (1969: 66–67). Compare also Levinson (1983: 238–240) and Bublitz (²2009: 106–110).

– Furthermore, a promise can only be uttered if it is not obvious to speaker and hearer that the speaker will carry out the promised action anyway.

(3) sincerity rule:[418]

– A promise can only be uttered if the speaker intends to carry out the action.

(4) essential rule:

– The utterance of a promise "counts as the undertaking of an obligation to do *A*" (Searle 1969: 63).

In contrast,

(23)$_{SP}$ *PICKERING. Higgins: I'm interested. What about the ambassador's garden party? I'll say youre the greatest teacher alive if you make that good. I'll bet you all the expenses of the experiment you cant do it. And I'll pay for the lessons.*

is a case of betting: again, there is a sentence which predicates some future act (teach Eliza proper English); the preparatory rules would be that the two people betting take different views as to the outcome of this act; the sincerity rule in this case requires that Pickering will pay for the experiment should Higgins succeed, and the essential rule can be seen as the undertaking of an obligation in very much the same way as with a promise.

17.3.4   Types of speech act

17.3.4.1   Searle's taxonomy

Both Austin and Searle propose classifications of speech acts which focus on the illocutionary aspect of the speech act. Austin's (1962: 150) classification has been criticized for not being a classification of speech acts but basically one of verbs describing illocutionary acts.[419] On the basis of a

---

[418] For insincere promises see Searle (1969: 62).

[419] Austin (1962: 150) distinguishes between (1) verdictives, (2) exercitives, (3) commissives, (4) behabitives, and (5) expositives. For a critical view see Bublitz (^{2}2009: 110–112). See also Leech (1983: 176) and Levinson (1983: 239). For Searle's classification see Bublitz (^{2}2009: 116–120). Compare also the approach taken by Leech (1983: 198–226).

number of different criteria, Searle (1979a) arrives at a distinction between five "basic categories of illocutionary acts":[420]

	Searle (1979a: 12–17)	paradigm cases (Levinson 1983: 240)
assertives (representatives)	"commit the speaker (in varying degrees) to something's being the case, to the truth of the expressed proposition"	asserting, concluding, etc.
directives	"attempts (of varying degrees ...) by the speaker to get the hearer to do something"	requesting, questioning
commissives	"commit the speaker (again in varying degrees) to some future course of action"	promising, threatening, offering
expressives	"express the psychological state specified in the sincerity condition about a state of affairs specified in the propositional content"	thanking, apologizing, welcoming, congratulating
declarations	"the successful performance ... brings about the correspondence between the propositional content and reality, successful performance guarantees that the propositional content corresponds to the world"	excommunicating, declaring war, christening, firing from employment

In these terms, the following passage from *Pygmalion* could be analysed as follows:

(15)$_{SP}$ *MRS HIGGINS: [dismayed] Henry!* <expressive> *[Scolding him] What are you doing here today?* <directive> *It is my at-home day* <representative>*: you promised not to come.* <representative> *[...]*

---

[420]   Searle (1979a: 12) lists as criteria "illocutionary point, and its corollaries, direction of fit and expressed sincerity conditions". See also Bublitz (²2009: 120–122) for a discussion of the criteria employed by Searle.

> HIGGINS: *Oh bother!* <expressive> *[...]*
> MRS HIGGINS: *Go home at once.* <directive>
> HIGGINS: *[kissing her] I know, mother.* <representative> *I came on purpose.* <representative>
> MRS HIGGINS: *But you mustn't.* <representative> *I'm serious, Henry.* <representative> *You offend all my friends:* <representative> *they stop coming whenever they meet you.* <representative>

17.3.4.2   *Direct and indirect speech acts*

One of the problems of this kind of analysis is that although *What are you doing here?* in (15) can be interpreted as the speech act of asking a question (which falls into the category of directives) in the context of situation its main communicative function can be described as an expression of surprise and disapproval and thus be classified as belonging to the category of expressives. Searle (1979b: 30) accounts for this dual function of illocutionary acts by introducing the notion of an indirect speech act:[421] in Searle's view, an utterance such as

(24)$_{QE}$ *Can you reach the salt?*

has two illocutionary forces – that of question and that of a request. The fact that such utterances can serve as requests can be explained by two factors: firstly, the addressee's ability to reach the salt can be seen as a preparatory condition for the request to pass it. Secondly, in particular contexts hearers will interpret such questions as only being relevant to the conversation if the speaker wishes them to carry out the action described according to the co-operative principle established by Grice (1975) (> 17.2).

Searle's view (1979b: 31) of indirect speech acts as "cases in which one illocutionary act is performed indirectly by way of performing another" has been criticized for a number of reasons. Thus while in the case of (24) one could argue that a "literal" (question) interpretation and an indirect inferred (request) interpretation are possible, Coulthard (^{2}1985: 27) points out that this is by no means always the case since, for instance, teacher directives such as the following "don't seem to admit verbal responses easily":

| T: How many times have I told you to ... | P: ? Seven, sir. |
| T: Who's talking now? | P: ? Me, sir |

---

[421]   Compare Levinson (1983: 263–276). See also 17.1.

T: Can I hear someone whistling?   P: ? Yes, sir

Such examples could be seen as an argument in favour of analysing such cases simply as idiomatic constructions. However, Levinson (1983: 270–271) argues that any such explanation "will need to be complemented by a powerful pragmatic theory that will account for which interpretation will be taken in which context" in cases in which more than one interpretation is possible.

Nevertheless, the notion of indirect speech act is by no means unproblematic. In particular, one has to bear in mind, as Levinson (1983: 274) and Bublitz (^{2}2009: 141) show, that the claim of indirectness is based on the assumption that there is a direct correlation between syntactic structures such as declarative, interrogative and imperative and speech act functions such as 'question' for interrogative. The "indirectness" then arises from the fact that the hearer infers from the context that the speaker may not have been meaning to ask a question at all so that the utterance has to be reinterpreted as, for example, a request. If one does not maintain such a strong link between syntactic form and illocutionary force, it is possible to attribute utterances illocutionary force independent of their form.[422] As a consequence, a distinction between direct and indirect speech acts as such is no longer possible or necessary. Rather, indirectness can be seen as "a matter of degree" (Leech 1983: 38) and be integrated into a general model of pragmatics.[423] Separating the classification of speech acts from syntactic structure also makes it considerably easier to assign certain utterances to particular types of speech act.

17.3.4.3   Problems of classification

Irrespective of the notion of indirect speech acts, one has to say that Searle's classification of speech acts is not entirely unproblematic. In particular, as Levinson (1983: 240) criticizes, there "is no reason ... to think that it is definitive or exhaustive".[424] Indeed, one may wonder, for instance, whether the fact that the class of directives comprises questions as well as

---

[422] Levinson (1983: 274) describes this position as follows: "Illocutionary force is then entirely pragmatic and moreover has no direct and simple correlation with sentence-form or -meaning."

[423] Cf. Bublitz (^{2}2009: 145–147) and Coulthard (1977: 26–28) for a discussion of indirectness.

[424] For further criticism of Searle's typology see Levinson (1983: 240).

commands is particularly well-founded – other linguists such as Leech (1983: 211) make a distinction between directive and rogative, for example. Similarly, one might argue, as Coulthard (^{2}1985: 25) does, that "propositionally empty items" such as *hello* cannot be accommodated easily in Searle's typology. On the other hand – and here there is a parallel to Fillmore's (1968) model of case grammar – any classification of this kind will have to provide for more discrete categories to be identified as subcategories of the major classes established. In fact, the level of discretion required depends very much on the purposes of the analysis.

What is perhaps the most surprising aspect of speech act theory as developed by Austin and Searle is that although it is concerned with what speakers "do" with language they do not investigate what "real speakers" have done in the sense that they would base their theories on the analysis of actual spoken or written text. Rather, speech act theory is developed on the basis of invented examples in envisaged linguistic and extra-linguistic situations of use. In the formulation of the theory, this is reflected in two ways: firstly, the utterances discussed within the framework of speech act theory mostly consist of sentences. One might argue that it might be appropriate to consider a sequence of several sentences as a single speech act with one illocutionary force. Thus, in (15), the whole passage uttered by Mrs Higgins could be seen as expressing 'reproach'.

A second consequence of the fact that speech act theory has not been driven by the analysis of real language use is that certain aspects of discourse structure such as the relation of different elements of a conversation to each other etc. have not been taken into account.[425] These issues are at the centre of work on discourse analysis.[426]

---

[425] Cf. Mey (1993: 181–185), Levinson (1983: 279).

[426] For an account of research on discourse analysis see Levinson (1983: 284–370) and Brown and Yule (1983) or Coulthard (^{2}1985).

18   Texts

18.1   The notion of text

18.1.1   Cohesion and coherence

Texts can be seen as a level of linguistic description above that of the sentence.[427] Such a level is needed for a number of reasons: one is that most utterances used in discourse comprise more than one sentence; another that it would be wrong to imagine texts as a mere series of unrelated sentences. This can be shown by looking at a sentence such as

(1)$_{TI}$ *From about 1950 until her death she also lived there.*

Sentence (1) is highly unlikely to occur as the first sentence of a text. In fact, it does not make much sense if read in isolation. This is because it contains four linguistic elements which can only be interpreted with reference to the sentence preceding it in the text from which it is taken – namely *her, she, also* and *there.*

(2)$_{TI}$ *Barbara Hepworth worked in Trewyn Studios from 1949, ten years after she first arrived in West Cornwall.*

Following (2), it is clear that *she* and *her* refer to Barbara Hepworth and *there* refers to Trewyn Studios since these are explicitly mentioned in the first sentence of the text. Similarly, *also* is used to express the contrast between *working in Trewyn Studios* and *living in Trewyn Studios.* These are examples of items that depend for their interpretation on elements of the surrounding text. Such items can thus be seen as establishing links between elements of a text or as creating **cohesion** within the text.

   The term cohesion can be applied to sentence-internal and inter-sentential relations: there does not seem to be any great difference in the function of *but* in (3^2) and (3^3) apart from the fact that in the first case it

---

[427]   This does not necessarily contradict the view expressed by the famous American linguist Leonard Bloomfield (1933/1935: 170), who said: "It is evident that the sentences in any utterance are marked off by the mere fact that each sentence is an independent linguistic form, not included by virtue of any grammatical construction in any larger linguistic form."

links two sentences and in the second it links two clauses belonging to the same sentence.[428]

(3)ₜᵢ   ¹*When Barbara Hepworth first arrived at Trewyn studios she was*
         still largely preoccupied with the stone and wood carving which
         was central to her work. ²*But during the 1950s she increasingly*
         made sculpture in bronze as well. ... ³*Some of the bronzes now in*
         the garden may be familiar to visitors from casts situated else-
         where, but here they are seen in the environment in which they
         were created.

It should be noted, however, that some linguists, in particular Halliday and Hasan in their influential book *Cohesion in English* (1976), tend to focus on relations across sentence boundaries because these have been studied less widely than sentence internal structures. [429]

Cohesion can arise from structural relations or parallels between different sentences in a text but also from the relations between the lexical items occurring in the text. The latter can be illustrated by text (4), in which the repeated use of the same words (*Cornwall* in sentences 4^1 and 4^3, *art* in 4^1, 4^2, 4^3 and 4^5 etc.) or of morphologically related words (such as *art* and *artist*) contributes to cohesion:

(4)ₜᵢ   ¹*Any account of modern art in Cornwall must begin by acknowl-*
         edging a three thousand year legacy of human activity in the re-
         gion now known as West Penwith. ²*The extraordinary presence of*
         Bronze Age standing stones and Celtic carvings and sculpture, as
         well as the heritage of indigenous craft traditions, have regularly
         surfaced in art made in the region in the twentieth century.
         ³*Nevertheless, most histories of modern art in Cornwall begin by*

---

[428]   The same is true of the function of *she* in (1) and (2), of course. The fact that, especially in spoken language, sentence boundaries are by no means always clear, provides a further argument for not restricting the use of the term cohesion.

[429]   For a more detailed survey of this model see Halliday and Hasan (1976) and Schubert (2008: 31–58). Although Halliday and Hasan restrict the use of the term cohesion to relations across sentence boundaries, it is important to realize that they only do this in order to focus on the textual aspect of cohesion. Halliday and Hasan (1976: 6) explicitly point out that the "parts of a sentence or a clause 'cohere' with each other" and thus also "display texture". Note that other linguists such as de Beaugrande and Dressler (1981: 50) apply the term cohesion to both sentence-internal and inter-sentential relations.

noting Turner's visit to the county in 1811. [4]Turner's sketches attest to the natural beauty of the region and the romance of visiting the furthest flung limb of Southern England. [5]They inaugurate the dialogue between artist and landscape that dominates the subsequent history of art in the region.

What is even more important for (4) to be perceived as a text, however, is that the different elements of the text can be related by the reader so that it appears as a meaningful whole. This property of texts is generally known as **coherence**. The notion of coherence thus refers not only to linguistic relations between certain words or constructions in a text but also to knowledge about real-world items and affairs: thus it requires extra-linguistic knowledge to know that Cornwall is a county of England (and thus to relate *the county* in (4^3) to Cornwall) just as it takes some geographical knowledge of the British Isles to relate *the furthest flung limb of Southern England* to West Penwith (or Cornwall). To what extent a text is perceived as making sense depends, to some extent at least, on the world knowledge and the inferences made by the reader: readers not aware of the fact that William Turner is a famous British painter will perhaps perceive the text as less coherent than those who are, although they may infer this from the phrase *Turner's sketches* in (4^4). It is thus important to note that, as de Beaugrande and Dressler (1981: 6) say, "[c]oherence is clearly not a mere feature of texts, but rather the outcome of cognitive processes among text users".

In a way, cohesion and coherence constitute different perspectives from which a text can be analysed. The analysis of cohesion focuses on the text-internal links between linguistic units such as words and structures, whereas the investigation of coherence concerns such aspects as to whether a sequence of words and linguistic structures presenting certain facts, events or relations between them make sense. In some cases, it is difficult to decide whether what one can call the texture of a text arises from cohesion or coherence: would one want to say that the repeated occurrence of words such as *art* and words related to art is a purely linguistic phenomenon that makes the text cohesive or is that the result of the way in which certain ideas are developed in the text? This question also concerns issues such as whether expressions such as *three thousand year, Bronze Age, twentieth century, 1811, history* can be analysed as being related in terms of the categories and relations identified in semantics and whether the occurrence of *histories* (4^3) and *history* (4^5) contributes to the cohesion of the text despite the fact that the word *history* occurs in two different senses here.

As far as the relation between cohesion and coherence is concerned, one should bear in mind that a sequence of utterances can be perceived as coherent without any obvious signs of cohesion:[430]

(5)_{QE}   A: *There's the doorbell.*
       B: *I'm in the bath.*

This example makes clear that whether an utterance appears as meaningful (and coherent) or not may depend on the world-knowledge of the speakers, the context of situation or the linguistic context. A sentence such as (6) can be perceived as a coherent utterance in different situations:

(6)_{TI}   *This is the first work by Barbara Hepworth to which she gave a title referring directly to landscape.*

If, for instance, sentence (6) is uttered by a guide showing visitors round a museum, they will interpret *this* as referring to the object which they are looking at and consider the utterance coherent in the context of the situation. In the book from which it is taken, it could be interpreted with respect to the headline

(7)_{TI}   [1]Dame Barbara Hepworth 1903–1975
       [2]**Landscape Sculpture 1944**, cast 1961 ...

       [3]This is the first work by Barbara Hepworth to which she gave a title referring directly to landscape.

or/and by looking at a photograph of the sculpture printed next to the text. In all of these cases the use of *this* would appear coherent but only when it is part of the text presented as (7) there is also cohesion.[431]

---

[430]   Example quoted from Brown and Yule (1983: 196).

[431]   Note in this context the following view by Sinclair (1994: 16): "Text is often described as a long string of sentences, and this encourages the practice of drawing links from one bit of the text to another. I would like to suggest, as an alternative, that the most important thing is what is happening in the current sentence. ... The state of the discourse is identified with the sentence which is currently being processed. ... The previous text is part of the immediately previous experience of the reader or listener and is no different from any other, non-linguistic experience."

18.1.2   Texts as utterances

Both cohesion and coherence are important aspects of the analysis of texts. Since there are texts which are coherent without being cohesive and there are also sequences of words that could be analysed as being cohesive but not as being coherent[432] (Brown and Yule 1983: 197) it makes sense to recur only on coherence in a definition of the notion of text. Further criteria have been suggested – for instance, by de Beaugrande and Dressler (1981) – of which the fact that a text should have a communicative function appears the most central.[433]

It is for this reason that Brinker ([3]1992: 17) and Schubert (2008: 26) identify coherence and communicative function as central to the definition of text.

A **text** can then be defined as a linguistic utterance – spoken or written – consisting of one or more sentences (minimally consisting of one word) that can be attributed the property of coherence and that has a communicative function.[434]

18.2   **Cohesive relations**

18.2.1   Explicit linking expressions

Perhaps the most obvious way in which the cohesion of texts manifests itself is the use of words or phrases that link two sentences or structure the

---

[432]   Cf. the example given by Enkvist (1978: 110–111): "I bought a Ford. A car in which President Wilson rode down the Champs Elysées was black. Black English has been widely discussed. The discussion between the presidents ended last week. A week has seven days. ..." Cf. Brown and Yule (1983: 197).

[433]   See also Esser (2009: 19–20).

[434]   Compare also Quirk, Greenbaum, Leech and Svartvik (CGEL 1985: 1423): "... a text – unlike a sentence – is not a grammatical unit but rather a semantic and even a pragmatic one. A text is a stretch of language which seems appropriately coherent in actual use. That is, the text 'coheres' in its real-world context, semantically and pragmatically, and it is also internally or linguistically coherent. For this latter facet, the term 'cohesive' has been applied, referring to the actual forms of linguistic linkage." See also the seven standards of textuality posited by de Beaugrande and Dressler (1981) and Schubert's (2008: 22–23) critique of that model.

text explicitly – a phenomenon for which Halliday and Hasan (1976) use the term **conjunction**.

(8)$_{PH}$ *I wish you could see the place today in its Mediterranean brilliance of light and colour! Yesterday, <u>though</u>, we were wreathed in mist all day ...*

(9)$_{TI}$ *Barbara Hepworth worked in Trewyn Studios from 1949, ten years after she first arrived in West Cornwall. From about 1950 until her death she <u>also</u> lived there.*

(10)$_{TI}$ *The involvement of the Tate in this project reflects the fact that, whilst it holds only a small group of major Newlyn School paintings, its holdings of painting and sculpture from St Ives are rich and broad, capable of providing changing displays of variety and quality at a new gallery. <u>But</u> the idea of a gallery for St Ives also chimed well with the Tate's declared policy of presenting the national collections of British and Modern Art to diverse audiences away from London. <u>That is why</u> the Trustees agreed to take responsibility for the gallery that Cornwall County Council had committed to build.*

While in the case of conjunction linguistic items are used that have an explicit linking function, in other cases of cohesion the link is less explicit but the presence of other items in the text is still presupposed for the interpretation of particular expressions.[435]

18.2.2   Grammatical aspects of relating referents and meanings

Many cohesive effects have to do with the fact that the same referent (of a real or imagined world) is being referred to more than once or that the same sense (i.e. meaning of a word) is being expressed more than once. This can be done in a number of ways, which have been described in great detail by Halliday and Hasan (1976).

(1) A phrase can depend on another element in the text for the identification of its referent. Halliday and Hasan (1976) use the term **reference** for this type of cohesion and make a distinction between

▷ **personal reference** – established by personal pronouns (including their genitive forms often called possessive pronouns)

---

[435]   For asyndetic coordination see CGEL (1985: 13.1).

▷ **demonstrative reference** – established by the definite article *the* and
the determiner-pronouns *this* – *these, that* – *those* or words such as
there.

(11)_{PH}   <u>Midsummer Reds: July 1982</u> *is a painting unique in Heron's work.* <u>*Its*</u>
robust textures and rugged forms, with the exception of the great lem-
ony disc and a couple of smaller shapes, are created entirely by palette-
knife.

(12)_{PH}   <u>*The maximal sensation created by a vast field of a subtly differentiated*</u>
<u>*pure hue, the optical vibrations generated by colour juxtaposition at*</u>
<u>*linear boundaries, and the dynamic equilibrium of disparate formal*</u>
<u>*elements by which motive and shape oscillate between negative and*</u>
<u>*positive:*</u> <u>*these*</u> *were the means to artistic purposes that only oil painting*
could fulfil.

In the case of personal reference and demonstrative reference there is co-
reference between the pro-form and the item to which the pro-form refers.
Thus in (11) both the noun phrase *Midsummer Reds: July 1982* and *its* refer
to the same painting by Patrick Heron. A slightly different situation is presented by (13), where the item *this* takes up the previous sentence (so that
the idea expressed by (13^1) can be regarded as the referent of *this* in
(13^2).[436]

(13)_{PH} ^{1}*'*<u>*The feeling of a sort of marriage of indoor and outdoor space, through*</u>
<u>*the aperture of the window frame, itself roughly rectilinear and parallel*</u>
<u>*to the picture surface, was really the main theme of all my paintings –*</u>
<u>*or nearly all – between 1945 and 1955.'*</u> ^{2}<u>*This,*</u> *as we have seen, is not*
entirely true of Heron's production in that period ...

(2) A word can take up another word, part of a phrase or a larger unit of the
text in terms of the meaning expressed by it. Halliday and Hasan (1976) use
the term **substitution** for this phenomenon and distinguish between

---

[436]   For the categories of extended reference and textual reference see Halliday
and Hasan (1976: 52–53). Note that Halliday and Hasan (1976: 89) describe
reference as "a relation between meanings". In the case of (13), there is no
co-reference since (13^1) as a sentence does not have a referent. Halliday and
Hasan (1976: 32–33) make a distinction between endophoric reference,
which can be anaphoric (i.e. to preceding text) or cataphoric (i.e. to following
text), and exophoric reference (i.e. to the context of situation). Only endophoric reference is cohesive since exophoric reference is text-external. Compare in this respect Sinclair (1994) (see note 431).

▷ nominal substitution where the pro-forms *one, ones* or *same* replace the head of a noun phrase

▷ verbal substitution in which *do* acts as a pro-form for a verb or a whole predicate (and possibly also adjuncts)

▷ clausal substitution by *so* or *not*.

(14)$_{TI}$ *This work exists in two versions. The original elmwood carving of 1944, is on permanent loan to the Barbara Hepworth Museum. The <u>one</u> illustrated is a bronze cast made in 1961.*

(15)$_{ZD}$ *'... They say you met Miss Coyne – the Treveals' Clare.'...*
        'I <u>did</u>'.

(16)$_{ZD}$ *Flushed, giggling, they start to put themselves to rights.*
        But <u>not</u> Clare.

(3) Cohesion can also arise if the element taken up from surrounding text is not expressed formally at all. This is the case, for example, if the participants of a verb (which are part of its semantic valency) are not expressed by complements in the same sentence but when their referents can be retrieved from the context.

(17)$_{ZD}$ *'Will you be going over to Newlyn?' she asks, collecting teacups. Her face is averted, her voice casual.*
        'Why, no – you know I only went there last Thursday. I have no business there today. Why do you ask?'
        'I only just <u>wondered</u> – I wasn't <u>sure</u>.' [unexpressed participant: *whether you were going over to Newlyn*]

(18)$_{ZD}$ *Go on, then – open it. I know you <u>want to</u>.* [unexpressed participant: *open it*]

(19)$_{ZD}$ *'I don't want to go home.' she says.*
        'No. Why <u>should</u> you?' he responds. [unexpressed participant: *want to go home*]

While the above cases can be accounted for in terms of contextually-optional valency slots of the corresponding verbs which have no formal expression (> 12.3.5), in the case of (20) and (21) certain elements of the clause could be seen as adjuncts and complements of the verb in the preceding sentence:

(20)$_{ZD}$ *'You been <u>walking</u> over to St Ives by the coast,' he remarks to Lawrence. It is not a question.*

'Yesterday, you mean? No, not all the way. But I walked along the cliff-path.'
'That's what I heard. ...'

(21)_{ZD} *'These are pencil drawings. And I do water-colours.'*
'What do you draw?'
'Flowers, mostly.'
'Do you? May I see?'

In Halliday and Hasan's (1976) model such cases are referred to as **ellipsis**.[437] However, they treat cases which are very similar in character such as (22) – (24) as **comparative reference**, although they can also be explained in terms of contextually-optional valency slots:

(22)_{TI} *'... I also don't like personal publicity which leads to being known or recognised by the general public or even art students as this interferes with my private life & it is this which produces the work.'*
Barbara Hepworth's situation was very different at the time. [unexpressed participant: *from what it is now*]

(23)_{PH} *... The exception was Rothko. ...* [unexpressed participant: *from the group of artists discussed*]

(24)_{TI} *I have always been intrigued by observing the way in which first the colour on one side and then the colour on the other side of a common but irregularly drawn frontier dividing them seems to come in front. As your eye moves along such a frontier the spatial positions of the colour-areas alternate ...* [unexpressed argument: *as the one mentioned*]

18.2.3   Lexical aspects of cohesion and coherence

Halliday and Hasan (1976) subsume all the above types of cohesion under grammatical cohesion, which they distinguish from lexical cohesion.[438] It has to be said that the same or at least very similar mechanisms are at work in lexical cohesion and in grammatical cohesion and also that different

---

[437]   It may seem preferable to speak of unexpressed participants here since the term ellipsis suggests a kind of underlying element which got deleted. The point is, however, that the referent of the participant can be identified, not that exact words should be retrieved.

[438]   For an account of lexical cohesion see Halliday and Hasan (1976: 274–292) and Schubert (2008: 45–54).

ways of making a text coherent interact or overlap. Thus the use of **general nouns** such as *works* or *event* is very similar to the relation described as reference with respect to items such as *it* or *this* in (11) – (13) and often goes hand in hand with the use of the article *the*:[439]

(25)ₜᵢ   *This painting is a turning point in Lanyon's work. It was one of the large <u>works</u> commissioned by the Arts Council for the Festival of Britain in 1951.*

(26)ₚₕ   *In July 1965, at the ICA in London, Heron made a short speech in which for the first time in public he criticized American aesthetic chauvinism in general and the role played by Clement Greenberg in the critical promotion of American painting in particular. <u>The event</u> caused something of a stir: ...*

The use of general nouns can be seen as a special type of **reiteration**, a term which also covers explicit **repetition** of a lexical item as in

(27)ₜᵢ   ¹*It may be hard news for new visitors to Tate Gallery St Ives to imagine that it is built on the <u>site</u> of the town's old gasworks.* ²*The <u>site</u> had, by the 1980s, become derelict and dangerous. However, it presented obvious attractions as a <u>site</u> for a future gallery of modern art: it overlooks Porthmeor Beach, but is also close to the old town around the harbour and the modern development to the north-west, including the streets where artists have lived for four generations.*

Repetition of lexical items certainly contributes to the cohesiveness of a text, but it could be argued that this also applies to groups of words and to parallels in syntactic construction.

In any case, there seem to be different levels at which cohesion between different items can be claimed. This can be illustrated by text (28):

(28)ₜᵢ   ¹*Since the mid-nineteenth century two 'schools' of art have grown up in West Cornwall, at Newlyn and at St Ives.* ²*The existing public galleries in Penzance and Newlyn provide for the display of Newlyn School painting but no similar arrangement has hitherto existed for St Ives.* ³*The idea of a permanent home in the region for the distinctive modern art of St Ives has long been cherished by many who live in or visit the area.* ⁴*The Tate Gallery St Ives is the realisation of that idea.*
        ⁵*The involvement of the Tate in this project reflects the fact that, whilst it holds only a small group of major Newlyn School paintings, its*

---

[439]   For the textual function of nouns see Götz-Votteler (2008: 135–141).

holdings of painting and sculpture from St Ives are rich and broad, ca-
pable of providing changing displays of variety and quality at a new
gallery. ⁶But the idea of a gallery for St Ives also chimed well with the
Tate's declared policy of presenting the national collections of British
and Modern Art to diverse audiences away from London. ⁷That is why
the Trustees agreed to take responsibility for the gallery that Cornwall
County Council had committed to build.

In this text we can identify (a) identical lexical forms representing the same
lexeme (*Cornwall, Newlyn, art* etc.), (b) different morphological forms of
the same lexeme (²*galleries* – ⁷*gallery* but also ¹*have*, ²*has*, ⁷*had* and ⁴*is* –
⁵*are*), (c) items related by word formation (⁵*holds* – ⁵*holdings*) and (d) lexical forms representing different senses of the same lexeme (²*painting* –
⁵*paintings* – ⁵*painting*).

Halliday and Hasan (1976: 284) argue that cohesion can also be
"achieved through the associations of lexical items that regularly co-occur"
(a type of cohesion for which they rather confusingly use the term collocation).[440] This type of cohesion can be based on semantic relations such as
synonymy, different types of oppositeness, and hyponymy or on the fact
that words belong to the same lexical field or to the same lexical set.[441] The
fact that Halliday and Hasan (1976: 284) are rather vague in their description of this category[442] and call it the "most problematical part of lexical
cohesion" may have to do with the fact that these relations between words
can be more appropriately described in terms of coherence than in terms of
purely linguistic relations between the words in question.

This applies in particular to cases such as the following, where the use
of the definite article is of interest.

---

[440] Cf. Schubert (2008: 51–54) and also Herbst (1996) for this use of the term
collocation.

[441] Schubert (2008: 52–53) makes use of Lipka's (³2002: 166–174) distinction
between lexical fields and lexical sets, where a lexical field is defined by its
members belonging to the same word class and sharing at least one semantic
feature, whereas lexical sets are not defined entirely on the basis of purely
linguistic criteria (> 16.1).

[442] Cf. Halliday and Hasan (1976: 285): "The members of any such set stand in
some kind of semantic relation to one another, but for textual purposes it does
not much matter what this relation is." Compare, however, Hasan's (1984)
more convincing account in terms of identity and similarity chains.

(29)$_{TI}$ [1]*Until he moved permanently to Cornwall, Heron and his family regularly stayed in St Ives in a house in St Andrew Street, overlooking the harbour. [2]This painting is one of a series based on the main room of the house and the view from its windows.*

The use of *the* in the noun phrase *the house* in (29[2]) can be explained by the fact that it refers to *a house* in (29[1]). There is no prior mention of *main room*, however. It would be difficult to describe the relation of *main room* and *house* as a semantic relation since not only houses but also other buildings such as inns, huts, etc. can have main rooms.[443] Such relations can be accounted for much more convincingly in terms of cognitive models of knowledge representation which have made use of concepts such as frame, scenario or script.[444] A **frame** can be defined as "a schematic representation of speakers' knowledge of the situations or states of affair that underlie the meanings of lexical items" (Fillmore 2007: 130).[445]

Within such models, one can then account for the use of the definite article in (29[2]) by saying that the word *house* opens up a *house*-frame, which accounts for the fact that it is part of the speaker's knowledge about houses that they can have a main room, (a kitchen, a bathroom etc.), which is why *main room* does not have to be introduced as a "new" entity. The same would hold for the use of *the* with *view* since it could be argued that speakers know that houses have windows and that windows can have views.

---

[443]   Cf., however, the discussion of the semantic relation of meronymy by Croft and Cruse (2004: 150–163).

[444]   For a discussion of frame, scenario, script and related concepts see Brown and Yule (1983: 236–256), Bublitz (2009: 179–194), Ungerer and Schmid ([2]2006: 207–217) and Schubert (2008: 71–75).

[445]   Compare also Fillmore and Atkins (1992: 76–77): "Semantic theories founded on the notion of *cognitive frames* or *knowledge schemata* ... approach the description of lexical meaning in a quite different way. In such theories, a word's meaning can be understood only with reference to a structured background of experience, beliefs, or practices, constituting a kind of conceptual prerequisite for understanding the meaning. Speakers can be said to know the meaning of the word only by first understanding the background frames that motivate the concept that the word encodes. Within such an approach, words or word senses are not related to each other directly, word to word, but only by way of their links to common background frames and indications of the manner in which their meanings highlight particular elements of such frames." See also Fillmore (1976).

In the same way one could explain the use of the definite article in *the sea* in (30^1) and (30^2) or of *the sand* in (30^4) on the grounds that a *beach*-frame contains knowledge of the fact that a beach is on the sea (or a lake etc.) and very often consists of a stretch of sand, whereas *trees* are not an integral part of such a frame.

(30)$_{PH}$ ^{1}*Take, for example, a beach extending as far as the eye can reach, bordered, on the one hand, by trees, and, on the other, by the sea. ^{2}There is enough green in the sea to relate it to the palms. ^{3}There is enough of the sky reflected in the water to create a resemblance, in some sense, between them. ^{4}The sand is yellow between the green and the blue.*

These examples show that certain aspects of the coherence of texts can be accounted for more satisfactorily by referring to the world-knowledge of speakers than to the language-internal relations that form the basis of cohesion.

18.3   Thematic structure and information structure

18.3.1   Theme and rheme – given and new information

Since the way that a message is presented in a sentence can depend on the surrounding text, the information structure of sentences is an important aspect of the analysis of texts. The framework most widely used to describe such phenomena was originally developed by scholars such as Mathesius (1975) and Firbas, important representatives of the Prague School, and applied to the description of English, for instance, by Halliday (1970b).

The first distinction to be made is that between **theme** and **rheme**. The theme can be defined as the left-most constituent of a clause, the rheme then being the remaining part of the sentence.

(2)	*Barbara Hepworth*	*worked in Trewyn Studios from 1949, ten years after she first arrived in West Cornwall.*
	theme	rheme

Halliday (1994: 37) describes the theme as the "element which serves as the point of departure of the message; it is that with which the clause is concerned". This distinction between theme and rheme bears a certain resemblance to that between subject (in the sense of an element 'about which something is said') and predicate ('what is said about the subject') in traditional grammar. However, the theme need not always be the subject of the clause:[446]

(31)_{TI}	*From the 1930s onwards*	*Barbara Hepworth made sculptures which consisted of a single upright form.*
	theme	rheme
(32)_{SP}	*Remember*	*that you are a human being with a soul and the divine gift of articulate speech: that your native language is the language of Shakespear and Milton and The Bible ...*
	theme	rheme

While many linguists – for example, Esser (2009: 32) – describe the theme as that part of the clause which is known to the hearer and the rheme as the part that contains new information, Halliday (1970: 160–164) makes a distinction between theme and rheme on the one hand and '**given**' and '**new**' on the other. Given information can be described as information that the speaker assumes to be familiar to the hearer, whereas new information is information that the speaker assumes not to be known to the hearer. It is obvious that theme and rheme and 'given' and 'new' represent distinctions that do not necessarily coincide, as can be illustrated by the first two sentences of the Foreword of a brochure sold at the Tate Gallery St Ives:

(33)_{TI}	[1]*The Tate Gallery St Ives project*	*is unique.*
	theme	rheme
	new	new
	[2]*It*	*allows the visitor to see the works of art in the area in which they were conceived and close to the landscape and the sea which influenced them.*
	theme	rheme
	given	new

While the categories of *given* and *new* serve to illustrate some aspects of the information structure quite well, one has to recognize that they are not always easy to apply to actual textual analysis and that more refined cate-

---

[446] For a detailed description of possible themes see Halliday (1994: 37–67). For a definition of theme and rheme in this sense see Hoffmann (2000).

gories recognizing different degrees of givenness or newness may be required.[447] Firbas's (1992: 8–11) notion of communicative dynamism tries to capture this by saying that the information value of the various units of a clause tends to increase with linear progression: this means that as a rule the first unit has a very low information value and the last unit has the highest information value in the sentence, while the other units of the clause have an information value that lies somewhere in between.

18.3.2   End-focus and marked focus

Quirk, Greenbaum, Leech and Svartvik (CGEL 1985: 18.3/9) use the terms theme and focus to describe the information structure of sentences (where focus is defined in terms of stress). They establish the principle of end-focus (which operates alongside the principle of end-weight) to say that new and important information is "most neutrally and normally" placed at the end of a clause.[448]

However, the information structure of sentences can deviate from this in a number of ways. For instance, the intonation nucleus of the sentence can be on elements other than the last one, thus creating marked focus. In a neutral context,

(25)$_{TI}$ *This painting is a turning point in Lanyon's work.*

will have the nucleus on *Lanyon's work* but marked focus can be achieved by putting the nucleus on *this, painting* or *turning point*. A similar effect of giving special prominence to an item can be achieved by a number of syntactic constructions such as a cleft sentence as in (34) or a pseudo-cleft sentences as in (35):[449]

---

[447]   For a discussion of different degrees of 'givenness' see Brown and Yule (1983: 179–188). See also Prince (1981: esp. 225–232). For an attempt to describe different types of thematic progression in texts see Daneš (1970). Compare Götz-Votteler (2008: 68–80). For a critical account of the Prague School concepts see Newmeyer (2001).

[448]   For a precise definition of the terms theme and focus see CGEL (1985: 18.1–18.11). The principle of end-weight refers to the fact that syntactically heavy (or long) constituents tend to occur at the ends of clauses: ... *the stripe paintings did seem to reduce to the bare minimum the formula for the making of pictures.*$_{PH}$

[449]   See CGEL (1985: 18.20–43) for grammatical devices and information structure.

(34)$_{PH}$ *It was in* Arts *in March 1956 that Heron wrote the celebrated article that recorded the first collective showing in London of the painters ...*

(35)$_{PH}$ *What has changed is the underlying formal structure of the paintings.*

18.4   Spoken and written texts

Texts can be classified from different perspectives and according to different criteria. Werlich (1975), for instance, distinguishes between different text types such as description, narration, exposition, argumentation and instruction with regard to the way in which texts are structured.[450] We will concentrate here on the difference between spoken and written texts, i.e. a difference caused by the medium of communication.

Spoken and written language differs in a number of respects, which can be attributed to a number of factors.[451] First of all, one has to consider the fact that the spoken and the written medium offer a different range of possibilities for expressing meaning. In the spoken language, there is variety of phonetic or prosodic means of expression which the written language lacks. For instance, as pointed out above, stress can be used to highlight particularly important elements of the message; similarly, intonation provides a way of expressing meanings such as 'statement' or 'question', or of signalling 'surprise', 'disbelief', 'encouragement' or 'disapproval' for instance.[452] In the written medium, punctuation or different typefaces can be used to express some of these meanings.[453]

---

[450]   Compare Werlich's (1976: 39) definition of text type as "an idealized norm of distinctive text structuring". For the distinction between text type and genre see Schubert (2008: 89). For different text types see Werlich (1975: 27–43) and Schubert (2008: 91–94).

[451]   For a detailed description of the features of the spoken and the written language see e.g. Barnickel (1980: II.84–151) or Brown and Yule (1983: 14–17). Compare also Schubert's (2008: 133–161) discussion of conversation analysis.

[452]   For a survey of such functions of different tones in English see Gut (2009: 121–126).

[453]   Note that the spoken language can also contain indications of meaning of a different kind when one considers factors such as speed of delivery, voice quality, which often, however, are not used intentionally. See Brown (1977: 125–155). For the relevance of intended and non-intended meaning elements to film translation cf. Herbst (1994: 226–237).

Further differences are related to the circumstances of the utterance and are thus to a much greater extent a matter of degree. In spoken conversation, for example, the interlocutors are usually in the same room and can see each other, which enables them to make use of visual symbols such as gestures or to establish reference by deictic words such as *this, over there* or *here*. This does not apply in the same way to telephone conversations, of course.[454]

Similarly, in real (as opposed to fictional) conversation, speech tends to be produced spontaneously, which means that speakers hesitate, produce false starts or change constructions while they are speaking – and sometimes carry out repairs of such performance phenomena. Most situations in which written texts are produced allow more time for planning and correction so that as a result written texts may appear more structured.[455]

Corpus analyses, such as the ones that form the basis of the *Longman Grammar of Spoken and Written English* (1999) by Biber et al. (LGSWE), provide evidence for the linguistic manifestation of differences between the written and the spoken language.[456] Thus it was found, for instance, that

▷ tags are typical of conversation or written representations of speech (LGSWE 3.4.4),

▷ noun phrases with a modifier are rare in conversation, whereas almost 60% of all NPs in academic prose contain a modifier (LGSWE 8.1.1) or that

▷ passives tend to be more frequent in written texts, especially academic prose, than in conversation (LGSWE 11.3).

---

[454] For a discussion of deixis see Bublitz (2009: 237–258).

[455] Cf. Crystal and Davy (1975: 86): "In the world of written English, discourse has a regular, predictable pattern of connectivity. Sentences are regularly identifiable ... The general impression is one of premeditation and conscious organization. Errors of expression and changes of mind, if they occur, can be carefully erased, and eliminated from a final draft. If a word or phrase does not come to mind, the writer may pause until he finds it, or choose some alternative. The page you are reading now is errorless: it does not show the various stages of revision from manuscript to printer's proof which gave it the form it now has." See also Brown and Yule (1983: 15), who point out that spoken language contains "many incomplete sentences, often simply sequences of phrases" and little subordination.

[456] LGSWE compares subcorpora of the four registers conversation, fiction, newspaper language and academic prose.

It is important to note that such features are not necessarily due to the spoken or the written medium but the circumstances in which one tends to use spoken or written language. Thus there is a wide range of texts in between the typical spoken text of spontaneous conversation and the typical written text as it is to be found in academic writing, for example. Novels may contain dialogues which show typical features of spontaneous conversation such as question tags or adjacency pairs of the type *hello – hello* or 'question' and 'answer'. The dialogues of plays or films differ from natural conversation in a number of ways, for example, with respect to hesitation phenomena, repairs, overlap or interruption. In fact, these kinds of dialogue belong to the category of texts that are written to be spoken. News broadcasts on the radio or TV also fall into this intermediate category. On the one hand, these texts clearly represent written language: since there is time to plan and construct the utterance, the text will usually be well-structured. On the other hand, radio news broadcasts have to be designed in such a way that they can be understood by listening because the hearer does not have the chance to go back and re-read a complex sentence as in a newspaper article, for instance. TV news often combines spoken text with written text and as such combines the two media of linguistic expression. In particular, it should be noticed that the use of the internet has resulted in new forms of texts which, although written, also display many characteristics of the spoken language.[457]

Thus – with the exception of differences directly caused by the medium of expression – it is very difficult to find general criteria for distinguishing between spoken and written texts. As a consequence, a classification of texts must be based on a number of criteria such as[458]

▷ whether a text is spoken to be heard (as in conversation), spoken to be written (dictation), written to be spoken (news broadcast, play) or written to be read (e-mail, novel),

▷ whether there is direct interaction between the people communicating (as in an oral conversation or an internet chatgroup) or not (as in the case of books or films),

---

[457] For a detailed discussion of the language of e-mails, virtual worlds, chatgroups etc. see Crystal (2001: esp. 24–48). See also Schubert (2008: 117–128).

[458] Compare Söll and Hausmann (1985: 46) and Herbst (1994: 150–153). See also Crystal (2001: 42–43).

▷ whether there is face-to-face contact between the participants (as in many conversations or also university lectures) or not (as in a telephone conversation, a chatgroup or, of course, a novel),

▷ to what extent the language produced is spontaneous (as would typically be the case in conversation or – to a lesser degree perhaps – chatgroups) or pre-planned (as in news broadcasts or written texts).

Recommended further reading:

– Bublitz (^{2}2009)
– Schubert (2008)

Variation

19 Variation in language

19.1 Registers and dialects

As was pointed out in Chapter 1, a language must not be imagined as a monolithic system but the use of language is characterized by a considerable amount of variation in the sense that there are different ways of expressing the same content or meaning. Some of this variation entails a choice on the part of the speakers; other types of variation are subject to external factors. Thus the form a particular utterance takes may depend on

▷ whether the medium of expression is spoken or written (as shown in the preceding chapter),

▷ what is being discussed and whether specialized vocabulary or terminology is being used in the discussion,

▷ whether the situation of utterance is (or is perceived by the speaker as) relatively formal or relatively informal,

▷ the regional and social background of the speaker (and the extent to which this is apparent from their use of language),

▷ whether the speaker is a woman or a man.[459]

Varieties that are determined by factors such as medium, field of discourse or attitude are often subsumed under the labels of **register** and **style** (the latter only referring to attitudinal variation). Biber et al., in the *Longman Grammar of Spoken and Written English* (1999: 15), characterize **registers** as "varieties relating to different circumstances and purposes" and distinguish them from **dialects** as "varieties associated with different groups of

---

[459] For differences between the language used by men and women see e.g. Coates (1986). For a corpus-based study of parameters such as the use of empty adjectives, colour terms, non-standard language, question tags by male and female speakers of British and American English see Grimm (2008).

speakers". Halliday, McIntosh, and Strevens (1964: 87) speak of varieties of a language "distinguished according to use" and "according to user" respectively.[460]

Such a distinction is too rigorous, however, because there are no clear-cut boundaries between the different varieties and because, up to a point, the factors determining the choice of a variety may be seen as interrelated. For instance, speakers may well be competent in more than one dialect, i.e. be able to speak, say, the standard language and some form of a regional dialect. For such speakers, the extent to which they make use of "regional elements" in their language may well be influenced by situational factors such as who they are talking to and how formal they perceive the situation to be.[461] It is for such reason that Hudson (1980: 51) rejects what he refers to as a variety-based model and argues in favour of an "item-based model", in which a linguistic item (lexical item, form of pronunciation, grammatical construction) "is associated with a social description which says who uses it, and when".[462]

Indeed, sociolinguistic experiments have shown considerable variation with respect to particular features. In a famous experiment the American sociolinguist Labov investigated whether people working in three different New York department stores pronounced an [r] in words such as *fourth floor* or not. Labov (1966: 63–87) found that the use of [r] correlates to social status because more [r]-forms occurred in the more prestigious shops and to careful speech because people used more [r]-forms when they repeated the forms because they thought the researcher had not understood them. So it seems that the use of this particular variable is typical of a

---

[460] For a survey see Barnickel (1980: esp. 18–21) or Esser (1993: 38–43).

[461] Compare Hudson's (1980: 56) remark about varieties: "... there are yet more reasons for not taking the notion seriously as a part of sociolinguistic theory, since so-called varieties may be hopelessly mixed up together even in the same stretch of speech". For the overlap between dialects and registers see also Hudson (1980: 51), for the concept of code-switching see Hudson (1980: 56–58).

[462] Note that the approach advocated by Hudson (1980: 232) shows strong parallels to the model of the mental lexicon as envisaged by Bybee (1995) in the context of morphology and other usage-based approaches (> 9.7 and 13.2) since he emphasizes the role of storage: "... the evidence that we have surveyed suggests that we do in fact remember a vast amount of information concerned with particular lexical and other types of item, and that *linguistic items may be related individually to social context*".

group of speakers (in the sense of a social dialect) as well as of a particular style of speech.[463] Similarly, studies carried out by Trudgill ([3]1995: 32, 35–36) revealed that the use of a word-final [n̩] (as opposed to RP [ŋ]) in words such as *walking*, "h-dropping" in words such as *hat*, the use of glottal stops as realizations of /t/ in words such as *better* or the use of third person singular verbs without an {S}-suffix (*She like him very much*) correlate with the social class of the speakers:[464]

class	percentage of [n̩]-realizations in *walking, running, etc.*	percentage of no realization of <h> in *hammer, hat,* etc.	percentage of glottal stops in *butter, bet* etc.	percentage of verbs without 3rd person singular {S}
middle middle	31	6	41	0
lower middle	42	14	62	2
upper working	87	40	89	70
middle working	95	59	92	87
lower working	100	61	94	97

One interesting factor determining this variation is accommodation, i.e. the phenomenon that speakers tend to adapt their own speech to that of their interlocutors. For instance, Trudgill (1986: 7–8) found that as an interviewer he tended to use more glottal stops in words such as *better* or *bet* when he was talking to informants with a high score of glottal stop realizations.[465] In any case, the figures presented above are a clear indication of the fact "that it is not possible to talk legitimately of discrete social-class accents – again there is a continuum, with most speakers using sometimes one pronunciation, sometimes another" (Trudgill [3]1995: 36).

---

[463] For a description of Labov's experiments and further studies on the correlation of social class and particular linguistic forms see Hudson (1980: 148–157) and Holmes (1992: 144–161). Compare also Trudgill ([3]1995: 31–38).

[464] For a detailed account of social and stylistic variation see Trudgill (1974: esp. 55–63, 90–96 and 130–132).

[465] This does not apply to the groups with the highest scores for glottal stops. For details see Trudgill (1978: 7–8).

19.2 Accent, dialect, standard and prestige

19.2.1 Standard English and its pronunciations

When we talk about regional and social varieties of language it is important to consider that such varieties should not be taken to exist in a discrete and clearly distinguishable form.[466] First of all, it is not really possible to draw a clear dividing line between one dialect and another because dialect boundaries tend to be gradual in character. Thus, the notion of dialect is already a generalization of some sort. Similarly, the distinction between social and regional dialects is artificial up to a point because there is strong interdependency between the two dimensions. Thus one can safely assume that the language typically used by speakers at the lower end of the social scale usually shows more regionally marked forms than that of so-called "educated speakers". Trudgill (1975: 21) uses the following representation to show the interrelatedness of the social and the regional dimension in Britain:

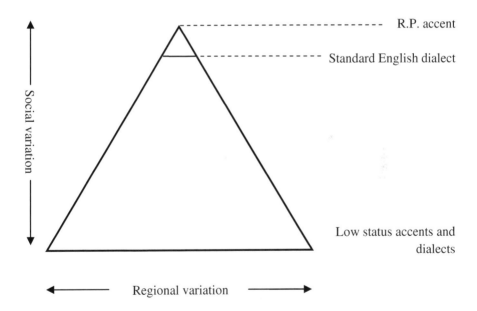

---

[466] Compare Chapter 1 for the global spread of English and regional varieties.

A special position is taken by the form of English usually referred to as Standard English. According to Barnickel (1980: 28–30), a standard can be defined as a variety[467]

▷ that is used for communication between speakers of different regional dialects and is intelligible to all speakers in a country

▷ that is generally used in printing

▷ that has received a certain form of codification in that it is the variety most usually described in grammar books and dictionaries

▷ that is usually taught to foreigners.

Although Quirk, Greenbaum, Leech, and Svartvik (CGEL 1985: 18) point out that the "degree of acceptance of a single standard of English throughout the world ... is a truly remarkable phenomenon", different national standards of English such as British and American English can be distinguished.[468] Trudgill and Hannah ([5]2008) identify two ENL (English as a native language) varieties that are most commonly used as models in EFL teaching – British English and North American English. The latter they describe as "English as it is written and spoken by educated speakers in the United States of America and Canada" ([5]2008: 5), whereas British English is characterized in very broad terms by Trudgill and Hannah ([5]2008: 4):

> As far as grammar and vocabulary are concerned, this generally means Standard English as it is normally written and spoken by educated speakers in England and, with certain differences, in Wales, Scotland, Northern Ireland, The Republic of Ireland, Australia, New Zealand and South Africa.

While Standard English allows for a certain amount of regional variation at the levels of vocabulary, grammar or pronunciation, within England and Wales there is one pronunciation of it, called **Received Pronunciation (RP)**, which shows no regional variation. RP is a highly prestigious **accent** which is defined entirely in social terms. Historically, it is associated with public school education and for a very long time RP was extremely important as a social marker in British society, as documented, for example, in

---

[467] Compare the criteria given by Haugen (1966/1972: 110): selection, codification, elaboration of function, acceptance by the community. For linguistic criteria of Standard English see Trudgill and Hannah ([5]2008: 2–3): See also Trudgill (1975: 18).

[468] CGEL (1985: 1.25), however, describes a variety such as Irish English as a national standard. For national varieties of English see also Barnickel (1980: 44–139) and Hansen, Carls, and Lucko (1996).

George Bernard Shaw's play *Pygmalion*. Since today this type of accent is more appropriately characterized in terms of its use on radio and television by BBC national newsreaders, for example, the term RP is sometimes replaced with **BBC English**.[469] While Trudgill and Hannah ([5]2008: 15) estimate that only 3–5 per cent of the population of England are RP speakers, Wells (1982: 10) points out that in the United States the majority of speakers use an accent that "reveals little or nothing of their geographical origins". This accent is referred to as **General American** or Network English.[470]

19.2.2   Quality judgements

It is important to realize that the standard language is, as Kortmann (2005: 256) or Trudgill ([3]1995: 8) emphasize, not in any way superior to other regional or social dialects of the language with respect to any structural aspects or intrinsic linguistic properties. The standard language rather has a special status because of its functions in a speech community. It is a variety used for certain purposes of communication and also a variety used by so-called "educated speakers".[471]

The use of the standard raises a number of highly relevant educational issues. For instance, one could argue that it is important to teach the standard at school because it is the variety of the language which is most appropriately used in certain communicative situations in which it would be a disadvantage not to be able to use the standard. Even Peter Trudgill (1975:

---

[469]   See, for instance, Gimson's introduction to the fourteenth edition of the *English Pronouncing Dictionary* (EPD14, 1977: x), where he points out that the term "Public School Pronunciation" used by Daniel Jones in the first editions of the EPD and his description of that type of pronunciation as "that most usually heard in everyday speech in the families of Southern English persons whose menfolk have been educated at the great public boarding-schools" is "hardly tenable today". EPD15 (1997: v) uses the term BBC English. For variability within RP today see Wells (1982: 279–301). See also Upton (2008: 237–240).

[470]   For a more detailed account of General American see Wells (1982: esp. 467–472).

[471]   Cf. CGEL (1985: 1.22). Kortmann (2005: 257) estimates that the standard variety is used by a minority of 12% to 15% of the population.

80), whose views on these matters can be regarded as relatively radical, says:

> We accept ... that the teaching of written standard English can be carried out in schools, not because this dialect is 'correct' or even 'appropriate', but because it may be socially and economically advantageous to children when they leave – and because it is possible.

However, it is important that when the standard is taught at school to children who do not normally use it, they learn to understand that this is a variety of the language that is useful for particular purposes and that the language they normally use is not in any way inferior and is equally useful for other purposes of communication.[472]

It is interesting to see that the use of a particular dialect or, especially perhaps in Britain, the use of a particular accent can influence the way a particular utterance or its speaker is perceived by interlocutors. One experiment that can be quoted in this context was carried out by Elyan, Smith, Giles, and Bourhis (1978: 128) in which it was tested how listeners react to utterances spoken by two women once using RP and once using a Northern English accent.

> It was found that listeners considered the RP speakers to be higher in self-esteem, clearer, more fluent, intelligent, self-confident, adventurous, independent, feminine and less weak than the regional accented speakers. In addition, the former were more likely to have a job which was well-paid and prestigious and an egalitarian relationship with their spouse in the home, but less likely to have children than Northern accented speakers. At the same time, regional speakers were perceived to be more sincere and likeable, and less aggressive and egotistic than their RP counterparts.

Irrespective of whether the results of such experiments are totally reliable in every detail, there is strong evidence to suggest that people connect certain qualities with particular varieties. It has been shown, however, that such judgements do not result from particular intrinsic features of those varieties. Thus, for example, not pronouncing word-initial *h* is considered ugly in an English context, where it occurs in low-prestige varieties such as the London accent of Cockney. At the same time it is a prominent feature of the French language, which is generally regarded as elegant. Rather, aesthetic judgements seem to reflect qualities associated with the speakers

---

[472] Cf. Trudgill (1975: 65–83). For a discussion of the deficit hypothesis, restricted and elaborated code cf. Hudson (1980: 214–230).

of the varieties in question or areas where they are spoken.[473] Within England, there is a tendency for Received Pronunciation, the standard pronunciation of England and Wales, to obtain high prestige scores, followed by accents of pleasant rural areas such as Somerset, with the Birmingham accent at the absolute bottom.[474] Edwards (1982: 25) concludes:

> Overall, these British (and Irish) studies of accent evaluation show that speech samples may evoke stereotyped reactions reflecting differential views of social groups. Standard accents usually connote high status and competence; regional accents may be seen to reflect greater integrity and attractiveness.

The fact that different varieties apparently evoke certain stereotypes indicates that different varieties are associated not only with particular user groups but also with particular situations of use.

19.3 Levels of differences between regional and social varieties

Differences between regional and social varieties can be observed at all levels of linguistic description:[475]

As far as **pronunciation** is concerned, it is interesting to see that some accents of English distinguish different words by different sounds which are pronounced the same in others: thus, RP and many other accents of English have two different vowels in words such as *put, book, push* and words such as *putt* (in golf), *cut* or *much*:

	RP	Northern English
put, book, push	ʊ	ʊ
putt, cut, much	ʌ	

---

[473] See the discussion of the social connotations hypothesis by Trudgill and Giles (1978).

[474] In a study by Giles (1970: 218) ten accents of English were ranked as to their aesthetic content in the following way: RP, Irish English, South Welsh, Northern England, Somerset, North American, Cockney, Affected RP, Birmingham. See also Coupland and Bishop (2007). For further such studies and possible objections see also Herbst (1994: 91). For German see Hundt (1992).

[475] For detailed descriptions of varieties of English world-wide see Trudgill and Hannah (^{5}2008).

In Northern accents of English, however, both groups of words are pronounced with the same vowel because they do not have a sound contrast corresponding to that between RP /ʊ/ and /ʌ/.

There are also cases where two varieties express the same sound contrast, i.e. they can be said to have the same phonemes (> 5.1.1) but use them in different sets of words. Both RP and Northern English and General American use different vowels in the words in lists (i) and (ii):[476]

		RP	Northern English General American
(i)	*park, father, calm, hard*	vowel 1	
(ii)	*ant, hat, latter*	vowel 2	

In words belonging to set (iii), however, RP has the vowel of group (i), whereas Northern English and General American have the vowel of group (ii):

		RP	Northern English General American
(iii)	*castle, aunt, banana,* *example*	vowel 1	vowel 2

These differences explain why "[i]n a northern accent, then, *put* and *putt* are typically homophones, [pʊt], while *gas* and *glass* rhyme perfectly, [gas, glas]" (Wells 1982: 349).

If we say that two accents make the same distinctions this does not mean that the sounds expressing these distinctions have to be phonetically identical. Thus, although from a certain point of view it makes sense to say that words such as *castle* or *aunt* have the same vowel phoneme in General American and Northern English, the pronunciation of these words in the two accents differs considerably, which can be represented like this:[477]

---

[476] For a description of different accents of English with reference to standard lexical sets see Wells (1982). See also Schneider (2008b).

[477] For the vowel systems and the use of the symbols compare Wells (1982: 118, 120, 363–365), who gives /ɑː/ for Birmingham and /aː/ for Leeds. For /æ/ in RP and American English see 5.2.3 and 7.5.

		RP	Northern English	General American
(i)	*park, father, calm, hard*	ɑː	ɑː	ɑ
(ii)	*ant, hat, latter, trap*	æ	a	æ
(iii)	*castle, aunt, banana, example, bath*	ɑː	aː	æ

A further very important distinction to be made in the case of accents of English is that between **rhotic** and **non-rhotic accents**. Rhotic accents have an overt /r/-realization before consonants (*park, farm*) or in word-final position (*far, core, here*), whereas non-rhotic accents do not. Rhotic pronunciation is typical of many American accents including General American and Canadian English, as well as the accents of Ireland, Scotland or the South West of England, whereas Received Pronunciation and most other accents of England and Wales, Australian English, New Zealand English or South African English are non-rhotic.[478]

One important feature distinguishing RP and American English concerns the pronunciation of /juː/ and /uː/ in words such as *knew, student* or *enthusiasm*.[479] Furthermore, there can be differences in pronunciation related to stress (*BrE* /ədˈvɜːtɪsmənt/ vs. *AmE* /ædvəˈtaɪzmənt/ or simply concerning individual words (*BrE* /təˈmɑːtəʊ/ vs. *AmE* /təˈmeɪɾoʊ/).

Lexical differences are also very important when it comes to identifying the differences between different varieties of a language. This becomes clear when we ask how a particular object or thing of the real world is referred to in a particular variety. Thus, for instance, if speakers of American English are talking about a 'railway system operating below the streets of a town or city', they will probably be using the word *subway*, whereas speakers of British English will use the word *underground*, when talking about what in German is called a *Fußgängerunterführung* speakers of British English will use *subway*, whereas speakers of American English will use the word *underpass*.

---

[478] See Wells (1982: 75–76).

[479] For Yod-dropping in British and American accents see Wells (1982: 147–148). Generally, /uː/ pronunciations can be regarded as more typical of American English, but note that the pronunciations given in EPD17 and LPD3 do not always coincide.

From the point of view of the lexicon, one can thus say that

▷ certain words only occur in particular varieties: thus words such as *lorry* are used in British English but not in American English,

▷ certain words have meanings that are exclusive to or typical of a particular variety: thus *subway* has the meaning of 'underground railway' in American English and the meaning of "a path that goes under a road …" (OALD6) in British English, British and American English share the general meaning of *waste disposal*, but using it to refer to a *waste disposal unit* is British English; the word *tea* is used for a meal only in British English; etc.

▷ some words occur in different varieties but with different meanings: *coffee shop* in American English is "a restaurant that serves cheap meals" and in British English "a place in a large shop or a hotel that serves meals and non-alcoholic drinks" (LDOCE5).

Some words marked *BrE* or *AmE* in LDOCE5	
BrE	AmE
communication cord – cooling off period – dustman – golden jubilee – motorway – post-code – school-leaver – tea brake – tea-cake	*attorney – blindside – boom box – freeway – garbage collector – heavy hitter – raise (noun) – restroom – soda fountain – zip code*
Some word meanings marked *BrE* or *AmE* in LDOCE5	
BrE	AmE
circle 'the upper floor of a theatre' – *copper* 'police officer' – *hide* 'place from which you can watch animals or birds' – *scoop* 'win a prize or award'– *way out* 'a door or passage through which you leave a building'	*blind* 'a small shelter from which you can watch birds or animals' – *figure* 'calculate an amount' – *outlet* 'place on a wall where you can connect electrical equipment to the supply of electricity'

Such differences in the lexicon do not only apply to individual words but also to multi-word units: the idioms *not give a monkey's* or *sail close to the wind* are typical of British English, for instance. Mittmann (2004) has demonstrated that certain clusters of words tend to be used in one variety rather than the other: for example, *kind of* or *kinda* was found significantly more often in a corpus of spoken American English than in a comparable corpus of spoken British English, whereas *sort of/sorta* is more typical of British spoken English. Similarly, combinations such as *I suppose, I reckon, I should think* are overwhelmingly used by British speakers, whereas *I guess* and *I figure* represent typical American usage. Similarly, more than 90 per cent of the occurrences of *a little bit* were found in the British corpus but more than 60 per cent of *a little* and *a bit* in the American corpus.[480]

It is important to realize that such differences concerning combinations of words are often a matter of frequency rather than absolute features of one variety. This is also true of some **grammatical features**: the *Grammar of Spoken and Written English* by Biber et al. (1999: 462) states that in conversation American English shows more uses of the progressive aspect than British English does, whereas British English news broadcasts show a higher proportion of forms of the perfect aspect.

Differences in the grammar of different varieties can, however, also be more dramatic. For instance, multiple negation can be found in many varieties of English world-wide (Kortmann 2008: 492, Schneider 2008a: 769). One further such feature is the occurrence of double modals (*I tell you what we might should do*) to be found in Britain in Northern English, Scottish and Shetland/Orkney English (Kortmann 2008: 491) but also in Southern American dialects and Jamaican Creole (Schneider 2008a: 766).[481]

As far as British and American English are concerned, there are a number of differences concerning inflexion (such as *BrE got – AmE gotten, BrE learnt – AmE learned*) or the use of the articles in certain phrases (*BrE go to university – AmE go to a university*).[482] Similarly, differences in valency can be found: Trudgill and Hannah ([5]2008: 70) give examples such as

– that uninflected *come* and *go* occur with an [INF]-complement in US English but not in English English (*Can I come have a cup of coffee with you?*)

– that verbs such as *seem* or *look* occur in English English with an [NP]-complement (*It seems a good idea*), whereas a [like NP]-complement

---

[480] Cf. Mittmann (2004: 212, 217). See also Herbst and Mittmann (2003).

[481] Compare Kortmann (2008) for a survey of morphological and syntactic variation in the British Isles and Schneider (2008a) for the Americas and the Carribean.

[482] For these and further differences between English English and American English see Hannah and Trudgill ([5]2008: 59–82).

can occur both in English English and US English (*It seems like a good idea*).

A further level where differences between British and American English can be observed is **spelling**:

	BrE	AmE
individual words	*cosy, monologue*	*cozy, monolog/monologue*
-our vs. *-or*	*colour, rigour, splendour*	*color, rigor, splendor*
-ise vs. *-ize*	*analyse, realize/realise*	*analyze, realize*
-re vs. *-er*	*centre, kilometre, theatre*	*center, kilometer, theater*
doubling of consonants	*travelled, travelling*	*traveled, traveling*

20   Linguistic change

20.1   Types of linguistic change

This chapter is concerned with linguistic change and illustrates some of the important changes that have taken place in the history of the English language in the areas of pronunciation, lexis and grammar.[483]

The causes of linguistic change are generally described as falling into two different categories. The first of these – **external causes** – are related to language contact situations in which a language, or a particular variety of a language, comes into contact with another language or another variety. Thus, for instance, the Scandinavian settlements in the Northern parts of England during the Old English period led to a considerable amount of contact between speakers of English and speakers of Norse and a situation of bilingualism in the North of England[484] just as the Norman Conquest resulted in contact between people who spoke Norman French and people who spoke English. Depending on the direction of the influence, one can distinguish between

▷ **substrate influence**, i.e. a situation in which a language (or variety) exerts influence on that of speakers in socially or politically superior position as in the case of Celtic influence on English,[485]

---

[483]   For a discussion of the nature of linguistic change see Traugott (2002: esp. 21): "From a 'functionalist' perspective ... change is the result of strategic interaction, specifically of choice-making on the part of speakers/writers in interactional negotiation with addressees/readers. This includes, but is not limited to, conveying of information. On this view, language change is the result of innovation in the individual *and* spread of the innovation to the community, as suggested by Weinreich, Labov and Herzog (1968)."

[484]   See Kastovsky (1992: 329–332).

[485]   See Lutz (2009: 229): "... a substratum language may exert far-reaching structural influence on the phonology, morphology, and syntax of the superstratum if many speakers of the substratum abandon their own language for the superstratum, i.e. in case of large-scale language shift. Thus, scholars looking for Celtic loanwords in English as a result of the Anglo-Saxon con-

▷ **superstrate influence**, i.e. a situation in which the language of a group of speakers in a socially or politically superior position influences that of the speakers in an inferior position as in the case of French influence on English after 1066, and

▷ **adstrate influence**, i.e. a situation in which a language influences a language or variety of a group of speakers of equal status.[486]

As opposed to such external causes of linguistic change there are also **internal causes**. Brinton and Arnovick (2006: 56–57) mention factors such as ease of articulation (which may show in assimilation or elision of sounds), perceptual clarity (which may conflict with ease of articulation) or tendencies such as the devoicing of final consonants or the loss of final [n].

20.2   Sound change

20.2.1   The phoneme systems of Old English and RP

That the sound system of a language is subject to constant modification is obvious. The extent of the changes becomes clear when one compares the phoneme system of Old English with that of RP today,[487] which for the purpose of easy comparison will be represented in the following form:

	Old English		**Present-Day British English (RP)**		
Monophthongs	/iː/ /i/ /yː/ /y/	/uː/ /u/	/iː/ /ɪ/		/uː/ /ʊ/
	/eː/ /e/	/oː/ /o/	/e/		
				/ɜː/ /ə/	/ɔː/
	/æː/ /æ/		/æ/		
				/ʌ/	
		/ɑː/ /ɑ/		/ɑː/	/ɒ/

---

quest are looking for the wrong type of traces of this kind of contact …". See also Vennemann (1998: esp. 245–248).

[486] For a more detailed discussion of the causes of change see Brinton and Arnovick (2006: 60–61). For a discussion of the notion of adstrate see also Schneider (2007).

[487] RP-system adapted from Gimson ([4]1989: 80 and 82), Old English system based on Hogg (1992: 85–86) and Lass (2006: 53–54). Lass (2006: 54) also includes double consonants; cf. also Hogg (1992: 89). For unstressed vowels see Hogg (1992: 88). For a more detailed account see Hogg (1992: 84–95).

Diphthongs	/e:o/ /eo/ /æɑ:/ /æɑ/	/eɪ, əʊ, aʊ, aɪ, ɪə, ʊə, ɔɪ, eə/
Consonants	/p/ /b/ /t/ /d/ /k/ /g/	/p/ /b/ /t/ /d/ /k/ /g/
	/f/ /θ/ /s/	/f/ /v/ /θ/ /ð/ /s/ /z/
	/ʃ/ /h/	/ʃ/ /ʒ/ /h/
	/tʃ/ /dʒ/	/tʃ/ /dʒ/
	/m/ /n/	/m/ /n/ /ŋ/
	/l/ /r/	/l/ /r/
	/j/ /w/	/j/ /w/

It is immediately obvious that there are fewer differences in the consonant system than in the vowel system. In the case of the vowels, Old English has rounded front vowel phonemes /y:/ and /y/ (in words such as *mys* [my:s] ('mice') and *cyning* [kynɪŋg] ('king')), which modern English lacks. What is also very noticeable is the fact that there are considerable discrepancies between the lists of diphthongs and in particular that RP (but not American English and other rhotic varieties) has the series /ɪə/ /eə/ /ʊə/. The most striking fact about the consonants is that the voiceless and voiced counterparts of the fricatives /f/ /θ/ /s/ are to be treated as allophones of a single phoneme since they are in complementary distribution:[488]

/f θ s/	[v ð z]	between voiced sounds	[su:ðan] 'from the South'
	[f θ s]	in all other positions	[sæ:] 'sea'
			[su:θ] 'South'

It should be clear that a comparison of the phoneme systems at two different stages of the language can lead to valuable insights about the nature of systems. However, it does not allow any conclusions as to the stability or development of the system or of individual sounds. Thus while both in Old English and in present-day RP an /i:/-phoneme can be identified, these do not occur in the same words: in fact, the /i:/ of *sea* must be traced back to Old English /æ:/ in *sæ*,[489] whereas /i:/ can be found in a word such as *drifan* /dri:fan/ in Old English, which has developed into /aɪ/.

---

[488] Similarly, [ŋ] occurs as an allophone of /n/ before velar consonants. The phoneme /h/ is analysed by Hogg (1992: 92) as having three allophones in Old English: [h] [x] [ç].

[489] Note that the symbol *æ* is meant to represent "æ".

20.2.2   Types of sound change

A distinction can thus be made between sound changes that affect the nature of the phonological system and those that do not. A **phoneme merger** occurs when a phonological distinction is given up. An example of this kind of change is the contrast between Old English /yː/ and /iː/, which was given up at the end of the Old English period when /yː/ developed into /iː/ (/myːs/ > /miːs/, which later became /maɪs/) and the opposition was lost. The opposite development is that of a **phoneme split**, which happens when a new phonological opposition is created. This happened, for instance, in the case of the fricatives /f θ s/, where, caused by a number of developments such as the loss of morphological endings and French influence in early Middle English,[490] the voiced sounds [v ð z] came to occur in the same positions as [f θ s]. Thus the sounds that had originally been allophones of each other were no longer in complementary distribution and created a phonological opposition. As a result, separate phonemes /f/ and /v/, /θ/ and /ð/ as well as /s/ and /z/ have to be identified. When a change just affects the quality of sounds but not the number of phonological oppositions in a language, one speaks of a **phoneme shift**. An example of a phoneme shift in English is the Great Vowel Shift, which will be discussed in 20.2.3.2.

While the distinction between phoneme mergers, phoneme splits and phoneme shifts refers to the phonological system of a language, the distinction between conditioned and unconditioned changes refers to the conditions under which a change can take place. An **unconditioned sound change** is one which affects the sound in question irrespective of the environment in which it occurs, whereas a **conditioned sound change** only happens under certain circumstances. The development of Old English /yː/ into /iː/ is an example of such an unconditioned change since /yː/ was subject to that change irrespective of its position in the word or any condition determining a particular phonetic context, in other words, all Old English /yː/s were affected by this change. On the other hand, the emergence of /yː/ in words such as /myːs/ in Old English can be traced back to a conditioned change that is known as **i-mutation** (> 20.2.3.1).

A third distinction concerns the phonetic character of sound changes, where **qualitative sound changes**, which (like i-mutation) affect the

---

[490]   For details see Lass (2006: 62).

quality of the sounds, must be distinguished from **quantitative sound changes** such as **lengthening** or **shortening.**

20.2.3 Important sound changes in the history of English

20.2.3.1 *I-mutation*

I-mutation (also called **i-umlaut**) took place between Germanic and Old English and is a good example of a conditioned sound change since it only affected vowels that were followed by a syllable containing [j] or [i]. Hogg (1992: 113) describes i-mutation as follows:

> … Old English vowels harmonised to an /i/ or /j/ following them in the same word. This caused all back vowels to front and all short front vowels (except, naturally, /i/) and diphthongs to raise when an /i/ or /j/ followed in the next syllable. We can tabulate this as follows:

Since some Germanic noun plural endings contained [i] and [j], i-mutation can be seen as the cause of those plural forms in modern English that show a different vowel from the singular such as *goose – geese, tooth – teeth* (Old English /oː/ and /eː/ < /oː/ in the forms that gave rise to the present-day singular and plural forms) or *mouse – mice* (Old English /uː/ and /yː/ < /uː/ respectively).[491]

20.2.3.2 *The Great Vowel Shift*

One of the most important sound changes in the history of English is the so-called **Great Vowel Shift**. It affected the Middle English long vowels, all of which were raised or diphthongized between the Middle English period and Present-Day English, as can be seen from the following examples:

---

[491] It is important to bear in mind that /ø(ː)/ was unrounded to /e(ː)/ in West Saxon. For a detailed description of i-mutation see Hogg (1992).

Middle English	GVS	Further changes up to Present-Day English	
/iː/	> /ei/	> /ai/	*life*
/eː/	> /iː/		*deed*
/ɛː/	> /eː/	> /iː/	*deal*
/aː/	> /ɛː/	> /eɪ/	*make*
/ɔː/	> /oː/	/ou/ > /əʊ/	*home*
/oː/	> /uː/		*food*
/uː/	> /ou/	/aʊ/	*house*

Part of this development is due to the Great Vowel Shift. There has been considerable discussion about what started the Great Vowel Shift, including explanations in terms of a "drag chain" or a "push chain": the idea of a drag chain, proposed by Otto Jespersen (1909: 232), rests on the assumption that the development started by a diphthongisation of the close vowels /iː/ and /uː/ as a result of which /eː/ and /oː/ moved upwards. Luick, however, saw the raising of /eː/ and /oː/ as the starting point of the development so that /iː/ and /uː/ were pushed out of their original positions.[492] More recently, Lass (1999: 80) proposes distinguishing between two phases, "the early push chain initiated by the raising of ME /eː oː/" and "the later raising of the lower vowels".[493] After the Great Vowel Shift, a number of qualitative changes can be observed as well as one major development, namely the phonological merger of Middle English /eː/ (*see*) and /ɛː/ (*sea*).

The fact that English spelling had widely been fixed by the time the Great Vowel Shift set in explains some of the major discrepancies between

---

[492] For a more detailed account of these controversial views see Lass (1999: 74–75). Compare Luick's (1940: 554) remarks about the "first impulse" ("erster Impuls") and Jespersen's (1909: 233) view "that the whole shift began at the upper end". See also Stockwell's (2002) discussions and the account given by Brinton and Arnovick (2006: 308), who also point out that "[s]cholars argue over whether this was really one shift or a series of separate ones".

[493] For the identification of a "First Push" in the form of an upward movement of the two late Old English vowels /æː / and /ɑː / see Lutz (2004: 220–221.)

pronunciation and spelling in English, as is reflected in the orthographic distinction between *sea* and *see*, for instance.[494]

20.2.3.3   Quantitative changes

As far as lengthening of vowels is concerned, two important conditions for such lengthening ought to be mentioned:[495]

– before consonant clusters consisting of a nasal or /l/ or /r/ followed by a plosive with the same place of articulation (a so-called homorganic plosive). It is due to this type of lengthening that words such as *climb* or *child* have /aɪ/ in present-day English. Since this lengthening did not take place when a third consonant followed, *children* has /ɪ/, for instance.

– in stressed open syllables of disyllabic words. This type of lengthening resulted in a long vowel which became diphthongized in words such as *name*.

Shortening occurs under the following conditions:

– before double consonants except homorganic clusters (*wisdom* < /iː/)

– in the first syllable of a trisyllabic word (*southern* < *suðerne* /uː/)

20.2.3.4   Present-day reflections

One interesting aspect of the operation of such sound laws is that although they can be regarded as regular processes taking place in the language, the result is one of increasing irregularity.[496] Thus, the successive operation of various of the sound laws described above can describe a considerable number of irregularities of present-day English:

---

[494] For a definition of the terms *grapheme* and *allograph* and an outline of correspondences between English pronunciation and spelling see Arnold and Hansen ([8]1992: 57–84); for the different ways in which English phonemes can be spelt compare also Gimson ([4]1989).

[495] See Brunner (1960/[2]1984: 251) and Bammesberger (1989: 58–60). For quantitative changes relevant to the Great Vowel Shift see also Lutz (2004).

[496] Compare Strang's (1970: 293) discussion of examples such as *clean* and *cleanse* or *wise* and *wisdom* in this context.

– The vowel change in the singular and plural forms of nouns such as *goose – geese* or *mouse – mice* can be explained by the fact that the Germanic plural suffix caused i-mutation, creating a difference of vowel between singular and plural. Both the vowels of the singular and the plural were later subject to the Great Vowel Shift.

– The difference in the vowels in the pairs /faɪv/ – /fɪfθ/ and /saʊθ/ – /sʌðən/ in present-day English can be explained by the fact that in *fifth* and *southern* the long vowels /iː/ and /uː/ were shortened, /ʊ/ later developing into /ʌ/, whereas the vowels in *five* and *south* remained unaffected by such shortening and were diphthongized in the Great Vowel Shift.

– The irregularity in verbs such as *keep – kept – kept* or *meet – met – met* has similar causes. In Old English, *cepan* and *metan* both had a long /eː/-vowel. Both verbs were weak verbs, forming their past tense with a suffix *–ed*, which resulted in forms such as *mette,* with long /eː/ and a double consonant, which caused shortening of the vowel to /e/. Since only long vowels were subject to the Great Vowel Shift, present-day English shows vowel alternation between /iː/ in the present tense forms and /e/ in the past tense forms and the past participle.

20.3 Lexis

20.3.1 New words

The most obvious type of lexical change is the use of new words. New words can come into existence on the basis of existing language material by productive word formation processes (> 9.1.2) or by a process of borrowing in which words are "taken over" from another language. The amount of loan words in present-day English is enormous – Kastovsky (2006: 202) estimates that about 70 per cent of the vocabulary of present-day English are loans, mostly from French or Latin and Greek.[497] The following list contains a few examples:[498]

---

[497] The influence of one language on another need not necessarily take the form of a complete word being taken over: in some cases, a word that exists in the language already may take over a new sense under the influence of another language (a process that can be referred to as semantic borrowing) or a new word or phrase may be coined on the model of another language but using

donor language

Latin	*abbot, mile, port, street* (Old English: continental period up to 1066) – *cause, contradiction, history, include, incredible, interrupt, polite, summary* (Middle English) – *focus, formula, nucleus, premium, status* (Early Modern English)
French	*appetite, authority, court, crown, dinner, government, justice, orange, parliament, plead, pork* (Middle English) – *grotesque, police, scene, soup* (Early Modern English)
Scandinavian	*law, knife* (Old English) – *against, anger, both, fog, give, husband, seem, sky, smile, take, they/their/them, Thursday, want, window* (Middle English)
Greek	*alphabet, drama* (via Latin; Early Modern English)
Italian	*bankrupt, volcano, sonata, umbrella* (Early Modern English)
Spanish	*creole, banana, sherry* (Early Modern English)

It is important to note that words taken from other languages differ with respect to the degree of integration. Thus for a word such as *corpus* the Latin plural *corpora* can be used in present-day English alongside a form *corpuses*, other words such as *stimulus* or *alumnus* only have *i*-plurals, whereas words such as *apparatus, bonus, campus* only take regularized plural forms in *-s*.[499]

---

existing language material – thus Kastovsky (2006: 258) gives *make/pay a visit, in detail, in particular* as examples of a category loan translation. It has to be pointed out, however, that such distinctions are by no means unproblematic. Cf. the classification suggested by Betz ([2]1965). See also Carstensen (1975). For the inadequacy of this classification for the description of anglicisms in German and an alternative approach see Carstensen (1993: 53–62). For a description of different types of anglicisms arising in film translation see Herbst (1994: 129–150).

[498] Examples taken from Kastovsky (2006) and Kastovsky (1992).

[499] Cf. CGEL (1985: 5.92–101). The degree of integration is often taken as the basis for a distinction between *Lehnwort* and *Fremdwort*. Cf. e.g. Gneuss (1955); for a discussion of the distinction see e.g. Herbst (1994: 146–150).

The reverse process should also be mentioned, namely that words discontinue being used. Thus Old English words such as *niman* (corresponding to German *nehmen*) or *eag-þyrel* ('window') died out.

20.3.2   Changes of meaning

Another important type of change in the field of vocabulary concerns changes of meaning: words can become polysemous, i.e. new lexical units can come into existence, or meanings may die out. That such changes of meaning can be quite dramatic is shown by the fact that the German word *Zaun* 'fence', the English word *town* and the Dutch word *tuin* 'garden' or English *silly* and German *selig* go back to the same Germanic words.

Changes of meaning can take different forms; thus *holiday* (originally 'holy day'), *sanctuary* (originally 'holy place') or *bonfire* (originally 'fire of bones') can be seen as examples of the sense of a word becoming more general, whereas in the case of *sermon* (originally 'speech') or *lust* (originally 'desire') the present-day meaning is more restricted or specialized.[500] Kastovsky (2006: 216) points out how such changes can affect words in the same semantic field – the meaning of *bird* having become more general (in Old English it meant 'young bird, chicken') and that of *fowl* (Old English *fugol* meaning 'bird') having been extended. New senses can develop through words being used metaphorically as in the case of *mouse* ('computer tool'). Interestingly, such "metaphorical" senses can come to be used more frequently than the original sense as seems to be the case with a word such as *treadmill*, for example.[501] These few examples can serve as an indication of the complex nature of semantic change and the difficulty in describing it in terms of such general categories as generalization, specialization etc.[502] In particular, one should remember that in many cases it may be a matter of debate whether one should analyse a word as having developed

---

[500]   For a discussion of these examples see Brinton and Arnovick (2006: 77).

[501]   For examples such as *current* and *mouse* see Kastovsky (2006: 216). For *treadmill* see Moon (1987: 92).

[502]   For categories such as weakening and strengthening, pejoration and amelioration, figurative shifts etc. see e.g. Brinton and Arnovick (2006: 76–85). Compare also Leisi (1973: 114–132), who points out the disparate nature of such criteria. For a detailed survey of types of change see also Hock (1991: 280–308).

a "new" sense (and thus polysemous) or regard the sense of a word as having become more general.

20.3.3   Homonymy

While semantic change can lead to polysemy (as in the case of *mouse*, for example), homonymy is caused by phonetic and orthographic changes in the language: thus both Old English *ear* ('ear') and Old English *eare* ('corn') developed into Modern English *ear*, which can then be analysed as a case of homonymy (> 15.1).

20.4   Grammar

20.4.1   Differences between Old English and Modern English

As far as grammatical differences between Old English and Modern English are concerned, it can be stated that Old English had a much more sophisticated system of inflexional endings than Modern English does.[503]

▷ Gender: Old English nouns can be classified according to grammatical gender (masculine, feminine and neuter), which is also reflected in adjective inflexion. Grammatical gender was lost during the Middle English period.

▷ Case: In Old English nouns have four distinct case forms (nominative, accusative, genitive and dative), and adjectives and some pronouns distinguish a fifth case (instrumental). In contrast, present-day English nouns show two morphologically marked case forms (a common case and an 's-genitive) and some pronouns three (nominative: *he* – genitive: *his* – accusative: *him*).

---

[503]   For details of Old English morphology see Quirk and Wrenn ([2]1957: 19–41) or Lass (1994: 123–174). For a justification of the use of terms such as nominative and accusative see CamG (2002: 456), for the use of the terms common case, subjective case and objective case see CGEL (1985: 5.112 and 6.2).

[504]   Traugott (1992: 273) points out that Old English word order was "not free; rather, different word order patterns co-existed". For a detailed description of word order in Old English see Traugott (1992: 273–285).

▷ Number: with respect to number, Old English personal pronouns do not only show a contrast between singular and plural but also have special dual forms (thus expressing a contrast between one, two, and more than two).

▷ Person: Old English verbs have three morphologically distinct forms for first, second and third person singular indicative present tense forms and a separate plural form for all persons, while Modern English only has {S} to mark third person singular.

These examples serve to illustrate how the English language developed from a predominantly synthetic towards an analytic language. It is important to realize the role of phonological and morphological changes between Old English and Middle English in this context: due to the reduction of vowels in unstressed syllables many inflexional endings were levelled or lost, which means that the role of inflexion as a means of expressing meaning (and assigning syntactic functions such as subject) was reduced. At the same time, the relatively free word order typical of Old English main clauses became more fixed (i.e. the number of word order patterns available in the language decreased)[504] and periphrastic constructions were increasingly being used.[505] Similarly, the semantic role of a BENEFICIARY or RECIPIENT typically associated with the dative case in Old English or German can be expressed by word order (traditionally described as the indirect object preceding the direct object) or by a *to_NP*-construction.

There does not seem to be agreement about the causes of these changes: on the one hand, the loss of inflexions is often seen as the reason of the emergence of periphrastic constructions and a more fixed type of word order. On the other hand, one could imagine that the fact that the respective meanings were expressed by new constructions meant that inflexions

---

[505] In Old English, as in present-day German, case still played an important role in distinguishing subjects and objects, for example. If there is no contrast between nominative and accusative in noun inflexions, case does not provide a means of indicating the subject of a clause, for instance – a function which can also be expressed by a word order in which subjects precede verbs in declarative clauses. Note, however, that nominative and accusative were by no means formally distinguished with all noun classes in Old English. Thus *a*-stems had identical forms for nominative and accusative (sg. *dæg* – pl. *dagas*), for example. See Lass (1994: 129–139) for case forms of nouns. For a more detailed account of these developments in Middle English see Brinton and Arnovick (2006: 266–297).

ceased to have an important function and were lost.[506] In any case, it is important to realize that the English language underwent dramatic changes between late Old English and Early Modern English in this area; in fact Brinton and Arnovick (2006: 295) describe the structural changes of the Middle English period as "the most significant and far-reaching grammatical changes in the history of the language".

20.4.2   Analogy

One important type of change in the field of grammar is presented by analogy.[507] This is particularly noticeable in the field of morphology, for instance, when speakers start using "regular" {S}-plurals with words that (used to) have irregular plural forms such as *corpuses* instead of *corpora*. In a similar way, the plural form of one of the Old English noun stems was extended to words of other classes so that plural forms such as *books, names* or *horses* can be seen as analogical.[508]

Similarly, the fact that a considerable number of Old English strong verbs (> 8.4) began developing regular {D}-past tense forms in the Middle English period can be seen as being caused by analogy to the large number of verbs following the regular pattern. This means that the ablaut-forms of a verb such *help* (*helpan – healp – hulpon – geholpen* in Old English) were regularized.[509] Bybee (1995: 426) argues that irregularity is linked to token frequency because irregular forms will only be stored in the mental lexicon if they occur frequently enough. Thus it is not surprising that the verb *be* should distinguish the greatest number of morphological forms of all verbs in English (e.g. *was – were*) because each of them is sufficiently frequent[510] (> 9.6).

---

[506]   See Brinton and Arnovick (2006: 295–297) for a discussion of different views; compare also the discussion and the references given in Fischer and van der Wurff (2006: esp. 185–187). See also Görlach (1974: 96–98).

[507]   For a detailed discussion of analogy see Hock (1991: 167–236).

[508]   Cf. Lass (1992: 96).

[509]   For a detailed outline of the development of the Old English strong verbs see Brunner (1962: 209–252).

[510]   Note, however, that the frequency criterion does not apply in the same way to irregular plural forms of nouns.

20.4.3 Grammaticalization

A further very important type of change can be described as grammaticalization, which Hopper and Traugott ([2]2003: xv) define "as the process whereby lexical items and constructions come in certain linguistic contexts to serve grammatical functions, and, once grammaticalized, continue to develop new grammatical functions".[511]

A good example of the concept of grammaticalization is the *be going to-* construction of present-day English, which is quite obviously related to the verb *go*. Following Hopper and Traugott ([2]2003: 2–3) one can imagine a sentence such as *I am going to marry Bill* to be interpreted originally as containing a main verb *go* (in the sense of *leave* or *travel*) and a purpose clause (*in order to marry Bill.*). A (new) meaning (of 'futurity') can be inferred from the meaning of 'purpose' and become prominent if no direction or motion is being expressed. A very important factor in grammaticalization is reanalysis: so one could argue that *I am going to marry Bill* can be reinterpreted with *marry* being the main verb and *am going to* having a kind of auxiliary function (as in the classification of *be going to* as a semi-auxiliary in CGEL (1985: 3.47). Hopper and Traugott ([2]2003: 3) point out that the reanalysis is manifest when *going to* is used with verbs or in contexts in which a 'purpose' reading is not possible or at least very unlikely as in *I am going to like Bill* or *I am going to go to London*. This reanalysis can also result in phonological reduction, which only occurs in cases of *going to* being used as a semi-auxiliary:

(1)$_{QE}$ *Bill's gonna go to college after all.*

(2)$_{QE}$ **Bill's gonna college after all.*

As far as the meaning of *go* is concerned, Hopper and Traugott argue that the components of motion and directionality of *go* (which it still has in main verb uses) have been lost in the process of grammaticalization but some new, specifically temporal meanings have been added.

There are numerous examples of grammaticalization: Brinton and Arnovick (2006: 74) mention the use of *of* as a marker of possession or the

---

[511]   For a discussion of the history of the term and different approaches to grammaticalization see Krug (2000: 11–18), Hopper and Traugott ([2]2003: 18–31), Traugott (2002) or Noël (2007). See also Lenker (2010: esp. 184–185) especially with respect to the aspect of uni-directionality in grammaticalization processes.

emergence of a category of modal verbs out of Old English full verbs, for example.[512] Krug (2000: 250–251), in a corpus-based study on the grammaticalization of combinations such as *have to*, stresses the importance of frequency in the development of new categories.[513] Fischer and van der Wurff (2006: 133) point out that the fact that the modal *will* is used with inanimate subjects can be seen as an example of grammaticalization. Whether in the light of the counterarguments provided in the major reference grammars of English this is a good enough reason for arguing in favour of a category future tense in present-day English depends on one's perspective and on one's definition of tense (> 2.3).[514]

The discussion of the grammaticalization phenomena in present-day historical linguistics can easily be related to the view expressed by corpus linguists such as Sinclair or construction grammarians that there is no clear dividing line between lexis and grammar (> 10.5 and 13.2).

---

[512] For the development of modal verbs out of preterite-present verbs see Krug (2000: 44–45). See also Lightfoot (1988: 311–313) and Fischer and van der Wurff (2006: 146–152).

[513] For the postulate of a new category of emerging modals see Krug (2000: 214).

[514] The position of Fischer and van der Wurff (2006: 131) or of Brinton and Arnovick (2006: 74) differs from that taken in CGEL (1985: 4.3) or CamG (2002: 208–210).

Postscript

I very much hope that this book has succeeded in giving readers an idea of the wide range of topics that fall under the scope of linguistics. The idea of an introduction of this kind can only be to provide a relatively selective survey of different fields of study and different approaches to their study and in particular to raise curiosity as to what else there is. I have tried to give a few hints as to where one could continue reading in order to get a more profound account of individual aspects or an alternative view of things from the one presented here.

Two points should perhaps be mentioned as a sort of personal conclusion: firstly, given the diversity of perspectives in the analysis of language, it is interesting to see that over the last few decades researchers in the fields of corpus linguistics, foreign language linguistics, historical linguistics and cognitive linguistics (in particular construction grammar and usage-based theories of language acquisition) have come to conclusions about the nature of language and the ways that the human mind processes language that point in a relatively similar direction, which opens up very encouraging perspectives for future research.

Secondly, it is important to realize that the insights gained by linguistic analysis can be fruitfully applied to many fields which have not been treated in this introduction. One particularly significant area that could be mentioned here is speech therapy. Other important fields are related to situations which involve more than one language. The insights that Sinclair subsumed under the term idiom principle are highly relevant to, for instance, translation studies and lexicography. In fact, the amount and type of coverage that multi-word units of different kinds have received in some of the more recent editions of English foreign learners' dictionaries is a good example of the direct relation between linguistic research and its applications. It should always be borne in mind that practical descriptive work, as is done in dictionaries, or the analysis of difficulties arising in translation can always be exploited for gaining theoretical insights into the nature of language because whatever creates a problem in the use of language ought to be accounted for in any theory of language. This applies equally to foreign language teaching, a field for which more recent developments in linguistic theory offer very interesting perspectives indeed.

A third point that I would like to add as a sort of personal conviction is that it is an extremely valuable exercise to try to put one's own ideas about language to the test by applying them to authentic language material. This is one of the reasons why most of the examples used in this book were either taken from corpora such as the British National Corpus or from books I happened to be reading while working on this text. To those who have read the examples carefully, it may not come as a great surprise to hear that parts of this book were written in Cornwall. Nevertheless, it was not the prime end of this book to create an interest in Cornish art (although this would be a not altogether unwelcome side-effect) but to demonstrate the immense fascination of the many facets and perspectives of the study of language.

Bibliography

Aarts, Bas
    2000   Corpus linguistics, Chomsky and fuzzy tree fragments. In *Corpus Linguistics and Linguistic Theory: Papers from the Twentieth International Conference on English Language Research on Computerized Corpora (ICAME)*, Christian Mair, and Marianne Hundt (eds.), 5–13. Amsterdam/Atlanta: Rodopi.

Aarts, Flor, and Jan Aarts
    ²1988   *English Syntactic Structures.* New York/Leyden: Prentice Hall/Martinus Nijhoff. First edition 1982.

Abercrombie, David
    1967   *Elements of General Phonetics.* Edinburgh: Edinburgh University Press.

Ágel, Vilmos
    2000   *Valenztheorie.* Tübingen: Narr.

Aijmer, Karin, and Bengt Altenberg (eds.)
    1991   *English Corpus Linguistics.* London/New York: Longman.

Aitchison, Jean
    ³2003   *Words in the Mind: An Introduction to the Mental Lexicon.* Oxford: Blackwell.

Alexander, Richard J.
    1992   Fixed expressions, phraseology and language teaching. *Zeitschrift für Anglistik und Amerikanistik* 40 (3): 238–249.

Allen, J. P. B., and P. van Buren
    1971   *Chomsky: Selected Readings.* London: Oxford University Press.

Allerton, David J.
    1982   *Valency and the English Verb.* London: Academic Press.

Allerton, David J.
    1990   Language as form and patterns: Grammar and its categories. In *An Encyclopaedia of Language*, N. E. Collinge (ed.), 68–111. London/New York: Routledge.

Altenberg, Bengt
    1998   On the phraseology of spoken English: The evidence of recurrent word-combinations. In *Phraseology: Theory, Analysis, and Applications*, A. P. Cowie (ed.), 101–121. Oxford: Clarendon Press.

Anderson, Stephen R.
1988   Morphological theory. In *Linguistics: The Cambridge Survey*, Frederick J. Newmeyer (ed.), 146–191. Cambridge: Cambridge University Press.

Arnold, Roland, and Klaus Hansen
[8]1992   *Englische Phonetik*. Leipzig: Langenscheidt/Enzyklopädie. First edition 1975.

Armstrong, Sharon Lee, Lila R. Gleitman, and Henry Gleitman
1999   What some concepts might not be. In *Core Readings*, Eric Margolis, and Stephen Laurence (eds.), 225–259. Cambridge, Mass./London: MIT Press.

Aronoff, Mark, and Frank Anshen
1998   Morphology and the lexicon: Lexicalization and Productivity. In *The Handbook of Morphology*, Andrew Spencer, and Arnold M. Zwicky (eds.), 237–247. Oxford/Malden: Blackwell.

Austin, John L.
1962   *How to Do Things with Words*. London: Oxford University Press.

Ayto, John
1996   Lexical life expectancy: A prognostic guide. In *Words: Proceedings of an International Symposium Lund, 25–26 August 1995, Konferenser 36*, Jan Svartvik (ed.), 181–188. Stockholm: Kungl. Vitterhets Historie och Antikvitets Akademien.

Bahns, Jens
1996   *Kollokationen als lexikographisches Problem: Eine Analyse allgemeiner und spezieller Lernerwörterbücher des Englischen*. Tübingen: Niemeyer.

Bammesberger, Alfred
1989   *English Linguistics*. Heidelberg: Winter.

Barnickel, Klaus Dieter
1980   *Sprachliche Varianten des Englischen*. 2 Vols. München: Hueber.

Bauer, Laurie
1983   *English Word-Formation*. Cambridge: Cambridge University Press.

Bauer, Laurie
1994   *Watching English Change: An Introduction to the Study of Linguistic Change in Standard Englishes in the Twentieth Century*. London/NewYork: Longman.

Baumgärtner, Alfred Clemens
1970   Konsistenz und Dependenz. In *Vorschläge für eine strukturale Grammatik des Deutschen*, H. Steger (ed.), 57–77. Darmstadt: Wissenschaftliche Buchgesellschaft.

de Beaugrande, Robert-Alain, and Wolfgang Ulrich Dressler
1981   *Introduction to Text Linguistics*. London/New York: Longman.

Behrens, Heike
1999   Was macht Verben zu einer besonderen Kategorie im Spracherwerb?
          In *Das Lexikon im Spracherwerb*, Jörg Meibauer, and Monika Roth-
          weiler (eds.), 32-50. Tübingen: Francke.
Behrens, Heike
2005   Wortartenerwerb durch Induktion. In *Wortarten und Grammatikali-
          sierung: Perspektiven in System und Erwerb*, Clemens Knobloch,
          and Burkhard Schaeder (eds.), 177–198. Berlin/New York: de
          Gruyter.
Behrens, Heike
2007   The acquisition of argument structure. In *Valency: Theoretical, De-
          scriptive and Cognitive Issues*, Thomas Herbst, and Katrin Götz-
          Votteler (eds.), 193–214. Berlin/New York: Mouton de Gruyter.
Behrens, Heike
2008   Corpora in language acquisition research: History, methods, perspec-
          tives. In *Corpora in Language Acquisition Research: History, Meth-
          ods,* Heike Behrens (ed.), xi–xxx. Amsterdam: Benjamins.
Behrens, Heike
2009   Usage-based and emergentist approaches to language acquisition.
          Linguistics 47 (2): 383–411.
Berlin, Brent, and Paul Kay
1969   *Basic Color Terms: Their Universality and Evolution.* Berkeley/ Los
          Angeles: University of California Press.
Betz, Werner
[2]1965   *Deutsch und Lateinisch: Die Lehnbildungen der althochdeutschen
          Benediktinerregel.* Bonn: Bouvier. First edition 1949.
Biber, Douglas, Stig Johansson, Geoffrey Leech, Susan Conrad, and Edward Fine-
          gan
1999   *Longman Grammar of Spoken and Written English.* Harlow: Long-
          man. [LGSWE]
Bloomfield, Leonard
1933   *Language.* New York: Holt. ([2]1935), London: Allen & Unwin Ltd.
Bolinger, Dwight
[2]1975   *Aspects of Language.* New York: Harcourt Brace Jovanovich.
Brekle, Herbert Ernst
1985   *Einführung in die Geschichte der Sprachwissenschaft.* Darmstadt:
          Wiss. Buchgesellschaft.
Brinker, Klaus
1977   *Modelle und Methoden der strukturalistischen Syntax.* Stuttgart:
          Kohlhammer.

Brinker, Klaus
³1992 *Linguistische Textanalyse: Eine Einführung in Grundbegriffe und Methoden.* Berlin: Schmidt.
Brinton, Laurel J., and Leslie K. Arnovick
2006 *The English Language: A Linguistic History.* Oxford: Oxford University Press
Brown, Gillian
1977 *Listening to Spoken English.* London: Longman.
Brown, Gillian, and George Yule
1983 *Discourse Analysis.* Cambridge: Cambridge University Press.
Brunner, Karl
1962 *Die englische Sprache. Vol. 2.* Tübingen: Niemeyer.
Brunner, Karl
²1984 *Die Englische Sprache. Vol. 1: Allgemeines. Lautgeschichte.* Tübingen: Niemeyer. First edition 1960.
Bublitz, Wolfram
²2009 *Englische Pragmatik: Eine Einführung.* Berlin: Schmidt.
Burgschmidt, Ernst
1973–5 *System, Norm und Produktivität in der Wortbildung: Aufsätze.* Erlangen: E. Burgschmidt. 3. Vols.
Burgschmidt, Ernst
1977 Strukturierung, Norm und Produktivität in der Wortbildung. In *Perspektiven der Wortbildungsforschung,* H. E. Brekle, und D. Kastovsky (eds.), 39–47. Bonn: Bouvier.
Burgschmidt, Ernst
1978 *Wortbildung im Englischen.* Dortmund: Lambert Lensing.
Burgschmidt, Ernst, and Dieter Götz
1974 *Kontrastive Linguistik Deutsch/Englisch.* München: Hueber.
Bußmann, Hadumod
⁴2008 *Lexikon der Sprachwissenschaft.* Stuttgart: Kröner.
Bybee, Joan
1995 Regular morphology and the lexicon. *Language and Cognitive Processes* 10 (5): 425–455.
Bybee, Joan
2005 From usage to grammar: The mind's response to repetition (manuscript: http://www.unm.edu/~jbybee/Bybee%20plenary.pdf [1.4.2007]).
Bybee, Joan
2007 The Emergent Lexicon. In *Frequency of Use and the Organization of Language,* Joan Bybee (ed.), 279–293. Oxford: Oxford University Press.

Bybee, Joan, and Paul Hopper
   2001   Introduction to frequency and emergence of linguistic structure. In
             Frequency and the Emergence of Linguistic Structure, Joan Bybee
             and Paul Hopper (eds.), 1–24. Amsterdam/Philadelphia: Benjamins.
Cameron-Faulkner, T., Elena Lieven, and Michael Tomasello
   2003   A Construction Based Analysis of Child Directed Speech. *Cognitive
             Science* 27: 843–873.
Carstensen, Broder
   1975   Amerikanische Einflüsse auf die deutsche Sprache. In *Jahrbuch für
             Amerikastudien*, Ernst Fraenkel, Hans Galinsky, Dietrich Gerhard,
             and H. J. Lang (eds.), 34–55. Heidelberg: Winter. First edition 1963.
Catford, J.C.
   1988   *A Practical Introduction to Phonetics*. Oxford: Clarendon Press.
Chomsky, Noam
   1957   *Syntactic Structures*. The Hague: Mouton.
Chomsky, Noam
   1959   Review of Skinner Verbal Behavior. *Language* 35: 26–58.
Chomsky, Noam
   1965   *Aspects of the Theory of Syntax*. Cambridge, Mass.: MIT Press.
Chomsky, Noam
   1966   *Topics in the Theory of Generative Grammar*. The Hague/Paris:
             Mouton.
Chomsky, Noam
   1967   Recent contributions to the theory of innate ideas. *Synthese* 17: 2–
             11.
Chomsky, Noam
   1970   Remarks on nominalization. In *Readings in English Transforma-
             tional Grammar*, R. A. Jacobs, and P. S. Rosenbaum (eds.), 184–
             221. Waltham, Mass./London: Ginn and Company.
Chomsky, Noam
   1981   *Lectures on Government and Binding*. Dordrecht: Foris.
Chomsky, Noam
   1986   *Knowledge of Language: Its Nature, Origin, and Use*. New
             York/Westport/London: Praeger.
Chomsky, Noam
   1988   *Language and Problems of Knowledge: The Managua Lectures*.
             Cambridge, Mass.: MIT Press.
Chomsky, Noam
   1995   *The Minimalist Program*. Cambridge, Mass./London: MIT Press.
Chomsky, Noam
   2004   Linguistics in the 21st Century. An Interview with Noam Chomsky.
             [Interviewed by Naoki Fukui and Mihoko Zushi, November 22,

2002], in *The Generative Enterprise Revisited*, Noam Chomsky, Berlin/New York: Mouton de Gruyter.

Chomsky, Noam, and Morris Halle
1968   *The Sound Pattern of English*. New York/Evanston/London: Harper & Row.

Clark, Eve V.
1998   Morphology in language acquisition. In *The Handbook of Morphology*, Andrew Spencer, and Arnold M. Zwicky (eds.), 374–389. Oxford/Malden: Blackwell.

Clark, Herbert H., and Eve V. Clark
1977   *Psychology and Language: An Introduction to Psycholinguistics*. San Diego: Harcourt Brace Jovanovich.

Coates, Jennifer
1986   *Women, Men and Language. A Sociolinguistic Account of Sex Differences in Language*. London/New York: Longman.

Coates, Richard
1987   Lexical morphology. In *New Horizons in Linguistics 2*, John Lyons, Richard Coates, Margaret Deuchar, and Gerald Gazdar (eds.), 103–121. Harmondsworth: Penguin.

de Cock, Sylvie
2000   Repetitive phrasal chunkiness and advanced EFL speech and writing. In *Corpus Linguistics and Linguistic Theory*, Christian Mair, and Marianne Hundt (eds.), 51–68. Amsterdam/Atlanta: Rodopi.

Cook, Vivian J.
1988   *Chomsky's Universal Grammar*. Oxford: Blackwell.

Coseriu, Eugenio
1973   *Probleme der strukturellen Semantik*. Tübingen: Narr.

Coulthard, Malcolm
²1985   *An Introduction to Discourse Analysis*. London/New York: Longman. First edition 1977.

Coupland, Nikolas, and Hywel Bishop
2007   Ideologised Values for British Accents. *Journal of Sociolinguistics* II/I: 74–93.

Cowie, Anthony P.
1981   The treatment of collocation and idioms in learners' dictionaries. *Applied Linguistics* 2 (3): 223–235.

Croft, William
2000   Lexical and grammatical meaning. In *Morphologie. Morphology. Ein internationals Handbuch zur Flexion und Wortbildung. An International Handbook on Inflection and Word-Formation 1.* Halbband, Vol. 1, Geert Booij, Christian Lehmann, and Joachim

Mugdan in collaboration with Wolfgang Kesselheim, Stavros Sko-
peteas (eds.), 257–263. Berlin/New York: Walter de Gruyter.

Croft, William, and David A. Cruse
2004   *Cognitive Linguistics*. Cambridge: Cambridge University Press.

Cruse, David A.
1986   *Lexical Semantics*. Cambridge: Cambridge University Press.

Cruttenden, Alan
1986   *Intonation*. Cambridge: Cambridge University Press.

Crystal, David
1988   *The English Language*. Harmondsworth: Penguin.

Crystal, David
²1997   *The Cambridge Encyclopedia of Language*. Cambridge/New
York/Melbourne: Cambridge University Press.

Crystal, David
2001   *Language and the Internet*. Cambridge: Cambridge University Press.

Crystal, David
²2003   *The Cambridge Encyclopaedia of the English Language*, Cambridge: Cambridge University Press.

Crystal, David
2006   English worldwide. In *A History of the English Language*, Richard
Hogg, and David Denison (eds.), 420–444. Cambridge: Cambridge
University Press.

Crystal, David, and Derek Davy
1975   *Advanced Conversational English*. London: Longman.

Culler, Jonathan
1976   *Saussure*. Glasgow: Fontana.

Daneš, František
1970   Zur linguistischen Analyse der Textstruktur. *Folia Linguistica* 1970,
72–78. [Also in *Sprachwissenschaft: Ein Reader*, Ludger Hoffmann,
(ed.), 591–597. Berlin/New York: Walter de Gruyter, 2000.]

Denison, David and Richard Hogg
2006   Overview. In *A History of the English Language*, Richard Hogg, and
David Denison (eds.), 1–42. Cambridge: Cambridge University
Press.

Dirven, René, and Günther Radden
1977   *Semantische Syntax des Englischen*. Frankfurt: Athenaion.

Dretzke, Burkhard
1985   *Fehlerbewertung im Aussprachebereich*. Hamburg: Buske.

Dretzke, Burkhard
1998   *Modern British and American English Pronunciation*. Paderborn:
Schöningh (UTB).

Dufter, Andreas, Jörg Fleischer, and Guido Seiler
  2009   Introduction. In *Describing and Modelling Variation in Grammar*, Andreas Dufter, Jörg Fleischer, and Guido Seiler (eds.), 1–18. Berlin/New York: Mouton de Gruyter.

Edwards, John R.
  1982   Language attitudes and their implications among English speakers. In *Attitudes towards Language Variation: Social and Applied Contexts*, E. B. Ryan, and H. Giles (eds.), 20–33. London: Arnold.

Ellis, Nick
  2003   Constructions, chunking, and connectionism: The emergence of second language structure. In *The Handbook of Second Language Acquisition*, Catherine J. Doughty, and Michael H. Long (eds.), 63–103. Malden/Oxford/Carlton: Blackwell.

Elyan, Olwen, Philip Smith, Howard Giles, and Richard Bourhis
  1978   RP-accented female speech: The voice of perceived androgyny? In *Sociolinguistic Patterns of British English*, P. Trudgill (ed.), 122–131. London: Arnold.

Emons, Rudolf
  1974   *Valenzen englischer Prädikatsverben*. Tübingen: Niemeyer.

Emons, Rudolf
  1978   *Valenzgrammatik für das Englische. Eine Einführung*. Tübingen: Niemeyer.

Engel, Ulrich
  1977   *Syntax der deutschen Gegenwartssprache*. Berlin: Schmidt.

Enkvist, Nils Erik
  1978   Coherence, pseudo-coherence, and non-coherence. In *Reports on Text Linguistics: Semantics and Cohesion*, Jan-Ola Östman (ed.), 109-128. Åbo: Stiftelsens för Åbo Akademi.

Esser, Jürgen
  1979   *Englische Prosodie: Eine Einführung*. Tübingen: Narr.

Esser, Jürgen
  1993   *English Linguistic Stylistics*. Tübingen: Niemeyer.

Esser, Jürgen
  2009   *Introduction to English Text-Linguistics*. Frankfurt: Peter Lang.

Fanselow, Gisbert, and Sascha W. Felix
  1987   *Sprachtheorie 2: Die Rektions- und Bindungstheorie*. Tübingen: Francke (UTB).

Faulhaber, Susen
  forthc.   *Verb valency patterns – challenging semantics-based accounts*. Berlin/New York: Mouton de Gruyter.

Fillmore, Charles
    1968   The case for case. In *Universals in Linguistic Theory*, Emmon Bach, and Robert T. Harms (eds.), 1–88. New York: Holt, Rinehart and Winston.

Fillmore, Charles
    1976   Frame semantics and the nature of language. In *Origins and Evolution of Language and Speech: Annals of the New York Academy of Sciences*, Stevan R. Harnad, Horst D. Steklis, and Jane Lancaster (eds.), 20–32. New York: The New York Academy of Sciences.

Fillmore, Charles
    1988   The mechanisms of "construction grammar". In *General Session and Parasession on Grammaticalization*, Shelley Axmaker, Annie Jassier, and Helen Singmaster (eds.), 35–55. Berkeley: Berkeley Linguistics Society.

Fillmore, Charles
    2007   Valency issues in FrameNet. In *Valency: Theoretical, Descriptive and Cognitive Issues*, Thomas Herbst, and Katrin Götz-Votteler (eds.), 129–160. Berlin/New York: Mouton de Gruyter.

Fillmore, Charles, and Beryl T. Atkins
    1992   Toward a frame-based lexicon: The semantics of RISK and its neighbors. In *Frames, Fields, and Contrasts: New Essays in Semantic and Lexical Organization*, Adrienne Lehrer, and Eva Feder Kittay (eds.), 75–188. Hillsdale/Hove/London: Lawrence Erlbaum Associates.

Fillmore, Charles, Paul Kay, and Catherine M. O'Connor
    1988   Regularity and idiomaticity in grammatical constructions: The case of *let alone*. *Language* 64: 501–538.

Firbas, Jan
    1992   *Functional sentence perspective in written and spoken communication*. Cambridge: Cambridge University Press.

Firth, John Rupert
    1968   A synopsis of linguistic theory: 1930–55. In *Selected Papers by J. R. Firth 1952–59*, F. R. Palmer (ed.), 168–205: London/Harlow: Longman. First edition 1957.

Fischer, Olga, and Win van der Wurff
    2006   Syntax. In *A History of the English Language*, Richard Hogg, and David Denison (eds.), 109–198. Cambridge: Cambridge University Press.

Fischer, Kerstin and Anatol Stefanowitsch
    2006   Konstruktionsgrammatik: Ein Überblick. In *Konstruktionsgrammatik: Von der Anwendung zur Theorie*, 3–17. Tübingen: Stauffenburg.

Frege, Gottlob
2000 Einleitung in die Logik. In *Sprachwissenschaft: Ein Reader*, Ludger Hoffmann (ed.), 682–686. Berlin /New York: Walter de Gruyter. First edition 1906.

Garman, Michael
1990 *Psycholinguistics*. Cambridge: Cambridge University Press.

Garside, Roger
1987 The CLAWS word–tagging system. In *The Computational Analysis of English: A Corpus-Based Approach,* Garside, Roger, Geoffrey Leech, and Geoffrey Sampson (eds.), 30–41, London/ New York: Longman.

Giegerich, Heinz J.
1992 *English Phonology: An Introduction*. Cambridge: Cambridge University Press.

Giles, Howard
1970 Evaluative reactions to accents. *Educational Review* 22: 211–227.

Gilquin, Gaëtanelle
2007 To err is not all: What corpus and elicitation can reveal about the use of collocations by learners. *Zeitschrift für Anglistik und Amerikanistik* 55 (3): 273–291.

Gimson, A. C.
⁴1989 *An Introduction to the Pronunciation of English*. London: Arnold. First edition 1962. Revised version by Susan Ramsaran.

Gimson, A.C., and Alan Cruttenden
⁶2001 *Gimson's Pronunciation of English*. London: Arnold. Revised by Alan Cruttenden.

Gläser, Rosemarie
²1990 *Phraseologie der englischen Sprache*. Leipzig: Verlag Enzyklopädie.

Gleason, Henry Allan
1961 Revised edition. *An Introduction to Descriptive Linguistics*. New York: Holt, Rinehart & Winston.

Gneuss, Helmut
1955 *Lehnbildungen und Lehnbedeutungen im Altenglischen*. Berlin/Bielefeld/München: Schmidt.

Görlach, Manfred
1974 *Einführung in die englische Sprachgeschichte*. Heidelberg: Quelle und Meyer.

Götz, Dieter
1971 *Studien zu den verdunkelten Komposita im Englischen*. Erlanger Beiträge zur Sprach- und Kunstwissenschaft. Nürnberg: Verlag Hans Carl.

Götz, Dieter
1976   *Stilistik und Idiomatik im Englischunterricht*. Dortmund: Lensing.
Götz-Votteler, Katrin
2008   *Aspekte der Informationsentwicklung im Erzähltext*. Tübingen: Narr.
Goldberg, Adele
1995   *Constructions: A Construction Grammar Approach to Argument Structure*. Chicago: Chicago University Press.
Goldberg, Adele
2006   *Constructions at Work*. Oxford/New York: Oxford University Press.
Granger, Sylviane
1998   Prefabricated patterns in advanced EFL writing: Collocations and formulae. In *Phraseology: Theory, Analysis, and Applications*, A. P. Cowie (ed.), 145–160. Oxford: Clarendon Press.
Granger, Sylviane
2009   The contribution of learner corpora to second language acquisition and foreign language teaching: A critical evaluation. In *Corpora and Language Teaching*, Karin Aijmer (ed.), 13–32. Amsterdam/Philadelphia: Benjamins.
Granger, Sylviane
forthc. From phraseology to pedagogy: Challenges and prospects. In *Chunks in the Description of Language: A Tribute to John Sinclair*, Thomas Herbst, Susen Faulhaber, and Peter Uhrig (eds.), Berlin/New York: Mouton de Gruyter.
Granger, Sylviane, and Magali Paquot
2008   Disentangling the phraseological web. In *Phraseology: An Interdisciplinary Perspective*, Sylviane Granger, and Fanny Meunier (eds.), 27–49. Amsterdam/Philadelphia: Benjamins.
Granger Sylviane, E. Dagneaux, F. Meunier, and Magali Paquot
2009   *International Corpus of Learner English*. Vol. 2. Louvain-la-Neuve: Presses universitaires de Louvain.
Greenbaum, Sidney
1974   Some verb-intensifier collocations in American and British English. *American Speech* 49: 79–89. First edition 1974. [Reprinted in S. Greenbaum (1988), 113–124.]
Greenbaum, Sidney
1988   *Good English and the Grammarian*. London/New York: Longman.
Greenbaum, Sidney, and Randolph Quirk
1970   *Elicitation Experiments in English: Linguistic Studies in Use and Attitude*. London: Longman.

Grice, Paul
1975   Logic and Conversation. In *Syntax and Semantics. Vol. 3: Speech Acts*, P. Cole, and J. L. Morgan (eds.), 41–58. New York: Academic Press.
Gries, Stefan Th.
2008   Phraseology and linguistic theory: A brief survey. In *Phraseology in Foreign Language Learning and Teaching*, Fanny Meunier, and Sylviane Granger (eds.), 3–25. Amsterdam/Philadelphia: Benjamins.
Gries, Stefan Th., and Anatol Stefanowitsch
forthc.   Cluster analysis and the identification of collexeme classes. In *Empirical and Experimental Methods in Cognitive/Functional Research*, John Newman, and Sally Rice (eds.), 73–90. Stanford: CSLI.
Grimm, Anne
2008   *"Männersprache" – "Frauensprache"? Eine korpusgestützte empirische Analyse des Sprachgebrauchs britischer und amerikanischer Frauen und Männer hinsichtlich Geschlechtsspezifika.* Hamburg: Verlag Dr Kovač.
Gut, Ulrike
2008   Nigerian English: Phonology. In *Varieties of English 4: Africa, South and Southeast Asia,* Rajend Mesthrie (ed.), 35–54. Berlin/New York: Mouton de Gruyter.
Gut, Ulrike
2009   *Introduction to English Phonetics and Phonology.* Frankfurt: Lang.
Haegeman, Liliane
1991   *Introduction to Government and Binding Theory.* Oxford/Cambridge, Mass.: Blackwell.
Halliday, Michael A. K.
1970a   *A Course in Spoken English: Intonation.* London: Oxford University Press.
Halliday, Michael A. K.
1970b   Language Structure and Language Function. In *Horizons in Linguistics*, John Lyons (ed.), 140–165. New Harmondsworth: Penguin.
Halliday, Michael A. K.
²1994   *An Introduction to Functional Grammar.* London/Melbourne/Auckland: Arnold.
Halliday, Michael, Angus McIntosh, and Peter Strevens
1964   *The Linguistic Sciences and Language Teaching.* London: Longman.
Halliday, Michael A. K., and Ruqaiya Hasan
1976   *Cohesion in English.* London: Longman.
Handl, Susanne
2008   Essential collocations for learners of English: The role of collocational direction and weight. In *Phraseology in Foreign Language*

Learning and Teaching, Fanny Meunier, and Sylviane Granger (eds.), 43–66. Amsterdam/Philadelphia: Benjamins.

Hansen, Barbara, Klaus Hansen, Albrecht Neubert, and Manfred Schentke
²1985   *Englische Lexikologie: Einführung in Wortbildung und Semantik.* Leipzig: Enzyklopädie.

Hansen, Klaus, Uwe Carls, and Peter Lucko
1996   *Die Differenzierung des Englischen in nationale Varianten.* Berlin: Schmidt.

Harris, Zellig
1957   Co-occurrence and transformation. In *Language* 33.3, 283–340. [Reprinted in Zellig S. Harris: *Papers on Syntax*, Henry Hiż (ed.), 143–210. Dordrecht/Boston/London: Reidel Publishing Company, 1981.]

Hasan, Ruqaiya
1984   Coherence and cohesive harmony. In *Understanding Reading Comprehension*, J. Flood (ed.), 181–219. Newark: International Reading Association.

Haugen, Einar
1966   Dialect, language, nation. In *American Anthropologist* 68: 922–935. [Reprinted in *Sociolinguistics*, J.B. Pride, and Janet Holmes (eds.), 97–111. Harmondsworth: Penguin, 1972]

Hausmann, Franz-Josef
1984   Wortschatzlernen ist Kollokationslernen. *Praxis des neusprachlichen Unterrichts* 31: 395–406.

Hausmann, Franz-Josef
1985   Kollokationen im deutschen Wörterbuch: Ein Beitrag zur Theorie des lexikographischen Beispiels. In *Lexikographie und Grammatik*, Henning Bergenholtz, and J. Mugdan (eds.), 118–129. Tübingen: Niemeyer.

Hausmann, Franz-Josef
2004   Was sind eigentlich Kollokationen? In *Wortverbindungen – mehr oder weniger fest*, Kathrin Steyer (ed.), 309–334. Berlin: de Gruyter.

Hausser, Roland
1999   *Foundations of Computational Linguistics: Man-Machine Communication in Natural Language.* Berlin: Springer.

Helbig, Gerhard
1970   *Geschichte der neueren Sprachwissenschaft.* Leipzig: VEB Bibliographisches Institut.

Helbig, Gerhard
1992   *Probleme der Valenz- und Kasustheorie.* Tübingen: Niemeyer.

Herbst, Thomas
1983   *Untersuchungen zur Valenz englischer Adjektive und ihrer Nomina-lisierungen.* Tübingen: Narr.
Herbst, Thomas
1992   Pro-Nunciation: Zur Bedeutung einer guten Aussprache in der Fremdsprache. *Die Neueren Sprachen* 91 (1): 2–18.
Herbst, Thomas
1994   *Linguistische Aspekte der Synchronisation von Fernsehserien: Phonetik, Textlinguistik, Übersetzungstheorie.* Tübingen: Niemeyer.
Herbst, Thomas
1996   What are collocations: *Sandy beaches* or *false teeth*? *English Studies* 77 (4): 379–393.
Herbst, Thomas
2005   Englische Grammatik ist nicht so kompliziert: Pro Minimalismus, Lücke und Polysemie – Kontra Prototypik und Semantik in grammatischer Terminologie. In *Linguistische Dimensionen des Fremdsprachenunterrichts*, Thomas Herbst (ed.), 11–28. Würzburg: Königshausen und Neumann.
Herbst, Thomas
2007   Valency complements or valency patterns? In *Valency: Theoretical, Descriptive and Cognitive Issues*, Thomas Herbst, and Katrin Götz-Votteler (eds.), 15–35. Berlin/New York: Mouton de Gruyter.
Herbst, Thomas
2009a   Valency: Item-specificity and idiom principle. In *Exploring the Lexis-Grammar Interface*, Ute Römer, and Rainer Schulze (eds.), 49–68. Amsterdam/Philadelphia: John Benjamins.
Herbst, Thomas
2009b   Introduction to the Erlangen Valency Patternbank. www.pattern-bank.uni-erlangen.de
Herbst, Thomas
2010   Valency constructions and clause constructions or how, if at all, valency grammarians might *sneeze the foam off the cappuccino*. In *Cognitive Foundations of Linguistic Usage Patterns*: Empirical Studies, Hans-Jörg Schmid, and Susanne Handl (eds.), 225–255. Berlin/New York: de Gruyter Mouton.
Herbst, Thomas, and Susen Faulhaber
forthc. Optionen der Valenzbeschreibung: Ein Valenzmodell für das Englische. In *Grammar and Corpora III: Conference Proceedings.* Tübingen: Gunter Narr.
Herbst, Thomas, David Heath, and Hans-Martin Dederding
1980   *Grimm's Grandchildren: Current Topics in German Linguistics.* London: Longman.

Herbst, Thomas, and Michael Klotz
2003   *Lexikografie.* Paderborn: Schöningh (UTB).

Herbst, Thomas, and Brigitta Mittmann
2003   How can American English and British English be recognised? – Arguments in favour of shifting the focus in the study of language varieties toward(s) use and perception. In *Cultural Encounters in the New World: Literatur- und kulturwissenschaftliche Beiträge zu kulturellen Begegnungen in der Neuen Welt*, Harald Zapf, and Klaus Lösch (eds.), 127–150. Tübingen: Narr.

Herbst, Thomas, and Susen Schüller
2008   *Introduction to Syntactic Analysis: A Valency Approach.* Tübingen: Narr.

Herbst, Thomas, Rita Stoll, und Rudolf Westermayr
1991   *Terminologie der Sprachbeschreibung.* Ismaning: Hueber.

Heringer, Hans Jürgen
1970   *Theorie der deutschen Syntax.* München: Hueber.

Heringer, Hans Jürgen
1993   Basic ideas and the classical model. In *Syntax: Ein internationales Handbuch zeitgenössischer Forschung.* Vol. 1, Joachim Jacobs, Armin von Stechow, Wolfgang Sternefeld, and Theo Vennemann (eds.), 298–316. Berlin/New York: Walter de Gruyter.

Heringer, Hans Jürgen
1996   *Deutsche Syntax dependentiell.* Tübingen: Stauffenburg.

Heringer, Hans Jürgen, Bruno Strecker, and Rainer Wimmer
1980   *Syntax: Fragen – Lösungen – Alternativen.* München: Fink (UTB).

Hjelmslev, Louis
1961   *Prolegomena to a Theory of Language*, transl. by Francis J. Whitfield. Madison: The University of Wisconsin Press. First edition 1943.

Hjelmslev, Louis
1974   *Prolegomena zu einer Sprachtheorie.* München: Hueber.

Hock, Hans Heinrich
[2]1991   *Principles of Historical Linguistics.* Berlin/New York: Mouton de Gruyter.

Hockett, Charles
1954   Two models of grammatical description. In *Word* 10: 210–231.

Hockett, Charles
1958   *A Course in Modern Linguistics.* New York/London: Holt, Rinehart & Winston. [Excerpts in *Sprachwissenschaft: Ein Reader*, Ludger Hoffmann (ed.). Berlin/New York: Walter de Gruyter, [2]2000.]

Hoffmann, Ludger (ed.)
  ²2000a   *Sprachwissenschaft: Ein Reader.* Berlin/New York: Walter de Gruyter.

Hoffmann, Ludger
  ²2000b   Thema und Rhema. In *Sprachwissenschaft: Ein Reader*, Ludger Hoffmann (ed.), 598–612. Berlin/New York: Walter de Gruyter.

Hoffmann, Sebastian
  2004   Using the OED quotations database as a corpus: A linguistic appraisal. *ICAME Journal* 28: 17–30.

Hoffmann, Sebastian, Stefan Evert, Nicholas Smith, David Lee, and Ylva Berglund Prytz
  2008   *Corpus Linguistics with* BNCweb*: A Practical Guide.* Frankfurt: Lang.

Hogg, Richard
  1992   Phonology and morphology. In *The Cambridge History of the English Language. Vol. I: The Beginnings to 1066*, R. Hogg (ed.), 67–167. Cambridge: Cambridge University Press.

Holmes, Janet
  1992   *An Introduction to Sociolinguistics.* London/New York: Longman.

Hopper, Paul
  1987   Emergent Grammar. *Berkeley Linguistics Society* 13: 39–157.

Hopper, Paul, and Elizabeth Closs Traugott
  ²2003   *Grammaticalization.* Cambridge: Cambridge University Press.

House, Juliane
  2002   Communicating in English as a lingua franca. *Eurosla Yearbook* 2: 243–261.

Huber, Markus
  2008   Ghanaian English: Phonology. In *Varieties of English 4: Africa, South and Southeast Asia,* Rajend Mesthrie (ed.), 67–92. Berlin/New York: Mouton de Gruyter.

Huddleston, Rodney
  1984   *Introduction to the Grammar of English.* Cambridge: Cambridge University Press.

Huddleston, Rodney, and Geoffrey K. Pullum (eds.)
  2002   *The Cambridge Grammar of the English Language.* Cambridge: Cambridge University Press. [CamG]

Hudson, Richard
  1976   *Arguments for a Non-Transformational Grammar.* Chicago/London: University of Chicago Press.

Hudson, Richard
  1980   *Sociolinguistics.* Cambridge: Cambridge University Press.

Hudson, Richard
    1984   *Word Grammar*. Oxford: Blackwell.
Hudson, Richard
    1993   Do we have heads in our minds? In *Heads in Grammatical Theory*, Greville G. Corbett, Norman M. Fraser, and Scott McGlashan (eds.), 266–291. Cambridge: Cambridge University Press.
Hundt, Markus
    1992   *Einstellungen gegenüber dialektal gefärbter Standardsprache*. Stuttgart: Steiner Verlag.
Hunston, Susan and, Gill Francis
    2000   *Pattern Grammar: A Corpus-Driven Approach to the Lexical Grammar of English*. Amsterdam: John Benjamins.
Jackendoff, Ray
    ²1997   *The Architecture of the Language Faculty*. Cambridge, Mass./London: MIT Press.
Jakobson, Roman, C. Gunnar Fant, and Morris Halle
    1951   *Preliminaries to Speech Analysis: The Distinctive Features and their Correlates*. Cambridge, Mass.: MIT Press.
Jespersen, Otto
    1909   *A Modern English Grammar on Historical Principles. Part I: Sounds and Spellings*. Heidelberg: Carl Winter's Universitätsbuchhandlung.
Johansson, Stig
    1991   Times change, and so do corpora. In *English Corpus Linguistics*, Karin Aijmer, and Bengt Altenberg (eds.), 305–314. London/New York: Longman.
Jones, Daniel
    ⁹1960   *An Outline of English Phonetics*. Cambridge: Heffer and Sons. First edition 1918.
Jones, Daniel
    1973   Some thoughts on the phoneme. In *Phonetics in Linguistics: A Book of Readings*, William Eric Jones and John Laver (eds.), 168–179. London/New York: Longman. First edition 1944.
Kaplan, R. M., and Joan Bresnan
    1982   Lexical-functional grammar: A formal system for grammatical representation. In *The Mental Representation of Grammatical Relations,* Joan Bresnan (ed.), 173–281. Cambridge, Mass.: MIT Press.
Kastovsky, Dieter
    1982   *Wortbildung und Semantik*. Düsseldorf/Bern/München: Schwann-Bagel, Francke.

Kastovsky, Dieter
   1992   Semantics and vocabulary. In *The Cambridge History of English Language. Vol. I: The Beginnings to 1066*. R. Hogg (ed.), 290–408. Cambridge: Cambridge University Press.
Kastovsky, Dieter
   2006   Vocabulary. In *A History of the English Language*, Richard Hogg, and David Denison (eds.), 199–270. Cambridge: Cambridge University Press.
Katz J. J., and J. A. Fodor
   1963   The structure of a semantic theory. *Language* 39: 170–210.
Kay, Paul
   2005   Argument structure constructions and the argument-adjunct distinction. In *Grammatical Constructions: Back to the Roots*, Mirjam Fried, and Hans C. Boas (eds.), 71–98. Amsterdam: Benjamins.
Klann-Delius, Gisela
   1999   *Spracherwerb*. Stuttgart: Metzler.
Klotz, Michael
   2000   *Grammatik und Lexik: Studien zur Syntagmatik englischer Verben*. ZAA Studies. Tübingen: Stauffenburg.
König, Ekkehard, and Volker Gast
   2007   *Understanding English-German Contrasts*. Berlin: Schmidt.
Kohler, Klaus J.
   1977   *Einführung in die Phonetik des Deutschen*. Berlin: Schmidt.
Kortmann, Bernd
   2005   *English Linguistics: Essentials (English edition)*. Berlin: Cornelsen.
Kortmann, Bernd
   2008   Synopsis: Morphological and syntactic variation in the British Isles. In *Varieties of English 1: The British Isles*, Bernd Kortmann, and Clive Upton (eds.), 478–495. Berlin/New York: Mouton de Gruyter.
Krug, Manfred G.
   2000   *Emerging English Modals: A Corpus-Based Study of Grammaticalization*. Berlin/New York: Mouton de Gruyter.
Labov, William
   1966   *The Social Stratification of English in New York City*. Washington: Center for Applied Linguistics.
Lakoff, George
   1987   *Women, Fire, and Dangerous Things: What Categories Reveal about the Mind*. Chicago/London: University of Chicago Press.
Langacker, Ronald W.
   1987   *Foundations of Cognitive Grammar. Volume 1: Theoretical Prerequisites*. Stanford, CA: Stanford University Press.

Lass, Roger
 1984 *Phonology: An Introduction to Basic Concepts.* Cambridge: Cambridge University Press.

Lass, Roger
 1992 Phonology and morphology. In *The Cambridge History of the English Language. Vol. II: 1066–1476*, Norman Blake (ed.), 23–155. Cambridge: Cambridge University Press.

Lass, Roger
 1994 *Old English: A Historical Linguistic Companion.* Cambridge: Cambridge University Press.

Lass, Roger
 1999 Phonology and morphology. In *The Cambridge History of the English Language. Vol. III: 1476–1776*, R. Lass (ed.), 56–186. Cambridge: Cambridge University Press.

Lass, Roger
 2006 Phonology and morphology. In *A History of the English Language*, Richard Hogg, and David Denison (eds.), 43–108. Cambridge: Cambridge University Press.

Lea, Diana
 2007 Making a collocations dictionary. *Zeitschrift für Anglistik und Amerikanistik* 55 (3): 261–271.

Leech, Geoffrey
 ²1981 *Semantics.* Harmondsworth: Penguin.

Leech, Geoffrey
 1983 *Principles of Pragmatics.* London/New York: Longman.

Leech, Geoffrey
 1991 The state of the art in corpus linguistics. In *English Corpus Linguistics*, Karin Aijmer, and Bengt Altenberg (eds.), 8–29. London/New York: Longman.

Leech, Geoffrey
 1992 Corpora and theories of linguistic performance. In *Directions in Corpus Linguistics: Proceedings of Nobel Symposium 82*, Jan Svartvik (ed.), 105–122. Berlin/New York: Mouton de Gruyter.

Leech, Geoffrey, and Jan Svartvik
 ²1994 *A Communicative Grammar of English.* London/New York: Longman.

Leech, Geoffrey, Marianne Hundt, Christian Mair, and Nicholas Smith
 2009 *Change in Contemporary English: A Grammatical Study.* Cambridge: Cambridge University Press.

Lees, Robert B.
 ⁵1968 *The Grammar of English Nominalizations.* Bloomington: Mouton & Co. First edition 1960.

Lehmann, Hans Martin, Peter Schneider, and Sebastian Hoffmann
    2000   BNCweb. In *Corpora Galore. Analyses and Techniques in Describing English*, J. Kirk, (ed.), 259–266. Amsterdam/Atlanta: Rodopi.

Leisi, Ernst
    ⁵1969   *Das heutige Englisch: Wesenszüge und Probleme*. Heidelberg: Winter. Revised edition: Ernst Leisi, and Christian Mair (⁸1999): Heidelberg: Winter.

Leisi, Ernst
    1973   *Praxis der englischen Semantik*. Heidelberg: Winter.

Lenker, Ursula
    2010   *Argument and rhetoric: Adverbial connectors in the history of English*. Berlin/New York: De Gruyter Mouton.

Levinson, Stephen C.
    1983   *Pragmatics*. Cambridge: Cambridge University Press.

Lieven, Elena
    2008   Learning the English auxiliary: A usage-based approach. In *Trends in Corpus Research* (Finding Structure in Data) TILAR Series. Vol. 6, Heike Behrens (ed.), 61–98. Amsterdam/Philadelphia: Benjamins.

Lieven, Elena, Heike Behrens, J. Speares, and Michael Tomasello
    2003   Early syntactic creativity: a usage-based approach. *Journal of Child Language* 30: 333–370.

Lightfood, David
    1988   Syntactic change. In *Linguistics: The Cambridge Survey. Vol. I. Linguistic Theory: Foundations*, Frederick J. Newmeyer (ed.), 303–323. Cambridge: Cambridge University Press.

Lipka, Leonhard
    1976   Topicalization, case grammar, and lexical decomposition in English. *Archivum Linguisticum* VII (2): 118–141.

Lipka, Leonhard
    ³2002   *English Lexicology*. Tübingen: Narr.

Lorenz, Gunter
    1999   *Adjective Intensification – Learners versus Native Speakers: A Corpus Study of Argumentative Writing*. Amsterdam/Atlanta: Rodopi.

Luick, Karl
    1903   *Studien zur englischen Lautgeschichte*. Wien et al.: Braumüller.

Luick, Karl
    1940   *Historische Grammatik der englischen Sprache*. Vol. 1. II. Abteilung. Leipzig: Tauchnitz.

Lutz, Angelika
    2002a   Sprachmischung in der deutschen und englischen Wortbildung. In *Historische Wortbildung des Deutschen*, Mechthild Habermann, Pe-

ter O. Müller, and Horst Haider Munske (eds.), 407–437. Tübingen: Niemeyer.

Lutz, Angelika
    2002b   When did English begin? In *Sounds, Words, Texts and Change*, Teresa Fanego, Belén Méntez-Naya, and Elena Seoane (eds.), 145–171. Amsterdam/Philadelphia: Benjamins.

Lutz, Angelika
    2004   The first push: A prelude to the Great Vowel Shift. *Anglia* 122 (2): 209–224.

Lutz, Angelika
    2009   Celtic influence on Old English and West Germanic. *English Language and Linguistics* 13 (2): 227–249.

Lyons, John
    1968   *Introduction to Theoretical Linguistics*. Cambridge: Cambridge University Press.

Lyons, John
    1977   *Semantics I*. Cambridge: Cambridge University Press.

Lyons, John
    [3]1991   *Chomsky*. London: Fontana.

Maclay, Howard
    1971   Overview. In *Semantics: An Interdisciplinary Reader in Philosophy, Linguistics and Psychology*, Danny D. Steinberg, and Leon A. Jakobovits (eds.), 157–182. Cambridge: Cambridge University Press.

MacWhinney, Brian
    1998   Models of the Emergence of Language. *Annual Review of Psychology* 49: 199–227.

Mair, Christian
    1997   *Einführung in die anglistische Sprachwissenschaft*. Darmstadt: Wissenschaftliche Buchgesellschaft.

Mair, Christian
    2008   *English Linguistics*: An Introduction. Tübingen: Narr.

Marchand, Hans
    [2]1969   *The Categories and Types of Present-Day English Word-Formation: A Synchronic-Diachronic Approach*. München: Beck.

Mathesius, Vilém
    1975   *A Functional Analysis of Present Day English on a General Linguistic Basis*. The Hague/Paris: Mouton.

Matthews, Peter H.
    1974   *Morphology: An Introduction to the Theory of Word-Structure*. Cambridge: Cambridge University Press.

Matthews, Peter H.
    1981   *Syntax*. Cambridge: Cambridge University Press.

Matthews, Peter
    1982   *Do Languages Obey General Laws?* Cambridge: Cambridge University Press.

Matthews, Peter
    1990   Language as mental faculty. In *An Encyclopaedia of Language*, N. E. Collinge (ed.), 112–138. London: Routledge.

Matthews, Peter H.
    1993   *Grammatical Theory in the United States from Bloomfield to Chomsky.* Cambridge: Cambridge University Press.

Matthews, Peter H.
    2007   *Syntactic Relations. A critical survey.* Cambridge: Cambridge University Press.

McQueen, James M., and A. Cutler
    1998   Morphology in word recognition. In *The Handbook of Morphology*, Andrew Spencer, and Arnold M. Zwicky (eds.), 406–427. Oxford//Malden: Blackwell.

Mey, Jacob L.
    1993   *Pragmatics: An Introduction.* Oxford, UK/Cambridge, Mass.: Blackwell.

Meyer, Matthias L. G.
    2009   Revisiting the evidence for objects in English. In *Exploring the Lexis-Grammar Interface*, Ute Römer, and Rainer Schulze (eds.), 211–227. Amsterdam/Philadelphia: John Benjamins.

Mindt, Dieter
    1988   *EDV in der Angewandten Linguistik: Ziele – Methoden – Ergebnisse.* Frankfurt: Diesterweg.

Mittmann, Brigitta
    2004   *Mehrwort-Cluster in der englischen Alltagskonversation: Unterschiede zwischen britischem und amerikanischem gesprochenem Englisch als Indikatoren für den präfabrizierten Charakter der Sprache.* Tübingen: Narr.

Moon, Rosamund
    1987   The analysis of meaning. In *Looking Up*, John Sinclair (ed.), 86–103. London/Glasgow: Collins.

Mugglestone, Lynda
    2009   The Oxford English Dictionary. In *The Oxford History of English Lexicography. Vol. I.*, A. P. Cowie (ed.), 230–259. Oxford: Oxford University Press.

Mukherjee, Joybrato
    2002   *Korpuslinguistik und Englischunterricht: Eine Einführung.* Frankfurt: Lang.

Mukherjee, Joybrato
2009   *Anglistische Korpuslinguistik.* Berlin: Schmidt.
Nesselhauf, Nadja
2004   Learner corpora and their potential for language teaching. In *How to Use Corpora in Language Teaching*, John Sinclair (ed.), 125–152. Amsterdam/Philadelphia: Benjamins.
Nesselhauf, Nadja
2005   *Collocations in a Learner Corpus.* Amsterdam: John Benjamins.
Neuhaus, Hans Joachim
1971   *Beschränkungen in der Grammatik der Wortableitungen im Englischen.* Dissertation: Saarbrücken.
Newmeyer, Frederick J.
2001   The Prague School and North American functionalist approaches to syntax. *Journal of Linguistics* 37: 101–126.
Noël, Dirk
2007   Verb valency patterns, constructions and grammaticalization. In *Valency: Theoretical, Descriptive and Cognitive Issues*, Thomas Herbst, and Katrin Götz-Votteler (eds.), 67–83. Berlin/New York: Mouton de Gruyter.
Ogden, Charles K., and I. A. Richards
[10]1956   *The Meaning of Meaning.* London: Routledge & Kegan Paul Ltd. First edition 1923.
Palmer, Frank
1971   *Grammar.* Harmondsworth: Penguin.
Palmer, Frank
[2]1981   *Semantics.* Cambridge: Cambridge University Press.
Palmer, Frank
1994   *Grammatical Roles and Relations.* Cambridge: Cambridge University Press.
Paquot, Magali
2009   Exemplification in learner writing: A cross-linguistic perspective. In *Phraseology in Foreign Language Learning and Teaching*, Fanny Meunier, and Sylviane Granger (eds.), 101–119. Amsterdam/Philadelphia: Benjamins.
Pike, Kenneth L.
1943   *Phonetics: A Critical Analysis of Phonetic Theory and a Technic for the Practical Description of Sounds.* Ann Arbor: The University of Michigan Press.
Pinker, Steven
1991   Rules of language. *Science* 253: 530–535.

Pinker, Steven, and Alan Prince
 1994 Regular and irregular morphology and the psychological status of rules of grammar. In *The Reality of Linguistic Rules*, S. D. Lima, R. L. Corrigan, and G. K. Iverson (eds.), 321–351. Amsterdam: Benjamins.

Plag, Ingo
 2003 *Word-Formation in English*. Cambridge: Cambridge University Press.

Plag, Ingo, Maria Braun, Sabine Lappe, and Mareile Schramm
 2007 *Introduction to English Linguistics*. Berlin/New York: Mouton de Gruyter.

Prince, Ellen F.
 1981 Toward a taxonomy of given-new information. In *Radical Pragmatics*, Peter Cole (ed.), 223–255. New York/London: Academic Press.

Pullum, Geoffrey K.
 2009 Lexical categorization in English dictionaries and traditional grammars. In *Classification in Linguistics and Lexicography. Zeitschrift für Anglistik und Amerikanistik* 57 (3): 255–273.

Quirk, Randolph, Sidney Greenbaum, Geoffrey Leech, and Jan Svartvik
 1972 *A Grammar of Contemporary English*. London: Longman. [GCE]

Quirk, Randolph, Sidney Greenbaum, Geoffrey Leech, and Jan Svartvik
 1985 *The Comprehensive Grammar of the English Language*. London/New York: Longman. [CGEL]

Quirk, Randolph, and C. L. Wrenn
 ²1957 *An Old English Grammar*. London: Methuen.

Radford, Andrew
 1993 Head-hunting: On the trail of the nominal Janus. In *Heads in Grammatical Theory*, Greville G. Corbett, Norman M. Fraser, and Scott McClashan (eds.), 73–113. Cambridge: Cambridge University Press.

Roach, Peter
 ⁴2009 *English Phonetics and Phonology: A Practical Course*. Cambridge: Cambridge University Press.

Robins, Robert H.
 1967 *A Short History of Linguistics*. London and Harlow: Longman.

Robins, Robert H.
 1971 *General Linguistics: An Introductory Survey*. London: Longman.

Robins, Robert H.
 2000 The development of the word class system of the European grammatical tradition. *Foundations of Language* 2: 3–19. First published in 1966. [In *Sprachwissenschaft: Ein Reader*, Ludger Hoffmann (ed.), 452–469. Berlin/New York: Walter de Gruyter, 2000.]

Rosch Heider, Eleanor
    1971   'Focal' color areas and the development of color names. *Developmental Psychology* 4 (3): 447–455.

Rosch Heider, Eleanor
    1972   Universals in color naming and memory. *Journal of Experimental Psychology* 93 (1): 10–20.

Rosch, Eleanor
    1973   On the Internal Structure of Perceptual and Semantic Categories. In *Cognitive Development and the Acquisition of Language*, Timothy E Moore (ed.), 111-144. New York/San Franciso/London: Academic Press.

Rosch, Eleanor
    1975   Cognitive Representations of Semantic Categories. *Journal of Experimental Psychology* 104 (3): 192–233.

Russell, Bertrand
    1919   *Introduction to Mathematical Philosophy*. London: George Allen and Unwin.

Sampson, Geoffrey
    1980   *Schools of Linguistics*. Stanford: Stanford University Press.

Sampson, Geoffrey
    2001   *Empirical Linguistics*. London/New York: Continuum.

Saussure, Ferdinand de
    1916   *Cours de linguistique générale*, Charles Bally, and Albert Séchehaye (eds.). Paris/Lausanne: Payot.

Saussure, Ferdinand de
    1964   Lettres de Ferdinand de Saussure à Antoine Meillet (4 janvier 1894). In Société Genevoise de Linguistique, *Cahiers Ferdinand de Saussure,* 21, 1964, Genève: Librairie Droz: 93–130. First edition 1894.

Saussure, Ferdinand de
    1983   *Course in General Linguistics*, translated and annotated by Roy Harris, London: Duckworth.

Scheler, Manfred
    1977   *Der englische Wortschatz*. Berlin: Schmidt.

Scherer, Günther, and Alfred Wollmann
    1972   *Englische Phonetik und Phonologie*. Berlin: Schmidt.

Schmid, Hans-Jörg
    2005   *Englische Morphologie und Wortbildung: Eine Einführung*. Berlin: Schmidt.

Schmid, Hans-Jörg
    2008   New words in the mind: Concept-formation and entrenchment of neologisms. *Anglia* 126: 1–36.

Schmid, Hans-Jörg
  forthc.   *English Morphology and Word-Formation*. Berlin: Schmidt.
Schmied, Josef
  1991   *English in Africa*. London/New York: Longman.
Schmied, Josef
  2008   East African English (Kenya, Uganda, Tanzania): Phonology. In *Varieties of English 4 Africa: South and Southeast Asia,* Rajend Mesthrie (ed.), 150–163. Berlin/New York: Mouton de Gruyter.
Schneider, Edgar
  2007   *Postcolonial English: Varieties around the World*. Cambridge: Cambridge University Press.
Schneider, Edgar
  2008a   Synopsis: Morphological and syntactic variation in the Americas and the Caribbean. In *Varieties of English 2: The Americas and the Caribbean,* Edgar Schneider (ed.), 763–776. Berlin/New York: Mouton de Gruyter.
Schneider, Edgar
  2008b   List of features: Phonology and phonetics. In *Varieties of English 1: The British Isles,* Bernd Kortmann, and Clive Upton (eds.), xix–xxiv. Berlin/New York: Mouton de Gruyter.
Schröder, Konrad
  2005   Einige unmaßgebliche Gedanken zur grammatischen Terminologie und zum Grammatikunterricht des Schulfaches Englisch: A somewhat personal account. In *Linguistische Dimensionen des Fremdsprachenunterrichts,* Thomas Herbst (ed.), 1–9. Würzburg: Königshausen und Neumann.
Schubert, Christoph
  2008   *Englische Textlinguistik: Eine Einführung*. Berlin: Schmidt Verlag.
Searle, John R.
  1969   *Speech Acts: An Essay in the Philosophy of Language*. Cambridge: Cambridge University Press.
Searle, John R.
  1971   What is a speech act? In *The Philosophy of Language,* John R. Searle (ed.), 39–53. London: Oxford University Press.
Searle, John R.
  1979a   A taxonomy of illocutionary acts. In *Expression and Meaning: Studies in the Theory of Speech Acts,* John R. Searle, 1–29. Cambridge: Cambridge University Press.
Searle, John R.
  1979b   Indirect speech acts. In *Expression and Meaning: Studies in the Theory of Speech Acts,* John R. Searle, 30–57. Cambridge: Cambridge University Press.

Sells, Peter
  1985   *Lectures on Contemporary Syntactic Theories.* Stanford: Center for
            the Study of Language and Information, Stanford University.
Siepmann, Dirk
  2005   Collocation, colligation and encoding dictionaries. Part I: Lexico-
            logical aspects. *International Journal of Lexicography* 18 (4): 409–
            444.
Siepmann, Dirk
  2007   Collocations and examples: Their relationship and treatment in a
            new corpus-based learner's dictionary. In *Zeitschrift für Anglistik
            und Amerikanistik* 55 (3): 235–260.
Siepmann, Dirk
  2008   Phraseology in learners' dictionaries: What, where and how? In
            Phraseology in Foreign Language Learning and Teaching, Fanny
            Meunier, and Sylviane Granger (eds.), 185–202. Amster-
            dam/Philadelphia: Benjamins.
Sinclair, John (ed.)
  1990   *Collins Cobuild English Grammar.* London/Glasgow: Collins.
Sinclair, John
  1991   *Corpus, Concordance, Collocation.* Oxford: Oxford University
            Press.
Sinclair, John
  1994   Trust the text. In *Advances in Written Text Analysis,* Malcolm
            Coulthard (ed.), 12–25 London/New York: Routledge.
Sinclair, John
  2004   *Trust the Text.* London/New York: Routledge.
Sinclair, John, and Anna Mauranen
  2006   *Linear Unit Grammar: Integrating Speech and Writing.* Amster-
            dam/Philadelphia: Benjamins.
Söll, Ludwig, and Franz-Josef Hausmann
  [3]1985   *Gesprochenes und geschriebenes Französisch.* Berlin: Schmidt.
Somers, Harold L.
  1987   *Valency and Case in Computational Linguistics.* Edinburgh: Edin-
            burgh University Press.
Stefanowitsch, Anatol
  2007   Linguistics beyond grammaticality. *Corpus Linguistics and Linguis-
            tic Theory* 3 (1): 57–71.
Stefanowistch, Anatol
  2008   Negative entrenchment: A usage-based approach to negative evi-
            dence. *Cognitive Linguistics* 19 (3): 513–531.

Stefanowitsch, Anatol, and Stefan Th. Gries
2003   Collostructions: Investigating the interaction between words and constructions. *International Journal of Corpus Linguistics* 8 (2): 209–243.

Steinberg, Danny D.
1982   *Psycholinguistics: Language, Mind and World.* London/New York: Longman.

Stockwell, Robert
2002   How much shifting actually occurred in the historical English vowel shift? In *Studies in the History of the English Language: A Millennial Perspective*, Donka Minkova, and Robert Stockwell (eds.), 267–281. Berlin/New York: Mouton de Gruyter.

Strang, Barbara
1970   *A History of English.* London: Methuen.

Stubbs, Michael
1996   *Text and Corpus Analysis.* Oxford/Cambridge, Mass.: Blackwell.

Stubbs, Michael
2009   Technology and phraseology: With notes on the history of corpus linguistics. In *Exploring the Lexis-Grammar Interface*, Ute Römer, and Rainer Schulze (eds.), 15–31. Amsterdam/ Philadelphia: John Benjamins.

Taylor, John R.
³2003   *Linguistic Categorization.* Oxford: Oxford University Press.

Tesnière, Lucien
1959   *Éléments de syntax structurale.* Paris: Klincksieck. [Excerpts in *Sprachwissenschaft: Ein Reader*, Ludger Hoffmann (ed.). Berlin/New York: Walter de Gruyter, ²2000.].

Tomasello, Michael
2003   *Constructing a Language.* Cambridge, Mass./London: Harvard University Press.

Traugott, Elizabeth Closs
1992   Syntax. In *The Cambridge History of the English Language. Vol. I*, Richard M. Hogg (ed.), 168–289. Cambridge: Cambridge University Press.

Traugott, Elizabeth Closs
2002   From etymology to historical pragmatics. In *Studies in the History of the English Language: A Millennial Perspective*, Donka Minkova, and Robert Stockwell (eds.), 19–49. Berlin/New York: Mouton de Gruyter.

Trier, Jost
1934   Das sprachliche Feld: Eine Auseinandersetzung. *Neue Jahrbücher für Wissenschaft und Jugendbildung* 10: 428–429.

Trudgill, Peter
  1974   *The Social Differentiation of English in Norwich.* London: Cambridge University Press.
Trudgill, Peter
  1975   *Accent, Dialect and the School.* London: Arnold.
Trudgill, Peter (ed.)
  1978   *Sociolinguistic Patterns of British English.* London: Arnold.
Trudgill, Peter
  1986   *Dialects in Contact.* Oxford: Blackwell.
Trudgill; Peter
  [3]1995   *Sociolinguistics.* Harmondsworth: Penguin. First edition 1974.
Trudgill, Peter, and Howard Giles
  1978   Sociolinguistic and linguistic value judgements: Correctness, adequacy and aesthetics. In *Functional Studies in Language and Literature*, P. Coppieters, and D. L. Goyvaerts (eds.), 167–190. Gent/Antwerpen/Brüssel: E. Story Scientia p.V.B.A. Scientific Publishers.
Trudgill, Peter, and Jean Hannah
  [5]2008   *International English: A Guide to Varieties of Standard English.* London: Hodder Education. First edition 1982, London: Arnold.
Ullmann, Stephen
  1972   *Semantics.* Oxford: Basil Blackwell.
Ungerer, Friedrich
  1999   *Englische Grammatik heute.* Stuttgart/Düsseldorf/Leipzig: Klett. [EGH]
Ungerer, Friedrich, and Hans-Jörg Schmid
  [2]2006   *An Introduction to Cognitive Linguistics.* London: Pearson Longman.
Upton, Clive
  2008   Received Pronunciation. In *Varieties of English 1: The British Isles*, Bernd Kortmann, and Clive Upton (eds.), 237–252. Berlin/New York: Mouton de Gruyter.
Vennemann, Theo
  1977   Konstituenz und Dependenz in einigen neueren Grammatiktheorien. *Sprachwissenschaft* 2: 259–301.
Vennemann, Theo
  1998   Germania Semitica: ⁺*plōg-/*⁺*pleg-*, ⁺*furh-/*⁺*farh-*, ⁺*folk-/*⁺*flokk*, ⁺*felh-/*⁺*folg-*. In *Deutsche Grammatik: Thema in Variationen. Festschrift für Hans-Werner Eroms zum 60. Geburtstag*, Karin Donhauser, Ludwig M. Eichinger (eds.), 245–261. Heidelberg: Winter.

Vennemann, Theo, and J. Jakobs
  2000   *Sprache und Grammatik*. Darmstadt: Wissenschaftliche Buchgesellschaft. First edition 1982. [Excerpts in *Sprachwissenschaft: Ein Reader*, Ludger Hoffmann (ed.). Berlin/New York: Walter de Gruyter,
          ²2000.]
Viereck, Wolfgang, Karin Viereck, and Heinrich Ramisch
  2002   *Dtv-Atlas Englische Sprache*. München: dtv.
Weinreich, Uriel, William Labov, and Marvin I. Herzog
  1968   Empirical foundations for a theory of language change. In *Directions
          for Historical Linguistics: A Symposium*, W.P. Lehmann, and Yakov
          Malkiel (eds.), 95–188. Austin/London: University of Texas Press.
Wells, John
  1982   *Accents of English, 3 vols*. Cambridge: Cambridge University Press.
Werlich, Egon
  1975   *Typologie der Texte*. Heidelberg: Quelle & Meyer.
Werlich Egon
  1976   *A Text Grammar of English*. Heidelberg: Quelle & Meyer.
Wiik, Kalevi
  1965   *Finnish and English Vowels: A Comparison with Special Reference
          to the Learning Problems Met by Native Speakers of Finnish Learning English*. Turku: Annales Universitatis Turkuensis Series B/94:
          Turun Yliopisto.
Wimmer, Heinz, and Josef Perner
  1979   *Kognitionspsychologie*. Stuttgart: Kohlhammer.
Wotjak, Gerd
  1971   *Untersuchung zur Struktur der Bedeutung*. München: Hueber.

Dictionaries:

A Dictionary of English Affixes: Their Function and Meaning
  2007   by Gabriele Stein. München: Lincom.
Advanced Learner's Dictionary of Current English
  ²1963   by A. S. Hornby, edited by E.V. Gatenby, and H. Wakefield. London: Oxford University Press. [OALD2]
A First Dictionary of Linguistics and Phonetics
  1980   by David Crystal. London: André Deutsch.
Anglizismen-Wörterbuch: Der Einfluß des Englischen auf den deutschen Wortschatz nach 1945
  1993   by Broder Carstensen [continued by Ulrich Busse]. Berlin/New
          York: de Gruyter.

A Valency Dictionary of English
  2004   by Thomas Herbst, David Heath, Ian Roe, and Dieter Götz. Berlin/New York: Mouton de Gruyter. [VDE]
Cambridge English Pronouncing Dictionary
  [17]2006   by Daniel Jones. Edited by Peter Roach, James Hartman, and Jane Setter. Cambridge: Cambridge University Press [EPD17].
Collins COBUILD English Language Dictionary
  1987   edited by John Sinclair. London: Collins.
Duden Aussprachewörterbuch
  [4]2000   by M. Mangold, and Dudenredaktion. Mannheim: Dudenverlag.
Duden: Deutsches Universalwörterbuch
  [4]2001   by Wissenschaftlicher Rat der Dudenredaktion: Anette Klosa, Kathrin Kunkel-Razum, Werner Scholze-Stubenrecht, and Matthias Wermke. Mannheim/Leipzig/Wien/Zürich: Dudenverlag.
Duden Oxford Großwörterbuch Englisch: Deutsch-Englisch / Englisch-Deutsch
  [2]1999   edited by Dudenredaktion, and Oxford University Press. Mannheim/Leipzig/Wien/Zürich: Dudenverlag.
English Pronouncing Dictionary
  [15]1997   by Daniel Jones, edited by Peter Roach, James Hartman, and Jane Setter. Cambridge/New York/Melbourne: Cambridge University Press (see also *Everyman's English Pronouncing Dictionary* and *Cambridge English Pronouncing Dictionary*).
Erlangen Valency Patternbank
  2009–   by Thomas Herbst and Peter Uhrig. Available online at: http://www.patternbank.uni-erlangen.de.
Everyman's English Pronouncing Dictionary
  [13]1967   by Daniel Jones. London: Dent & Sons/New York: E.P. Dutton & Co. [EPD13]
Everyman's English Pronouncing Dictionary
  [14]1977   by Daniel Jones, edited by A. C. Gimson. London: Dent & Sons. [EPD14]
Framenet   http://framenet.icsi.berkeley.edu/
Longman Dictionary of Contemporary English
  1978   edited by Paul Procter. Harlow: Longman. [LDOCE1]
Longman Dictionary of Contemporary English
  [4]2003   edited by Della Summers. Harlow: Longman. [LDOCE4]
Longman Dictionary of Contemporary English
  [5]2009   edited by Michael Mayor. Harlow: Pearson Longman. [LDOCE5]
Longman Pronunciation Dictionary
  [3]2008   by John Wells. Harlow: Pearson-Longman. First edition 1990. [LPD3]

New Shorter Oxford English Dictionary on Historical Principles
  1993   edited by Lesley Brown. Oxford: Clarendon Press. [NSOED]
Oxford Advanced Learner's Dictionary of Current English
  ⁶2000   by A. S. Hornby, edited by Sally Wehmeier. Oxford: Oxford University Press. [OALD6]
Oxford Advanced Learner's Dictionary of Current English
  ⁷2005   by A. S. Hornby, edited by Sally Wehmeier. Oxford: Oxford University Press. [OALD7]
Oxford Collocations Dictionary for Students of English
  2002   edited by Jonathan Crowther, Sheila Dignen, and Diana Lea. Oxford: Oxford University Press.
Oxford Dictionary of Current Idiomatic English. Vol. 1: Verbs with Prepositions and Particles
  1974   by Anthony P. Cowie, and R. Mackin. London: Oxford University Press.
Oxford Dictionary of Current Idiomatic English. Vol 2: Phrase, Clause and Sentence Idioms
  1983   edited by Anthony Paul Cowie, Ronald Mackin, and Isabel R. McCaig. Oxford: Oxford University Press. [ODCIE2]
Oxford English Dictionary
  ²1989   edited by John Simpson, and E. S. C. Weiner. Oxford: Clarendon. [OED2]
VALBU – Valenzwörterbuch deutscher Verben
  2004   by Helmut Schumacher, Jacqueline Kubczak, Renate Schmidt, and Vera de Ruiter. Tübingen: Narr.
Wörterbuch zur Valenz und Distribution deutscher Verben
  ²1973   by Gerhard Helbig, and Wolfgang Schenkel. Leipzig: Enzyklopädie. First edition 1969.

Sources used:

AE	Authentic example
BNC	British National Corpus
HM	http://www.henry-moore.org/pg/henry-moore-research/henry-moores-life/1898–1925 (last accessed 14 April 2010).
NF	*125 Jahre Reederei Norden Frisia.* By Heinz Busching (1996). Norden: Soltau-Kurier-Norden.
NW	*Nice Work.* By David Lodge (1989). Harmondsworth: Penguin. First published 1988.
PH	*Patrick Heron.* By Mel Gooding (1994). London: Phaidon.

PW *Painting the Warmth of the Sun.* By Tom Cross (1995). Tiverton: Westcountry Books/Cambridge: Lutterworth Press.

QE Quoted example

SP *Pygmalion.* By George Bernard Shaw (1916). Harmondsworth: Penguin.

TI *Tate St Ives. Tate Gallery St Ives. Barbara Hepworth Museum and Sculptore Garden. An Illustrated Companion.* By Michael Tooby (1993). London: Tate Gallery Publications.

TS *The Shining Sands. Artists in Newlyn and St Ives 1880–1930.* By Tom Cross (1994). Tiverton: Westcountry Books/Cambridge: Lutterworth Press.

VDE *A Valency Dictionary of English* (see bibliography).

WG *Patrick Heron: Paintings 1970–1984.* By James Beechey (2004). Waddington Galleries London.

ZD *Zennor in Darkness.* By Helen Dunmore (1994). Harmondsworth: Penguin.

Index

abbreviation 105
ablaut 91, 105, 206, 327
accent 4, 55, 82, 119, 305–311
acoustic phonetics 45
acronymisation 105, 108, 109, 112
adjective 40, 99, 101, 102, 109, 110,
    150, 153, 155, 156, 158, 159, 162–
    164, 187, 195, 253, 325
adjunct 152, 184, 185, 193, 198
adverbial 107, 135, 147, 152, 153, 184
affixation 103, 105, 108
affricate 50, 59
allomorph 84, 87, 89, 90
allophone 57, 71, 79, 317
alveolar 49, 50, 53, 59, 70
antonymy 245, 246
approximant 50, 59, 77
argument structure construction 192,
    212, 214, 215, 218, 219
articulatory phonetics 46
aspiration 45, 51, 57, 58, 69, 79
assimilation 73, 75, 316
back vowel 51, 319
back-formation 104, 105, 111–113
bilabial 49, 58, 59
blending 108, 112
blocked morpheme 94
blocking 114, 117, 122
bound morpheme 85, 103, 217
cardinal vowel 51, 52, 61
case grammar 107, 171, 176, 178,
    179, 183, 204, 282
clipping 109, 112
coherence 283, 285–287, 291, 293,
    295
cohesion 283–288, 291–293, 295

collocation 40, 129, 131–134, 139,
    206, 293
competence 28–32, 112–115, 200,
    209, 216, 219, 309
complement 107, 147, 149, 150, 152,
    153, 156, 175, 179, 184–191, 193,
    196–198, 214, 215, 227, 313
complementarity 245, 246, 251
complementary distribution 57, 60,
    85, 89, 317, 318
componential analysis 248–251, 260
compounding 102–104, 108
concordance 37
consonant 54, 58, 66, 69, 71, 81, 82,
    317, 321, 322
construction grammar 30, 42, 138,
    139, 141, 191, 205, 207, 210–212,
    217, 329
contextually optional 190
conversational implicatures 270
converseness 246, 251, 252
conversion 103, 105, 109–113
co-operative principle 268–270, 280
corpus 9, 33–42, 125, 129, 130, 206
cranberry morpheme 94
denotation 220, 223, 224, 228, 229,
    231
dental 49, 53, 59
determinative 155, 166, 169
determiner 96, 103, 110, 155, 166,
    167, 169, 170, 194, 195, 289
diachronic 14, 16–18, 36, 93, 100,
    111, 235
dialect 3, 4, 206, 303–305, 308
distinctive feature 58, 60, 61, 68, 249
elision 73, 75, 316

familiarity marker 105
foreign language teaching 4, 22, 23, 25, 40, 69, 131, 134, 136, 137
fortis 51, 53, 60, 61, 66, 69, 71, 79
free morpheme 85, 87, 102
fricative 50, 53, 59, 60, 70, 77
front vowel 317, 319
functional morpheme 85
generative grammar 20, 28, 35, 201, 202, 204, 207, 210, 212
glottal 50, 59, 69, 70, 71, 82, 304
gradation series 91
grammatical morpheme 85–87
grammaticalization 120, 328, 329
Great Vowel Shift 6, 318–322
head 102, 106, 108, 135, 154–156, 167, 169, 191, 193–198, 226, 235, 276, 290
homonymy 202, 233–238, 325
hyponymy 240, 247, 293
idiolect 3
idiom 134, 136–138, 207, 212, 268
idiom principle 136–138, 207, 212
i-mutation 91, 318, 319, 322
incompatibility 251
intonation 44, 54, 55, 80, 81, 230, 297, 298
intuition 27, 31, 32, 35, 72, 205
language acquisition 26, 28, 30, 31, 39, 93, 112, 124, 170, 200, 208–210, 215–219
langue 14, 29, 30
lateral 46, 50, 59, 77
lenis 51, 53, 60, 61, 69
lexeme 97, 98, 100, 101, 109, 118, 119, 127, 131, 136, 233–235, 239, 250, 293
lexical field 239, 247, 248, 293
lexical morpheme 85–87
lexical unit 73, 98, 100, 121, 186, 188, 191, 233–235, 237–240, 242, 243, 247–249, 251–324

lexicalization 108, 117, 119–121
loan word 8, 322
manner of articulation 50
meaning 14–16, 19, 23, 56, 58, 67, 71, 81, 84, 92, 94, 98, 107, 119, 131, 132, 134, 136, 152, 153, 176, 177, 204, 211, 213–215, 220–226, 229–240, 242, 247–253, 258–261, 263, 265–267, 288, 289, 294, 298, 312, 324, 326, 328
minimal pair 58, 60
modifier 106, 108, 156, 299
morph 87, 88, 90
morpheme 67, 83–90, 92, 94, 97, 102, 108, 115, 120, 143, 161, 220
morphological conditioning 90
morphological process 86
nasal 48–50, 53, 59, 321
nasalized 49, 77, 78
New Englishes 4
nonce formation 115, 118, 119
object 107, 142, 145, 147–153, 173, 176, 179, 184, 204, 214, 215, 326
obligatory 124, 146, 152, 156, 184, 190
open-choice principle 136, 137
optional 75, 110, 122, 146, 152, 184, 190, 290, 291
oral 46, 48, 49, 53, 77, 301
palato-alveolar 50, 59
paradigmatic 19, 20
parole 14, 29, 30
particle 135, 136, 160, 168, 169, 188, 197
performance 28–32, 39, 200, 201, 206, 274, 277, 279, 299
phone 44, 48, 67–71, 74, 76, 79, 104, 233
phoneme 57–60, 63–65, 67–72, 74, 76, 78–82, 84, 90, 97, 220, 249, 310, 316–318
phoneme merger 318

phoneme shift 318
phoneme split 318
phonological conditioning 67, 89
phonotactics 65
phrase 102, 126, 127, 136, 143, 146, 152–157, 162, 165–167, 169, 171, 172, 174, 176, 179, 185, 187, 188, 194–198, 201, 203, 204, 215, 224, 226, 227, 288–290, 299
place of articulation 49, 321
plosive 50, 53, 59, 60, 66, 68, 69, 321
polysemy 215, 234–238, 266, 325
portmanteau morph 87
post-alveolar 50, 59
pragmatics 25, 228, 267, 268, 274, 281
predicate 144–147, 152, 155, 174, 189, 192, 193, 198, 290, 295
prefixation 104, 114
productivity 113, 114
reference 155, 220, 221, 224–228, 262, 275, 276, 288, 289, 291, 292, 299
relational opposition 246
rheme 295, 296
Sapir-Whorf-hypothesis 255, 256
semantic role 148, 176, 178–180, 191, 198, 204, 326
semantics 19, 25, 188, 228, 229, 231, 234, 239, 241, 247, 249, 252, 256, 257, 266–268, 270, 285
semi-vowel 47, 74, 77
signifiant 14, 15, 220
signifié 14, 15, 220
sound change 107, 318, 319
speech act 25, 29, 140, 224, 228, 271, 274, 277, 278, 280–282
standard 6, 11, 24, 61, 93, 238, 302, 303, 305–309
stress 54, 55, 75, 102, 103, 120, 297, 298, 311
strong verb 91, 92, 327

subject 107, 142, 144–149, 152, 153, 174, 176, 177, 184, 189, 191, 193, 198, 204, 295
suffixation 104, 112–114, 162
suprasegmental element 54
synchronic 14, 16–18, 31, 91–93, 111, 113, 236, 237
synonymy 241–243, 247, 293
syntagmatic 19, 20, 251
theme 213, 289, 295–297
token 96, 216
type 96
unique morpheme 94
usage-based 30, 31, 124, 215, 217, 219, 303
valency 20, 37, 110, 138, 139, 141, 146, 151, 168, 176, 178, 179, 183–193, 195, 197, 204, 206, 212–215, 218, 290, 291, 313
variety 3, 4, 21, 22, 27, 34, 42, 49, 64, 149, 217, 288, 293, 298, 303, 306–308, 312, 313, 315, 316
velar 50, 53, 59, 317
verb 20, 32, 39, 91, 103, 107, 109–113, 120, 135–138, 142, 145–148, 151–153, 155, 156, 158–162, 164, 165, 168–170, 173, 174, 176, 177, 180, 181, 183–191, 193, 197, 204, 212–215, 217, 218, 274, 290, 327, 328
voiced 47, 49, 53, 59–61, 68–70, 80, 82, 85, 90, 317, 318
voiceless 49, 53, 59–61, 68–70, 80, 81, 85, 90, 317
vowel 47, 51–54, 60–65, 68–71, 73–75, 77–80, 82, 88, 90, 91, 309–310, 317, 319, 321, 322
weak form 75, 82
weak verb 91, 92, 322
word class 12, 23, 95, 96, 105, 110, 142, 147, 157–170, 187, 188, 197, 198, 237, 247, 293

word formation 25, 83, 94, 99–108, 110–115, 117–121, 131, 134, 136, 256, 293, 322

zero-derivation 103, 104, 109–111
zero-morph 88, 89, 104, 109
zero-morpheme 88, 104, 109

2671009R00227

Printed in Germany
by Amazon Distribution
GmbH, Leipzig